COMING TO TERMS

American Plays & the Vietnam War

COMING TO TERMS
American Plays & the Vietnam War

Introduction by *James Reston, Jr.*

Theatre Communications Group
New York • 2016

A Note on the New Edition

Theatre Communications Group (TCG), the national organization for the American not-for-profit professional theatre, in partnership with Blue Star Families, launched the Blue Star Theatres Program in 2012. The program is designed to build connections between resident theatre companies in cities and towns across the U.S. and the military families in their communities.

Blue Star Theatres Program activities have included a regrant program to support projects that strengthen relationships between theatres and military communities, special events at theatres around the country, an online directory of theatres offering discounted and free tickets and programs for military families, and a publishing program.

Coming to Terms: American Plays and the Vietnam War was originally published in 1985. As American troops return home from Iraq and Afghanistan, and as we face the prospect of ongoing conflict in other parts of the world, it seems timely to reprint *Coming to Terms* as one component of TCG's Blue Star Theatres Program.

TCG's Blue Star Theatres Program is meant to bring greater familiarity and understanding between the military community and the theatre community, so that there will be an expanded awareness of opportunities for healing and connection. We hope this program is an excellent example of how returning veterans can be engaged with a national community that cares. TCG is committed to honoring the extraordinary dedication of our service members and their families and facilitating these connections on a national scale.

This reprint of *Coming to Terms* is published by the generosity and leadership support of the MetLife Foundation.

 MetLife Foundation

Contents

Introduction

by James Reston, Jr.

Memory, especially collective memory, is a subtle and in many ways fragile act. Normally, we think of it as the dominion of historians, as if they always have the last word. They deliver with their fat biographies, "The Life and Times of . . .," and their grand generalizations, "The Tragic Era . . .," and their trenchant analyses, "The Short and Long Range Causes of . . .," and it can sometimes be pretty dry stuff. Almost inevitably, such tracts recount in splendid detail the perambulations of men in power. Stock questions are asked of every historical epoch. What will HISTORY record? What will the historians think one hundred years later? How will reputations stand the "test of time"?

Vietnam will be different. For once, traditional historical method is inadequate. Facts and men in power are not at the core of this story, but rather the emotions of the generation which shouldered the profound consequences of this ill-conceived enterprise. The Vietnam generation, reacting to the decisions from on high, changed American society forever, and so the heart of the matter is emotional and cultural.

In the past several years we've heard quite a bit about the "lessons of Vietnam." Briefly, it became a point of argument in the campaign for the Democratic nomination in 1984 between Gary Hart and Walter Mondale. A spate of books, usually churned out by former policy makers and historians of public policy, have purported to address the issue. Even a label now exists—Vietnam revisionism—for this brand of scholarship. The problem has been bandied around as the United States flirts with "another Vietnam" in Central America.

And yet, for all the books, for all its mention in political debate, a sense of disquiet reigns. Vietnam is not yet, by any measure, a digested event of American history. It is a national experience that is still denied and repressed, not one which is folded into the sweep of our history and which we calmly acknowledge as the downside of American potentiality.

This is partly the failure of political leadership. Gerald Ford and Jimmy Carter were too weak as men and as leaders to educate the country on the resonance of the first American defeat in war. They needed to be the leaders of the Second Reconstruction of American history, comparable to the first after the American Civil War. If, after our first divisive war, America became a more racially equal society, then after Vietnam America needed to become a less militarist society. It did not happen. Instead, these presidents presided over amnesia and malaise. And in the great malaise, the victims were left to sort out their lives without help or respect or even acknowledgment.

Perhaps it is not entirely the politician's fault. Their silence or their half-hearted attempts at reconciliation, like their clemencies and pardon for Vietnam War resisters, were reflections of a national mood. For 10 years, the American people did not want to think about Vietnam. And since they did not want to think about it, politicians—and, yes, publishers and theatrical directors too—did not provide the public with food for thought. In effect, the whole culture together shut down on the subject.

Ronald Reagan changed all that. When his soldiers died in Lebanon and Grenada and El Salvador, and American patriotism again came to represent mainly anti-Communism; when Caspar Weinberger fashioned those empty phrases at the gravesites of Vietnam veterans, like "We never again will commit American boys to a war we don't intend to win," and Reagan himself declared Vietnam to have been a noble cause, the culture began to wake up from its long sleep. It was time to think again about the longest, costliest war in American history, for a Vietnam mythology was in the making.

But by the time it became fashionable to "think" about Vietnam, the nation had forgotten the total agony of the experience. If one reads the revisionist histories, it is as if Vietnam were only a question of whether Congress and domestic dissent shackled the military and didn't allow it to exercise its full measure of violence. If only we had bombed North Vietnam more and sooner, or picked some spot on the coast for another Inchon invasion early on, or invaded Cambodia when it would do some good. If only . . . if only: it is the standard refuge of losers. The lessons of Vietnam somehow got focused on policy questions to the exclusion of emotional and generational questions. The next time you enter a guerrilla war in a jungle, be sure. . . . What? . . . Sock it to the sanctuaries soon and hard! Deny the flow of arms from the outside! Then, by God, you'll show 'em you intend to win. . . . Such lessons are minor indeed, if they are lessons at all.

The real lessons lie in what happened to one generation of Americans. The Vietnam generation is unique in American history. The choices it faced, the manner in which it dealt with those choices, the problems it faced in the aftermath: that is the story of Vietnam. Only in dealing with that can the country come to terms with the war.

In 1985, this is far from an idle concern for some musty academic. For the Vietnam generation may not forever be unique. The truth is that at this moment there is not a sufficient appreciation of the Vietnam agony in our political community, in our culture, or in our youth, who are the candidates for the next Vietnam. We do not know it well enough to loathe it sufficiently. Without loathing, how can we prevent it from happening again? We have conveniently forgotten much of what is distasteful to remember. Memory is always that way, but this amnesia has consequences.

In my view, the most accurate, most profound memory of Vietnam lies in the arts. The novels, the plays, the painting and sculpture, the poetry—these all go to the emotional truth of the experience, and when they are good they are worth more than a mountain of books on the military campaigns or the chief political figures or the chapter-and-verse facts about the era. That is one more unique aspect of the Vietnam age. The playwright becomes more important than the historian, for in no other war of our history was the private word more important than the public pronouncements, the whispered intimacies between friends—whether dignitaries or the boys in the streets and trenches—more important than statements from lecterns or barricades or muddy foxholes. For such whisperings are seldom recorded. With the Vietnam experience, the history is the subtext.

But there is here also a question of the audience. We of the Vietnam generation, particularly the artists who have something to say about our experience, have the problem of how to get people to listen. Our message is not nice and jolly, although we may employ humor or satire or parody or the absurd to get it across. In the current mood of America, strong voices easily drown us out. These voices are not only loud but soothing, especially so since the country avoided the issue for a decade. It is flattering to be told now, if you are a Vietnam veteran, that yours was a noble cause, even though you never thought of it as a cause or as yours while you were enduring it. It is flattering to have memorials erected to your bravery and sacrifice, not only in Washington but in many state capitals. That veterans became passionate, almost hysterical, over whether their symbolic representation in a statue has a heroic or merely reflective air goes to their own internal conflicts within their own memory. Such internal conflicts are the very stuff of the stage.

The wall in Washington, after all, is not the only memorial which bears the names of the war dead. There is another memorial to the American soldier—smudged and nearly overgrown by the relentless jungle—in a village in Vietnam called My Lai. Upon its cement surface are the names of 504 Vietnamese dead. Over there, a different mythology is being created: that all

American soldiers were Lieutenant Calleys. The American soldier as devil competes with the American soldier as misunderstood, scorned, rediscovered and, finally, ennobled warrior. One does not have to travel halfway around the world to appreciate these competing images. They exist, dramatically and poignantly, within the soul of veterans and Vietnam avoiders alike.

The literature of Vietnam is now vast, and it is quite possible that before the final coming to terms is over, this war will compete even with the American Civil War in its literary output. If you want to know more about the "post-traumatic stress syndrome" that Emily Mann dramatizes so unflinchingly in *Still Life* and Steve Metcalfe highlights in that cruel line of *Strange Snow* where the sister speaks to her veteran brother of "generosity and love, feelings you've forgotten," there are reams of psychological tracts available. If you want to know more about those who said no, the dirges on the anti-war movement exist, but you will do far better to see a sprightly production of Michael Weller's wickedly funny and wonderful *Moonchildren*. If you want to delve into the latent violence the fear of Vietnam induced, the psychiatrists have looked at that too, of course, but it's all there in a much more arresting form in David Rabe's *Streamers*. Thick government studies have the statistics about how 80 percent of Vietnam veterans either disagreed with Vietnam policy or did not understand it, but as you regard the carnage on the stage at the end of *Streamers* and hear Richie say "I didn't even know what it was about exactly . . .," you will understand better what fighting and killing for no apparent reason means to the individual. In *Still Life*, you will learn that it means drugs, and divorce, and jail, and a loss of manhood. These are the social costs of fighting a war so adverse to the noble and radical principles upon which the country was founded.

The same dense studies show that the Vietnam veteran was distinguished not so much by the color of his skin as by his lack of education. Standards of leadership had to be lowered as in no other war in American history. The best, the brightest and the most cultured stayed away. Lieutenant Calley could never have been an American officer in any other war. In *Botticelli* Terrence McNally skillfully turns this situation upside down by giving us two wildly cultured grunts playing a parlor game outside a tunnel entrance in the jungle. Thus, the playwright teaches by inversion, a technique that artists can bring off best. Likewise it took an artist like Amlin Gray, in *How I Got That Story*, to make an essentially absurd war even more grotesquely absurd than it actually was, thereby making us laugh while we hurt. And by exploring the relation between madness and bravery and the hypocrisy of official honor, Tom Cole's *Medal of Honor Rag* will give you a powerful point of view for the next time the Pentagon hands out 8,000 medals.

In short, all the important lessons of Vietnam are here in this fine and varied collection of plays, in forms that enable the lessons to be felt and understood *totally* with the heart and soul, as well as with the mind. Such total understanding, with the total acceptance that understanding brings in its wake, is the only way that American culture will come to terms with the Vietnam memory.

The collection also demonstrates a point that many, even in the theatre, will not readily accept: that the stage has a special role in presenting living issues of the day. Its tools are beyond those of the historian and the journalist, for the stage is at home with the interior of things. In that sacred precinct, very often a deeper truth lies. The theatre is not at its best when it attempts to reproduce history or contemporary politics, but rather when it presents a *concept* of history against which the audience can test its own perceptions. The stage can humanize history and bring it alive, while professional historians and the television are dehumanizing. Such dehumanization is especially common with terrible events like Vietnam and Jonestown, where the public is shocked by the unthinkable.

The stage must recapture its proper confrontational role, making itself important not just by dealing with emotional issues of recollection and memory, but with issues that the society debates now, today. For the stage can pierce the shroud with which television covers our world. This book shows that playwrights are ready to apply their special gifts to the contemporary scene, to reclaim their special wisdom in relation to the affairs of today. It's up to the theatres to dare to let these voices be heard. Audiences, even in 1985, *will* respond.

Born in New York City in 1941, James Reston, Jr., a graduate of the University of North Carolina, spent three years in U.S. Army Intelligence. He is the author of two novels, several nonfiction books and two plays, *Sherman, the Peacemaker* and *Jonestown Express*. His latest book, *Sherman's March and Vietnam* (Macmillan), appeared earlier in 1985, after being excerpted in *The New Yorker*.

COMING TO TERMS
American Plays & the Vietnam War

STREAMERS

David Rabe

About David Rabe

Born in Dubuque, Iowa in 1940, David Rabe was doing graduate work in theatre at Villanova University when he was drafted into the army. Assigned to a support group for hospitals, he spent 11 months in Vietnam. Returning to Villanova to complete his M.A., Rabe saw his first Vietnam play, *Sticks and Bones*, produced there in 1969. *The Basic Training of Pavlo Hummel* was premiered by Joseph Papp's New York Shakespeare Festival in May 1971; *Sticks and Bones* opened there less than six months later, and was subsequently moved to Broadway, winning the Tony Award for Best Play in 1972. Other plays by Rabe include *The Orphan*, *In the Boom Boom Room* and *Goose and Tom-Tom*, all first produced by Papp. Rabe's most recent play, *Hurlyburly*, was originally staged at Chicago's Goodman Theatre by Mike Nichols and then moved to Broadway, where as of early 1985 it is still running. Rabe also wrote the screenplay for *I'm Dancing as Fast as I Can*. In addition to his Tony, Rabe's many awards include an Obie for Distinguished Playwriting and the Dramatists Guild's Hull-Warriner Award.

Production History

Streamers opened at the Long Wharf Theatre in New Haven in January 1976, under the direction of Mike Nichols, and in April of that year was produced by Joseph Papp at Lincoln Center, with Nichols again directing. *Streamers* won the New York Drama Critics Circle Award as the best American play of 1976. Rabe wrote the screenplay for the Robert Altman film based on the play.

Characters

MARTIN
RICHIE
CARLYLE
BILLY
ROGER
COKES
ROONEY
M.P. LIEUTENANT
PFC HINSON (M.P.)
PFC CLARK (M.P.)
FOURTH M.P.

Time

The mid-1960s.

Place

An army barracks in Virginia.

MASTER SSU, MASTER YÜ, MASTER LI AND MASTER LAI

All at once Master Yü fell ill, and Master Ssu went to ask how he was.
"Amazing!" exclaimed Master Yü. "Look, the Creator is making me all
crookedy! My back sticks up like a hunchback's so that my vital organs are
on top of me. My chin is hidden down around my navel, my shoulders are
up above my head, and my pigtail points at the sky. It must be due to some
dislocation of the forces of the yin and the yang. . . . "

"Do you resent it?" asked Master Ssu.

"Why, no," replied Master Yü. "What is there to resent . . .?"

Then suddenly Master Lai also fell ill. Gasping for breath, he lay at the
point of death. His wife and children gathered round in a circle and wept.
Master Li, who had come to find out how he was, said to them, "Shooooo!
Get back! Don't disturb the process of change."

And he leaned against the doorway and chatted with Master Lai. "How
marvelous the Creator is!" he exclaimed. "What is he going to make out
of you next? Where is he going to send you? Will he make you into a rat's
liver? Will he make you into a bug's arm?"

"A child obeys his father and mother and goes wherever he is told, east
or west, south or north," said Master Lai. "And the yin and the yang—
how much more are they to a man than father or mother! Now that they
have brought me to the verge of death, how perverse it would be of me to refuse
to obey them. . . . So now I think of heaven and earth as a great furnace
and the Creator as a skilled smith. What place could he send me that would
not be all right? I will go off peacefully to sleep, and then with a start I will
wake up."

—CHUANG-TZU

They so mean around here, they steal your sweat.

—SONNY LISTON

The Play

Streamers

ACT ONE

The set is a large cadre room thrusting angularly toward the audience. The floor is wooden and brown. Brightly waxed in places, it is worn and dull in other sections. The back wall is brown and angled. There are two lights at the center of the ceiling. They hang covered by green metal shades. Against the back wall and to the stage right side are three wall lockers, side by side. Stage center in the back wall is the door, the only entrance to the room. It opens onto a hallway that runs off to the latrines, showers, other cadre rooms and larger barracks rooms. There are three bunks. BILLY's bunk is parallel to ROGER's bunk. They are upstage and on either side of the room, and face downstage. RICHIE's bunk is downstage and at a right angle to BILLY's bunk. At the foot of each bunk is a green wooden footlocker. There is a floor outlet near ROGER's bunk. HE uses it for his radio. A reading lamp is clamped onto the metal piping at the head of RICHIE's bunk. A wooden chair stands beside the wall lockers. Two mops hang in the stage left corner near a trash can.

It is dusk as the lights rise on the room. RICHIE is seated and bowed forward wearily on his bunk. HE wears his long-sleeved khaki summer dress uniform. Upstage behind him is MARTIN, a thin, dark young man, pacing, worried. A white towel stained red with blood is wrapped around his wrist. HE paces several steps and falters, stops. HE stands there.

5

RICHIE: Honest to God, Martin, I don't know what to say anymore. I don't
know what to tell you.

MARTIN (*Beginning to pace again*): I mean it. I just can't stand it. Look at me.

RICHIE: I know.

MARTIN: I hate it.

RICHIE: We've got to make up a story. They'll ask you a hundred questions.

MARTIN: Do you know how I hate it?

RICHIE: Everybody does. Don't you think I hate it, too?

MARTIN: I enlisted, though. I enlisted and I hate it.

RICHIE: I enlisted, too.

MARTIN: I vomit every morning. I get the dry heaves. In the middle of every
night. (HE *flops down on the corner of* BILLY*'s bed and sits there, slumped forward, shaking his head*)

RICHIE: You can stop that. You can.

MARTIN: No.

RICHIE: You're just scared. It's just fear.

MARTIN: They're all so mean; they're all so awful. I've got two years to go.
Just thinking about it is going to make me sick. I thought it would be
different from the way it is.

RICHIE: But you could have died, for God's sake. (HE *has turned now;* HE *is facing*
MARTIN)

MARTIN: I just wanted out.

RICHIE: I might not have found you, though. I might not have come up here.

MARTIN: I don't care. I'd be out.

*The door opens and a black man in filthy fatigues—they are grease-stained and
dark with sweat—stands there.* HE *is* CARLYLE, *looking about.* RICHIE, *seeing
him, rises and moves toward him.*

RICHIE: No. Roger isn't here right now.

CARLYLE: Who isn't?

RICHIE: He isn't here.

CARLYLE: They tole me a black boy livin' in here. I don't see him. (HE *looks
suspiciously about the room*)

RICHIE: That's what I'm saying. He isn't here. He'll be back later. You can
come back later. His name is Roger.

MARTIN: I slit my wrist. (*Thrusting out the bloody, towel-wrapped wrist toward*
CARLYLE)

RICHIE: Martin! Jesus!

MARTIN: I did.

RICHIE: He's kidding. He's kidding.

CARLYLE: What was his name? Martin? (HE *is confused and the confusion has made
him angry.* HE *moves toward* MARTIN) You Martin?

MARTIN: Yes.

BILLY, *a white in his mid-twenties, blond and trim, appears in the door, whistling, carrying a slice of pie on a paper napkin. Sensing something,* HE *falters, looks at* CARLYLE, *then* RICHIE.

BILLY: Hey, what's goin' on?

CARLYLE (*Turning, leaving*): Nothin', man. Not a thing.

BILLY *looks questioningly at* RICHIE. *Then, after placing the piece of pie on the chair beside the door,* HE *crosses to his footlocker.*

RICHIE: He came in looking for Roger, but he didn't even know his name.

BILLY (*Sitting on his footlocker,* HE *starts taking off his shoes*): How come you weren't at dinner, Rich? I brought you a piece of pie. Hey, Martin.

MARTIN *thrusts out his towel-wrapped wrist.*

MARTIN: I cut my wrist, Billy.

RICHIE: Oh, for God's sake, Martin! (HE *whirls away*)

BILLY: Huh?

MARTIN: I did.

RICHIE: You are disgusting, Martin.

MARTIN: No. It's the truth. I did. I am not disgusting.

RICHIE: Well, maybe it isn't disgusting, but it certainly is disappointing.

BILLY: What are you guys talking about? (*Sitting there,* HE *really doesn't know what is going on*)

MARTIN: I cut my wrists, I slashed them, and Richie is pretending I didn't.

RICHIE: I am not. And you only cut one wrist and you didn't slash it.

MARTIN: I can't stand the army anymore, Billy. (HE *is moving now to petition* BILLY, *and* RICHIE *steps between them*)

RICHIE: Billy, listen to me. This is between Martin and me.

MARTIN: It's between me and the army, Richie.

RICHIE: (*Taking* MARTIN *by the shoulders as* BILLY *is now trying to get near* MARTIN): Let's just go outside and talk, Martin. You don't know what you're saying.

BILLY: Can I see? I mean, did he really do it?

RICHIE: No!

MARTIN: I did.

BILLY: That's awful. Jesus. Maybe you should go to the infirmary.

RICHIE: I washed it with peroxide. It's not deep. Just let us be. Please. He just needs to straighten out his thinking a little, that's all.

BILLY: Well, maybe I could help him?

MARTIN: Maybe he could.

RICHIE *is suddenly pushing at* MARTIN. RICHIE *is angry and exasperated.* HE *wants* MARTIN *out of the room.*

RICHIE: Get out of here, Martin. Billy, you do some push-ups or something.

Having been pushed toward the door, MARTIN *wanders out.*

BILLY: No.

RICHIE: I know what Martin needs. (HE *whirls and rushes into the hall after* MAR-TIN, *leaving* BILLY *scrambling to get his shoes on*)

BILLY: You're no doctor, are you? I just want to make sure he doesn't have to go to the infirmary, then I'll leave you alone. (*One shoe on,* HE *grabs up the second and runs out the door into the hall after them*) Martin! Martin, wait up!

Silence. The door has been left open. Fifteen or twenty seconds pass. Then some-one is heard coming down the hall. HE *is singing "Get a Job" and trying to do the voices and harmonies of a vocal group.* ROGER, *a tall, well-built black in long-sleeved khakis, comes in the door.* HE *has a laundry bag over his shoulder, a pair of clean civilian trousers and a shirt on a hanger in his other hand. After dropping the bag on his bed,* HE *goes to his wall locker, where* HE *carefully hangs up the civilian clothes. Returning to the bed,* HE *picks up the laundry and then, as if struck,* HE *throws the bag down on the bed, tears off his tie and sits down angrily on the bed. For a moment, with his head in his hands,* HE *sits there. Then, resolutely,* HE *rises, takes up the position of attention, and simply topples forward, his hands leaping out to break his fall at the last in-stant and put him into the push-up position. Counting in a hissing, whisper-ing voice,* HE *does ten push-ups before giving up and flopping onto his belly.* HE *simply doesn't have the will to do any more. Lying there,* HE *counts rapid-ly on.*

ROGER: Fourteen, fifteen. Twenty. Twenty-five.

BILLY, *shuffling dejectedly back in, sees* ROGER *lying there.* ROGER *springs to his feet, heads toward his footlocker, out of which* HE *takes an ashtray and a pack of cigarettes.*

You come in this area, you come in here marchin', boy: standin' tall.

BILLY, *having gone to his wall locker, is tossing a* Playboy *magazine onto his bunk.* HE *will also remove a towel, a Dopp kit and a can of foot powder.*

BILLY: I was marchin'.

ROGER: You call that marchin'?

BILLY: I was as tall as I am; I was marchin'—what do you want?

ROGER: Outa here, man; outa this goddamn typin'-terrors outfit and into some kinda real army. Or else out and free.

BILLY: So go; who's stoppin' you; get out. Go on.

ROGER: Ain't you a bitch.

BILLY: You and me more regular army than the goddamn sergeants around this place,·you know that?

ROGER: I was you, Billy boy, I wouldn't be talkin' so sacrilegious so loud, or they be doin' you like they did the ole sarge.

BILLY: He'll get off.

ROGER: Sheee-it, he'll get off. (*Sitting down on the side of his bed and facing* BILLY, HE *lights up a cigarette.* BILLY *has arranged the towel, Dopp kit and foot powder on his own bed*) Don't you think L.B.J. want to have some sergeants in that Vietnam, man? In Disneyland, baby? Lord have mercy on the ole sarge. He goin' over there to be Mickey Mouse.

BILLY: Do him a lot of good. Make a man outa him.

ROGER: That's right, that's right. He said the same damn thing about himself and you, too, I do believe. You know what's the ole boy's MOS? His Military Occupation Specialty? Demolitions, baby. Expert is his name.

BILLY (*Taking off his shoes and beginning to work on a sore toe,* HE *hardly looks up*): You're kiddin' me.

ROGER: Do I jive?

BILLY: You mean that poor ole bastard who cannot light his own cigar for shakin' is supposed to go over there blowin' up bridges and shit? Do they wanna win this war or not, man?

ROGER: Ole sarge was over in Europe in the big one, Billy. Did all kinds a bad things.

BILLY (*Swinging his feet up onto the bed,* HE *sits, cutting the cuticles on his toes, powdering his feet*): Was he drinkin' since he got the word?

ROGER: Was he breathin', Billy? Was he breathin'?

BILLY: Well, at least he ain't cuttin' his fuckin' wrists.

Silence. ROGER *looks at* BILLY, *who keeps on working.*

Man, that's the real damn army over there, ain't it? That ain't shinin' your belt buckle and standin' tall. And we might end up in it, man.

Silence. ROGER, *rising, begins to sort his laundry.*

Roger . . . you ever ask yourself if you'd rather fight in a war where it was freezin' cold or one where there was awful snakes? You ever ask that question?

ROGER: Can't say I ever did.

BILLY: We used to ask it all the time. All the time. I mean, us kids sittin' out on the back porch tellin' ghost stories at night. 'Cause it was Korea time and the newspapers were fulla pictures of soldiers in snow with white frozen beards; they got these rags tied around their feet. And snakes. We hated snakes. Hated 'em. I mean, it's bad enough to be in the jungle duckin' bullets, but then you crawl right into a goddamn snake. That's awful. That's awful.

ROGER: It don't sound none too good.

BILLY: I got my draft notice, goddamn Vietnam didn't even exist. I mean, it existed, but not as in a war we might be in. I started crawlin' around the floor a this house where I was stayin' 'cause I'd dropped outa school, and I was goin' "Bang, bang," pretendin'. Jesus.

ROGER (*Continuing with his laundry,* HE *tries to joke*): My first goddamn formation in basic, Billy, this NCO's up there jammin' away about how some a us are goin' to be dyin' in the war. I'm sayin', "What war? What that crazy man talkin' about?"

BILLY: Us, too. I couldn't believe it. I couldn't believe it. And now we got three people goin' from here.

ROGER: Five.

ROGER *and* BILLY *look at each other, and then turn away, each returning to his task.*

BILLY: It don't seem possible. I mean, people shootin' at you. Shootin' at you to kill you. (*Slight pause*) It's somethin'.

ROGER: What did you decide you preferred?

BILLY: Huh?

ROGER: Did you decide you would prefer the snakes or would you prefer the snow? 'Cause it look like it is going to be the snakes.

BILLY: I think I had pretty much made my mind up on the snow.

ROGER: Well, you just let 'em know that, Billy. Maybe they get one goin' special just for you up in Alaska. You can go to the Klondike. Fightin' some snowmen.

RICHIE *bounds into the room and shuts the door as if to keep out something dreadful.* HE *looks at* ROGER *and* BILLY *and crosses to his wall locker, pulling off his tie as* HE *moves. Tossing the tie into the locker,* HE *begins unbuttoning the cuffs of his shirt.*

RICHIE: Hi, hi, hi, everybody. Billy, hello.

BILLY: Hey.

ROGER: What's happenin', Rich?

Moving to the chair beside the door, RICHIE *picks up the pie* BILLY *left there.* HE *will place the pie atop the locker, and then, sitting,* HE *will remove his shoes and socks.*

RICHIE: I simply did this rather wonderful thing for a friend of mine, helped him see himself in a clearer, more hopeful light—little room in his life for hope? And I feel very good. Didn't Billy tell you?

ROGER: About what?

RICHIE: About Martin.

ROGER: No.

BILLY (*Looking up and speaking pointedly*): No.

RICHIE *looks at* BILLY *and then at* ROGER. RICHIE *is truly confused.*

RICHIE: No? No?

BILLY: What do I wanna gossip about Martin for?

RICHIE (HE *really can't figure out what is going on with* BILLY. *Shoes and socks in hand,* HE *heads for his wall locker*): Who was planning to gossip? I mean, it did happen. We could talk about it. I mean, I wasn't hearing his goddamn confession. Oh, my sister told me Catholics were boring.

BILLY: Good thing I ain't one anymore.

RICHIE (*Taking off his shirt,* HE *moves toward* ROGER): It really wasn't anything, Roger, except Martin made this rather desperate, pathetic gesture for attention that seems to have brought to the surface Billy's more humane and protective side. (*Reaching out,* HE *tousles* BILLY's *hair*)

BILLY: Man, I am gonna have to obliterate you.

RICHIE (*Tossing his shirt into his locker*): I don't know what you're so embarrassed about.

BILLY: I just think Martin's got enough trouble without me yappin' to everybody.

RICHIE *has moved nearer* BILLY, *his manner playful and teasing.*

RICHIE: "Obliterate"? "Obliterate," did you say? Oh, Billy, you better say "shit," "ain't" and "motherfucker" real quick now or we'll all know just how far beyond the fourth grade you went.

ROGER (*Having moved to his locker, into which* HE *is placing his folded clothes*): You hear about the ole sarge, Richard?

BILLY (*Grinning*): You ain't . . . shit . . . motherfucker.

ROGER (*Laughing*): All right.

RICHIE (*Moving center and beginning to remove his trousers*): Billy, no, no. Wit is my domain. You're in charge of sweat and running around the block.

ROGER: You hear about the ole sarge?

RICHIE: What about the ole sarge? Oh, who cares? Let's go to a movie. Billy, wanna? Let's go. C'mon. (*Trousers off,* HE *hurries to his locker*)

BILLY: Sure. What's playin'?

RICHIE: I don't know. Can't remember. Something good, though.

With a Playboy *magazine* HE *has taken from his locker,* ROGER *is settling down on his bunk, his back toward both* BILLY *and* RICHIE.

BILLY: You wanna go, Rog?

RICHIE (*In mock irritation*): Don't ask Roger! How are we going to kiss and hug and stuff if he's there?

BILLY: That ain't funny, man. (HE *is stretched out on his bunk, and* RICHIE *comes bounding over to flop down and lie beside him*)

RICHIE: And what time will you pick me up?

BILLY (HE *pushes at* RICHIE, *knocking him off the bed and onto the floor*): Well, you just fall down and wait, all right?

RICHIE: Can I help it if I love you? (*Leaping to his feet,* HE *will head to his locker, remove his shorts, put on a robe*)

ROGER: You gonna take a shower, Richard?

RICHIE: Cleanliness is nakedness, Roger.

ROGER: Is that right? I didn't know that. Not too many people know that. You may be the only person in the world who know that.

RICHIE: And godliness is in there somewhere, of course. (*Putting a towel around his neck,* HE *is gathering toiletries to carry to the shower*)

ROGER: You got your own way a lookin' at things, man. You cute.

RICHIE: That's right.

ROGER: You g'wan, have a good time in that shower.

RICHIE: Oh, I will.

BILLY (*Without looking up from his feet, which* HE *is powdering*): And don't drop your soap.

RICHIE: I will if I want to. (*Already out the door,* HE *slams it shut with a flourish*)

BILLY: Can you imagine bein' in combat with Richie—people blastin' away at you—he'd probably want to hold your hand.

ROGER: Ain't he somethin'?

BILLY: Who's zat?

ROGER: He's all right.

BILLY (*Rising,* HE *heads toward his wall locker, where he will put the powder and Dopp kit*): Sure he is, except he's livin' underwater.

Looking at BILLY, ROGER *senses something unnerving; it makes* ROGER *rise, and return his magazine to his footlocker.*

ROGER: I think we oughta do this area, man. I think we oughta do our area. Mop and buff this floor.

BILLY: You really don't think he means that shit he talks, do you?

ROGER: Huh? Awwww, man . . . Billy, no.

BILLY: I'd put money on it, Roger, and I ain't got much money.

BILLY *is trying to face* ROGER *with this, but* ROGER, *seated on his bed, has turned away.* HE *is unbuttoning his shirt.*

ROGER: Man, no, no. I'm tellin' you, lad, you listen to the ole Rog. You seen that picture a that little dolly he's got in his locker? He ain't swish, man, believe me—he's cool.

BILLY: It's just that ever since we been in this room, he's been different somehow. Somethin'.

ROGER: No, he ain't.

BILLY. *turns to his bed, where* HE *carefully starts folding the towel. Then* HE *looks at* ROGER.

BILLY: You ever talk to any a these guys—queers, I mean? You ever sit down, just rap with one of 'em?

ROGER: Hell, no; what I wanna do that for? Shit, no.

BILLY (*Crossing to the trash can in the corner, where* HE *will shake the towel empty*): I mean, some of 'em are okay guys, just way up this bad alley, and you say to 'em, "I'm straight, be cool," they go their own way. But then there's these other ones, these bitches, man, and they're so crazy they think anybody can be had. Because they been had themselves. So you tell 'em you're straight and they just nod and smile. You ain't real to 'em. They can't see nothin' but themselves and these goddamn games they're always playin'. (*Having returned to his bunk,* HE *is putting on his shoes*) I mean, you can be decent about anything, Roger, you see what I'm sayin'? We're all just people, man, and some of us are hardly that. That's all I'm sayin'. (*There is a slight pause as* HE *sits there thinking. Then* HE *gets to his feet*) I'll go get some buckets and stuff so we can clean up, okay? This area's a mess. This area ain't standin' tall.

ROGER: That's good talk, lad; this area a midget you put it next to an area standin' tall.

BILLY: Got to be good fuckin' troopers.

ROGER: That's right, that's right. I know the meanin' of the words.

BILLY: I mean, I just think we all got to be honest with each other—you understand me?

ROGER: No, I don't understand you; one stupid fuckin' nigger like me—how's that gonna be?

BILLY: That's right; mock me, man. That's what I need. I'll go get the wax.

Out BILLY *goes, talking to himself and leaving the door open. For a moment* ROGER *sits, thinking, and then* HE *looks at* RICHIE'*s locker and gets to his feet and walks to the locker.* HE *opens it and looks at the pinup hanging on the inside of the door.* HE *takes a step backward, looking.*

ROGER: Sheee-it.

Through the open door comes CARLYLE. ROGER *doesn't see him. And* CARLYLE *stands there looking at* ROGER *and the picture in the locker.*

CARLYLE: Boy . . . whose locker you lookin' into?

ROGER (HE *is startled, but recovers*): Hey, baby, what's happenin'?

CARLYLE: That ain't your locker, is what I'm askin', nigger. I mean, you ain't got no white goddamn woman hangin' on your wall.

ROGER: Oh, no—no, no.

CARLYLE: You don't wanna be lyin' to me, 'cause I got to turn you in you lyin' and you do got the body a some white goddamn woman hangin' there for you to peek at nobody around but you—you can be thinkin' about that sweet wet pussy an' maybe it hot an' maybe it cool.

ROGER: I could be thinkin' all that, except I know the penalty for lyin'.

CARLYLE: Thank God for that. (*Extending his hand, palm up*)

ROGER: That's right. This here the locker of a faggot. (*And* HE *slaps* CARLYLE*'s hand, palm to palm*)

CARLYLE: Course it is; I see that; any damn body know that. (ROGER *crosses toward his bunk and* CARLYLE *swaggers about, pulling a pint of whiskey from his hip pocket*) You want a shot? Have you a little taste, my man.

ROGER: Naw.

CARLYLE: C'mon. C'mon. I think you a Tom you don't drink outa my bottle. (HE *thrusts the bottle toward* ROGER *and wipes a sweat- and grease-stained sleeve across his mouth*)

ROGER (*Taking the bottle*): Shit.

CARLYLE: That right. How do I know? I just got in. New boy in town. Somewhere over there; I dunno. They dump me in amongst a whole bunch a pale, boring motherfuckers. (HE *is exploring the room. Finding* BILLY*'s* Playboy, HE *edges onto* BILLY*'s bed and leafs nervously through the pages*) I just come in from P Company, man, and I been all over this place, don't see too damn many of us. This outfit look like it a little short on soul. I been walkin' all around, I tell you, and the number is small. Like one hand you can tabulate the lot of 'em. We got few brothers I been able to see, is what I'm sayin'. You and me and two cats down in the small bay. That's all I found. (*As* ROGER *is about to hand the bottle back,* CARLYLE, *almost angrily, waves him off*) No, no, you take another; take you a real taste.

ROGER: It ain't so bad here. We do all right.

CARLYLE (HE *moves, shutting the door. Suspiciously,* HE *approaches* ROGER): How about the white guys? They give you any sweat? What's the situation? No jive. I like to know what is goin' on within the situation before that situation get a chance to be closin' in on me.

ROGER (*Putting the bottle on the footlocker,* HE *sits down*): Man, I'm tellin' you, it ain't bad. They're just pale, most of 'em, you know. They can't help it; how they gonna help it? Some of 'em got little bit of soul, couple real good boys around this way. Get 'em little bit of Coppertone, they be straight, man.

CARLYLE: How about the NCOs? We got any brother NCO watchin' out for us or they all white, like I goddamn well KNOW all the officers are? Fuckin' officers always white, man; fuckin' snow cones and bars everywhere you look. (HE *cannot stay still.* HE *moves to his right, his left;* HE *sits,* HE *stands*)

ROGER: First sergeant's a black man.

CARLYLE: All right; good news. Hey, hey, you wanna go over the club with me, or maybe downtown? I got wheels. Let's be free. (*Now* HE *rushes at* ROGER) Let's be free.

ROGER: Naw . . .

CARLYLE: Ohhh, baby . . . ! (HE *is wildly pulling at* ROGER *to get him to the door*)

ROGER: Some other time. I gotta get the area straight. Me and the guy sleeps in here too are gonna shape the place up a little.

ROGER *has pulled free, and* CARLYLE *cannot understand. It hurts him, depresses him.*

CARLYLE: You got a sweet deal here an' you wanna keep it, that right? (HE *paces about the room, opens a footlocker, looks inside*) How you rate you get a room like this for yourself—you and a couple guys?

ROGER: Spec 4. The three of us in here Spec 4.

CARLYLE: You get a room then, huh? (*And suddenly, without warning or transition,* HE *is angry*) Oh, man I hate this goddamn army. I hate this bastard army. I mean, I just got outa basic—off leave—you know? Back on the block for two weeks—and now here. They don't pull any a that petty shit, now, do they—that goddamn petty basic training bullshit? They do and I'm gonna be bustin' some head—my hand is gonna be upside all kinds a heads, 'cause I ain't gonna be able to endure it, man, not that kinda crap—understand? (*And again,* HE *is rushing at* ROGER) Hey, hey, oh, c'mon, let's get my wheels and make it, man, do me the favor.

ROGER: How'm I gonna? I got my obligations.

And CARLYLE *spins away in anger.*

CARLYLE: Jesus, baby, can't you remember the outside? How long it been since you been on leave? It is so sweet out there, nigger; you got it all forgot. I had such a sweet, sweet time. They doin' dances, baby, make you wanna cry. I hate this damn army. (*The anger overwhelms him*) All these mother-actin' jacks givin' you jive about what you gotta do and what you can't do. I had a bad scene in basic—up the hill and down the hill; it ain't somethin' I enjoyed even a little. So they do me wrong here, Jim, they gonna be sorry. Some-damn-body! And this whole Vietnam THING—I do not dig it. (HE *falls on his knees before* ROGER. *It is a gesture that begins as a joke, a mockery. And then a real fear pulses through him to nearly fill the pose* HE *has taken*) Lord, Lord, don't let 'em touch me. Christ, what will I do, they DO! Whoooooooooooooo! And they pullin' guys outa here, too, ain't they? Pullin' 'em like weeds, man; throwin' 'em into the fire. It's shit, man.

ROGER: They got this ole sarge sleeps down the hall—just today they got him.

CARLYLE: Which ole sarge?

ROGER: He sleeps just down the hall. Little guy.

CARLYLE: Wino, right?

ROGER: Booze hound.

CARLYLE: Yeh; I seen him. They got him, huh?

ROGER: He's goin'; gotta be packin' his bags. And three other guys two days ago. And two guys last week.

CARLYLE (*Leaping up from* BILLY's *bed*): Ohhh, them bastards. And everybody just takes it. It ain't our war, brother. I'm tellin' you. That's what gets me, nigger. It ain't our war nohow because it ain't our country, and that's what burns my ass—that and everybody just sittin' and takin' it. They gonna be bustin' balls, man—kickin' and stompin'. Everybody here maybe one week from shippin' out to get blown clean away and, man, whata they doin'? They doin' what they told. That what they doin'. Like you? Shit! You gonna straighten up your goddamn area! Well, that ain't for me; I'm gettin' hat, and makin' it out where it's sweet and the people's livin'. I can't cut this jive here, man. I'm tellin' you. I can't cut it.

CARLYLE *has moved toward* ROGER, *and behind him now* RICHIE *enters, running, his hair wet, traces of shaving cream on his face. Toweling his hair,* HE *falters, seeing* CARLYLE. *Then* HE *crosses to his locker.* CARLYLE *grins at* ROGER, *looks at* RICHIE, *steps toward him and gives a little bow.*

My name is Carlyle; what is yours?

RICHIE: Richie.

CARLYLE (HE *turns toward* ROGER *to share his joke*): Hello. Where is Martin? That cute little Martin. (*And* RICHIE *has just taken off his robe as* CARLYLE *turns back*) You cute, too, Richie.

RICHIE: Martin doesn't live here. (*Hurriedly putting on underpants to cover his nakedness*)

CARLYLE (*Watching* RICHIE, HE *slowly turns toward* ROGER): You ain't gonna make it with me, man?

ROGER: Naw . . . like I tole you. I'll catch you later.

CARLYLE: That's sad, man; make me cry in my heart.

ROGER: You g'wan get your head smokin'. Stop on back.

CARLYLE: Okay, okay. Got to be one man one more time. (*On the move for the door, his hand extended palm up behind him, demanding the appropriate response*) Baby! Gimme! Gimme!

Lunging, ROGER *slaps the hand.*

ROGER: G'wan home! G'wan home.

CARLYLE: You gonna hear from me. (*And* HE *is gone out the door and down the hallway*)

ROGER: I can . . . and do . . . believe . . . that.

RICHIE, *putting on his T-shirt, watches* ROGER, *who stubs out his cigarette, then·crosses to the trash can to empty the ashtray.*

RICHIE: Who was that?

ROGER: Man's new, Rich. Dunno his name more than that "Carlyle" he said. He's new—just outa basic.

RICHIE (*Powdering his thighs and under his arms*): Oh, my God . . .

> BILLY *enters, pushing a mop bucket with a wringer attached and carrying a container of wax.*

ROGER: Me and Billy's gonna straighten up the area. You wanna help?

RICHIE: Sure, sure; help, help.

BILLY (*Talking to* ROGER, *but turning to look at* RICHIE, *who is still putting powder under his arms*): I hadda steal the wax from Third Platoon.

ROGER: Good man.

BILLY (*Moving to* RICHIE, *joking, yet really irritated in some strange way*): What? Whata you doin', singin'? Look at that, Rog. He's got enough jazz there for an entire beauty parlor. (*Grabbing the can from* RICHIE'*s hand*) What is this? Baby Powder! BABY POWDER!

RICHIE: I get rashes.

BILLY: Okay, okay, you get rashes, so what? They got powder for rashes that isn't baby powder.

RICHIE: It doesn't work as good; I've tried it. Have you tried it?

> *Grabbing* BILLY'*s waist,* RICHIE *pulls him close.* BILLY *knocks* RICHIE'*s hands away.*

BILLY: Man, I wish you could get yourself straight. I'll mop, too, Roger—okay? Then I'll put down the wax and you can spread it? (HE *has walked away from* RICHIE)

RICHIE: What about buffing?

ROGER: In the morning. (HE *is already busy mopping up near the door*)

RICHIE: What do you want me to do?

BILLY (*Grabbing up a mop,* HE *heads downstage to work*): Get inside your locker and shut the door and don't holler for help. Nobody'll know you're there; you'll stay there.

RICHIE: But I'm so pretty.

BILLY: NOW! (*Pointing to* ROGER. HE *wants to get this clear*) Tell that man you mean what you're sayin', Richie.

RICHIE: Mean what?

BILLY: That you really think you're pretty.

RICHIE: Of course I do; I am. Don't you think I am? Don't *you* think I am, Roger?

ROGER: I tole you—you fulla shit and you cute, man. Carlyle just tole you you cute, too.

RICHIE: Don't you think it's true, Billy?

BILLY: It's like I tole you, Rog.

RICHIE: What did you tell him?

BILLY: That you go down; that you go up and down like a yo-yo and you go blowin' all the trees like the wind.

> RICHIE *is stunned.* HE *looks at* ROGER, *and then* HE *turns and stares into his own locker. The* OTHERS *keep mopping.* RICHIE *takes out a towel, and putting it around his neck,* HE *walks to where* BILLY *is working.* HE *stands there, hurt, looking at* BILLY.

RICHIE: What the hell made you tell him I been down, Billy?

BILLY (*Still mopping*): It's in your eyes; I seen it.

RICHIE: What?

BILLY: You.

RICHIE: What is it, Billy, you think you're trying to say? You and all your wit and intelligence—your *humanity.*

BILLY: I said it, Rich; I said what I was tryin' to say.

RICHIE: *Did* you?

BILLY: I think I did.

RICHIE: *Do* you?

BILLY: Loud and clear, baby. (*Still mopping*)

ROGER: They got to put me in with the weirdos. Why is that, huh? How come the army *hate* me, do this shit to me—*know* what to do. (*Whimsical and then suddenly loud, angered, violent*) Now you guys put socks in your mouths, right now—get shut up—or I am gonna beat you to death with each other. Roger got work to do. To be doin' it!

RICHIE (*Turning to his bed,* HE *kneels upon it*): Roger, I think you're so innocent sometimes. Honestly, it's not such a terrible thing. Is it, Billy?

BILLY: How would I know? (HE *slams his mop into the bucket*) Oh, go fuck yourself.

RICHIE: Well, I can give it a try, if that's what you want. Can I think of you as I do?

BILLY (*Throwing down his mop*): GODDAMMIT! That's it! IT! (HE *exits, rushing into the hall and slamming the door behind him.* ROGER *looks at* RICHIE. *Neither quite knows what is going on. Suddenly the door bursts open and* BILLY *storms straight over to* RICHIE, *who still kneels on the bed*) Now I am gonna level with you. Are you gonna listen? You gonna hear what I say, Rich, and not what you think I'm sayin'? (RICHIE *turns away as if to rise, his manner flippant, disdainful*) No! Don't get cute; don't turn away cute. I wanna say somethin' straight out to you and I want you to hear it!

RICHIE: I'm all ears, goddammit! For what, however, I do not know, except some boring evasion.

BILLY: At least wait the hell till you hear me!

RICHIE (*In irritation*): Okay, okay! What?

BILLY: Now this is level, Rich; this is straight talk. (HE *is quiet, intense. This is difficult for him.* HE *seeks the exactly appropriate words of explanation*) No b.s. No tricks. What you do on the side, that's your business and I don't care about it. But if you don't cut the cute shit with me, I'm gonna turn you off. Completely. You ain't gonna get a good mornin' outa me, you understand, because it's gettin' bad around here. I mean, I know how you think—how you keep lookin' out and seein' yourself, and that's what I'm tryin' to tell you because that's all that's happenin', Rich. That's all there is to it when you look out at me and think there's some kind of approval or whatever you see in my eyes—you're just seein' yourself. And I'm talkin' the simple quiet truth to you, Rich. I swear I am.

BILLY *looks away from* RICHIE *now and tries to go back to the mopping. It is embarrassing for them all.* ROGER *has watched, has tried to keep working.* RICHIE *has flopped back on his bunk. There is a silence.*

RICHIE: How . . . do . . . you want me to be? I don't know how else to be.
BILLY: Ohhh, man, that ain't any part of it. (*The mop is clenched in his hands*)
RICHIE: Well, I don't come from the same kind of world as you do.
BILLY: Damn, Richie, you think Roger and I come off the same street?
ROGER: Shit . . .
RICHIE: All right. Okay. But I've just done what I wanted all my life. If I wanted to do something, I just did it. Honestly. I've never had to work or anything like that and I've always had nice clothing and money for cab fare. Money for whatever I wanted. Always. I'm not like you are.
ROGER: You ain't sayin' you really done that stuff, though, Rich.
RICHIE: What?
ROGER: That fag stuff.
RICHIE (HE *continues looking at* ROGER *and then* HE *looks away*): Yes.
ROGER: Do you even know what you're sayin', Richie? Do you even know what it means to be a fag?
RICHIE: Roger, of course I know what it is. I just told you I've done it. I thought you black people were supposed to understand all about suffering and human strangeness. I thought you had depth and vision from all your suffering. Has someone been misleading me? I just told you I did it. I know all about it. Everything. All the various positions.
ROGER: Yeh, so maybe you think you've tried it, but that don't make you it. I mean, we used to . . . in the old neighborhood, man, we had a couple dudes swung that way. But they was weird, man. There was this one little fella, he was a screamin' goddamn faggot . . . uh . . . (HE *considers* RICHIE, *wondering if perhaps* HE *has offended him*) Ohhh, ohhh, you ain't no screamin' goddamn faggot, Richie, no matter what you say. And the baddest man on the block was my boy Jerry Lemon. So one day Jerry's got the faggot

in one a them ole deserted stairways and he's bouncin' him off the walls. I'm just a little fella, see, and I'm watchin' the baddest man on the block do his thing. So he come bouncin' back into me instead of Jerry, and just when he hit, he gave his ass this little twitch, man, like he thought he was gonna turn me on. I'd never a thought that was possible, man, for a man to be twitchin' his ass on me, just like he thought he was a broad. Scared me to death. I took off runnin'. Oh, oh, that ole neighborhood put me into all kinds a crap. I did some sufferin', just like Richie says. Like this once, I'm swingin' on up the street after school, and outa this phone booth comes this man with a goddamned knife stickin' outa his gut. So he sees me and starts tryin' to pull his motherfuckin' coat out over the handle, like he's worried about how he looks, man. "I didn't know this was gonna happen," he says. And then he falls over. He was just all of a sudden dead, man; just all of a sudden dead. You ever seen anything like that, Billy? Any crap like that?

BILLY, *sitting on* ROGER*'s bunk, is staring at* ROGER.

BILLY: You really seen that?
ROGER: Richie's a big-city boy.
RICHIE: Oh, no; never anything like that.
ROGER: "Momma, help me," I am screamin'. "Jesus, Momma, help me." Little fella, he don't know how to act, he sees somethin' like that.

For a moment THEY *are still, each thinking.*

BILLY: How long you think we got?
ROGER: What do you mean?

ROGER *is hanging up the mops;* BILLY *is now kneeling on* ROGER*'s bunk.*

BILLY: Till they pack us up, man, ship us out.
ROGER: To the war, you mean? To Disneyland? Man, I dunno; that up to them IBMs. Them machines is figurin' that. Maybe tomorrow, maybe next week, maybe never.

The war—the threat of it—is the one thing THEY *share.*

RICHIE: I was reading they're planning to build it all up to more than five hundred thousand men over there. Americans. And they're going to keep it that way until they win.
BILLY: Be a great place to come back from, man, you know? I keep thinkin' about that. To have gone there, to have been there, to have seen it and lived.
ROGER (*Settling onto* BILLY*'s bunk,* HE *lights a cigarette*): Well, what we got right here is a fool, gonna probably be one a them five hundred thousand, too. Do you know I cry at the goddamn anthem yet sometimes? The flag is

flyin' at a ball game, the ole Roger gets all wet in the eye. After all the shit been done to his black ass. But I don't know what I think about this war. I do not know.

BILLY: I'm tellin' you, Rog—I've been doin' a lot a readin' and I think it's right we go. I mean, it's just like when North Korea invaded South Korea or when Hitler invaded Poland and all those other countries. He just kept testin' everybody and when nobody said no to him, he got so committed he couldn't back out even if he wanted. And that's what this Ho Chi Minh is doin'. And all these other Communists. If we let 'em know somebody is gonna stand up against 'em, they'll back off, just like Hitler would have.

ROGER: There is folks, you know, who are sayin' L.B.J. is the Hitler, and not ole Ho Chi Minh at all.

RICHIE (*Talking as if this is the best news* HE's *heard in years*): Well, I don't know anything at all about all that, but I am certain I don't want to go—whatever is going on. I mean, those Vietcong don't just shoot you and blow you up, you know. My God, they've got these other awful things they do: putting elephant shit on these stakes in the ground and then you step on 'em and you got elephant shit in a wound in your foot. The infection is horrendous. And then there's these caves they hide in and when you go in after 'em, they've got these snakes that they've tied by their tails to the ceiling. So it's dark and the snake is furious from having been hung by its tail and you crawl right into them—your face. My God.

BILLY: They do not.

> BILLY *knows* HE *has been caught;* THEY ALL *know it.*

RICHIE: I read it, Billy. They do.

BILLY (*Completely facetious, yet the fear is real*): That's bullshit, Richie.

ROGER: That's right, Richie. They maybe do that stuff with the elephant shit, but nobody's gonna tie a snake by its tail, let ole Billy walk into it.

BILLY: That's disgusting, man.

ROGER: Guess you better get ready for the Klondike, my man.

BILLY: That is probably the most disgusting thing I ever heard of. I DO NOT WANT TO GO! NOT TO NOWHERE WHERE THAT KINDA SHIT IS GOIN' ON! L.B.J. is Hitler; suddenly I see it all very clearly.

ROGER: Billy got him a hatred for snakes.

RICHIE: I hate them, too. They're hideous.

BILLY (*And now, as a kind of apology to* RICHIE, HE *continues his self-ridicule far into the extreme*): I mean, that is one of the most awful things I ever heard of any person doing. I mean, any person who would hang a snake by its tail in the dark of a cave in the hope that some other person might crawl into it and get bitten to death, that first person is somebody who oughta be shot. And I hope the five hundred thousand other guys that get sent over there kill 'em all—all them gooks—get 'em all driven back into Ger-

many, where they belong. And in the meantime, I'll be holding the nor-
thern border against the snowmen.

ROGER (*Rising from* BILLY's *bed*): And in the meantime before that, we better
be gettin' at the ole area here. Got to be strike troopers.

BILLY: Right.

RICHIE: Can I help?

ROGER: Sure. Be good. (*And* HE *crosses to his footlocker and takes out a radio*) Think
maybe I put on a little music, though it's gettin' late. We got time. Billy,
you think?

BILLY: Sure. (*Getting nervously to his feet*)

ROGER: Sure. All right. We can be doin' it to the music. (HE *plugs the radio into the floor outlet as* BILLY *bolts for the door*)

BILLY: I gotta go pee.

ROGER: You watch out for the snakes.

BILLY: It's the snowmen, man; the snowmen.

> BILLY *is gone and "Ruby," sung by Ray Charles, comes from the radio. For
> a moment, as the music plays,* ROGER *watches* RICHIE *wander about the room,
> pouring little splashes of wax onto the floor. Then* RICHIE *moves to his bed and
> lies down, and* ROGER, *shaking his head, starts leisurely to spread the wax,
> with* RICHIE *watching.*

RICHIE: How come you and Billy take all this so seriously—you know.

ROGER: What?

RICHIE: This army nonsense. You're always shining your brass and keeping your
footlocker neat and your locker so neat. There's no point to any of it.

ROGER: We here, ain't we, Richie? We in the army. (*Still working the wax*)

RICHIE: There's no point to any of it. And doing those push-ups, the two of
you.

ROGER: We just see a lot a things the same way is all. Army ought to be a
serious business, even if sometimes it ain't.

RICHIE: You're lucky, you know, the two of you. Having each other for friends
the way you do. I never had that kind of friend ever. Not even when I
was little.

ROGER (*After a pause during which* HE, *working, sort of peeks at* RICHIE *every now
and then*): You ain't really inta that stuff, are you, Richie? (*It is a question
that is a statement*)

RICHIE (*Coyly* HE *looks at* ROGER): What stuff is that, Roger?

ROGER: That fag stuff, man. You know. You ain't really into it, are you? You
maybe messed in it a little is all—am I right?

RICHIE: I'm very weak, Roger. And by that I simply mean that if I have an
impulse to do something, I don't know how to deny myself. If I feel like
doing something, I just do it. I . . . will . . . admit to sometimes wishin'

I . . . was a little more like you . . . and Billy, even, but not to any severe extent.

ROGER: But that's such a bad scene, Rich. You don't want that. Nobody wants that. Nobody wants to be a punk. Not nobody. You wanna know what I think it is? You just got in with the wrong bunch. Am I right? You just got in with a bad bunch. That can happen. And that's what I think happened to you. I bet you never had a chance to really run with the boys before. I mean, regular normal guys like Billy and me. How'd you come in the army, huh, Richie? You get drafted?

RICHIE: No.

ROGER: That's my point, see. (HE *has stopped working.* HE *stands, leaning on the mop, looking at* RICHIE)

RICHIE: About four years ago, I went to this party. I was very young, and I went to this party with a friend who was older and . . . this "fag stuff," as you call it, was going on . . . so I did it.

ROGER: And then you come in the army to get away from it, right? Huh?

RICHIE: I don't know.

ROGER: Sure.

RICHIE: I don't know, Roger.

ROGER: Sure; sure. And now you're gettin' a chance to run with the boys for a little, you'll get yourself straightened around. I know it for a fact; I know that thing.

From off there is the sudden loud bellowing sound of SERGEANT ROONEY.

ROONEY (*Offstage*): THERE AIN'T BEEN NO SOLDIERS IN THIS CAMP BUT ME. I BEEN THE ONLY ONE—I BEEN THE ONLY ME!

And BILLY *comes dashing into the room.*

BILLY: Oh, boy.

ROGER: Guess who?

ROONEY (*Offstage*): FOR SO LONG I BEEN THE ONLY GODDAMN ONE!

BILLY (*Leaping onto his bed and covering his face with a* Playboy *magazine as* RICHIE *is trying to disappear under his sheets and blankets and* ROGER *is trying to get the wax put away so* HE *can get into his own bunk*): Hut who hee whor—he's got some yo-yo with him, Rog!

ROGER: Huh?

COKES *and* ROONEY *enter.* BOTH *are in fatigues and drunk and big-bellied.* THEY *are in their fifties, their hair whitish and cut short.* BOTH MEN *carry whiskey bottles, beer bottles.* COKES *is a little neater than* ROONEY, *his fatigue jacket tucked in and not so rumpled, and* HE *wears canvas-sided jungle boots.* ROONEY, *very disheveled, chomps on the stub of a big cigar.* THEY *swagger in, looking for fun, and stand there side by side.*

ROONEY: What kinda platoon I got here? You buncha shit sacks. Everybody look sharp. (*The* THREE BOYS *lie there, unmoving*) Off and on!

COKES: OFF AND ON! (HE *seems barely conscious, wavering as* HE *stands*)

ROGER: What's happenin', Sergeant?

ROONEY (*Shoving his bottle of whiskey at* ROGER, *who is sitting up*): Shut up, Moore! You want a belt? (*Splashing whiskey on* ROGER's *chest*)

ROGER: How can I say no?

COKES: My name is Cokes!

BILLY (*Rising to sit on the side of his bed*): How about me, too?

COKES: You wait your turn.

ROONEY (HE *looks at the three of them as if* THEY *are fools. Indicates* COKES *with a gesture*): Don't you see what I got here?

BILLY: Who do I follow for my turn?

ROONEY (*Suddenly, crazily petulant*): Don't you see what I got here? Everybody on their feet and at attention!

> BILLY *and* ROGER *climb from their bunks and stand at attention.* THEY *don't know what* ROONEY *is mad at.*

I mean it!

> RICHIE *bounds to the position of attention.*

This here is my friend, who in addition just come back from the war! The goddamn war! He been to it and he come back. (HE *is patting* COKES *gently, proudly*) The man's a fuckin' hero! (HE *hugs* COKES, *almost kissing him on the cheek*) He's always been a fuckin' hero.

> COKES, *embarrassed in his stupor, kind of wobbles a little from side to side.*

COKES: No-o-o-o-o-o . . . (*And* ROONEY *grabs him, starts pushing him toward* BILLY's *footlocker*)

ROONEY: Show 'em your boots, Cokes. Show 'em your jungle boots. (*With a long, clumsy step,* COKES *climbs onto the footlocker,* ROONEY *supporting him from behind and then bending to lift one of* COKES's *booted feet and display it for the boys*) Lookee that boot. That ain't no everyday goddamn army boot. That is a goddamn jungle boot! That green canvas is a jungle boot 'cause a the heat, and them little holes in the bottom are so the water can run out when you been walkin' in a lotta water like in a jungle swamp. (HE *is extremely proud of all this;* HE *looks at them*) The army ain't no goddamn fool. You see a man wearin' boots like that, you might as well see he's got a chestful a medals, 'cause he been to the war. He don't have no boots like that unless he been to the war! Which is where I'm goin' and all you slaphappy motherfuckers, too. Got to go kill some gooks. (HE *is nodding at them, smiling*) That's right.

COKES (*Bursting loudly from his stupor*): Gonna piss on 'em. Old booze. 'At's what I did. Piss in the rivers. Goddamn GIs secret weapon is old booze and he's pissin' it in all their runnin' water. Makes 'em yellow. Ahhhha ha, ha, ha! (HE *laughs and laughs, and* ROONEY *laughs, too, hugging* COKES)

ROONEY: Me and Cokesy been in so much shit together we oughta be brown. (*And then* HE *catches himself, looks at* ROGER) Don't take no offense at that, Moore. We been swimmin' in it. One Hundred and First Airborne, together. One-oh-one. Screamin' goddamn Eagles! (*Looking at each other, face to face, eyes glinting,* THEY *make sudden loud screaming-eagle sounds*) This ain't the army; you punks ain't in the army. You ain't ever seen the army. The army is Airborne! Airborne!

COKES (*Beginning to stomp his feet*): Airborne, Airborne! ALL THE WAY!

RICHIE, *amused and hoping for a drink, too, reaches out toward* ROONEY.

RICHIE: Sergeant, Sergeant, I can have a little drink, too.

ROONEY (*Looks at* RICHIE *and clutches the bottle*): Are you kiddin' me? You gotta be kiddin' me. (HE *looks to* ROGER) He's kiddin' me, ain't he, Moore? (*And then to* BILLY *and then to* COKES) Ain't he, Cokesy?

COKES *steps forward and down with a thump, taking charge for his bewildered friend.*

COKES: Don't you know you are tryin' to take the booze from the hand a the future goddamn Congressional Honor winner . . . Medal . . . ? (*And* HE *looks lovingly at* ROONEY. HE *beams*) Ole Rooney, Ole Rooney. (HE *hugs* ROONEY's *head*) He almost done it already.

And ROONEY, *overwhelmed, starts screaming "Agggggghhhhhhhhhh," a screaming-eagle sound, and making clawing eagle gestures at the air.* HE *jumps up and down, stomping his feet.* COKES *instantly joins in, stomping and jumping and yelling.*

ROONEY: Let's show these shit sacks how men are men jumpin' outa planes. Agggggghhhhhhhhhh. (*Stomping and yelling,* THEY *move in a circle,* ROONEY *followed by* COKES) A plane fulla yellin' stompin' men!

COKES: All yellin' stompin' men!

COKES *and* ROONEY *yell and stomp, making eagle sounds, and then* ROONEY *leaps up on* BILLY's *bed and runs the length of it until* HE *is on the footlocker,* COKES *still on the floor, stomping.* ROONEY *makes a gesture of hooking his rip cord to the line inside the plane.* THEY *yell louder and louder and* ROONEY *leaps high into the air, yelling "GERONIMO-O-O-O!" as* COKES *leaps onto the locker and then high into the air, bellowing "GERONIMO-O-O-O!"* THEY *stand side by side, their arms held up in the air as if grasping the shroud lines of open chutes.* THEY *seem to float there in silence.*

What a feelin' . . .

ROONEY: Beautiful feelin' . . .

For a moment more THEY *float there, adrift in the room, the sky, their memory.*
COKES *smiles at* ROONEY.

COKES: Remember that one guy, O'Flannigan . . . ?

ROONEY (*Nodding, smiling, remembering*): O'Flannigan . . .

COKES: He was this one guy . . . O'Flannigan . . . (HE *moves now toward the
boys,* BILLY, ROGER *and* RICHIE, *who have gathered on* ROGER'*s bed and footlocker.*
ROONEY *follows several steps, then drifts backward onto* BILLY'*s bed, where* HE *sits
and then lies back, listening to* COKES) We was testing chutes where you could
just pull a lever by your ribs here when you hit the ground—see—and the
chute would come off you, because it was just after a whole bunch a guys·
had been dragged to death in an unexpected and terrible wind at Fort Bragg.
So they wanted you to be able to release the chute when you hit if there
was a bad wind when you hit. So O'Flannigan was this kinda joker who
had the goddamn sense a humor of a clown and nerves, I tell you, of steel,
and he says he's gonna release the lever midair, then reach up, grab the lines
and float on down, hanging. (*His hand paws at the air, seeking a rope that
isn't there*) So I seen him pull the lever at five hundred feet and he reaches
up to two fistfuls a air, the chute's twenty feet above him, and he went
into the ground like a knife. (*The bottle, held high over his head, falls through
the air to the bed,* ALL *watching it*)

BILLY: Geezus.

ROONEY (*Nodding gently*): Didn't get to sing the song, I bet.

COKES (*Standing, staring at the fallen bottle*): No way.

RICHIE: What song?

ROONEY (HE *rises up, mysteriously angry*): Shit sack! Shit sack!

RICHIE: What song, Sergeant Rooney?

ROONEY: "Beautiful streamer," shit sack.

COKES, *gone into another reverie, is staring skyward.*

COKES: I saw this one guy—never forget it. Never.

BILLY: That's Richie, Sergeant Rooney. He's a beautiful screamer.

RICHIE: He said "streamer," not "screamer," asshole.

COKES *is still in his reverie.*

COKES: This guy with his chute goin' straight up above him in a streamer, like
a tulip, only white, you know. All twisted and never gonna open. Like a
big icicle sticking straight up above him. He went right by me. We met
eyes, sort of. He was lookin' real puzzled. He looks right at me. Then he
looks up in the air at the chute, then down at the ground.

ROONEY: Did *he* sing it?

COKES: He didn't sing it. He started going like this. (HE *reaches desperately up-*

ward with both hands and begins to claw at the sky while his legs pump up and down) Like he was gonna climb right up the air.

RICHIE: Ohhhhh, Geezus.

BILLY: God.

ROONEY *has collapsed backward on* BILLY*'s bed and* HE *lies there and then* HE *rises.*

ROONEY: Cokes got the Silver Star for rollin' a barrel a oil down a hill in Korea into forty-seven chinky Chinese gooks who were climbin' up the hill and when he shot into it with his machine gun, it blew them all to grape jelly.

COKES, *rocking a little on his feet, begins to hum and then sing "Beautiful Streamer," to the tune of Stephen Foster's "Beautiful Dreamer."*

COKES: "Beautiful streamer, open for me . . . . The sky is above me . . . " (*And then the singing stops*) But the one I remember is this little guy in his spider hole, which is a hole in the ground with a lid over it. (*And* HE *is using* RICHIE*'s footlocker before him as the spider hole.* HE *has fixed on it, is moving toward it*) And he shot me in the ass as I was runnin' by, but the bullet hit me so hard (*His body kind of jerks and* HE *runs several steps*) it knocked me into this ditch where he couldn't see me. I got behind him. (*Now at the head of* RICHIE*'s bed,* HE *begins to creep along the side of the bed as if sneaking up on the footlocker*) Crawlin'. And I dropped a grenade into his hole. (HE *jams a whiskey bottle into the footlocker, then slams down the lid*) Then sat on the lid, him bouncin' and yellin' under me. Bouncin' and yellin' under the lid. I could hear him. Feel him. I just sat there.

Silence. ROONEY *waits, thinking, then leans forward.*

ROONEY: He was probably singin' it.

COKES (*Sitting there*): I think so.

ROONEY: You think we should let 'em hear it?

BILLY: We're good boys. We're good ole boys.

COKES (*Jerking himself to his feet,* HE *staggers sideways to join* ROONEY *on* BILLY*'s bed*): I don't care who hears it, I just wanna be singin' it.

ROONEY *rises;* HE *goes to the boys on* ROGER*'s bed and speaks to them carefully, as if lecturing people on something of great importance.*

ROONEY: You listen up; you just be listenin' up, 'cause if you hear it right you can maybe stop bein' shit sacks. This is what a man sings, he's goin' down through the air, his chute don't open.

Flopping back down on the bunk beside COKES, ROONEY *looks at* COKES *and then at the boys. The* TWO OLDER MEN *put their arms around each other and* THEY *begin to sing.*

ROONEY and COKES (*Singing*):   Beautiful streamer,
                                  Open for me,
                                  The sky is above me,
                                  But no canopy.

BILLY (*Murmuring*): I don't believe it.

ROONEY and COKES: Counted ten thousand,
                                  pulled on the cord.
                                  My chute didn't open,
                                  I shouted, "Dear Lord."

                                  Beautiful streamer,
                                  This looks like the end,
                                  The earth is below me,
                                  My body won't bend.

                                  Just like a mother
                                  Watching o'er me,
                                  Beautiful streamer,
                                  Ohhhhh, open for me.

ROGER: Un-fuckin'-believable.
ROONEY (*Beaming with pride*): Ain't that a beauty.

> *And then* COKES *topples forward onto his face and flops limply to his side. The* THREE BOYS *leap to their feet.* ROONEY *lunges toward* COKES.

RICHIE: Sergeant!
ROONEY: Cokie! Cokie!
BILLY: Jesus.
ROGER: Hey!
COKES: Huh? Huh? (HE *sits up.* ROONEY *is kneeling beside him*)
ROONEY: Jesus, Cokie.
COKES: I been doin' that; I been doin' that. It don't mean nothin'.
ROONEY: No, no.
COKES (*Pushing at* ROONEY, *who is trying to help him get back to the bed.* ROONEY *agrees with everything* HE *is now saying and the noises* ROONEY *makes are little animal noises*): I told 'em when they wanted to send me back I ain't got no leukemia; they wanna check it. They think I got it. I don't think I got it. Rooney? Whata you think?
ROONEY: No.
COKES: My mother had it. She had it. Just 'cause she did and I been fallin' down.
ROONEY: It don't mean nothin'.

COKES (HE *lunges back and up onto the bed*): I tole 'em I fall down 'cause I'm drunk. I'm drunk all the time.

ROONEY: You'll be goin' back over there with me, is what I know, Cokie. (HE *is patting* COKES, *nodding, dusting him off*) That's what I know.

BILLY *comes up to them, almost seeming to want to be a part of the intimacy* THEY *are sharing.*

BILLY: That was somethin', Sergeant Cokes. Jesus.

ROONEY *whirls on* BILLY, *ferocious, pushing him.*

ROONEY: Get the fuck away, Wilson! Whata you know? Get the fuck away. You don't know shit. Get away! You don't know shit. (*And* HE *turns to* COKES, *who is standing up from the bed*) Me and Cokes are goin' to the war zone like we oughta. Gonna blow it to shit. (HE *is grabbing at* COKES, *who is laughing.* THEY *are both laughing.* ROONEY *whirls on the boys*) Ohhh, I'm gonna be so happy to be away from you assholes; you pussies. Not one regular army people among you possible. I swear it to my mother who is holy. You just be watchin' the papers for doin' darin' brave deeds. 'Cause we're old hands at it. Makin' shit disappear. Goddamn whooosh!

COKES: Whooosh!

ROONEY: Demnalitions. Me and . . . (*And then* HE *knows* HE *hasn't said it right*) Me and Cokie . . . . Demnal . . . . Demnali . . .

RICHIE (*Still sitting on* ROGER'*s bed*): You can do it, Sergeant.

BILLY: Get it. (HE *stands by the lockers and* ROONEY *glares at him*)

ROGER: 'Cause you're cool with dynamite, is what you're tryin' to say.

ROONEY (*Charging at* ROGER, *bellowing*): Shut the fuck up, that's what you can do; and go to goddamn sleep. You buncha shit . . . sacks. Buncha mothers—know-it-all motherin' shit sacks—that's what you are.

COKES (*Shoulders back,* HE *is taking charge*): Just goin' to sleep is what you can do, 'cause Rooney and me fought it through two wars already and we can make it through this one more and leukemia that comes or doesn't come— who gives a shit? Not guys like us. We're goin' just pretty as pie. And it's lights-out time, ain't it, Rooney?

ROONEY: Past it, goddammit. So the lights are goin' out.

There is fear in the room, and the THREE BOYS *rush to their wall lockers, where* THEY *start to strip to their underwear, preparing for bed.* ROONEY *paces the room, watching them, glaring.*

Somebody's gotta teach you soldierin'. You hear me? Or you wanna go outside and march around awhile, huh? We can do that if you wanna. Huh? You tell me? Marchin' or sleepin'? What's it gonna be?

RICHIE (*Rushing to get into bed*): Flick out the ole lights, Sergeant; that's what we say.

BILLY (*Climbing into bed*): Put out the ole lights.

ROGER (*In bed and pulling up the covers*): Do it.

COKES: Shut up. (HE *rocks forward and back, trying to stand at attention.* HE *is saying good night*) And that's an order. Just shut up. I got grenades down the hall. I got a pistol. I know where to get nitro. You don't shut up, I'll blow . . . you . . . to . . . fuck. (*Making a military left face*, HE *stalks to the wall switch and turns the lights out.* ROONEY *is watching proudly, as* COKES *faces the boys again.* HE *looks at them*) That's right.

In the dark, there is only a spill of light from the hall coming in the open door. COKES *and* ROONEY *put their arms around each other and go out the door, leaving it partly open.* RICHIE, ROGER *and* BILLY *lie in their bunks, staring.* THEY *do not move.* THEY *lie there. The* SERGEANTS *seem to have vanished soundlessly once* THEY *went out the door. Light touches each of the boys as* THEY *lie there.*

ROGER (HE *does not move*): Lord have mercy, if that ain't a pair. If that ain't one pair a beauties.

BILLY: Oh, yeh. (HE *does not move*)

ROGER: Too much, man—too, too much.

RICHIE: They made me sad; but I loved them, sort of. Better than movies.

ROGER: Too much. Too, too much.

Silence.

BILLY: What time is it?

ROGER: Sleep time, men. Sleep time.

Silence.

BILLY: Right.

ROGER: They were somethin'. Too much.

BILLY: Too much.

RICHIE: Night.

ROGER: Night. (*Silence*) Night, Billy.

BILLY: Night.

RICHIE *stirs in his bed.* ROGER *turns onto his side.* BILLY *is motionless.*

I . . . had a buddy, Rog—and this is the whole thing, this is the whole point—a kid I grew up with, played ball with in high school, and he was a tough little cat, a real bad man sometimes. Used to have gangster pictures up in his room. Anyway, we got into this deal where we'd drive on down to the big city, man, you know, hit the bad spots, let some queer pick us up . . . sort of . . . long enough to buy us some good stuff. It was kinda the thing to do for a while, and we all did it, the whole gang of us.

So we'd let these cats pick us up, most of 'em old guys, and they were hurt-in' and happy as hell to have us, and we'd get a lot of free booze, maybe a meal, and we'd turn 'em on. Then pretty soon they'd ask us did we want to go over to their place. Sure, we'd say, and order one more drink, and then when we hit the street, we'd tell 'em to kiss off. We'd call 'em fag and queer and jazz like that and tell 'em to kiss off. And Frankie, the kid I'm tellin' you about, he had a mean streak in him and if they gave us a bad time at all, he'd put 'em down. That's the way he was. So that kinda jazz went on and on for sort of a long time and it was a good deal if we were low on cash or needed a laugh and it went on for a while. And then Frankie—one day he come up to me—and he says he was goin' home with the guy he was with. He said, what the hell, what did it matter? And he's sayin'—Frankie's sayin'—why don't I tag along? What the hell, he's sayin', what does it matter who does it to you, some broad or some old guy, you close your eyes, a mouth's a mouth, it don't matter—that's what he's sayin'. I tried to talk him out of it, but he wasn't hearin' anything I was sayin'. So the next day, see, he calls me up to tell me about it. Okay, okay, he says, it was a cool scene, he says; they played poker, a buck minimum, and he made a fortune. Frankie was eatin' it up, man. It was a pretty way to live, he says. So he stayed at it, and he had this nice little girl he was goin' with at the time. You know the way a real bad cat can sometimes do that— have a good little girl who's crazy about him and he is for her, too, and he's a different cat when he's with her?
ROGER: Uh-huh.

The hall light slants across BILLY's *face.*

BILLY: Well, that was him and Linda, and then one day he dropped her, he cut her loose. He was hooked, man. He was into it, with no way he knew out—you understand what I'm sayin'? He had got his ass hooked. He had never thought he would and then one day he woke up and he was on it. He just hadn't been told, that's the way I figure it; somebody didn't tell him somethin' he shoulda been told and he come to me wailin' one day, man, all broke up and wailin', my boy Frankie, my main man, and he was a fag. He was a faggot, black Roger, and I'm not lyin'. I am not lyin' to you.
ROGER: Damn.
BILLY: So that's the whole thing, man; that's the whole thing.

Silence. THEY *lie there.*

ROGER: Holy . . . Christ. Richie . . . you hear him? You hear what he said?
RICHIE: He's a storyteller.
ROGER: What you mean?

RICHIE: I mean, he's a storyteller, all right; he tells stories, all right.

ROGER: What are we into now? You wanna end up like that friend a his, or you don't believe what he said? Which are you sayin'?

The door bursts open. The sounds of machine guns and cannon are being made by someone, and CARLYLE, *drunk and playing, comes crawling in.* ROGER, RICHIE *and* BILLY *all pop up, startled, to look at him.*

Hey, hey, what's happenin'?

BILLY: Who's happenin'?

ROGER: You attackin' or you retreatin', man?

CARLYLE (*Looking up; big grin*): Hey, baby . . . ? (*Continues shooting, crawling. The* THREE BOYS *look at each other*)

ROGER: What's happenin', man? Whatcha doin'?

CARLYLE: I dunno, soul; I dunno. Practicin' my duties, my new abilities. (*Half sitting,* HE *flops onto his side, starts to crawl*) The low crawl, man; like I was taught in basic, that's what I'm doin'. You gotta know your shit, man, else you get your ass blown so far away you don't ever see it again. Oh, sure, you guys don't care. I know it. You got it made. You got it made. I don't got it made. You got a little home here, got friends, people to talk to. I got nothin'. You got jobs they probably ain't ever gonna ship you out, you got so important jobs. I got no job. They don't even wanna give me a job. I know it. They are gonna kill me. They are gonna send me over there to get me killed, goddammit. WHAT'S A MATTER WITH ALL YOU PEOPLE?

The anger explodes out of the grieving and ROGER *rushes to kneel beside* CARLYLE. HE *speaks gently, firmly.*

ROGER: Hey, man, get cool, get some cool; purchase some cool, man.

CARLYLE: Awwwww . . . (*Clumsily,* HE *turns away*)

ROGER: Just hang in there.

CARLYLE: I don't wanna be no DEAD man. I don't wanna be the one they all thinkin' is so stupid he's the only one'll go, they tell him; they don't even have to give him a job. I got thoughts, man, in my head; alla time, burnin', burnin' thoughts a understandin'.

ROGER: Don't you think we know that, man? It ain't the way you're sayin' it.

CARLYLE: It is.

ROGER: No. I mean, we all probably gonna go. We all probably gonna have to go.

CARLYLE: No-o-o-o-o.

ROGER: I mean it.

CARLYLE (*Suddenly* HE *nearly topples over*): I am very drunk. (*And* HE *looks up at* ROGER) You think so?

ROGER: I'm sayin' so. And I am sayin', "No sweat." No point.

CARLYLE *angrily pushes at* ROGER, *knocking him backward.*

CARLYLE: Awwwww, dammit, dammit, mother . . . shit . . . it . . . ohhhhhhh. (*Sliding to the floor, the rage and anguish softening into only breathing*) I mean it. I mean it. (*Silence.* HE *lies there*)

ROGER: What . . . a you doin' . . . ?

CARLYLE: Huh?

ROGER: I don't know what you're up to on our freshly mopped floor.

CARLYLE: Gonna go sleep—okay? No sweat . . . (*Suddenly very polite,* HE *is looking up*) Can I, soul? Izzit all right?

ROGER: Sure, man, sure, if you wanna, but why don't you go where you got a bed? Don't you like beds?

CARLYLE: Dunno where's zat. My bed. I can' fin' it. I can' fin' my own bed. I looked all over, but I can' fin' it anywhere. GONE! (*Slipping back down now,* HE *squirms to make a nest.* HE *hugs his bottle*)

ROGER (*Moving to his bunk, where* HE *grabs a blanket*): Okay, okay, man. But get on top a this, man. (HE *is spreading the blanket on the floor, trying to help* CARLYLE *get on it*) Make it softer. C'mon, c'mon . . . get on this.

BILLY *has risen with his own blanket, and is moving now to hand it to* ROGER.

BILLY: Cat's hurtin', Rog.

ROGER: Ohhhhh, yeh.

CARLYLE: Ohhhhh . . . it was so sweet at home . . . it was so sweet, baby; so-o-o good. They doin' dances make you wanna cry . . . . (*Hugging the blankets now,* HE *drifts in a kind of dream*)

ROGER: I know, man.

CARLYLE: So sweet . . . !

BILLY *is moving back to his own bed, where, quietly,* HE *sits.*

ROGER: I know, man.

CARLYLE: So sweet . . . !

ROGER: Yeh.

CARLYLE: How come I gotta be here?

On his way to the door to close it, ROGER *falters, looks at* CARLYLE, *then moves on toward the door.*

ROGER: I dunno, Jim.

BILLY *is sitting and watching, as* ROGER *goes on to the door, gently closes it and returns to his bed.*

BILLY: I know why he's gotta be here, Roger. You wanna know? Why don't you ask me?

ROGER: Okay. How come he gotta be here?

BILLY (*Smiling*): Freedom's frontier, man. That's why.

ROGER (*Settled on the edge of his bed and about to lie back*): Oh . . . yeh . . .

A distant bugle begins to play taps and RICHIE, *carrying a blanket, is approaching* CARLYLE. ROGER *settles back;* BILLY *is staring at* RICHIE; CARLYLE *does not stir; the bugle plays.*

Bet that ole sarge don't live a year, Billy. Fuckin' blow his own ass sky high.

RICHIE *has covered* CARLYLE. HE *pats* CARLYLE's *arm, and then straightens in order to return to his bed.*

BILLY: Richie . . . !

BILLY's *hissing voice freezes* RICHIE. HE *stands, and then* HE *starts again to move, and* BILLY's *voice comes again and* RICHIE *cannot move.*

Richie . . . how come you gotta keep doin' that stuff?

ROGER *looks at* BILLY, *staring at* RICHIE, *who stands still as a stone over the sleeping* CARLYLE.

How come?

ROGER: He dunno, man. Do you? You dunno, do you, Rich?

RICHIE: No.

CARLYLE (*From deep in his sleep and grieving*): It . . . was . . . so . . . pretty . . . !

RICHIE: No.

The lights are fading with the last soft notes of taps.

End of Act One

ACT TWO

Scene 1

Lights come up on the cadre room. It is late afternoon and BILLY *is lying on his stomach, his head at the foot of the bed, his chin resting on his hands.* HE *wears gym shorts and sweat socks; his T-shirt lies on the bed and his sneakers are on the floor.* ROGER *is at his footlocker, taking out a pair of sweat socks. His sneakers and his basketball are on his bed.* HE *is wearing his khakis.*

A silence passes, and then ROGER *closes his footlocker and sits on his bed, where* HE *starts lacing his sneakers, holding them on his lap.*

BILLY: Rog . . . you think I'm a busybody? In any way? (*Silence.* ROGER *laces his sneakers*) Roger?

ROGER: Huh? Uh-uh.

BILLY: Some people do. I mean, back home. (HE *rolls slightly to look at* ROGER) Or that I didn't know how to behave. Sort of.

ROGER: It's time we maybe get changed, don't you think? (HE *rises and goes to his locker.* HE *takes off his trousers, shoes and socks*)

BILLY: Yeh. I guess. I don't feel like it, though. I don't feel good, don't know why.

ROGER: Be good for you, man; be good for you. (*Pulling on his gym shorts,* HE *returns to his bed, carrying his shoes and socks*)

BILLY: Yeh. (HE *sits up on the edge of his bed.* ROGER, *sitting, is bowed over, putting on his socks*) I mean, a lot of people thought like I didn't know how to behave in a simple way. You know? That I overcomplicated everything. I didn't think so. Don't think so. I just thought I was seein' complications that were there but nobody else saw. (HE *is struggling now to put on his T-shirt.* HE *seems weary, almost weak*) I mean, Wisconsin's a funny place. All those clear-eyed people sayin' "Hello" and lookin' you straight in the eye. Everybody's good, you think, and happy and honest. And then there's all of a sudden a neighbor who goes mad as a hatter. I had a neighbor who came out of his house one morning with axes in both hands. He started then attackin' the cars that were driving up and down in front of his house. An' we all knew why he did it, sorta. (HE *pauses;* HE *thinks*) It made me wanna be a priest. I wanted to be a priest then. I was sixteen. Priests could help people. Could take away what hurt 'em. I wanted that, I thought. Somethin', huh?

ROGER (HE *has the basketball in his hands*): Yeh. But everybody's got feelin's like that sometimes.

BILLY: I don't know.

ROGER: You know, you oughta work on a little jump shot, my man. Get you some kinda fall-away jumper to go with that beauty of a hook. Make you tough out there.

BILLY: Can't fuckin' do it. Not my game. I mean, like that bar we go to. You think I could get a job there bartendin', maybe? I could learn the ropes. (HE *is watching* ROGER, *who has risen to walk to his locker*) You think I could get a job there off-duty hours?

ROGER (*Pulling his locker open to display the pinup on the inside of the door*): You don't want no job. It's that little black-haired waitress you wantin' to know.

BILLY: No, man. Not really.

ROGER: It's okay. She tough, man. (HE *begins to remove his uniform shirt.* HE *will put on an O.D. T-shirt to go to the gym*)

BILLY: I mean, not the way you're sayin' it, is all. Sure, there's somethin' about her. I don't know what. I ain't even spoke to her yet. But somethin'. I mean, what's she doin' there? When she's dancin', it's like she knows somethin'. She's degradin' herself, I sometimes feel. You think she is?

ROGER: Man, you don't even know the girl. She's workin'.

BILLY: I'd like to talk to her. Tell her stuff. Find out about her. Sometimes I'm thinkin' about her and it and I got a job there, I get to know her and she and I get to be real tight, man—close, you know. Maybe we screw, maybe we don't. It's nice . . . whatever.

ROGER: Sure. She a real fine-lookin' chippy, Billy. Got nice cakes. Nice little titties.

BILLY: I think she's smart, too. (ROGER *starts laughing so hard* HE *almost falls into his locker*) Oh, all I do is talk. "Yabba-yabba." I mean, my mom and dad are really terrific people. How'd they ever end up with somebody so weird as me?

ROGER (*Moves to* BILLY, *jostles him*): I'm tellin' you, the gym and a little ball is what you need. Little exercise. Little bumpin' into people. The soul is tellin' you.

BILLY *rises and goes to his locker, where* HE *starts putting on his sweat clothes.*

BILLY: I mean, Roger, you remember how we met in P Company? Both of us brand-new. You started talkin' to me. You just started talkin' to me and you didn't stop.

ROGER (*Hardly looking up*): Yeh.

BILLY: Did you see somethin' in me made you pick me?

ROGER: I was talkin' to everybody, man. For that whole day. Two whole days. You was just the first one to talk back friendly. Though you didn't say much, as I recall.

BILLY: The first white person, you mean. (*Wearing his sweat pants,* HE *is now at his bed, putting on his sneakers*)

ROGER: Yeh. I was tryin' to come outa myself a little. Do like the fuckin' headshrinker been tellin' me to stop them fuckin' headaches I was havin', you know. Now let us do fifteen or twenty push-ups and get over to that gymnasium, like I been sayin'. Then we can take our civvies with us—we can shower and change at the gym. (HE *crosses to* BILLY, *who flops down on his belly on the bed*)

BILLY: I don't know . . . I don't know what it is I'm feelin'. Sick like.

ROGER *forces* BILLY *up onto his feet and shoves him playfully downstage, where* THEY *both fall forward into the push-up position, side by side.*

ROGER: Do 'em, trooper. Do 'em. Get it.

ROGER *starts.* BILLY *joins in. After five,* ROGER *realizes that* BILLY *has his knees on the floor.* THEY *start again. This time,* BILLY *counts in double time.* THEY *start again. At about "seven,"* RICHIE *enters. Neither* BILLY *nor* ROGER *sees him.* THEY *keep going.*

ROGER and BILLY: . . . seven, eight, nine, ten . . .

RICHIE: No, no; no, no; no, no, no. That's not it; that's not it.

ROGER and BILLY (THEY *keep going, yelling the numbers louder and louder*): . . . eleven, twelve, thirteen . . .

RICHIE crosses to his locker and gets his bottle of cologne, and then returning to the center of the room to stare at them, HE *stands there dabbing cologne on his face.*

. . . fourteen, fifteen.

RICHIE: You'll never get it like that. You're so far apart and you're both humping at the same time. And all that counting. It's so unromantic.

ROGER (*Rising and moving to his bed to pick up the basketball*): We was exercisin', Richard. You heard a that?

RICHIE: Call it what you will, Roger.

With a flick of his wrist, ROGER *tosses the basketball to* BILLY.

Everybody has their own cute little pet names for it.

BILLY: Hey!

And BILLY *tosses the ball at* RICHIE, *hitting him in the chest, sending the cologne bottle flying.* RICHIE *yelps, as* BILLY *retrieves the ball and, grabbing up his sweat jacket from the bed, heads for the door.* ROGER, *at his own locker, has taken out his suit bag of civilian clothes.*

You missed.

RICHIE: Billy, Billy, Billy, please, please, the ruffian approach will not work with me. It impresses me not even one tiny little bit. All you've done is spill my cologne. (HE *bends to pick up the cologne from the floor*)

BILLY: That was my aim.

ROGER: See you.

BILLY *is passing* RICHIE. *Suddenly* RICHIE *sprays* BILLY *with cologne, some of it getting on* ROGER, *as* ROGER *and* BILLY, *groaning and cursing at* RICHIE, *rush out the door.*

RICHIE: Try the more delicate approach next time, Bill. (*Having crossed to the door,* HE *stands a moment, leaning against the frame. Then* HE *bounces to* BILLY*'s bed, sings "He's just my Bill," and squirts cologne on the pillow. At his locker,* HE *deposits the cologne, takes off his shirt, shoes and socks. Removing a hard-cover copy of Pauline Kael's* I Lost It at the Movies *from the top shelf of the locker,* HE *bounds to the center of the room and tosses the book the rest of the way to the bed. Quite pleased with himself,* HE *fidgets, pats his stomach, then lowers himself into the push-up position, goes to his knees and stands up*) Am I out of my fucking mind? Those two are crazy. I'm not crazy.

RICHIE *pivots and strides to his locker. With an ashtray, a pack of matches and a pack of cigarettes,* HE *hurries to his bed and makes himself comfortable to read, his head propped up on a pillow. Settling himself, HE opens the book, finds his place, thinks a little, starts to read. For a moment HE lies there. And then CARLYLE steps into the room. HE comes through the doorway looking to his left and right. HE comes several steps into the room and looks at RICHIE. RICHIE sees him. THEY look at each other.*

CARLYLE: Ain't nobody here, man?

RICHIE: Hello, Carlyle. How are you today?

CARLYLE: Ain't nobody here? (HE *is nervous and angrily disappointed*)

RICHIE: Who do you want?

CARLYLE: Where's the black boy?

RICHIE: Roger? My God, why do you keep calling him that? Don't you know his name yet? Roger. Roger. (HE *thickens his voice at this, imitating someone very stupid.* CARLYLE *stares at him*)

CARLYLE: Yeh. Where is he?

RICHIE: I am not his keeper, you know. I am not his private secretary, you know.

CARLYLE: I do not know. I do not know. That is why I am asking. I come to see him. You are here. I ask you. I don't know. I mean, Carlyle made a fool outa himself comin' in here the other night, talkin' on and on like how he did. Lay on the floor. He remember. You remember? It all one hype, man; that all one hype. You know what I mean. That ain't the real Carlyle was in here. This one here and now the real Carlyle. Who the real Richie?

RICHIE: Well . . . the real Richie . . . has gone home. To Manhattan. I, however, am about to read this book. (*Which HE again starts to try to do*)

CARLYLE: Oh. Shit. Jus' you the only one here, then, huh?

RICHIE: So it would seem. (HE *looks at the air and then under the bed as if to find someone*) So it would seem. Did you hear about Martin?

CARLYLE: What happened to Martin? I ain't seen him.

RICHIE: They are shipping him home. Someone told about what he did to himself. I don't know who.

CARLYLE: Wasn't me. Not me. I keep that secret.

RICHIE: I'm sure you did. (*Rising, walking toward* CARLYLE *and the door, cigarette pack in hand*) You want the cigarette? Or don't you smoke? Or do you have to go right away? (*Closing the door*) There's a chill sometimes coming down the hall, I don't know from where. (*Crossing back to his bed and climbing in*) And I think I've got the start of a little cold. Did you want the cigarette?

CARLYLE *is staring at him. Then* HE *examines the door and looks again at* RICHIE. HE *stares at* RICHIE, *thinking, and then* HE *walks toward him.*

CARLYLE: You know what I bet? I been lookin' at you real close. It just a way

I got about me. And I bet if I was to hang my boy out in front of you, my big boy, man, you'd start wanting to touch him. Be beggin' and talkin' sweet to ole Carlyle. Am I right or wrong? (HE *leans over* RICHIE) What do you say?

RICHIE: Pardon?

CARLYLE: You heard me. Ohhh. I am so restless, I don't even understand it. My big black boy is what I was talkin' about. My thing, man; my rope, Jim. HEY, RICHIE! (*And* HE *lunges, then moves his fingers through* RICHIE'*s hair*) How long you been a punk? Can you hear me? Am I clear? Do I talk funny? (HE *is leaning close*) Can you smell the gin on my mouth?

RICHIE: I mean, if you really came looking for Roger, he and Billy are gone to the gymnasium. They were—

CARLYLE: No. (HE *slides down on the bed, his arm placed over* RICHIE'*s legs*) I got no athletic abilities. I got none. No moves. I don't know. HEY, RICHIE! (*Leaning close again*) I just got this question I asked. I got no answer.

RICHIE: I don't know . . . what . . . you mean.

CARLYLE: I heard me. I understood me. "How long you been a punk?" is the question I asked. Have you got a reply?

RICHIE (*Confused, irritated, but fascinated*): Not to that question.

CARLYLE: Who do if you don't? I don't. How'm I gonna? (*Suddenly there is a whistling in the hall, as if someone might enter, footsteps approaching, and* RICHIE *leaps to his feet and scurries away toward the door, tucking in his undershirt as* HE *goes*) Man, don't you wanna talk to me? Don't you wanna talk to ole Carlyle?

RICHIE: Not at the moment.

CARLYLE (HE *is rising, starting after* RICHIE, *who stands nervously near* ROGER'*s bed*): I want to talk to you, man; why don't you want to talk to me? We can be friends. Talkin' back and forth, sharin' thoughts and bein' happy.

RICHIE: I don't think that's what you want.

CARLYLE (HE *is very near to* RICHIE): What do I want?

RICHIE: I mean, to talk to me. (*As if repulsed,* HE *crosses away. But it is hard to tell if the move is genuine or coy*)

CARLYLE: What am I doin'? I am talkin'. DON'T YOU TELL ME I AIN'T TALKIN' WHEN I AM TALKIN'! COURSE I AM. Bendin' over backwards. (*And pressing his hands against himself in his anger,* HE *has touched the grease on his shirt, the filth of his clothing, and this ignites the anger*) Do you know they still got me in that goddamn P Company? That goddamn transient company. It like they think I ain't got no notion what a home is. No nose for no home—like I ain't never had no home. I had a home. IT LIKE THEY THINK THERE AIN'T NO PLACE FOR ME IN THIS MOTHER ARMY BUT K.P. ALL SUDSY AND WRINKLED AND SWEATIN'. EVERY DAY SINCE I GOT TO THIS SHIT HOUSE,

MISTER! HOW MANY TIMES YOU BEEN ON K.P.? WHEN'S THE
LAST TIME YOU PULLED K.P.? (HE *has roared down to where* RICHIE *had
moved, the rage possessing him*)

RICHIE: I'm E.D.

CARLYLE: You E.D.? You E.D.? You Edie, are you? I didn't ask you what you
friends call you, I asked you when's the last time you had K.P.?

RICHIE (*Edging toward his bed.* HE *will go there, get and light a cigarette*): E.D. is
"Exempt from Duty."

CARLYLE (*Moving after* RICHIE): You ain't got no duties? What shit you talkin'
about? Everybody in this fuckin' army got duties. That what the fuckin'
army all about. You ain't got no duties, who got 'em?

RICHIE: Because of my job, Carlyle. I have a very special job. And my friends
don't call me Edie. (*Big smile*) They call me Irene.

CARLYLE: That mean what you sayin' is you kiss ass for somebody, don't it?
Good for you. (*Seemingly relaxed and gentle,* HE *settles down on* RICHIE's *bed.*
HE *seems playful and charming*) You know the other night I was sleepin' there.
You know.

RICHIE: Yes.

CARLYLE (*Gleefully, enormously pleased*): You remember that? How come you
remember that? You sweet.

RICHIE: We don't have people sleeping on our floor that often, Carlyle.

CARLYLE: But the way you crawl over in the night, gimme a big kiss on my
joint. That nice.

RICHIE (*Shocked,* HE *blinks*): What?

CARLYLE: Or did I dream that?

RICHIE (*Laughing in spite of himself*): My God, you're outrageous!

CARLYLE: Maybe you dreamed it.

RICHIE: What . . . ? No. I don't know.

CARLYLE: Maybe you did it, then; you didn't dream it.

RICHIE: How come you talk so much?

CARLYLE: I don't talk, man, who's gonna talk? YOU? (HE *is laughing and
amused, but there is an anger near the surface now, an ugliness*) That bore me
to death. I don't like nobody's voice but my own. I am so pretty. Don't
like nobody else face. (*And then viciously,* HE *spits out at* RICHIE) You goddamn face ugly fuckin' queer punk!

And RICHIE *jumps in confusion.*

RICHIE: What's the matter with you?

CARLYLE: You goddamn ugly punk face. YOU UGLY!

RICHIE: Nice mouth.

CARLYLE: That's right. That's right. And you got a weird mouth. Like to suck
joints.

RICHIE *storms to his locker, throwing the book inside.* HE *pivots, grabbing a towel, marching toward the door.*

Hey, you gonna jus' walk out on me? Where you goin'? You c'mon back. Hear?

RICHIE: That's my bed, for chrissake. (HE *lunges into the hall*)

CARLYLE: You'd best. (*Lying there,* HE *makes himself comfortable.* HE *takes a pint bottle from his back pocket*) You come back, Richie, I tell you a good joke. Make you laugh, make you cry. (HE *takes a big drink*) That's right. Ole Frank and Jesse, they got the stagecoach stopped, all the peoples lined up—Frank say, "All right, peoples, we gonna rape all the men and rob all the women." Jesse say, "Frank, no, no—that ain't it—we gonna . . . ." And this one little man yell real loud, "You shut up, Jesse; Frank knows what he's doin'. "

Loudly, HE *laughs and laughs.* BILLY *enters. Startled at the sight of* CARLYLE *there in* RICHIE'S *bed,* BILLY *falters, as* CARLYLE *gestures toward him*)

Hey, man . . . ! Hey, you know, they send me over to that Vietnam, I be cool, 'cause I been dodgin' bullets and shit since I been old enough to get on pussy make it happy to know me. I can get on, I can do my job.

BILLY *looks weary and depressed. Languidly* HE *crosses to his bed.* HE *still wears his sweat clothes.* CARLYLE *studies him, then stares at the ceiling.*

Yeh. I was just layin' here thinkin' that and you come in and out it come, words to say my feelin'. That my problem. That the black man's problem altogether. You ever considered that? Too much feelin'. He too close to everything. He is, man; too close to his blood, to his body. It ain't that he don't have no good mind, but he BELIEVE in his body. Is . . . that Richie the only punk in this room, or is there more?

BILLY: What?

CARLYLE: The punk; is he the only punk? (*Carefully* HE *takes one of* RICHIE'S *cigarettes and lights it*)

BILLY: He's all right.

CARLYLE: I ain't askin' about the quality of his talent, but is he the only one, is my question?

BILLY (HE *does not want to deal with this.* HE *sits there*): You get your orders yet?

CARLYLE: Orders for what?

BILLY: To tell you where you work.

CARLYLE: I'm P Company, man. I work in P Company. I do K.P. That all. Don't deserve no more. Do you know I been in this army three months and ten days and everybody still doin' the same shit and sayin' the same shit and wearin' the same green shitty clothes? I ain't been happy one day, and that a lotta goddamn misery back to back in this ole boy. Is that Richie a good punk? Huh? Is he? He takes care of you and Roger—that how come you in this room, the three of you?

BILLY: What?

CARLYLE (*Emphatically*): You and Roger are hittin' on Richie, right?

BILLY: He's not queer, if that's what you're sayin'. A little effeminate, but that's all, no more; if that's what you're sayin'.

CARLYLE: I'd like to get some of him myself if he a good punk, is what I'm sayin'. That's what I'm sayin'! You don't got no understandin' how a man can maybe be a little diplomatic about what he's sayin' sorta sideways, do you? Jesus.

BILLY: He don't do that stuff.

CARLYLE (*Lying there*): What stuff?

BILLY: Listen, man. I don't feel too good, you don't mind.

CARLYLE: What stuff?

BILLY: What you're thinkin'.

CARLYLE: What . . . am I thinkin'?

BILLY: You . . . know.

CARLYLE: Yes, I do. It in my head, that how come I know. But how do you know? I can see your heart, Billy boy, but you cannot see mine. I am unknown. You . . . are known.

BILLY (*As if* HE *is about to vomit, and fighting it*): You just . . . talk fast and keep movin', don't you? Don't ever stay still.

CARLYLE: Words to say my feelin', Billy boy.

> RICHIE *steps into the room.* HE *sees* BILLY *and* CARLYLE, *and freezes.*

There he is. There he be.

> RICHIE *moves to his locker to put away the towel.*

RICHIE: He's one of them who hasn't come down far out of the trees yet, Billy; believe me.

CARLYLE: You got rudeness in your voice, Richie—you got meanness I can hear about ole Carlyle. You tellin' me I oughta leave—is that what you think you're doin'? You don't want me here?

RICHIE: You come to see Roger, who isn't here, right? Man like you must have important matters to take care of all over the quad; I can't imagine a man like you not having extremely important things to do all over the world, as a matter of fact, Carlyle.

CARLYLE (HE *rises.* HE *begins to smooth the sheets and straighten the pillow.* HE *will put the pint bottle in his back pocket and cross near to* RICHIE): Ohhhh, listen— don't mind all the shit I say. I just talk bad, is all I do; I don't do bad. I got to have friends just like anybody else. I'm just bored and restless, that all; takin' it out on you two. I mean, I know Richie here ain't really no punk, not really. I was just talkin', just jivin' and entertainin' my own self.

Don't take me serious, not ever. I get on out and see you all later. (HE *moves for the door,* RICHIE *right behind him, almost ushering him*) You be cool, hear? Man don't do the jivin', he the one gettin' jived. That what my little brother Henry tell me and tell me.

Moving leisurely, CARLYLE *backs out the door and is gone.* RICHIE *shuts the door. There is a silence as* RICHIE *stands by the door.* BILLY *looks at him and then looks away.*

BILLY: I am gonna have to move myself outa here, Roger decides to adopt that sonofabitch.

RICHIE: He's an animal.

BILLY: Yeh, and on top a that, he's a rotten person.

RICHIE (HE *laughs nervously, crossing nearer to* BILLY): I think you're probably right. (*Still laughing a little,* HE *pats* BILLY'*s shoulder and* BILLY *freezes at the touch. Awkwardly* RICHIE *removes his hand and crosses to his bed. When* HE *has lain down,* BILLY *bends to take off his sneakers, then lies back on his pillow staring, thinking, and there is a silence.* RICHIE *does not move.* HE *lies there, struggling to prepare himself for something*) Hey . . . Billy? (*Very slight pause*) Billy?

BILLY: Yeh.

RICHIE: You know that story you told the other night?

BILLY: Yeh . . . ?

RICHIE: You know . . .

BILLY: What . . . about it?

RICHIE: Well, was it . . . about you? (*Pause*) I mean, was it . . . ABOUT you? Were you Frankie? (*This is difficult for him*) Are . . . you Frankie? Billy?

BILLY *is slowly sitting up.*

BILLY: You sonofabitch . . . !

RICHIE: Or was it really about somebody you knew . . . ?

BILLY (*Sitting, outraged and glaring*): You didn't hear me at all!

RICHIE: I'm just asking a simple question, Billy, that's all I'm doing.

BILLY: You are really sick. You know that? Your brain is really, truly rancid! Do you know there's a theory now it's genetic? That it's all a matter of genes and shit like that?

RICHIE: Everything is not so ungodly cryptic, Billy.

BILLY: You. You, man, and the rot it's makin' outa your feeble fuckin' brain.

ROGER, *dressed in civilian clothes, bursts in and* BILLY *leaps to his feet.*

ROGER: Hey, hey, anyone got a couple bucks he can loan me?

BILLY: Rog, where you been?

ROGER (*Throwing the basketball and his sweat clothes into his locker*): I need five. C'mon.

BILLY: Where you been? That asshole friend a yours was here.

ROGER: I know, I know. Can you gimme five?

RICHIE (HE *jumps to the floor and heads for his locker*): You want five. I got it. You want ten or more, even?

BILLY, *watching* RICHIE, *turns, and nervously paces down right, where* HE *moves about, worried.*

BILLY: I mean, we gotta talk about him, man; we gotta talk about him.

ROGER (*As* RICHIE *is handing him two fives*): 'Cause we goin' to town together. I jus' run into him out on the quad, man, and he was feelin' real bad 'bout the way he acted, how you guys done him, he was fallin' down apologizin' all over the place.

BILLY (*As* RICHIE *marches back to his bed and sits down*): I mean, he's got a lotta weird ideas about us; I'm tellin' you.

ROGER: He's just a little fucked up in his head is all, but he ain't trouble. (HE *takes a pair of sunglasses from the locker and puts them on*)

BILLY: Who needs him? I mean, we don't need him.

ROGER: You gettin' too nervous, man. Nobody said anything about anybody needin' anybody. I been on the street all my life; he brings back home. I played me a little ball, Billy; took me a shower. I'm feelin' good! (HE *has moved down to* BILLY)

BILLY: I'm tellin' you there's something wrong with him, though.

ROGER (*Face to face with* BILLY, HE *is a little irritated*): Every black man in the world ain't like me, man; you get used to that idea. You get to know him, and you gonna like him. I'm tellin' you. You get to be laughin' just like me to hear him talk his shit. But you gotta relax.

RICHIE: I agree with Billy, Roger.

ROGER: Well, you guys got it all worked out and that's good, but I am goin' to town with him. Man's got wheels. Got a good head. You got any sense, you'll come with us.

BILLY: What are you talkin' about—come with you? I just tole you he's crazy.

ROGER: And I tole you you're wrong.

RICHIE: We weren't invited.

ROGER: I'm invitin' you.

RICHIE: No, I don't wanna.

ROGER (HE *moves to* RICHIE; *it seems* HE *really wants* RICHIE *to go*): You sure, Richie? C'mon.

RICHIE: No.

ROGER: Billy? He got wheels, we goin' in drinkin', see if gettin' our heads real bad don't just make us feel real good. You know what I mean. I got him right; you got him wrong.

BILLY: But what if I'm right?

ROGER: Billy, Billy, the man is waitin' on me. You know you wanna. Jesus. Bad cat like that gotta know the way. He been to D.C. before. Got cousins here. Got wheels for the weekend. You always talkin' how you don't do nothin'—you just talk it. Let's do it tonight—stop talkin'. Be cruisin' up and down the strip, leanin' out the window, bad as we wanna be. True cool is a car. We can flip a cigarette out the window—we can watch it bounce. Get us some chippies. You know we can. And if we don't, he knows a cathouse, it fulla cats.

BILLY: You serious?

RICHIE: You mean you're going to a whorehouse? That's disgusting.

BILLY: Listen who's talkin'. What do you want me to do? Stay here with you?

RICHIE: We could go to a movie or something.

ROGER: I am done with this talkin'. You goin', you stayin'? (HE *crosses to his locker, pulls into view a wide-brimmed black and shiny hat, and puts it on, cocking it at a sharp angle*)

BILLY: I don't know.

ROGER (*Stepping for the door*): I am goin'.

BILLY (*Turning,* HE *sees the hat*): I'm going. Okay! I'm going! Going, going, going! (*And* HE *runs to his locker*)

RICHIE: Oh, Billy, you'll be scared to death in a cathouse and you know it.

BILLY: BULLSHIT! (HE *is removing his sweat pants and putting on a pair of gray corduroy trousers*)

ROGER: Billy got him a lion-tamer 'tween his legs!

The door bangs open and CARLYLE *is there, still clad in his filthy fatigues, but wearing a going-to-town black knit cap on his head and carrying a bottle.*

CARLYLE: Man, what's goin' on? I been waitin' like throughout my fuckin' life.

ROGER: Billy's goin', too. He's gotta change.

CARLYLE: He goin', too! Hey! Beautiful! That beautiful! (*His grin is large, his laugh is loud*)

ROGER: Didn't I tell you, Billy?

CARLYLE: That beautiful, man; we all goin' to be friends!

RICHIE (*Sitting on his bed*): What about me, Carlyle?

CARLYLE looks at RICHIE, and then at ROGER and then HE and ROGER begin to laugh. CARLYLE pokes ROGER and THEY laugh as THEY are leaving. BILLY, grabbing up his sneakers to follow, stops at the door, looking only briefly at RICHIE. Then BILLY goes and shuts the door. The lights are fading to black.

Scene 2

In the dark, taps begins to play. And then slowly the lights rise, but the room remains dim. Only the lamp attached to RICHIE's bed burns and there is the glow and spill of the hallway coming through the transom. BILLY, CARLYLE,

ROGER *and* RICHIE *are sprawled about the room.* BILLY, *lying on his stomach, has his head at the foot of his bed, a half-empty bottle of beer dangling in his hand.* HE *wears a blue oxford-cloth shirt and his sneakers lie beside his bed.* ROGER, *collapsed in his own bed, lies upon his back, his head also at the foot, a* Playboy *magazine covering his face and a half-empty bottle of beer in his hands, folded on his belly. Having removed his civilian shirt,* HE *wears a white T-shirt.* CARLYLE *is lying on his belly on* RICHIE's *bed, his head at the foot, and* HE *is facing out.* RICHIE *is sitting on the floor, resting against* ROGER's *footlocker.* HE *is wrapped in a blanket. Beside him is an unopened bottle of beer and a bottle opener.*

THEY *are all dreamy in the dimness as taps plays sadly on and then fades into silence.* NO ONE *moves.*

RICHIE: I don't know where it was, but it wasn't here. And we were all in it—it felt like—but we all had different faces. After you guys left, I only dozed for a few minutes, so it couldn't have been long. Roger laughed a lot and Billy was taller. I don't remember all the details exactly, and even though we were the ones in it, I know it was about my father. He was a big man. I was six. He was a very big man when I was six and he went away, but I remember him. He started drinking and staying home making model airplanes and boats and paintings by the numbers. We had money from Mom's family, so he was just home all the time. And then one day I was coming home from kindergarten, and as I was starting up the front walk he came out the door and he had these suitcases in his hands. He was leaving, see, sneaking out, and I'd caught him. We looked at each other and I just knew and I started crying. He yelled at me, "Don't you cry; don't you start crying." I tried to grab him and he pushed me down in the grass. And then he was gone. G-O-N-E.

BILLY: And that was it? That was it?

RICHIE: I remember hiding my eyes. I lay in the grass and hid my eyes and waited.

BILLY: He never came back?

RICHIE: No.

CARLYLE: Ain't that some shit. Now, I'm a jive-time street nigger. I knew where my daddy was all the while. He workin' in this butcher shop two blocks up the street. Ole Mom used to point him out. "There he go. That him—that your daddy." We'd see him on the street, "There he go."

ROGER: Man couldn't see his way to livin' with you—that what you're sayin'?

CARLYLE: Never saw the day.

ROGER: And still couldn't get his ass outa the neighborhood?

RICHIE *begins trying to open his bottle of beer.*

CARLYLE: Ain't that a bitch. Poor ole bastard just duck his head—Mom point-in' at him—he git this real goddamn hangdog look like he don't know who we talkin' about and he walk a little faster. Why the hell he never move away I don't know, unless he was crazy. But I don't think so. He come up to me once—I was playin'. "Boy," he says, "I ain't your daddy. I ain't. Your momma's crazy." "Don't you be callin' my momma crazy, Daddy," I tole him. Poor ole thing didn't know what to do.

RICHIE (*Giving up;* HE *can't get the beer open*): Somebody open this for me? I can't get this open.

BILLY *seems about to move to help, but* CARLYLE *is quicker, rising a little on the bunk and reaching.*

CARLYLE: Ole Carlyle get it.

RICHIE *slides along the floor until* HE *can place the bottle in* CARLYLE's *outstretched hand.*

RICHIE: Then there was this once—there was this TV documentary about these bums in San Francisco, this TV guy interviewing all these bums, and just for maybe ten seconds while he was talkin' . . . (*Smiling,* CARLYLE *hands* RICHIE *the opened bottle*) to this one bum, there was this other one in the background jumpin' around like he thought he was dancin' and wavin' his hat, and even though there wasn't anything about him like my father and I didn't really ever see his face at all, I just kept thinkin': That's him. My dad. He thinks he's dancin'.

THEY *lie there in silence and suddenly, softly,* BILLY *giggles, and then* HE *giggles a little more and louder.*

BILLY: Jesus!

RICHIE: What?

BILLY: That's ridiculous, Richie; sayin' that, thinkin' that. If it didn't look like him, it wasn't him, but you gotta be makin' up a story.

CARLYLE (*Shifting now for a more comfortable position,* HE *moves his head to the pillow at the top of the bed*): Richie first saw me, he didn't like me much nohow, but he thought it over now, he changed his way a thinkin'. I can see that clear. We gonna be one big happy family.

RICHIE: Carlyle likes me, Billy; he thinks I'm pretty.

CARLYLE (*Sitting up a little to make his point clear*): No, I don't think you pretty. A broad is pretty. Punks ain't pretty. Punk—if he good-lookin'—is cute. You cute.

RICHIE: He's gonna steal me right away, little Billy. You're so slow, Bill. I prefer a man who's decisive. (HE *is lying down now on the floor at the foot of his bed*)

BILLY: You just keep at it, you're gonna have us all believin' you are just what you say you are.

RICHIE: Which is more than we can say for you.

Now ROGER *rises on his elbow to light a cigarette.*

BILLY: Jive, jive.

RICHIE: You're arrogant, Billy. So arrogant.

BILLY: What are you—on the rag?

RICHIE: Wouldn't it just bang your little balls if I were!

ROGER (*To* RICHIE): Hey, man. What's with you?

RICHIE: Stupidity offends me; lies and ignorance offend me.

BILLY: You know where we was? The three of us? All three of us, earlier on? To the wrong side of the tracks, Richard. One good black upside-down whorehouse where you get what you buy, no jive along with it—so if it's a lay you want and need, you go! Or don't they have faggot whorehouses?

ROGER: IF YOU GUYS DON'T CUT THIS SHIT OUT I'M GONNA BUST SOMEBODY'S HEAD! (*Angrily* HE *flops back on his bed. There is a silence as* THEY *all lie there*)

RICHIE: "Where we was," he says. Listen to him. "Where we was." And he's got more school, Carlyle, than you have fingers and . . . (HE *has lifted his foot onto the bed; it touches, presses,* CARLYLE's *foot*) toes. It's this pseudo-earthy quality he feigns—but inside he's all cashmere.

BILLY: That's a lie. (*Giggling,* HE *is staring at the floor*) I'm polyester, worsted and mohair.

RICHIE: You have a lot of school, Billy; don't say you don't.

BILLY: You said "fingers and toes"; you didn't say "a lot."

CARLYLE: I think people get dumber the more they put their butts into some schoolhouse door.

BILLY: It depends on what the hell you're talkin' about. (*Now* HE *looks at* CARLYLE, *and sees the feet touching*)

CARLYLE: I seen cats back on the block, they knew what was shakin'—then they got into all this school jive and, man, every year they went, they come back they didn't know nothin'.

BILLY *is staring at* RICHIE's *foot pressing and rubbing* CARLYLE's *foot.* RICHIE *sees* BILLY *looking.* BILLY *cannot believe what* HE *is seeing. It fills him with fear. The silence goes on and on.*

RICHIE: Billy, why don't you and Roger go for a walk?

BILLY: What? (HE *bolts to his knees.* HE *is frozen on his knees on the bed*)

RICHIE: Roger asked you to go downtown, you went, you had fun.

ROGER (*Having turned,* HE *knows almost instantly what is going on*): I asked you, too.

RICHIE: You asked me; you *begged* Billy. I said no. Billy said no. You took my ten dollars. You begged Billy. I'm asking you a favor now—go for a walk. Let Carlyle and me have some time.

Silence.

CARLYLE (HE *sits up, uneasy and wary*): That how you work it?

ROGER: Work what?

CARLYLE: Whosever turn it be.

BILLY: No, no, that ain't the way we work it, because we don't work it.

CARLYLE: See? See? There it is—that goddamn education showin' through. All them years in school. Man, didn't we have a good time tonight? You rode in my car. I showed you a good cathouse, all that sweet black pussy. Ain't we friends? Richie likes me. How come you don't like me?

BILLY: 'Cause if you really are doin' what I think you're doin', you're a fuckin' animal!

CARLYLE leaps to his feet, hand snaking to his pocket to draw a weapon.

ROGER: Billy, no.

BILLY: NO, WHAT?!

ROGER: Relax, man; no need. (HE *turns to* CARLYLE; *patiently, wearily,* HE *speaks*) Man, I tole you it ain't goin' on here. We both tole you it ain't goin' on here.

CARLYLE: Don't you jive me, nigger. You goin' for a walk like I'm askin', or not? I wanna get this clear.

ROGER: Man, we live here.

RICHIE: It's my house, too, Roger; I live here, too. (HE *bounds to his feet, flinging the blanket that has been covering him so it flies and lands on the floor near* ROGER's *footlocker*)

ROGER: Don't I know that? Did I say somethin' to make you think I didn't know that?

Standing, RICHIE *is removing his trousers and throwing them down on his footlocker.*

RICHIE: Carlyle is my guest.

Sitting down on the side of his bed and facing out, RICHIE *puts his arms around* CARLYLE's *thigh.* ROGER *jumps to his feet and grabs the blanket from the foot of his bed. Shaking it open,* HE *drops onto the bed, his head at the foot of the bed and facing off as* HE *covers himself.*

ROGER: Fine. He your friend. This your home. So that mean he can stay. It don't mean I gotta leave. I'll catch you all in the mornin'.

BILLY: Roger, what the hell are you doin'?

ROGER: What you better do, Billy. It's gettin' late. I'm goin' to sleep.

BILLY: What?

ROGER: Go to fucking bed, Billy. Get up in the rack, turn your back and look at the wall.

BILLY: You gotta be kiddin'.

ROGER: DO IT!

BILLY: Man . . . !

ROGER: Yeah . . . !

BILLY: You mean just . . .

ROGER: It been goin' on a long damn time, man. You ain't gonna put no stop to it.

CARLYLE: You . . . ain't . . . serious.

RICHIE (*Both* HE *and* CARLYLE *are staring at* ROGER *and then* BILLY, *who is staring at* ROGER): Well, I don't believe it. Of all the childish . . . infantile . . .

CARLYLE: Hey! (*Silence*) HEY! Even I got to say this is a little weird, but if this the way you do it . . . (*And* HE *turns toward* RICHIE *below him*) it the way I do it. I don't know.

RICHIE: With them right there? Are you kidding? My God, Carlyle, that'd be obscene. (*Pulling slightly away from* CARLYLE)

CARLYLE: Ohhh, man . . . they backs turned.

RICHIE: No.

CARLYLE: What I'm gonna do? (*Silence.* HE *looks at them, all three of them*) Don't you got no feelin' for how a man feel? I don't understand you two boys. Unless'n you a pair of motherfuckers. That what you are, you a pair of motherfuckers? You slits, man. DON'T YOU HEAR ME!? I DON'T UNDERSTAND THIS SITUATION HERE. I THOUGHT WE MADE A DEAL! (RICHIE *rises, starts to pull on his trousers.* CARLYLE *grabs him*) YOU GET ON YOUR KNEES, YOU PUNK, I MEAN NOW, AND YOU GONNA BE ON MY JOINT FAST OR YOU GONNA BE ONE BUSTED PUNK. AM I UNDERSTOOD? (HE *hurls* RICHIE *down to the floor*)

BILLY: I ain't gonna have this going on here; Roger, I can't.

ROGER: I been turnin' my back on one thing or another all my life.

RICHIE: Jealous, Billy?

BILLY (*Getting to his feet*): Just go out that door, the two of you. Go. Go on out in the bushes or out in some field. See if I follow you. See if I care. I'll be right here and I'll be sleepin', but it ain't gonna be done in my house. I don't have much in this goddamn army, but *here* is mine. (HE *stands beside his bed*)

CARLYLE: I WANT MY FUCKIN' NUT! HOW COME YOU SO UPTIGHT? HE WANTS ME! THIS BOY HERE WANTS ME! WHO YOU TO STOP IT?

ROGER (*Spinning to face* CARLYLE *and* RICHIE): *That's right,* Billy. Richie one a those people want to get fucked by niggers, man. It what he know was gonna happen all his life—can be his dream come true. Ain't that right, Richie! (*Jumping to his feet,* RICHIE *starts putting on his trousers*) Want to make it real in the world, how a nigger is an animal. Give 'em an inch, gonna take a mile. Ain't you some kinda fool, Richie? Hear me, Carlyle.

CARLYLE: Man, don't make me no nevermind what he think he's provin' an' shit, long as I get my nut. I KNOW I ain't no animal, don't have to prove it.

RICHIE (*Pulling at* CARLYLE's *arm, wanting to move him toward the door*): Let's go. Let's go outside. The hell with it.

But CARLYLE *tears himself free;* HE *squats furiously down on the bunk, his hands seizing it, his back to all of them.*

CARLYLE: Bull shit. Bullshit! I ain't goin' no-fuckin'-where—this jive ass ain't runnin' me. Is this you house or not? (HE *doesn't know what is going on;* HE *can hardly look at any of them*)

ROGER (*Bounding out of bed, hurling his pillow across the room*): I'm goin' to the fuckin' john, Billy. Hang it up, man; let 'em be.

BILLY: No.

ROGER: I'm smarter than you—do like I'm sayin'.

BILLY: It ain't right.

ROGER: Who gives a big rat's ass!

CARLYLE: Right on, bro! That boy know; he do. (HE *circles the bed toward them*) Hear him. Look into his eyes.

BILLY: This fuckin' army takin' everything else away from me, they ain't takin' more than they got. I see what I see—I don't run, don't hide.

ROGER (*Turning away from* BILLY, HE *stomps out the door, slamming it*): You fuckin' well better learn.

CARLYLE: That right. Time for more schoolin'. Lesson number one. (*Stealthily* HE *steps and snaps out the only light, the lamp clamped to* RICHIE's *bed*) You don't see what you see so well in the dark. It dark in the night. Black man got a black body—he disappear.

The darkness is so total THEY *are all no more than shadows.*

RICHIE: Not to the hands; not to the fingers. (*Moving from across the room toward* CARLYLE)

CARLYLE: You do like you talk, boy, you gonna make me happy.

BILLY, *nervously clutching his sneaker, is moving backward.*

BILLY: Who says the lights go out? Nobody goddamn asked me if the lights go out.

BILLY, *lunging to the wall switch, throws it. The overhead lights flash on, flooding the room with light.* CARLYLE *is seated on the edge of* RICHIE's *bed,* RICHIE *kneeling before him.*

CARLYLE: I DO, MOTHERFUCKER, I SAY! (*And the switchblade seems to leap from his pocket to his hand*) I SAY! CAN'T YOU LET PEOPLE BE?

BILLY *hurls his sneaker at the floor at* CARLYLE's *feet. Instantly* CARLYLE *is across the room, blocking* BILLY's *escape out the door.*

Goddamn you, boy! I'm gonna cut your ass, just to show you how it feel—
and cuttin' can happen. This knife true.

RICHIE: Carlyle, now c'mon.

CARLYLE: Shut up, pussy.

RICHIE: Don't hurt him, for chrissake.

CARLYLE: Goddamn man throw a shoe at me, he don't walk around clean in
the world thinkin' he can throw another. He get some shit come back at
him.

BILLY doesn't know which way to go, and then CARLYLE, *jabbing the knife at
the air before* BILLY's *chest, has* BILLY *running backward, his eyes fixed on the
moving blade.* HE *stumbles, having run into* RICHIE's *bed.* HE *sprawls backward
and* CARLYLE *is over him.*

No, no; no, no. Put you hand out there. Put it out. (*Slight pause;* BILLY
is terrified) DO THE THING I'M TELLIN'! (BILLY *lets his hand rise in the
air and* CARLYLE *grabs it, holds it*) That's it. That's good. See? See?

The knife flashes across BILLY's *palm; the blood flows.* BILLY *winces, recoils,
but* CARLYLE's *hand still clenches and holds.*

BILLY: Motherfucker.

Again the knife darts, cutting, and BILLY *yelps.* RICHIE, *on his knees beside
them, turns away.*

RICHIE: Oh, my God, what are you—

CARLYLE (*In his own sudden distress,* HE *flings the hand away*): That you blood.
The blood inside you, you don't ever see it there. Take a look how easy
it come out—and enough of it come out, you in the middle of the worst
goddamn trouble you ever gonna see. And know I'm the man can deal
that kinda trouble, easy as I smile. And I smile . . . easy. Yeah.

BILLY is curled in upon himself, holding the hand to his stomach as RICHIE
now reaches tentatively and shyly out as if to console BILLY, *who repulses the
gesture.* CARLYLE *is angry and strangely depressed. Forlornly* HE *slumps onto
BILLY's footlocker as* BILLY *staggers up to his wall locker and takes out a towel.*

Bastard ruin my mood, Richie. He ruin my mood. Fightin' and lovin' real
different in the feelin's I got. I see blood come outa somebody like that,
it don't make me feel good—hurt me—hurt on somebody I thought was
my friend. But I ain't supposed to see. One dumb nigger. No mind, he
thinks, no heart, no feelings a gentleness. You see how that ain't true, Richie.
Goddamn man threw a shoe at me. A lotta people woulda cut his heart
out. I gotta make him know he throw shit, he get shit. But I don't hurt
him bad, you see what I mean?

BILLY*'s back is to them, as* HE *stands hunched at his locker, and suddenly his voice, hissing, erupts.*

BILLY: Jesus . . . H. . . . Christ . . . ! Do you know what I'm doin'? Do you know what I'm standin' here doin'? (HE *whirls now;* HE *holds a straight razor in his hand. A bloody towel is wrapped around the hurt hand.* CARLYLE *tenses, rises, seeing the razor*) I'm a twenty-four-year-old goddamn college graduate—intellectual goddamn scholar type—and I got a razor in my hand. I'm thinkin' about comin' up behind one black human being and I'm thinkin' nigger this and nigger that—I wanna cut his throat. THAT IS RIDICULOUS. I NEVER FACED ANYBODY IN MY LIFE WITH ANYTHING TO KILL THEM. YOU UNDERSTAND ME? I DON'T HAVE A GODDAMN THING ON THE LINE HERE!

The door opens and ROGER *rushes in, having heard the yelling.* BILLY *flings the razor into his locker.*

Look at me, Roger, look at me. I got a cut palm—I don't know what happened. Jesus Christ, I got sweat all over me when I think a what I was near to doin'. I swear it. I mean, do I think I need a reputation as a killer, a bad man with a knife? (HE *is wild with the energy of feeling free and with the anger at what these others almost made him do.* CARLYLE *slumps down on the footlocker;* HE *sits there*) Bullshit! I need shit! I got sweat all over me. I got the mile record in my hometown. I did four forty-two in high school and that's the goddamn record in Windsor County. I don't need approval from either one of the pair of you. (*And* HE *rushes at* RICHIE) You wanna be a goddamn swish—a goddamn faggot-queer—GO! Suckin' cocks and takin' it in the ass, the thing of which you dream—GO! AND YOU— (*Whirling on* CARLYLE) You wanna be a bad-assed animal, man, get it on—go—but I wash my hands. I am not human as you are. I put you down, I put you down—(HE *almost hurls himself at* RICHIE) you gay little piece of shit cake—SHIT CAKE. AND YOU—(*Hurt, confused,* RICHIE *turns away, nearly pressing his face into the bed beside which* HE *kneels, as* BILLY *has spun back to tower over the pulsing, weary* CARLYLE) you are your own goddamn fault, SAMBO! SAMBO! (*And the knife flashes up in* CARLYLE*'s hand into* BILLY*'s stomach, and* BILLY *yelps*) Ahhhhhhhhh. (*And pushes at the hand.* RICHIE *is still turned away*)

RICHIE: Well, fuck you, Billy.

BILLY (HE *backs off the knife*): Get away, get away.

RICHIE (*As* ROGER, *who could not see because* BILLY*'s back is to him, is approaching* CARLYLE *and* BILLY *goes walking up toward the lockers as if* HE *knows where* HE *is going, as if* HE *is going to go out the door and to a movie, his hands holding his belly*): You're so-o messed up.

ROGER (*To* CARLYLE): Man, what's the matter with you?

CARLYLE: Don't nobody talk that weird shit to me, you understand?

ROGER: You jive, man. That's all you do—jive!

> BILLY, *striding swiftly, walks flat into the wall lockers;* HE *bounces, turns.* THEY *are all looking at him.*

RICHIE: Billy! Oh, Billy!

> ROGER *looks at* RICHIE.

BILLY: Ahhhhhhh. Ahhhhhhh.

> ROGER *looks at* CARLYLE *as if* HE *is about to scream, and beyond him,* BILLY *turns from the lockers, starts to walk again, now staggering and moving toward them.*

RICHIE: I think . . . he stabbed him. I think Carlyle stabbed Billy. Roger!

> ROGER *whirls to go to* BILLY, *who is staggering downstage and angled away, hands clenched over his belly.*

BILLY: Shut up! It's just a cut, it's just a cut. He cut my hand, he cut gut. (HE *collapses onto his knees just beyond* ROGER'S *footlocker*) It took the wind out of me, scared me, that's all. (*Fiercely* HE *tries to hide the wound and remain calm*)

ROGER: Man, are you all right?

> ROGER *moves to* BILLY, *who turns to hide the wound. Till now* NO ONE *is sure what happened.* RICHIE *only "thinks"* BILLY *has been stabbed.* BILLY *is pretending* HE *isn't hurt. As* BILLY *turns from* ROGER, HE *turns toward* RICHIE *and* RICHIE *sees the blood.* RICHIE *yelps and* THEY *all begin talking and yelling simultaneously.*

CARLYLE: You know what I was learnin', he was learnin' to talk all that weird shit, cuttin', baby, cuttin', the ways and means a shit, man, razors.

ROGER: You all right? Or what? He slit you?

BILLY: Just took the wind outa me, scared me.

RICHIE: Carlyle, you stabbed him; you stabbed him.

CARLYLE: Ohhhh, pussy, pussy, pussy, Carlyle know what he do.

ROGER (*Trying to lift* BILLY): Get up, okay? Get up on the bed.

BILLY (*Irritated, pulling free*): I am on the bed.

ROGER: What?

RICHIE: No, Billy, no, you're not.

BILLY: Shut up!

RICHIE: You're on the floor.

BILLY: I'm on the bed. I'm on the bed. (*Emphatically. And then* HE *looks at the floor*) What?

ROGER: Let me see what he did. (BILLY's *hands are clenched on the wound*) Billy, let me see where he got you.

BILLY (*Recoiling*): NO-O-O-O-O-O, you nigger!

ROGER (HE *leaps at Carlyle*): What did you do?

CARLYLE (*Hunching his shoulders, ducking his head*): Shut up.

ROGER: What did you do, nigger—you slit him or stick him? (*And then* HE *tries to get back to* BILLY) Billy, let me see.

BILLY (*Doubling over till his head hits the floor*): NO-O-O-O-O-O! Shit, shit, shit.

RICHIE (*Suddenly sobbing and yelling*): Oh, my God, my God, ohhhh, ohhhh, ohhhh. (*Bouncing on his knees on the bed*)

CARLYLE: FUCK IT, FUCK IT, I STUCK HIM. I TURNED IT. This mother army break my heart. I can't be out there where it pretty, don't wanna live! Wash me clean, shit face!

RICHIE: Ohhhh, ohhhhh, ohhhhhhhhhh. Carlyle stabbed Billy, oh, ohhhh, I never saw such a thing in my life. Ohhhhhh. (*As* ROGER *is trying gently, fearfully, to straighten* BILLY *up*) Don't die, Billy; don't die.

ROGER: Shut up and go find somebody to help. Richie, go!

RICHIE: Who? I'll go, I'll go. (*Scrambling off the bed*)

ROGER: I don't know. JESUS CHRIST! DO IT!

RICHIE: Okay. Okay. Billy, don't die. Don't die. (*Backing for the door,* HE *turns and runs*)

ROGER: The sarge, or C.Q.

BILLY (*Suddenly doubling over, vomiting blood.* RICHIE *is gone*): Ohhhhhhhhhh. Blood. Blood.

ROGER: Be still, be still.

BILLY (*Pulling at a blanket on the floor beside him*): I want to stand up. I'm . . . vomiting . . . (*Making no move to stand, only to cover himself*) blood. What does that mean?

ROGER (*Slowly standing*): I don't know.

BILLY: Yes, yes, I want to stand up. Give me blanket, blanket. (HE *rolls back and forth, fighting to get the blanket over him*)

ROGER: RIICCHHHIIIEEEE! (*As* BILLY *is furiously grappling with the blanket*) No, no. (HE *looks at* CARLYLE, *who is slumped over, muttering to himself.* ROGER *runs for the door*) Wait on, be tight, be cool.

BILLY: Cover me. Cover me.

At last BILLY *gets the blanket over his face. The dark makes him grow still.* HE *lies there beneath his blanket. Silence.* NO ONE *moves. And then* CARLYLE *senses the quiet;* HE *turns, looks. Slowly, wearily,* HE *rises and walks to where* BILLY *lies.* HE *stands over him, the knife hanging loosely from his left hand as* HE *reaches with his right to gently take the blanket and lift it slowly from* BILLY*'s face.* THEY *look at each other.* BILLY *reaches up and pats* CARLYLE*'s hand holding the blanket.*

I don't want to talk to you right now, Carlyle. All right? Where's Roger? Do you know where he is? (*Slight pause*) Don't stab me anymore, Carlyle, okay? I was dead wrong doin' what I did. I know that now. Carlyle, promise me you won't stab me anymore. I couldn't take it. Okay? I'm cold . . . my blood . . . is . . .

From off comes a voice.

ROONEY (*Offstage*): Cokesy? Cokesy wokesy? (*And* HE *staggers into the doorway, very drunk, a beer bottle in his hand*) Ollie-ollie oxen-freeee. (HE *looks at them.* CARLYLE *quickly, secretly, slips the knife into his pocket*) How you all doin'? Everybody drunk, huh? I los' my friend. (HE *is staggering sideways toward* BILLY*'s bunk, where* HE *finally drops down, sitting*) Who are you, soldier? (CARLYLE *has straightened, his head ducked down as* HE *is edging for the door*) Who are you, soldier?

And RICHIE, *running, comes roaring into the room.* HE *looks at* ROONEY *and cannot understand what is going on.* CARLYLE *is standing.* ROONEY *is just sitting there. What is going on?* RICHIE *moves along the lockers, trying to get behind* ROONEY, *his eyes never off* CARLYLE.

RICHIE: Ohhhhhh, Sergeant Rooney, I've been looking for you everywhere— where have you been? Carlyle stabbed Billy, he stabbed him.
ROONEY (*Sitting there*): What?
RICHIE: Carlyle stabbed Billy.
ROONEY: Who's Carlyle?
RICHIE: He's Carlyle. (*As* CARLYLE *seems about to advance, the knife again showing in his hand*) Carlyle, don't hurt anybody more!
ROONEY (*On his feet,* HE *is staggering toward the door*): You got a knife there? What's with the knife? What's goin' on here?

CARLYLE *steps as if to bolt for the door, but* ROONEY *is in the way, having inserted himself between* CARLYLE *and* RICHIE, *who has backed into the doorway.*

Wait! Now wait!
RICHIE (*As* CARLYLE *raises the knife*): Carlyle, don't! (HE *runs from the room*)
ROONEY: You watch your step, you understand. You see what I got here? (HE *lifts the beer bottle, waves it threateningly*) You watch your step, motherfucker. Relax. I mean, we can straighten all this out. We—(CARLYLE *lunges at* ROONEY, *who tenses*) I'm just askin' what's goin' on, that's all I'm doin'. No need to get all—(*And* CARLYLE *swipes at the air again;* ROONEY *recoils*) Motherfucker. Motherfucker. (HE *seems to be tensing, his body gathering itself*

for some mighty effort. And HE *throws his head back and gives the eagle yell)* Eeeeeeeeeeaaaaaaaaaaaaaaaaahhhhhh! Eeeeaaaaaaaaaaaaaahhhhhhhhhhhhh! (CARLYLE *jumps;* HE *looks left and right)* Goddammit, I'll cut you good. (HE *lunges to break the bottle on the edge of the wall lockers. The bottle shatters and* HE *yelps, dropping everything)* Ohhhhhhhh! Ohhhhhhhhhhhhhhh! (CARLYLE *bolts, running from the room)* I hurt myself, I cut myself. I hurt my hand. (*Holding the wounded hand,* HE *scurries to* BILLY's *bed, where* HE *sits on the edge, trying to wipe the blood away so* HE *can see the wound)* I cut— (*Hearing a noise,* HE *whirls, looks;* CARLYLE *is plummeting in the door and toward him.* ROONEY *stands)* I hurt my hand, goddammit! (*The knife goes into* ROONEY's *belly.* HE *flails at* CARLYLE) I HURT MY HAND! WHAT ARE YOU DOING? WHAT ARE YOU DOING? WAIT! WAIT! (HE *turns away, falling to his knees, and the knife goes into him again and again)* No fair. No fair!

ROGER, *running, skids into the room, headed for* BILLY, *and then* HE *sees* CARLYLE *on* ROONEY, *the leaping knife.* ROGER *lunges, grabbing* CARLYLE, *pulling him to get him off* ROONEY. CARLYLE *leaps free of* ROGER, *sending* ROGER *flying backward. And then* CARLYLE *begins to circle* ROGER's *bed.* HE *is whimpering, wiping at the blood on his shirt as if to wipe it away.* ROGER *backs away as* CARLYLE *keeps waving the knife at him.* ROONEY *is crawling along the floor under* BILLY's *bed and then* HE *stops crawling, lies there.*

CARLYLE: You don't tell nobody on me you saw me do this, I let you go, okay? Ohhhhhhhhh. (*Rubbing, rubbing at the shirt*) Ohhhhhh, how'm I gonna get back to the world now, I got all this mess to—
ROGER: What happened? That you—I don't understand that you did this! That you did—
CARLYLE: YOU SHUT UP! Don't be talkin' all that weird shit to me—don't you go talkin' all that weird shit!
ROGER: Nooooooooooooo!
CARLYLE: I'm Carlyle, man. You know me. You know me.

CARLYLE *turns,* HE *flees out the door.* ROGER, *alone, looks about the room.* BILLY *is there.* ROGER *moves toward* BILLY, *who is shifting, undulating on his back.*

BILLY: Carlyle, no; oh, Christ, don't stab me anymore. I'll die. I will—I'll die. Don't make me die. I'll get my dog after you. I'LL GET MY DOG AFTER YOU!

ROGER *is saying, "Oh, Billy, man, Billy."* HE *is trying to hold* BILLY. *Now* HE *lifts* BILLY *into his arms.*

ROGER: Oh, Billy; oh, man. GODDAMMIT, BILLY!

A MILITARY POLICE LIEUTENANT *comes running in the door, his .45 automatic drawn, and* HE *levels it at* ROGER.

LIEUTENANT: Freeze, soldier! Not a quick move out of you. Just real slow, straighten your ass up.

ROGER *has gone rigid; the* LIEUTENANT *is advancing on him. Tentatively* ROGER *turns, looks.*

ROGER: Huh? No.

LIEUTENANT: Get your ass against the lockers.

ROGER: Sir, no. I—

LIEUTENANT (*Hurling* ROGER *away toward the wall lockers*): MOVE! (*Another M.P.,* PFC HINSON, *comes in, followed by* RICHIE, *flushed and breathless*) Hinson, cover this bastard.

HINSON (*Drawing his .45 automatic, moving on* ROGER): Yes, sir.

The LIEUTENANT *frisks* ROGER, *who is spread-eagled at the lockers.*

RICHIE: What? Oh, sir, no, no. Roger, what's going on?

LIEUTENANT: I'll straighten this shit out.

ROGER: Tell 'em to get the gun off me, Richie.

LIEUTENANT: SHUT UP!

RICHIE: But, sir, sir, he didn't do it. Not him.

LIEUTENANT (*Fiercely* HE *shoves* RICHIE *out of the way*): I told you, all of you, to shut up. (HE *moves to* ROONEY'*s body*) Jesus, God, this Sfc is cut to shit. He's cut to shit. (HE *hurries to* BILLY'*s body*) This man is cut to shit.

CARLYLE *appears in the doorway, his hands cuffed behind him, a third M.P.,* PFC CLARK, *shoving him forward.* CARLYLE *seems shocked and cunning, his mind whirring.*

CLARK: Sir, I got this guy on the street, runnin' like a streak a shit.

CLARK *hurls the struggling* CARLYLE *forward and* CARLYLE *stumbles toward the head of* RICHIE'*s bed as* RICHIE, *seeing him coming, hurries away along* BILLY'*s bed and toward the wall lockers.*

RICHIE: He did it! Him, him!

CARLYLE: What is going on here? I don't know what is going on here!

CLARK (*Club at the ready,* HE *stations himself beside* CARLYLE): He's got blood all over him, sir. All over him.

LIEUTENANT: What about the knife?

CLARK: No, sir. He must have thrown it away.

A FOURTH M.P. *has entered to stand in the doorway, and* HINSON, *leaving* ROGER, *bends to examine* ROONEY. HE *will also kneel and look for life in* BILLY.

LIEUTENANT: You throw it away, soldier?

CARLYLE: Oh, you thinkin' about how my sister got happened, too. Oh, you ain't so smart as you think you are! No way!

ROGER: Jesus God almighty.

LIEUTENANT: What happened here? I want to know what happened here.

HINSON (*Rising from* BILLY's *body*): They're both dead, sir. Both of them.

LIEUTENANT (*Confidential, almost whispering*): I know they're both dead. That's what I'm talkin' about.

CARLYLE: Chicken blood, sir. Chicken blood and chicken hearts is what all over me. I was goin' on my way, these people jump out the bushes be pourin' it all over me. Chicken blood and chicken hearts. (*Thrusting his hands out at* CLARK) You goin' take these cuffs off me, boy?

LIEUTENANT: Sit him down, Clark. Sit him down and shut him up.

CARLYLE: This my house, sir. This my goddamn house.

CLARK *grabs* CARLYLE, *begins to move him.*

LIEUTENANT: I said to shut him up.

CLARK: Move it; move! (*Struggling to get* CARLYLE *over to* ROGER's *footlocker as* HINSON *and the* FOURTH M.P. *exit*)

CARLYLE: I want these cuffs taken off my hands.

CLARK: You better do like you been told. You better sit and shut up!

CARLYLE: I'm gonna be thinkin' over here. I'm gonna be thinkin' it all over. I got plannin' to do. I'm gonna be thinkin' in my quietness; don't you be makin' no mistake.

CARLYLE *slumps over, muttering to himself.* HINSON *and the* FOURTH M.P. *return, carrying a stretcher.* THEY *cross to* BILLY, *chatting with each other about how to go about the lift.* THEY *will lift him;* THEY *will carry him out.*

LIEUTENANT (*To* RICHIE): You're Wilson?

RICHIE: No, sir. (*Indicating* BILLY) That's Wilson. I'm Douglas.

LIEUTENANT (*To* ROGER): And you're Moore. And you sleep here.

ROGER: Yes, sir.

RICHIE: Yes, sir. And Billy slept here and Sergeant Rooney was our platoon sergeant and Carlyle was a transient, sir. He was a transient from P Company.

LIEUTENANT (*Scrutinizing* ROGER): And you had nothing to do with this? (*To* RICHIE) He had nothing to do with this?

ROGER: No, sir, I didn't.

RICHIE: No, sir, he didn't. I didn't either. Carlyle went crazy and he got into a fight and it was awful. I didn't even know what it was about exactly.

LIEUTENANT: How'd the Sfc get involved?

RICHIE: Well, he came in, sir.

ROGER: I had to run off to call you, sir. I wasn't here.

RICHIE: Sergeant Rooney just came in—I don't know why—he heard all the yelling, I guess—and Carlyle went after him. Billy was already stabbed.

CARLYLE (*Rising, his manner that of a man who is taking charge*): All right now, you gotta be gettin' the fuck outa here. All of you. I have decided enough of the shit has been goin' on around here and I am tellin' you to be gettin' these motherfuckin' cuffs off me and you be gettin' me a bus ticket home. I am quittin' this jive-time army.

LIEUTENANT: You are doin' what?

CARLYLE: No, I ain't gonna be quiet. No way. I am quittin' this goddamn—

LIEUTENANT: You shut the hell up, soldier. I am ordering you.

CARLYLE: I don't understand you people! Don't you people understand when a man be talkin' English at you to say his mind? I have quit the army!

> HINSON *returns.*

LIEUTENANT: Get him outa here!

RICHIE: What's the matter with him?

LIEUTENANT: Hinson! Clark!

> HINSON *and* CLARK *move, grabbing* CARLYLE, *and* THEY *drag him, struggling, toward the door.*

CARLYLE: Oh, no. Oh, no. You ain't gonna be doin' me no more. I been tellin' you. To get away from me. I am stayin' here. This my place, not your place. You take these cuffs off me like I been tellin' you! My poor little sister Lin Sue understood what was goin' on here! She tole me! She knew! (HE *is howling in the hallway now*) You better be gettin' these cuffs off me!

> *Silence.* ROGER, RICHIE *and the* LIEUTENANT *are all staring at the door. The* LIEUTENANT *turns, crosses to the foot of* ROGER'S *bed.*

LIEUTENANT: All right now. I will be getting to the bottom of this. You know I will be getting to the bottom of this. (HE *is taking two forms from his clipboard*)

RICHIE: Yes, sir.

> HINSON *and the* FOURTH M.P. *return with another stretcher.* THEY *walk to* ROONEY, *talking to one another about how to lift him.* THEY *drag him from under the bed.* THEY *will roll him onto the stretcher, lift him and walk out.* ROGER *moves, watching them, down along the edge of* BILLY'S *bed.*

LIEUTENANT: Fill out these forms. I want your serial number, rank, your MOS, the NCOIC of your work. Any leave coming up will be canceled. Tomorrow at 0800 you will report to my office at the provost marshal's headquarters. You know where that is?

ROGER (*As the* TWO M.P.'*s are leaving with the stretcher and* ROONEY'*s body*): Yes, sir.

RICHIE: Yes, sir.

LIEUTENANT (*Crossing to* ROGER, HE *hands him two cards*): Be prepared to do some talking. Two perfectly trained and primed strong pieces of U.S. Army property got cut to shit up here. We are going to find out how and why. Is that clear?

RICHIE: Yes, sir.

ROGER: Yes, sir.

The LIEUTENANT *looks at each of them.* HE *surveys the room.* HE *marches out.*

RICHIE: Oh, my God. Oh. Oh.

RICHIE *runs to his bed and collapses, sitting hunched down at the foot.* HE *holds himself and rocks as if very cold.* ROGER, *quietly, is weeping.* HE *stands and then walks to his bed.* HE *puts down the two cards.* HE *moves purposefully up to the mops hanging on the wall in the corner.* HE *takes one down.* HE *moves with the mop and the bucket to* BILLY*'s bed, where* ROONEY*'s blood stains the floor.* HE *mops.* RICHIE, *in horror, is watching.*

What . . . are you doing?

ROGER: This area a mess, man. (*Dragging the bucket, carrying the mop,* HE *moves to the spot where* BILLY *had lain.* HE *begins to mop*)

RICHIE: That's Billy's blood, Roger. His blood.

ROGER: Is it?

RICHIE: I feel awful.

ROGER (HE *keeps mopping*): How come you made me waste all that time talkin' shit to you, Richie? All my time talkin' shit, and all the time you was a faggot, man; you really was. You shoulda jus' tole ole Roger. He don't care. All you gotta do is tell me.

RICHIE: I've been telling you. I did.

ROGER: Jive, man, jive!

RICHIE: No!

ROGER: You did bullshit all over us! ALL OVER US!

RICHIE: I just wanted to hold his hand, Billy's hand, to talk to him, go to the movies hand in hand like he would with a girl or I would with someone back home.

ROGER: But he didn't wanna; *he* didn't wanna.

Finished now, ROGER *drags the mop and bucket back toward the corner.* RICHIE *is sobbing;* HE *is at the edge of hysteria.*

RICHIE: He did.

ROGER: No, man.

RICHIE: He did. He did. It's not my fault.

ROGER *slams the bucket into the corner and rams the mop into the bucket. Furious,* HE *marches down to* RICHIE. *Behind him* SERGEANT COKES, *grinning and lifting a wine bottle, appears in the doorway.*

COKES: Hey! (RICHIE, *in despair, rolls onto his belly.* COKES *is very, very happy*) Hey! What a day, gen'l'men. How you all doin'?

ROGER (*Crossing up near the head of his own bed*): Hello, Sergeant Cokes.

COKES (*Affectionate and casual,* HE *moves near to* ROGER): How you all doin'? Where's ole Rooney? I lost him.

ROGER: What?

COKES: We had a hell of a day, ole Rooney and me, lemme tell you. We been playin' hide-and-go-seek, and I was hidin', and now I think maybe he started hidin' without tellin' me he was gonna and I can't find him and I thought maybe he was hidin' up here.

RICHIE: Sergeant, he—

ROGER: No. No, we ain't seen him.

COKES: I gotta find him. He knows how to react in a tough situation. He didn't come up here looking for me?

ROGER *moves around to the far side of his bed, turning his back to* COKES. *Sitting,* ROGER *takes out a cigarette, but* HE *does not light it.*

ROGER: We was goin' to sleep, Sarge. Got to get up early. You know the way this mother army is.

COKES (*Nodding, drifting backward,* HE *sits down on* BILLY*'s bed*): You don't mind I sit here a little. Wait on him. Got a little wine. You can have some. (*Tilting his head way back,* HE *takes a big drink and then, looking straight ahead, corks the bottle with a whack of his hand*) We got back into the area—we had been downtown—he wanted to play hide-and-go-seek. I tole him okay, I was ready for that. He hid his eyes. So I run and hid in the bushes and then under this Jeep. 'Cause I thought it was better. I hid and I hid and I hid. He never did come. So finally, I got tired—I figured I'd give up, come lookin' for him. I was way over by the movie theater. I don't know how I got there. Anyway, I got back here and I figured maybe he come up here lookin' for me, figurin' I was hidin' up with you guys. You ain't seen him, huh?

ROGER: No, we ain't seen him. I tole you that, Sarge.

COKES: Oh.

RICHIE: Roger!

ROGER: He's drunk, Richie! He's blasted drunk. Got a brain turned to mush!

COKES (*In deep agreement*): That ain't no lie.

ROGER: Let it be for the night, Richie. Let him be for the night.

COKES: I still know what's goin' on, though. Never no worry about that. I always know what's goin' on. I always know. Don't matter what I drink or how much I drink. I always still know what's goin' on. But . . . I'll be goin' maybe and look for Rooney. (*But rising,* HE *wanders down center*) But . . . I mean, we could be doin' that forever. Him and me. Me under the Jeep. He wants to find me, he goes to the Jeep. I'm over here. He comes here. I'm gone. You know, maybe I'll just wait a little while more I'm here.

He'll find me then if he comes here. You guys want another drink. (*Turning,* HE *goes to* BILLY'*s footlocker, where* HE *sits and takes another enormous guzzle of wine*) Jesus, what a goddamn day we had. Me and Rooney started drivin' and we was comin' to this intersection and out comes this goddamn Chevy. I try to get around her, but no dice. BINGO! I hit her in the left rear. She was furious. I didn't care. I gave her my name and number. My car had a headlight out, the fender bashed in. Rooney wouldn't stop laughin'. I didn't know what to do. So we went to D.C. to this private club I know. Had ten or more snorts and decided to get back here after playin' some snooker. That was fun. On the way, we picked up this kid from the engineering unit, hitchhiking. I'm starting to feel real clear-headed now. So I'm comin' around this corner and all of a sudden there's this car stopped dead in front of me. He's not blinkin' to turn or anything. I slam on the brakes, but it's like puddin' the way I slide into him. There's a big noise and we yell. Rooney starts laughin' like crazy and the kid jumps outa the back and says he's gonna take a fuckin' bus. The guy from the other car is swearin' at me. My car's still workin' fine, so I move it off to the side and tell him to do the same, while we wait for the cops. He says he wants his car right where it is and he had the right of way 'cause he was makin' a legal turn. So we're waitin' for the cops. Some cars go by. The guy's car is this big fuckin' Buick. Around the corner comes this little red Triumph. The driver's this blond kid got this blond girl next to him. You can see what's gonna happen. There's this fuckin' car sittin' there, nobody in it. So the Triumph goes crashin' into the back of the Buick with nobody in it. BIFF-BANG-BOOM. And everything stops. We're staring. It's all still. And then that fuckin' Buick kinda shudders and starts to move. With nobody in it. It starts to roll from the impact. And it rolls just far enough to get where the road starts a downgrade. It's driftin' to the right. It's driftin' to the shoulder and over it and onto this hill, where it's pickin' up speed 'cause the hill is steep and then it disappears over the side, and into the dark, just rollin' real quiet. Rooney falls over, he's laughin' so hard. I don't know what to do. In a minute the cops come and in another minute some guy comes runnin' up over the hill to tell us some other guy had got run over by this car with nobody in it. We didn't know what to think. This was fuckin' unbelievable to us. But we found out later from the cops that this wasn't true and some guy had got hit over the head with a bottle in a bar and when he staggered out the door it was just at the instant that this fuckin' Buick with nobody in it went by. Seein' this, the guy stops cold and turns around and just goes back into the bar. Rooney is screamin' at me how we been in four goddamn accidents and fights and how we have got out clean. So then we got everything all straightened out and we come back here to play hide-and-seek 'cause that's what ole Rooney wanted. (HE *is taking another drink, but finding the bottle empty*) Only now I can't find him. (*Near* RICHIE'*s footlocker stands a beer bottle and* COKES *begins to move toward it. Slowly* HE *bends and grasps the bottle;* HE *straightens, looking at it.* HE *drinks. And settles down on* RICHIE'*s footlocker*) I'll just sit a little.

RICHIE, *lying on his belly, shudders. The sobs burst out of him.* HE *is shaking.* COKES, *blinking, turns to study* RICHIE.

What's up? Hey, what're you cryin' about, soldier? Hey? (RICHIE *cannot help himself*) What's he cryin' about?

ROGER (*Disgustedly,* HE *sits there*): He's cryin' 'cause he's a queer.

COKES: Oh. You a queer, boy?

RICHIE: Yes, Sergeant.

COKES: Oh. (*Pause*) How long you been a queer?

ROGER: All his fuckin' life.

RICHIE: I don't know.

COKES (*Turning to scold* ROGER): Don't be yellin' mean at him. Boy, I tell you it's a real strange thing the way havin' leukemia gives you a lotta funny thoughts about things. Two months ago—or maybe even yesterday—I'da called a boy who was a queer a lotta awful names. But now I just wanna be figurin' things out. I mean, you ain't kiddin' me out about ole Rooney, are you, boys, 'cause of how I'm a sergeant and you're enlisted men, so you got some idea a vengeance on me? You ain't doin' that, are you, boys?

ROGER: No.

RICHIE: Ohhhh. Jesus. Ohhhh. I don't know what's hurtin' in me.

COKES: No, no, boy. You listen to me. You gonna be okay. There's a lotta worse things in this world than bein' a queer. I seen a lot of 'em, too. I mean, you could have leukemia. That's worse. That can kill you. I mean, it's okay. You listen to the ole sarge. I mean, maybe I was a queer, I wouldn't have leukemia. Who's to say? Lived a whole different life. Who's to say? I keep thinkin' there was maybe somethin' I coulda done different. Maybe not drunk so much. Or if I'd killed more gooks, or more krauts or more dinks. I was kindhearted sometimes. Or if I'd had a wife and I had some kids. Never had any. But my mother did and she died of it anyway. Gives you a whole funny different way a lookin' at things, I'll tell you. Ohhhhh, Rooney, Rooney. (*Slight pause*) Or if I'd let that little gook outa that spider hole he was in, I was sittin' on it. I'd let him out now, he was in there. (HE *rattles the footlocker lid under him*) Oh, how'm I ever gonna forget it? That funny little guy. I'm runnin' along, he pops up outa that hole. I'm never gonna forget him—how'm I ever gonna forget him? I see him and dive, goddamn bullet hits me in the side, I'm midair, everything's turnin' around. I go over the edge of this ditch and I'm crawlin' real fast. I lost my rifle. Can't find it. Then I come up behind him. He's half out of the hole. I bang him on top of his head, stuff him back into the hole with a grenade for company. Then I'm sittin' on the lid and it's made outa steel.

I can feel him in there, though, bangin' and yellin' under me, and his yelling I can hear is begging for me to let him out. It was like a goddamn Charlie Chaplin movie, everybody fallin' down and clumsy, and him in there yellin' and bangin' away, and I'm just sittin' there lookin' around. And he was Charlie Chaplin. I don't know who I was. And then he blew up. (*Pause*) Maybe I'll just get a little shut-eye right sittin' here while I'm waitin' for ole Rooney. We figure it out. All of it. You don't mind I just doze a little here, you boys?

ROGER: No.

RICHIE: No.

> ROGER *rises and walks to the door.* HE *switches off the light and gently closes the door. The transom glows.* COKES *sits in a flower of light.* ROGER *crosses back to his bunk and settles in, sitting.*

COKES: Night, boys.

RICHIE: Night, Sergeant.

> COKES *sits there, fingers entwined, trying to sleep.*

COKES: I mean, he was like Charlie Chaplin. And then he blew up.

ROGER (*Suddenly feeling very sad for this old man*): Sergeant . . . maybe you was Charlie Chaplin, too.

COKES: No. No. (*Pause*) No. I don't know who I was. Night.

ROGER: You think he was singin' it?

COKES: What?

ROGER: You think he was singin' it?

COKES: Oh, yeah. Oh, yeah; he was singin' it. (*Slight pause. Sitting on the footlocker,* HE *begins to sing a makeshift language imitating Korean, to the tune of "Beautiful Streamer."* HE *begins with an angry, mocking energy that slowly becomes a dream, a lullaby, a farewell, a lament*)

> Yo no som lo no
> Ung toe lo knee
> Ra so me la lo
> La see see oh doe.
>
> Doe no tee ta ta
> Too low see see
> Ra mae me lo lo
> Ah boo boo boo eee.
>
> Boo boo eee booo eeee
> La so lee lem
> Lem lo lee da ung
> Uhhh so ba booooo ohhhh.

Boo booo eee ung ba
Eee eee la looo
Lem lo lala la
Eeee oohhh ohhh ohhh ohhhhh.

In the silence, COKES *makes the soft, whispering sound of a child imitating an explosion, and his entwined fingers come apart. The dark figures of* RICHIE *and* ROGER *are near. The lingering light fades.*

END OF PLAY

BOTTICELLI

Terrence McNally

About Terrence McNally

Born in St. Petersburg, Florida in 1939 and raised in Corpus Christi, Texas, Terrence McNally is a Phi Beta Kappa graduate of Columbia University. Mc-Nally's first important play, *And Things That Go Bump in the Night*, premiered at The Guthrie Theater in Minneapolis in 1964; it opened on Broadway the following year. Other Broadway credits include *Noon, Bad Habits, The Ritz*, which was later adapted for film, and the 1984 musical *The Rink*, with a score by John Kander and Fred Ebb. Off Broadway productions include *Sweet Eros* and *Witness, Next, Where Has Tommy Flowers Gone?* and *Whiskey. The 5:48* and the recent *Mama Malone* were written for television. McNally has received two Guggenheim fellowships, an Obie award and a citation from the American Academy of Arts and Letters. Currently Vice President of the Dramatists Guild, he is a former winner of its Hull-Warriner Award.

Production History

Botticelli was first produced by Channel 13 in New York City in March 1968, directed by Glen Jordan. Its stage premiere was in August of that year, at the Berkshire Theatre Festival in Stockbridge, Massachusetts.

Playwright's Note

If the play is produced in an arena-type theatre, I would suggest the Man make his appearance through the audience. In a proscenium theatre, he might make his way down the center aisle with a follow spot on him. He must be center stage at the end of the play, a single light on his face.

Characters

WAYNE
STU
MAN

Time

An afternoon in the mid-1960s.

Place

A jungle in Vietnam.

The Play

Botticelli

Jungle foliage. Afternoon sun and shadows. Insect noises. Two soldiers, WAYNE *and* STU, *crouching with rifles.*

WAYNE: No, I'm not Marcel Proust.

STU: Proust was a stylist.

WAYNE: And he died *after* World War I.

STU: You sure?

WAYNE: 1922.

STU: Yeah?

WAYNE: November 4, 19—

STU: All right! (*Then*) What's up?

WAYNE (*Stiffening*): I thought I heard something. (*Relaxes*)

STU: Are you a . . . let's see . . . are you a Polish concert pianist who donated a large part of the proceeds from his concerts to the cause of Polish nationalism?

WAYNE: Oh, that's a real braincrusher, that one is!

STU: Well are you?

WAYNE: No I'm not Paderewski.

STU: Are you sure you're dead?

WAYNE: Oh brother!

STU: A dead European male in the arts beginning with P?

WAYNE: Why don't you write it down?

STU: Got it! You're a controversial Russian poet, novelist, dramatist and short-story writer.

WAYNE: Sorry. I'm not Pushkin.

STU: Pushkin wasn't considered controversial.

WAYNE: Who says?

STU: I do.

WAYNE: He was part Negro.

STU: What's controversial about that?

WAYNE: Dumas *père*?

STU: Don't change the subject. Controversial Russian writer. Come on. I've got you stumped, hunh? Look at you. Drew a blank. Hunh? Hunh?

WAYNE: I hope it's not Boris Pasternak you're crowing about.

STU: Drop dead, will you?

WAYNE: Then give up, hunh? (*Tenses*) Sshh! (*Relaxes*) Not yet.

STU: You'd think he'd starve in there by now.

WAYNE: Maybe he has. Why don't you go see?

STU: And get a grenade in the face. That tunnel could be half a mile long for all we know. He's buried in there like a groundhog. No, sir, I'm holding tight, staying right where I am, sergeant's orders. I got all the time in the world to wait for that bugger to stick his head out. (WAYNE *starts making cigarette*) Are you a . . .? I'm running dry. P's the hardest letter in the alphabet.

WAYNE: Wanna turn on?

STU: How much we got left?

WAYNE: If he's not out of there by tonight we're in trouble.

STU: Do you keep a diary?

WAYNE: Sure. Every night.

STU: No, who you are! Does he keep a diary?

WAYNE: I'm not Samuel Pepys.

STU: Smart-ass! (THEY *smoke*) Would you say this is the best part of the whole war?

WAYNE: What is?

STU: This. Pot.

WAYNE: No. I'd say Raquel Welch.

STU: Yeah.

WAYNE: What'd you think of her?

STU: I didn't.

WAYNE: Those goddam white leather boots up to here . . . and that yellow miniskirt . . .

STU: Hey, are you the outstanding English Baroque composer?

WAYNE: I'm not Henry Purcell. I thought Raquel Welch looked like a sexy . . . ostrich.

STU: Do the words "Rape of the Lock" mean anything to you?

WAYNE: No, and they don't mean anything to Alexander Pope either.

STU: Nuts!

WAYNE: Look, let me tell you who I am, hunh?

STU: No I said.

WAYNE: Brother, you're stubborn.

STU: And *you're* a Victorian playwright!

WAYNE: I'm not Arthur Wing Pinero.

STU: Sir.

WAYNE: Hunh?

STU: Sir Arthur Wing Pinero.

WAYNE: I know!

STU: You didn't say it.

WAYNE: I'd rather talk about Raquel Welch.

STU: Sure you would. You're getting stoned.

WAYNE: I'm not getting anything else.

STU: You still worrying about that letter from Susan?

WAYNE: Not since Raquel Welch I'm not.

STU: I bet.

WAYNE: Let her get a divorce. I don't care. Hell, the only mistake I made was thinking I had to marry her. I should've sent her to Puerto Rico. She could've had a vacation on me, too.

STU: Only you had scruples.

WAYNE: Leave me alone.

STU: Jesuit high school, Dominican college scruples.

WAYNE: God, you're insensitive. Wait'll *you* get married.

STU: Maybe I never will.

WAYNE: Yeah!

STU: I might not.

WAYNE: You'd marry the first girl who looked twice at you. Yours is one wedding I wouldn't want to miss. There's always Marlene Schroll.

STU: *As You Desire Me!*

WAYNE: What the—?

STU: You wrote *As You Desire Me.*

WAYNE: I'm not Luigi Pirandello.

STU: Okay, but simmer down, hunh?

WAYNE: It's a dumb game.

STU: Your idea.

WAYNE: I was trying to kill time.

STU: Well if we had something intelligent to discuss . . .

WAYNE: What's wrong with Raquel Welch?

STU: Nothing. She's the quintessence of intelligence.

WAYNE: I'm gonna bust you in the mouth. (*Pause*) I wish I'd burned my draft card.

STU: Are you a Russian composer?

WAYNE: I'm not Prokofiev.

STU: An Italian composer?

WAYNE: I'm not Puccini.

STU: An Italian composer?

WAYNE: I'm not Ponchielli.

STU: An Italian composer?

WAYNE: What are you, a record?

STU: An Italian composer?

WAYNE: All right, who?

STU: Pizzarella.

WAYNE: Go to hell.

STU: What's wrong with Pizzarella?

WAYNE: There's no Italian composer named Pizzarella.

STU: How do you know?

WAYNE: I know!

STU: Well maybe there is.

WAYNE: Yeah and you just made him up. Pizzarella. Look, if you're gonna play, play fair. Boy, you haven't changed since college. Even in charades you'd try to put something over.

STU: Like when?

WAYNE: Like when you did *The Brothers Karamazov*. Only you did it in Russian. How could anybody guess *The Brothers Karamazov* in a game of charades when *you* were doing it in Russian?

STU: It would've been too easy in English.

WAYNE: No wonder you never made the chess and bridge teams. Those are precise games. You don't muck with the rules in *them*. (*Pause*) Typical. Sulk now.

STU: I'm thinking.

WAYNE (*Rolls over on back, looks up at sky*): You know what I can't get over?

STU: Mmmmmm.

WAYNE: Poor Father Reilly.

STU: Yeah.

WAYNE: I mean just dropping dead like that. God, we were lucky having him for a teacher. And of all places to drop dead. He loved Rome the same way some men love women. I think he lived for his summer vacations. As much as he gave his students, his heart was always in Rome on the Spanish Steps or the Pincio. And I guess it was all those steps and hills that finally killed him. A great man.

STU: Wayne?

WAYNE: Yeah?

STU: An Italian composer?

WAYNE: You see this fist?

STU: I just thought of two more.

WAYNE: Real ones?

STU: Give up, you'll see.

WAYNE: If they're not, buddy . . . !

STU (*Looking at watch*): You've got fifteen seconds.

WAYNE: Unh . . . unh . . . unh . . . quit making me nervous . . . unh . . .

STU: Ten!

WAYNE: Palestrina!

STU: Who else?

WAYNE: Palestrina and . . . unh . . .

STU: Pizzarella?

WAYNE: Can it! Palestrina and . . .

STU: Five seconds.

WAYNE: Pergolesi. Giovanni Pergolesi! (*Burst of machine-gun fire,* THEY *both flatten out*) That dirty little . . . (*Aims, ready to fire*)

STU (*Terse whisper*): Homosexual Greek philosopher.

WAYNE: Brother, are you warped. I mean that's disgusting.

STU: Come on.

WAYNE: Plato wasn't homosexual.

STU: You were right there, climbing the Acropolis.

WAYNE: Your mind is really sick. A remark like that turns my stomach.

STU: Who made any remarks?

WAYNE: It's not even funny. (*Firing stops*) Where the hell is he? Come on, buster, stick your neck out. He's shooting to see if anybody's out here. We'll just have to sit tight.

STU: Apropos the Parthenon, did you by any chance supervise the rebuilding of it?

WAYNE: I'm not Phidias. What are we on now? Your Greek kick?

STU: You're a fine one to talk about *that.*

WAYNE: There's something crawling on you.

STU: Hey! What the hell is it? This country. Bugs in your shoes, bugs in your hair, bugs in your food. Look at him go. Eight legs . . . no, ten! . . . I guess those are wings . . . nice antennae . . . I used to be scared of bugs.

WAYNE: Do you have to have a conversation with him?

STU: Bon soir, bug. (*Crushes bug*)

WAYNE: I could never do that.

STU: Bugs have souls now, too?

WAYNE: Shut up about all that, will you?

STU: I don't suppose you're an Italian poet?

WAYNE: I'm not Petrarch, Einstein.

STU: It was just a wild guess.
WAYNE: You're never going to get me.
STU: I'm not going to give up either.
WAYNE: Stubborn, stubborn, stubborn!
STU: I'd lose all self-respect if I weren't.
WAYNE: Sshh.
STU: I mean the only reason to begin a game is to win it.
WAYNE: I said shut up!

The MAN *has come out of the tunnel.* HE's *young, emaciated.* HE *pauses at the entrance, quivering like a frightened rabbit. Spot on him.*

Look at the little bugger.
STU: Not so little through these sights.
WAYNE: Not yet! He has to come this way. Wait'll he's closer.
STU: You're not a French painter? A great master of the classical school?
WAYNE: I'm not Poussin.
STU: I've got another one. Impressionist.
WAYNE: French.
STU: Yeah.
WAYNE: I'm not Pissarro.
STU: I can't think of any more P's.
WAYNE: All right, *you* gave up, I'm—
STU: No!

MAN *has begun to move cautiously away from tunnel opening.*

WAYNE: Here he comes. Quiet now.
STU: Were you an Italian sculptor working with Giotto on the campanile in Florence.
WAYNE: I'm not Pisano. Get ready.
STU: Okay, and this is it, Wayne. Did you write a famous "Lives"?
WAYNE: I'm not Plutarch. Let's go.

MAN's *face contorts with pain as* HE *is cut down by a seemingly endless volley of gunfire.* HE *falls, twitches, finally lies still.* WAYNE *and* STU *approach.*

STU: Is he dead? I just asked!
WAYNE: Let's get back to camp.
STU: Okay, I give up. Who are you?
WAYNE: Pollaiuolo.
STU: Who?
WAYNE: Pollaiuolo. Antonio del Pollaiuolo.
STU: That's like Pizzarella.

WAYNE *and* STU *start moving off. Spot stays on* MAN's *face.*

WAYNE: Italian painter, sculptor and goldsmith. 1432-1498.

STU: Well I never heard of him.

WAYNE: Famous for his landscapes and the movement he put into the human body.

STU: Never heard of him.

WAYNE: He influenced Dürer, Signorelli and Verrocchio.

WAYNE *and* STU *are just voices now.*

STU: *Them* I've heard of.

WAYNE: Portrait of a Man? The Labors of Hercules? David? The Martyrdom of St. Sebastian? Tobias and the Angel?

STU: Never heard of him.

WAYNE: The tomb of Sixtus IV?

STU: Never heard of him.

WAYNE: Good God, he was a contemporary of Botticelli!

STU: Never heard of him.

WAYNE: Christ, you're dumb.

STU: I NEVER HEARD OF HIM.

Spot stays on MAN's *face. Slow fade.*

END OF PLAY

HOW I GOT THAT STORY

Amlin Gray

About Amlin Gray

Born in New York City in 1946, Amlin Gray was drafted in 1966. A conscientious objector, he served as a medic in Vietnam. Trained as an actor after his army discharge, by the early 1970s Gray had taken up playwriting; his first two plays were presented at the O'Neill Theater Center in 1974 and 1976. He became a resident playwright at Milwaukee Repertory Theater in 1977, since which time 13 of his original plays, adaptations and translations have first been seen there. These include *Kingdom Come, Zones of the Spirit* and, most recently, an adaptation of *Christmas Carol*. Commissioned by Milwaukee's Theatre X, *The Fantod* was cited by the American Theatre Critics Association as one of nine outstanding new plays produced in regional theatre during the 1978-79 season. Gray has been the recipient of Guggenheim, Rockefeller and National Endowment for the Arts grants, and is a 1985 McKnight Fellow.

Production History

How I Got That Story was first presented by Milwaukee Repertory Theater in April 1979, under the direction of Sharon Ott. The play's New York premiere, directed by Carole Rothman, took place at The Second Stage in December 1980. In February 1982 the play re-opened Off Broadway, again under Rothman's direction.

Playwright's Note

Every sound effect in the play is made, live or on tape, by the Event actor. Where possible, the audience should be able to recognize his voice.

The setting is a wide, shallow space, as bare of props and set pieces as possible. This will help to characterize the Event as the Reporter sees it: broadly, shallowly, and in sharply isolated fragments.

The back wall should be textured in a range of shades from green to greenish brown, perhaps with collage materials (bamboo, scraps of Asian writing, etc.) blended in. The backdrop must serve alike for city scenes and scenes set in the countryside. To facilitate the Event's transformations, masked breaks should be provided in the back wall. Slides announcing the titles of the scenes, etc., appear on the back wall, as do photographs of the Event, as described.

A list of scenes follows:

ACT ONE   1 *Accreditation*
           2 *Tip*
           3 *Audience*
           4 *Strip*
           5 *Field*
           6 *Imprintment*
           7 *Planes*
           8 *Run*

ACT TWO   1 *Village*
           2 *Self-Criticism*
           3 *Rescue*
           4 *Proposal*
           5 *Work*
           6 *Orphanage*
           7 *Home*

Characters

THE REPORTER. An eager young man in his late 20s.

THE HISTORICAL EVENT. The actor playing this part appears at times as the entire Event, at other times as people who make up parts of the Event, as follows:

THE DEPUTY COORDINATOR

MR. KINGSLEY

AN AMBONESE PEDESTRIAN

A BONZE

MADAME ING

A STREET URCHIN

A G.I. IN MIMI'S FLAMBOYANT

LIEUTENANT THIBODEAUX (pronounced "TIH-buh-doe")

PFC PROCHASKA

A GUERRILLA

SERGEANT PEERS

LI (pronounced "Lee")

A CIVILIAN FLIGHT ANNOUNCER

AN AMERICAN PHOTOGRAPHER

AN AIR FORCE PILOT
AN AMBONESE PSYCHOLOGICAL WARFARE OFFICER
AN AMBONESE SOLDIER
A GUERRILLA INFORMATION OFFICER
OFFICER X
AN AMBONESE NUN

Time

The mid-1960s.

Place

Vietnam.

The Play

How I Got That Story

This play is dedicated to
SHARON OTT

ACT ONE

As the audience is just about getting settled, the EVENT *walks into the play-ing area, stands utterly impassive, and, his mouth moving minimally, begins to articulate a strange and Asian-sounding musical piece. If any stage light is on him, it goes out with the house lights.* HE *continues his instrumental-sounding version of the foreign melody in the darkness.*

Slide: HOW I GOT THAT STORY

Slide: starring

Slide: (Actor's name) as The Reporter

A light comes up as the slide goes off, showing the REPORTER *with pencil poised over his notepad, trying to locate the source of the elusive music. The light goes out.*

Slide: and

Slide: (Actor's name) as The Historical Event

A light comes up on the EVENT, *from whose passive presence music continues to issue.* HE *is now standing on his head.*

81

Slide: ACCREDITATION

Lights come up on the REPORTER. HE *is wearing a rumpled lightweight jacket with ink stains around the pockets.* HE *holds a somewhat crushed felt hat in one hand and speaks to the audience.*

REPORTER: Hello there. This is Am-bo Land. My new job with the Trans-PanGlobal Wire Service brought me here. It's not the safest place right now, but this is how I figure it. The last two years I've been reporting on the western part of East Dubuque. A lot goes on there. If you add it all up right, then you've got western East Dubuque. That's fine. But if you add up Am-bo Land, it's everyplace. It's *it.* It's what the world is like. If I just keep my eyes wide open I can understand the whole world. That's how I figure it. These are the Am-bo Land offices of TransPanGlobal. Good-sized outfit, hey? I'm here to pick up my accreditation card so I can work incountry. Spell that word without a hyphen.

VOICE: Next.

The REPORTER *walks over to a desk. The* DEPUTY COORDINATOR *is sitting behind it.*

COORDINATOR: May I help you?

REPORTER: I'm here to see Mr. Kingsley.

COORDINATOR: May I ask your business?

REPORTER: I'm just picking up my card so I can work incountry.

COORDINATOR: You'll see Mr. Kingsley.

REPORTER: Thank you.

COORDINATOR: Straight back, third door to the right, first left, and down the hall.

REPORTER: Thanks.

COORDINATOR: He's expecting you.

REPORTER: He is?

COORDINATOR: Yes.

REPORTER: How?

COORDINATOR: You said you work for TransPanGlobal?

REPORTER: Yes.

COORDINATOR: I'm sure you know, then, that our business is communication.

REPORTER: Thank you very much.

The REPORTER *moves off and into the maze of the* COORDINATOR's *directions. When* HE *gets to* KINGSLEY's *office,* KINGSLEY *is waiting for him.* KINGSLEY *stands up from his desk and shakes the* REPORTER's *hand.*

KINGSLEY: I'm so happy to meet you. Please sit down. (HE *indicates a chair in front of his desk. The* REPORTER *sits*) Don't mind if I stare. It's one of the

little pleasures of my job when a byline changes to a face. You look quite
like your byline, I might say. I couldn't be more pleased.

REPORTER: Well, thank you.

KINGSLEY: I admire your work. Before I'd read two pages of the samples that
you sent us, I said, "Bob"—please call me Bob, that's what I call myself—

REPORTER: Okay, Bob.

KINGSLEY: I said, "Bob, this is a man for TransPanGlobal. An impartial man.
He views all sides and then he writes the truth as he believes it."

REPORTER: If I may, sir—

KINGSLEY: Bob.

REPORTER: Bob, I'm not sure I'd put it quite that way. I don't think belief
is too much help to a reporter. What I try to do is *see*, then write the truth—
Bob—as I *see* it.

KINGSLEY: My mistake. Poor choice of words. My meaning was, you don't
allow some pietistic preconception to subvert your objectivity. You write
what you see.

REPORTER: That's very nicely said, Bob. I'll subscribe to that.

KINGSLEY: On the other hand, you don't write *everything* you see.

REPORTER: I'm not quite sure I—

KINGSLEY: If your wife farts in church you don't run it on the human interest
page.

REPORTER: I'm not married.

KINGSLEY: No, I know you're not. That was a figure of speech.

REPORTER (*"Go on"*): Okay.

KINGSLEY: To bring this down to cases. The Government of Madame Ing is
fighting for its life. You probably know that the guerrillas don't confine
themselves to Robert's Rules of Order. Madame Ing is forced, in kind, to
bite and scratch a little. You may see a few examples. Some abridgement
of the freedom of internal opposition. Some abridgement of the outer limbs
of those involved. These things may rock you. Nothing wrong with that—as
long as you keep one thing very firmly in mind. When we send out reports,
the nearest terminal for them is the Imperial Palace. Madame Ing eats ticker
tape like eel in fish sauce. That's the A-1 delicacy here, you'll have to try
it. Can you handle chopsticks?

REPORTER: Yes, I—

KINGSLEY: Madame Ing is very sensitive to how she's viewed from overseas.
Let's face it. When we applied for permission to set up an agency here,
we didn't apply to the guerrillas. It's Ing who allowed us to come here,
and it's Ing who has the power to send us back. (*Sliding a card across the
desk to the* REPORTER) Let's have a signature.

REPORTER: What's this?

KINGSLEY: Your press card.

REPORTER (*Pleased*): Oh. (HE *signs*)

KINGSLEY (*Deftly seals the card in plastic*): You'll find this plastic proof against the rainy season, jungle rot . . . . I took a card like this intact right off the body of a newsman who had all but decomposed.

REPORTER: What happened to him?

KINGSLEY: Madame Ing expelled him but he didn't leave. The will of a developing government will find a way. (HE *hands the* REPORTER *his sealed card*) We're very glad you're with us.

Gray-out. KINGSLEY *disappears as the* REPORTER, *somewhat overloaded, retraces his steps through the maze of "corridors" and out onto the streets. His journey is accompanied by the sounds—made on tape, like all the sounds that follow, by the voice of the* EVENT—*of a ticker-tape machine, crossfading with the putt-beep-swish of Hondas.*

Slide: TIP

Lights full up on the REPORTER, *still a bit nonplussed as* HE *makes his way along the street.* HE *puts the press card in his hatband and the hat back on his head. The tape ends with a whooshing sound as a sudden wind blows the* REPORTER *to a standstill, makes him grab his hat.* HE *stands quite puzzled.*

REPORTER: That was odd. A sudden breeze, now nothing. (HE *wets his finger and holds it up; shrugs*) Oriental weather. (*Starts walking again*) I've heard that the guerrillas move so fast you feel a wind and don't see anything, but sitting in your pocket is a bomb. (*A moment's delay, then frantically* HE *pats his pockets from the chest down. Gives a sigh of relief. Then, registering something, returns to the first pocket that* HE *checked. Slowly* HE *draws out a neatly folded sheet of rice paper. Carefully* HE *opens it. It contains a single wooden match.* HE *reads the message on the paper*) "Han Sho Street and Perfume Boulevard in twenty minutes. A man will ask you for a light." (*Checking his watch*) Twenty minutes. That would be at two o'clock. What time is it now? (*Checking*) Twenty minutes of two! Excuse me, sir? (*A* MAN *in a conical reed hat has walked on*) Sir. Han Sho Street and Perfume Boulevard. Which way? (*The* AMBONESE PEDESTRIAN *snatches the* REPORTER'S *hat off his head and runs*) Hey! Hey! (*A chase ensues, with the* MAN *appearing from unexpected places, then vanishing, the* REPORTER *farther and farther behind him. A continuation of the street-sounds tape accompanies the chase*) Hey, come back here! Stop! I need that! (*Finally the* MAN *strolls on with his reed hat in his hand and the* REPORTER'S *on his head. Puffing, the* REPORTER *comes in sight*) Sir, it's not the hat I want. I won't begrudge you that. I know you probably live in very straitened circumstances. I just want the press card. (*The* MAN *points at an offstage sign*) Oh. Han Sho Street and Perfume Boulevard. (*The* MAN *holds out his own hat, bottom up. The* REPORTER *puts money in it. The* MAN *takes the* REPORTER'S *hat from his head and flips it to its owner. Then the* MAN *ambles off, counting his money*) I made it. No one here though. (HE *takes the match out of his pocket and holds it awkwardly in front of him. After a moment*) I'll take the opportunity to absorb a little atmosphere. (*Writing in a little spiral notebook*) Busy intersection. People. Hondas. Over there a big pagoda. Lots of Buddhists in the windows, dressed in saffron robes. (*As* HE *goes on, the* BONZE— *in saffron robes—comes on, unseen by him. The* BONZE *is carrying a large red gasoline can*) All ages. Every window filled with faces. They're all looking over here in my direction. Not at me, though. I don't *think* at me. (*The* BONZE *has "poured" a pool of gasoline on the pavement*) I can smell their incense. (*The* BONZE *has set the can down and come up behind the* REPORTER. *The* REPORTER *spins around*) Oh! You startled me. (*Pause. The* BONZE *just stands there*) Are you my contact? (*Pause*) You're supposed to ask me something. (*The* BONZE *stands. The* REPORTER *starts to hold the match up again, to give the man a hint. The* BONZE *takes it*) That's not incense! That's gas!

In one resolute movement, the BONZE *walks back to the puddle of gas and sits down cross-legged in the middle of it.* HE *"empties" the rest of the can over his head.*

BONZE: Down with Madame Ing! Down with the repressive government of Am-bo Land! (HE *scrapes the match on the pavement and at once is "burning" [a red special and a piece of paper crackled in each hand can give the effect]. The* REPORTER *stands rooted with horror*)

REPORTER: Oh my god. He's burning. People up and down the street are watching. I am too. I'm watching. (*Quickly*) I'm not watching. I'm not here! I'm a reporter! I'm recording this! (HE *writes*) "The monk was sitting in the center of a column of fire. From time to time a light wind blew the flames away from his face. His face was twisted with the pain." The pain, my god—! (*To himself*) No! You're not here. You're just recording this. You look at it, you take the pencil, and you write it down. (*The* BONZE *topples sideways*) My god. (HE *forces his pencil to his pad and writes. Tape fades up: a low repeating chant in an Asian-sounding language*) "Charred black . . . black circle on the pavement . . . wisps of orange fabric drifted down the street."

The lights fade out. The chant continues in the darkness.

Slide: AUDIENCE

Lights come up on the REPORTER, *still shaken from his experience at the street corner.*

REPORTER: I went and talked this morning to the Reverend Father of the Han Sho Street Pagoda. Here. (HE *takes out his notebook*) I think I've got it clear now. He explained to me that the—what's that? (HE *can't read his writing*) —the immolation was a political act and a spiritual act at the same time. There are six thousand monks in Am-bo Land. Of these six thousand, one hundred and fifty have applied for permission to kill themselves. They wish to demonstrate their faith. But the Reverend Father withholds permission till the worldly motive—political protest—is sufficient by itself to justify the act. (*Quoting*) "The spiritual act must be politically pure; the political act must be spiritually pure." It's both at once. And so it's sort of—neither. . . . If I'd had some sand or water—or I might have tried to damp the fire with my jacket—but that would have been unethical. . . . I've got it all down here, though. (*A gong sounds.* HE *starts*) The most amazing thing has happened! I'm about to talk to Madame Ing! She summoned me! Reporters have waited years without getting an audience. I can't believe this is happening.

The gong sounds again, a little louder. The REPORTER *walks awestruck into the Presence.* MADAME ING *is seated, regally.*

ING: Here I sit and stand.
REPORTER: Um . . . yes. (*At a loss what to say*) I've seen you on the cover of *Time* magazine.
ING: Do not mention that loathsome publication in my presence.
REPORTER: But they named you "Woman of the Year."
ING: What year?
REPORTER: Why, last year.
ING: Why not this year?
REPORTER: They never give it to anyone twice in a row.
ING: In my country one must grow in honor as one grows in years. *Time* should have named me "Woman of the Decade," next year "Woman of the Century," and so on. I have summoned you.
REPORTER: I'm flabbergasted.
ING: I wish not to know what that word means.
REPORTER: To what do I owe the extraordinary honor of your summons?
ING: To your crime.
REPORTER: My crime?
ING: You bribed the monks of Han Sho Street Pagoda to set one of their fellows on fire.
REPORTER: What?
ING: They filled his veins with morphine till his blood was thin. They led him to the street and they set fire to him.
REPORTER: That's not true.
ING: Not true?
REPORTER: No. The man was alone. Nobody led him to the street.

ING: Then he was hypnotized.

REPORTER: He wasn't.

ING: How do you know?

REPORTER: Because I heard him speak.

ING: A man can speak under hypnosis.

REPORTER: Well, I'm sure he wasn't hypnotized.

ING: Men of the press are expected to have documentation for what they say. Do you have proof?

REPORTER: I saw him.

ING: Look at me. You see my face?

REPORTER: Yes . . . .

ING: Am I smiling?

REPORTER (*Peering as through darkness at her unreadable expression*): I don't know.

ING: The monk was hypnotized.

REPORTER: *You* have no proof.

ING: I know. You have admitted you do not know. Madame Ing has won that argument.

REPORTER: All right, then, let's just say that he was hypnotized. What makes you think I was behind it?

ING: I have proof.

REPORTER: What proof?

ING: Sheer logic. Highly valued in the West. Tell me what reason might this monk have had to light himself on fire?

REPORTER: Well, I've done a little work on that. His motives were political, exclusively—and therefore they were purely of the spirit. Only by being entirely the one and not at all the other could they be entirely the other and I really thought I had that.

ING: On his first day in my country, a reporter puts this barbecue on ticker tapes that go to every land. Is this not good for his career?

REPORTER: No—!

ING: No?

REPORTER: Well, yes—

ING: You are the one man with a motive for this foolishness.

REPORTER: I didn't do it.

ING: You have proof?

REPORTER: No—.

ING: I have shown you *my* proof. Madame Ing has won *that* argument. It is time to do my dance for you. (SHE *breaks toward a standing screen*)

REPORTER: Madame Ing, I hope you won't expel me.

ING: No. You may be wrong.

REPORTER: Wrong?

ING: You may *not* have bribed the monks to burn their friend. (*The gong sounds.*

SHE *passes behind the screen; emerges draped in a flowing costume*) I have an army and I have a private army. (*Dancing a prelude*) My private army is made
up entirely of women.

REPORTER: Yes, I know.

ING (*Silencing him*): I speak to speak. I do not speak to give you information.
Objections have been raised because I pay my women more than my regular
army. But my women are all officers, down to the lowest private. Now I
present the guerrilla chief. (SHE *assumes the posture of a bent-haunched, quaver-
ing man*) And this is the lowest of my Paramilitary Girls. (SHE *strikes the
stance of a tall, fierce woman. In the dance that follows—a solo version of the entire
Peking Opera—the Paramilitary Girl fights with the guerrilla and defeats him.
ING withdraws behind her screen. Unseen, SHE uses a device to alter her voice—
say a #10 can. Reverberant*) You find us inscrutable here in the East.

REPORTER: It's not just you. It's the Americans here too. I can't—

ING: Be patient. Soon you will understand even less. Your ignorance will be
whipped with wind until it is pure as mist above the mountains. But you
must await this time with patience—patient as the rocks. We will never be
perfectly inscrutable to you till we have killed you and you do not know
why. (*The gong sounds*)

REPORTER: Does that mean I go now?

Silence. The REPORTER *starts off as the lights fade out. Slides: on the back wall
appear glimpses of parts of the face of the actor playing the* EVENT. *Each slide
shows just a single feature. The slides are in exaggerated half-tone—broken into
dots as if for reproduction—and thus suggestive of pictures in a newspaper. If
the slides come from more than one projector, they should alternate
arrhythmically.*

Slide: STRIP

The REPORTER *is standing on the sidewalk of the Strip.*

REPORTER: These people in power are a little hard to fathom. So I've come
here, to the street they call the Strip. This is where the real people come,
the normal, regular people. And what better place to look for the reality
of this moment in history? Who better to talk to than the G.I.'s and the
Government troops, the bar girls and the peddlers, people trying just to
get along, to live their lives, to snatch a moment of pleasure or excitement
in the midst of the horror and confusion of this war? (HE *starts to walk*)
The bars have names like China Doll, Las Vegas, there's the Dragon Bar,
that one's the Playboy. Up and down the street are skinny men in short
sleeves selling local soda dyed bright red and blue. Little barefoot boys are
selling·dirty pictures. That is, I'm sure they're dirty. I assume they're dirty.

Filthy, probably. (A STREET URCHIN *has pattered on.* HE *thrusts three or four pictures at the* REPORTER, *arrayed like playing cards*) No thank you, I don't want to see them. No, but wait a minute. I should look. They're part of local color. (HE *pays the* BOY *and takes the pictures. Quickly joking to the audience*) Nope, they're black-and-white. (*Back to the pictures*) That's awful. Would you look at that? That's terrible. (*Putting the pictures in his pocket*) These are documents. These say it all. (*A* G.I. *passes the* REPORTER. HE *is looking very wired*) There's a G.I. going into that bar. I'm going to interview him. (*Reading the sign above the "door" the* G.I. *has gone through*) "Mimi's Flamboyant." Here I go—(HE *chokes off, coughing, fans the smoke away from his face. There is a blast of instrumental music—a tinny imitation of Western rock-and-roll, say, "Satisfaction"*) The music's so loud I can hardly see the people's faces. Where did my G.I. go? It's dark in here but all the girls are wearing sunglasses. The girls look very young. They're pretty. No, that's not objective. Stick to what's objective. But they are. (*The* G.I. *comes in from the back, carrying a drink.* HE *looks spent.* HE *sits down at a table*) Look, there's my G.I. now. Excuse me, soldier, can I talk to you?

G.I. (*Looks at* REPORTER *stonily*): About what?

REPORTER: All this.

G.I.: All what?

REPORTER: The whole thing.

G.I.: You in the army?

REPORTER: No.

G.I.: Then what in the fuck are you doin' over here?

REPORTER: It's my beat. I'm a reporter.

G.I.: A reporter? All right. Ask your questions.

REPORTER: What's it like?

G.I.: What's what like?

REPORTER: Combat.

G.I.: Scary.

REPORTER: Scary?

G.I.: What the fuck you think?

REPORTER: I figured it was scary.

G.I.: You're a fuckin' genius. Ask some more.

REPORTER: I don't think we've exhausted that subject yet.

G.I.: Naw, you got it figured, man. It's scary. You got that one fuckin' *down*.

REPORTER: Tell me some stories.

G.I.: Stories?

REPORTER: Anecdotes. Some things that happened.

G.I.: Only one thing happens, baby. You're out there in the jungle, right? The fuckin' boonies. Everything is green. And then the bullet comes. Your name is on it. That's the story.

REPORTER: Your name is on it?

G.I.: That's a rodge.

REPORTER: What if your name's not on it?

G.I.: Then it misses you and hits your buddy.

REPORTER: Do you have to duck?

G.I.: What?

REPORTER: Do you duck?

G.I.: Your mamma drop you on your head when you was little?

REPORTER: So you duck then?

G.I.: Man, you hug that ground like it was Raquel fuckin' Welch.

REPORTER: But if the bullet hasn't got your name, it isn't going to hit you.

G.I.: Right.

REPORTER: And if it's got your name—

G.I.: Man, if it's got your name, you can dig a hole and roll an APC on top of you, don't make no never mind.

REPORTER: Then why do you duck?

G.I.: Someone's shooting at your ass, you duck!

REPORTER: It still seems like a contradiction. Guess you've got to go out there and see it for yourself.

G.I.: Out where?

REPORTER: The boonies.

G.I.: Are you batshit?

REPORTER: Huh?

G.I.: You're going out there?

REPORTER: Yeah.

G.I.: What for?

REPORTER: I want to see. (*Showing his notebook*) I've got a job to do.

G.I.: You want to see. Tomorrow morning you wake up in your hotel room, you say, fine day, think I'll grab a chopper, go on out and hump the boonies. That ain't it, man. You can't want to go. Somebody got to make you go. Some mean old sergeant, damnfool captain got to tell you, soldier, grab your gear and get your ass out there and hump. You can't want to go.

REPORTER: I won't get out there if it's not by choice. I have to want to.

G.I.: I'm gonna tell you something, hombre. I'm gonna tell you once, so listen. You go out there if you're gonna, but you don't come near my unit. Do you read me? We get hit for sure. You're *bad luck*. You come close to my platoon, I'm gonna waste your ass. You'll never know what hit you. (*Exiting into the back*) Mama! Mamasan! Hey mama!

Blackout. Tape: the sound of helicopters in flight, then setting down—without, however, turning off their rotors.

Slide: FIELD

The REPORTER *in the field.* HE *has put a mottled green flak jacket over his shirt, and is wearing a tiger-fatigue hat with his accreditation card tucked in the camouflage band.* HE *speaks into the microphone of a cassette recorder that hangs off his hip.*

REPORTER: This is your correspondent in Am-bo Land, reporting from the field. I've gone out with an American reconnaissance platoon. The choppers dropped us in a clearing. We've regrouped behind the treeline.

Lights up on LIEUTENANT THIBODEAUX, *speaking to the troops.*

LIEUTENANT: Sweet Jesus fuckin' string my balls and hang me from a fuckin' tree, Christ fuckin' motherfuck god damn! Because this war has taught me two things, men. It's taught me how to kill and it's taught me how to swear. God fuckin' crap-eye son of a bee, and cunt my fuckin' jungle rot and hang me fuckin' upside-down and jangle my cojones. Joy roll! Fuckin²-A! You hear me, men?

REPORTER: That's Lieutenant Thibodeaux. He's trying to help his troops achieve the right aggressive attitude.

LIEUTENANT: You hear me, men?

SOLDIERS (*On tape; with no trace of enthusiasm*): Yeah.

LIEUTENANT: Sound off like you got a pair! We're Airborne! Say it!

SOLDIERS: Airborne.

LIEUTENANT: Well, that's not outstanding, but it's better. Slip my disc and tie my tubes, god damn and fuckin' motherfuck!

REPORTER: He has to win the absolute confidence of the men in his command. If he's not able to, in combat, when he's giving them an order that requires them to risk their lives, it's possible that one of them may shoot him in the back. The soldiers call this "fragging."

LIEUTENANT: I won't lie to you. This is a dangerous mission. But I want you to know, men, I've been out there and I've come back. I've come back every god damn time. That's every motherloving asslick shitbrick pick your nose and fuck me time. I don't wear decorations in the field, but if any man here doesn't believe me he can come to my hootch when this thing is over and I'll show him my Sharpshooter's Badge with four bars and my two Good Conduct Medals. Suck my dick and kick my ass six ways from Sunday. Sing it with me. I wanna be an Airborne Ranger. I wanna be an Airborne Ranger. I wanna lead a life of danger.

SOLDIERS (*Barely audible*): I wanna lead a life of danger.

LIEUTENANT: 'Cause I fight out there beside my men. And here's one thing I promise you. If I give any of you men an order that requires you to lay down your life, it's because I'm wearing army green. I love this uniform. I love the army. Good luck, men. Let's move out!

The LIEUTENANT *turns and takes a step away. A shot rings out.* THIBODEAUX*'s limbs sprawl outwards as the lights black out. Almost immediately, the lights pick up the* REPORTER *in the same spot where* HE *stood at the beginning of the scene. Once more,* HE *speaks into his tape recorder.*

REPORTER: This is your correspondent in Am-bo Land, reporting from the field. Our mission was almost aborted by a circumstance the facts aren't quite all in on yet. We'll proceed with Sergeant Peers in charge. He's forming the platoon into a line. I'm supposed to walk at the end. The men say that'll give me the best view of everything that happens. (HE *walks in a circle, falling in behind the last soldier*—PFC PROCHASKA. PROCHASKA *carries an M-16 rifle.* THEY *hump the boonies during the following, the* REPORTER *carefully copying everything* PROCHASKA *does*) Excuse me? Soldier?

PFC (*Turning*): Yeah? Hey, stagger!

REPORTER: Stagger?

PFC: Don't walk in a line with me! Some sniper hits you gets me too.

REPORTER (*Sidestepping*): Check. Soldier?

PFC: Don't call me soldier. I got drafted. Call me Prochaska.

REPORTER: Check.

PFC: And keep it down.

REPORTER (*More quietly*): Is this your first patrol?

PFC: Do pigs shit ice cream?

REPORTER (*Not understanding*): No . . . (*Speaking furtively into his cassette recorder*) "Do pigs shit ice cream?" Look that up. (*To* PROCHASKA) What's the purpose—the objective—of this patrol?

PFC: Find the enemy.

REPORTER: Do you expect it to succeed?

PFC: I hope not.

REPORTER: Are you afraid?

PFC: Do cows have titties?

REPORTER: Yes . . . (*Into his recorder*) Check "Do cows have titties?" (*To* PROCHASKA) You don't think I'm bad luck, do you?

PFC: No, you good luck, brother.

REPORTER: Good luck? Super. Although it would defeat my entire purpose to affect the outcome of the mission in any way. But why am I good luck?

PFC: You're walking behind me.

REPORTER: Huh?

PFC: Go-rillas spring an ambush, the man in the back gets shot first.

REPORTER: Sure. That stands to reason.

PFC: You're not carrying a rifle either. They gonna take you for a medic.

REPORTER: What does that mean?

PFC: First they shoot the officer. Then they shoot the medic.

REPORTER: I thought they shot the man in back first.

PFC: Brother, either way . . .

REPORTER: I want to get this straight. Let's say for now that I'm not here, so you're the man in back. Good. Now the officer is Sergeant Peers, and there's the medic. Okay. So, the man in back and the officer get shot before the medic. But which of you gets shot first?

PFC: Man, we all get shot if you keep talking.

REPORTER: The sergeant is raising his hand. What does that mean?

PFC: Break time. You smoke?

REPORTER: No.

PFC: Save me your ciggies from your C's, okay?

REPORTER: Sure.

PFC: Don't sit near the radio. You do, they shoot you first. (HE *walks off. The* REPORTER *sits in place*)

REPORTER: When Pfc Prochaska said "C's," his reference was to C-rations, the G.I.'s meal-in-a-box. I'm about to open my first box of C's. (HE *takes a small box out of his pack. Reading*) "Meal, Combat, Individual." (HE *opens the box and finds a paper napkin on top; tucks it into his shirt like a bib. Then* HE *goes through the assorted tins and packets, reading their printed contents*) Cigarettes. (HE *puts the little four-pack of cigarettes aside for* PROCHASKA) Beans with Frankfurter Chunks in Tomato Sauce. Towel, Paper, Cleansing, Wet, Antiseptic. Interdental Stimulator. Cream substitute, Dry, Non-dairy. Chiclets. (HE *takes out a book of matches with an olive-drab cover*) "These matches are designed especially for damp climates. They will not light when wet."

While the REPORTER *has been busy with his C's, a* GUERRILLA *has appeared behind him, wearing foliage for camouflage.* HE *has watched the* REPORTER *for a moment, inhumanly still; then, with very small gestures to right and left, has closed in his fellow guerrillas—who are unseen—around the Americans for an ambush, and has vanished. Now the* REPORTER *fingers a small white wad.*

Toilet paper.

The ambush is sprung. The REPORTER *holds up his accreditation card. The firing is deafening, intolerably loud. It continues longer than its intensity would seem to allow, then quite suddenly it stops completely; all at once explodes again. The* REPORTER *low-crawls frantically away, nearly running into* SERGEANT PEERS, *who, having reached low ground, starts tuning in the field phone* HE *is carrying. It has a receiver like a regular telephone, leaving one of the* SERGEANT's *ears free.*

SERGEANT (*To the* REPORTER): Cover my back.

REPORTER: What? Sergeant Peers, it's—(HE *was going to say "me"*)

SERGEANT: All behind my back's your field of fire.

REPORTER: I haven't got a weapon.

SERGEANT (*Looking at him for the first time*): Christ, it's that one. (HE *goes back to the radio*)

REPORTER: What happens now?

SERGEANT: I try and get my god damn channel.

REPORTER: Where's the radio man?

SERGEANT: Which piece of him?

REPORTER (*Taking out his notebook*): What was his name?

SERGEANT (*Into the radio*): HQ!

REPORTER: Was he a draftee or did he enlist?

SERGEANT: At ease, god damn it!

REPORTER: Sarge, I've got to get some facts. If I'm not getting facts there isn't any purpose to my being here.

SERGEANT: HQ!

REPORTER: I mean, consider for a moment what my situation is. I don't know anything I didn't know before I got here. What if I get killed? I don't know why that monk was burning, what my boss wants. . . . What's the word for this? Condition Red?

SERGEANT (*Into the phone*): HQ! We're pinned down. Our coordinates are 5730 by 9324.

REPORTER: What's your serial number?

SERGEANT: Will you shut the fuck up?

REPORTER: I'm not getting any news! If I'm not getting any news then what in Christ's name am I doing here? (*A grenade bursts.* HE *is hit in the rump*) I'm hit.

SERGEANT: Don't move. (HE *quickly checks the wound*) You're all right.

REPORTER: No I'm not all right. I'm hit.

SERGEANT: You're okay.

REPORTER: Is there blood?

SERGEANT: No sweat. You're gonna see that girl. (*Handing him a pressure dressing*) Here. Hold this on the wound.

REPORTER: It hurts! I'm going to die! They're going to kill me! Get me out of here! Christ Jesus, get me out of here!

A whistling.

SERGEANT: Here comes the artillery! Flatten!

With the SERGEANT'*s last word there comes a blackout, then a monstrous crashing, ten times louder than before. The barrage continues in the darkness.*

Slide: IMPRINTMENT

Lights come up on the REPORTER *in a hospital bed.* HE *is sleeping. There is a little cabinet next to the bed, with a phone on it. The* REPORTER's *field clothes are folded on a shelf underneath. His cassette recorder is on top. A knock comes at the door—a very soft one. The* REPORTER *doesn't register it, but* HE *stirs, rearranges himself for more sleep—sees the audience.*

REPORTER: Where am I? (HE *sits partway up and feels a rush of pain*) Ow! Excuse me. (*Discreetly,* HE *lifts the sheet and turns his hip; remembers*) Oh yeah. What day is this? The last thing I remember is the medic and the morphine. I should find out where I am. (HE *makes a move to get up; stops mid-motion*) I feel dizzy. (*The soft knock is repeated*) Come in? (LI *enters: a small, pretty Ambonese bar girl.* SHE *walks with little steps into the room*) Hello.

LI: You sleep?

REPORTER: No, I'm awake. Are you the nurse?

LI: My name Li. Bar girl. I work Coral Bar. You know?

REPORTER: Um—no, I've never been there.

LI: I come here too. Man downstairs who sometime let me in. Are you G.I.?

REPORTER: No.

LI: See? I know you not G.I. I like you better than G.I. (*Coming further into the room*) You very nice.

REPORTER (*Holding her off*): No, I'm not nice. I'm a reporter.

LI: Li not understand.

REPORTER: I'm someone who's not here—who's here but can't—do anything, except report.

LI (*Puzzled*): You like I go away?

REPORTER: No, you don't have to go away. . . .

LI: You lonely.

REPORTER: No I'm not. Not *lonely.* . .

LI: Yes, you lonely. I see.

REPORTER: I'm *alone.* It's a condition of the job.

LI: You tired.

REPORTER: Well, they've given me some medication. . . .

LI: You lie down.

REPORTER: I'm lying down.

LI: You lie down all the way—

REPORTER (*Escapes by jumping out of bed—*HE *is wearing blue institutional pajamas*): I've got a wonderful idea.

LI: No, where you go?

REPORTER: You sit down. Sit down on the bed. (*Going into the pockets of his field clothes*) Look, here's some money for your time. There's fifty *hoi*. Is that enough? I'm going to interview you.

LI (*Not knowing the word*): In-ter-view?

The REPORTER *has laid two small colored bills on the bed.* LI *picks them up and, somewhat uncertainly, sits down on the bed. The* REPORTER *sets up his tape recorder.*

REPORTER: I've been feeling, lately, quite confused. I think that maybe, if I just can try and understand one person who's involved in all this, then I might be onto something. Will you tell me your story?

LI: Oh, you like me tell you *story.* Now I see. I have G.I. friend teach me tell him your Jack and the Beanstalk. When I get to part where beanstalk grow I stop and he say "Fee Fi Fo Fum"–

REPORTER: Not that kind of story. Just your life. Where do you come from?

LI: Where you like I come from?

REPORTER: From wherever you were born.

LI: Okay. I try. (*Thinks a second, sizing the* REPORTER *up*) I was born in little village. I hate the guerrillas. Was so glad when many helicopters come all full of big Americans. Americans with big guns. You have gun?

REPORTER: No.

LI: Yes you do. I know you have gun.

REPORTER: No, I don't.

LI: Yes, great big huge big gun and shoot so straight—

REPORTER (*Turns off the tape*): No, no. That isn't what I want, Li. I just want your story. Nothing else.

LI: You shy.

REPORTER: It's just a question of professional procedure.

LI: You like woman to be like a man. I see now. Now I tell my story.

REPORTER: Wait. (HE *switches on his tape*) Go.

LI: I am spy. My name not Li at all.

REPORTER: What is it?

LI: My name *Gad Da Lai I Rang Toi Doung.* That mean Woman Who Love to Watch Foreigners Die. I hate Americans.

REPORTER: Now we're getting down to cases. I'll bet all you girls hate Americans.

LI (*Encouraged*): Yes. I love to kill them.

REPORTER: Have you killed very many?

LI: Every day I kill one or I no can sleep. I like to pull their veins out with my little white sharp teeth. This is only thing can make Li happy with a man.

REPORTER (*Getting drawn in*): Wow. That's *political.*

LI: I like to climb on top of you and bite you, chew your neck until your bones are in my teeth and then I crack them—

REPORTER: Stop! You're making this up too. Li, don't you understand. I want your real story. (LI *has found the light switch on the wall above the bed and turned it off*) Li, turn the lights back on.

LI: You tired.

REPORTER: I'm not tired, I just *feel* tired.

LI: You come here.

REPORTER: I'll bring the tape recorder and we'll talk some more.

LI: You like it in my country?

REPORTER (*Sitting on the bed*): No. I hate it. I don't understand what anybody's doing. I don't like it here at all.

LI: You like I turn lights on?

REPORTER: Yes.

LI: There. (*The lights are still off*)

REPORTER: There what?

LI: You no see lights? Then you have eyes closed.

REPORTER: No—

LI: I turn lights off again. (SHE *leaves them off*) You like that?

REPORTER: Are they on or off?

LI: You lie down.

REPORTER (*Does*): Do you wear sunglasses indoors? At Mimi's all the girls wear very dark dark glasses. Are you touching me? You're not supposed to touch me.

LI: I no touch you. (SHE *is touching him*)

REPORTER: I saw a man burn with a lot of people watching. I saw Ing dance. I was in the jungle and a piece of flying metal flew so fast you couldn't see it but it stopped inside my body. I'm in Am-bo Land. (*The phone rings*) The phone? (HE *picks it up*) Hello? (*Pause*) Mr. Kingsley, yes, hello! (*Pause*) You're here? Wait just a little second, Mr. Kingsley. (*Turning the lights on*) Li? (SHE *is gone. The* REPORTER *looks puzzled but relieved.* HE *takes the phone back up—interrupts his movement to make a quick check under the bed, but* LI *is truly gone. Into the phone*) I'm sorry, sir. . . . Hello?

KINGSLEY (*Bursts in, bearing flowers*): Hey there, how's the Purple Heart?

REPORTER: Hello, sir—

KINGSLEY (*Points a mock-stern finger at the* REPORTER): Sir?

REPORTER: Bob! Hello, Bob. You're so thoughtful to come visit me.

KINGSLEY (*Seeing the cassette recorder, which is still in the* REPORTER's *lap*): I see you made a tape. You gonna pay the girl residuals? (*The* REPORTER *looks at the machine, then turns it off*) I got here half an hour ago and saw her coming in here. Figured this'd give you time enough. Hell, just in from the field most guys don't need but twenty seconds. (HE *plunks down the flowers on the cabinet*)

REPORTER: I was interviewing her.

KINGSLEY: Here's something else you'll need. (HE *takes a red-white-and-blue card out of his vest pocket and hands it to the* REPORTER)

REPORTER: What's this?

KINGSLEY: A business card.

REPORTER (*Looks at it*): It's just a number.

KINGSLEY: You hold on to that.

REPORTER (*Slips it in his shirt pocket*): Who is it?

KINGSLEY: Officer X.

REPORTER: Who's that?

KINGSLEY: He's probably lots of people. First-rate resource. He's got access to army supply lines. Got a couple of straws in the Ambonese milkshake too. You'll want a stereo system for starters. And an ice machine.

REPORTER: I don't need—

KINGSLEY: It's all on TransPanGlobal. X already has your name. Hey, you're our boy! We wouldn't want you cooped up here without a few amenities.

REPORTER: I've only got a flesh wound. I'll be out of here tomorrow, or today.

KINGSLEY: Today. Tomorrow.

REPORTER: Next day at the latest.

KINGSLEY: I guess you know you got off pretty easy.

REPORTER: Yes, I guess I did.

KINGSLEY: Good luck, huh?

REPORTER: Guess it was.

KINGSLEY: Good luck for you. Bad luck for TransPanGlobal.

REPORTER: How?

KINGSLEY: This thing has hit us right smack in the middle of a gore gap.

REPORTER: Gore gap?

KINGSLEY: Little guy from *Aujourd'hui* lost his esophagus last week. Two weeks ago some wop from *Benvenuto* got his ear blown off. We haven't had an injury for five months. God damn outlets don't believe you're really covering a war unless some blood flows with the ink. So let's say we announce your little contretemps the way it really happened. "On such-and-such a day our correspondent sallied forth to get the news. In the performance of his duty, he was wounded." (*As a questioner*) "Where?" "He took a little shrapnel." "Where?" "He took a little shrapnel in the ass." (*To the* REPORTER) Not too impressive. Let me ask you something. Why should we accept that you were wounded where you were and let the whole of TransPanGlobal look like shitheads—are you with me?—when a half a foot— six inches—from your perforated fanny is your spine?

REPORTER: My spine?

KINGSLEY: We're going to say the shrapnel lodged against your lower vertebrae. That's nothing that a brilliant surgeon, luck, and a short convalescence can't cure.

REPORTER: How short?

KINGSLEY: Three months.

REPORTER: Three months?

KINGSLEY: The spine's a very tricky area.

REPORTER: Why do you assume I'll go along with this?

KINGSLEY: We brought you here.

REPORTER: You brought me where?

KINGSLEY: To Am-bo Land.

REPORTER: That's supposed to make me grateful?

KINGSLEY: Don't you like it here?

REPORTER: What makes you even possibly imagine that I like it here?

KINGSLEY: By this point in their tour, we've found that most reporters have experienced imprintment.

REPORTER: What's—

KINGSLEY: Imprintment. A reporter goes to cover a country and the country covers him.

REPORTER: You think that Am-bo Land is covering me?

KINGSLEY: It's just a guess.

REPORTER: A guess.

KINGSLEY: That's all.

REPORTER: All right. I'm going to show you just how good a guess it is. (HE *gets out of bed*)

KINGSLEY: What are you doing?

REPORTER (*Getting his clothes out of the cabinet*): You see these socks? They're decomposing with the climate. Not the rain and mud. The *air*. The air is putrid in this country. When I go to put on clean socks in the morning they all smell as if some stranger took and *wore* them in the night. (HE *flings the socks away and starts to pull on his field clothes over his pajamas*) I can't *believe* you thought that Am-bo Land was covering me. It's true that I can't do my job, if that's the same thing. I can never tell what's going on. Nobody ever gives me any answers. If they do I'm asking stupid questions. That's not how my life is supposed to go! I won't accept that! I refuse! It doesn't rain here when it rains. It sweats. The palm leaves drip sweat even in the sunshine. Have you tried the beer? It's great. Tastes like the inside of a monkey's armpits.

KINGSLEY: Where are you going?

REPORTER: First I'm going to the airbase. That's four miles. From there, eleven thousand miles to East Dubuque.

KINGSLEY: You're leaving?

REPORTER: That's eleven thousand four miles. I'll be counting every centimeter.

KINGSLEY: What about the gore gap?

REPORTER: Blow your brains out. That'll fill it.

KINGSLEY: This is highly unprofessional. You know that.

REPORTER: No I don't. I don't know anything. I only know I'm going.

KINGSLEY: If you're going, I won't try to stop you.

REPORTER: Great. Goodbye. (*Limping slightly,* HE *starts out*)

KINGSLEY: You're sure you want to go?
REPORTER: I'm sure!
KINGSLEY: Enjoy your flight.
REPORTER: You bet I will! I'll savor every second.

The REPORTER *slams out. Blackout. Tape: A* CIVILIAN FLIGHT ANNOUNCER *speaks over an outdoor loudspeaker.*

FLIGHT ANNOUNCER (*In a voice that reeks routine*): Attention on the runway please. . . . Attention on the runway please. . . . Lone Star Airlines Flight 717 has completed its boarding procedure. . . . Clear the runway please. . . . Please clear the runway. . . . No more passengers may board at this time. . . . (*With a little more urgency*) Will the gentleman please clear the runway. . . . Flight 717 is taking off. . . . The gentleman is standing in the backblast. . . . Will the gentleman please limp a little faster, he is about to be cremated. . . .

Slide: PLANES

Simultaneously with the slide, the REPORTER *shouts from offstage.*

REPORTER: Okay! Okay!

Lights up on a black-and-yellow barrier with the legend, "DO NOT PASS BEYOND THIS POINT."

FLIGHT ANNOUNCER (*Still on tape*): Will the gimp in the pajama top accelerate his pace please . . . .
REPORTER (*Still offstage, but closer*): Yes, o-kay!
FLIGHT ANNOUNCER: Now will the moron kindly haul his ass behind the yellow barrier and await the next plane out at that location.
REPORTER (*Rushing on in total disarray*): Yes, all *right*! I'm here! I'm *here*!

The REPORTER *crawls under the barrier, ending up on the downstage side. The* PHOTOGRAPHER *hobbles on from the opposite direction.* HE *is missing an arm. One foot is in a huge cast. His clothes are multi-layered and multi-colored, and include a Clint Eastwood-style serape. Sundry cameras, lens cases, filter cases hang from straps around his neck and shoulders. A sign on his floppy field hat reads, "SAY CHEESE."*

PHOTOGRAPHER: Hey, man, I need a little help with something, can you help me out?
REPORTER (*Just sits on the asphalt, panting*): Damn it! *Damn* it!
PHOTOGRAPHER: Missed your plane, huh? That's a drag.
REPORTER: There's not another plane for seven hours.

PHOTOGRAPHER: There's one in fifteen minutes. That's the help I need.

REPORTER (*Pulls himself up by the barrier*): In fifteen minutes? Where?

PHOTOGRAPHER (*Pointing offstage*): Right over there. The Weasel. See? She's sleeping. But in fifteen minutes she'll be up there in the sky. It fucks your mind up.

REPORTER: That's a bomber.

PHOTOGRAPHER: Dig it.

REPORTER: I need a passenger plane.

PHOTOGRAPHER (*Enlightened*): You mean a plane to *go* somewhere. Okay, man. Not too zen, but. . . . Wanna help me out?

REPORTER: If I can.

PHOTOGRAPHER (*Extends his foot cast to be pulled off like a boot*): Here. Help me ditch this plaster, willya?

REPORTER: What's it on for?

PHOTOGRAPHER: German paper that I sometimes sell my snaps to wanted pictures of a minefield. Who knows why, right? Only, dig it man, the thing about a minefield is it looks like any other field. I mean like that's the whole idea, right? So I tramped a lot of paddies before I found one. Got an action shot, though. KRUUMP!

REPORTER: What happend to your arm?

PHOTOGRAPHER: Ooh that was righteous. It was nighttime. I was standing getting pictures of the tracer patterns. BAMMO! from behind! I got an incredible shot of that arm flying off. WHOOSH! Little bit underexposed, but something else, man. WHOOSH!

REPORTER: I think you ought to take my flight with me.

PHOTOGRAPHER: You wouldn't wanna leave if you could make these bomb runs.

REPORTER: I could make the bomb runs.

PHOTOGRAPHER: Nix. They just give seats to newsmen.

REPORTER: I'm a reporter.

PHOTOGRAPHER: Yeah? Well shit man, what you waiting for? Come help me get my foot up in the cockpit and then climb on in yourself.

REPORTER: No way. I've got a plane to catch.

PHOTOGRAPHER: These babies drop their goodies and they come right back. Takes half an hour.

REPORTER: They come back in half an hour?

PHOTOGRAPHER: Like a boomerang. Come on.

REPORTER: Not me.

PHOTOGRAPHER: I'm telling you, these flights are ab-*stract*.

REPORTER: Even if I wanted to, I couldn't.

PHOTOGRAPHER: Why not?

REPORTER: 'Cause they wouldn't let me on.

PHOTOGRAPHER: You're a reporter.

REPORTER: No I'm not. I was. I quit.

PHOTOGRAPHER: You quit?

REPORTER: That's right.

PHOTOGRAPHER: You give your card back?

REPORTER (*Lies*): —Yes.

PHOTOGRAPHER: You didn't, man. It's right there on your hat.

REPORTER (*Taking it out of the hatband*): I still have the card.

PHOTOGRAPHER: Come on! We're gonna miss the takeoff! It's outrageous, man, it pulls your smile till it's all the way back of your head! (HE *disappears*)

REPORTER (*Calling after him*): I'm not going to go. I'll help you load your cast in, but I'm not going to go.

PHOTOGRAPHER (*Off*): Come *on*, man!

REPORTER: Okay, but I'm only going to help you with your cast. . . .

The REPORTER *follows the* PHOTOGRAPHER *off. Blackout. Tape: an orientation by the* AIR FORCE PILOT, *crackling as if over earphones in a helmet.*

PILOT: I'm gonna tell you right off I don't want you here. I don't know why they let reporters on bomb runs and I'm damned if I'm gonna worry about you. This is a vertical mission. If they hit us while we're diving, I'll try to get the plane in a horizontal position, then I'll jump.

Slide: RUN

PILOT: That means there won't be any pilot, so you'll probably want to jump too.

Lights come up on the REPORTER *and the* PHOTOGRAPHER *seated in the plane.* THEY *are both wearing helmets. As the* PILOT *continues, the* REPORTER *tries to locate the devices* HE *mentions.*

There are two handles beside your seat. Move the one on the right first down then up. Your seat will eject you and your chute will open automatically. If the chute doesn't open you've got a spare, pull the cord on the front of your flight jacket. If that chute doesn't open you can lodge a complaint. Have a good flight and don't bother me.

The REPORTER *and the* PHOTOGRAPHER *lurch backwards in their seats as the plane takes off.*

PHOTOGRAPHER: Okay, man. When the pilot dives, you push a button on the left side of your helmet.

REPORTER: What does that do?

PHOTOGRAPHER: Try it, man. You see the nozzle there? Pure oxygen! (HE *takes a hit. The* REPORTER *follows suit*) You dive. The jungle gets closer and closer like it's flying up to slam you. You can see the tree that's going to hit you, then the leaves on the tree, then the veins on the leaves—and then the pilot pulls out and he starts to climb. The sky comes crushing down on you, your eyes go black, it's like you're being crushed by darkness. Then you level off and everything goes back to normal. Then you dive again. It's outa sight.

REPORTER: Can you see the victims on the ground?

PHOTOGRAPHER: Man, you can see their *faces*! You can see the little lights coming out of the end of their machine guns. Bullets flying up at just below the speed of sound, you screaming straight down toward 'em. Hit one and you cashed your checks!

REPORTER: One bullet couldn't bring a plane down.

PHOTOGRAPHER: Man, at that speed a stiff stream of piss could bring a plane down. Hey! We're diving!

REPORTER: Wait! I haven't got my background done! What's the pilot's hometown? I don't even know what the pilot's hometown is!

PHOTOGRAPHER: Wooo!

REPORTER: Stop the plane! I have to do an interview!

PHOTOGRAPHER: I thought you quit.

REPORTER: I did, but—(*The plane pitches sharply as it steepens its dive*) Oh-h-h—

PHOTOGRAPHER: Fifty meters in two seconds! Woo! This guy is good!

REPORTER: My stomach just went out with the exhaust fumes.

PHOTOGRAPHER: See that little man? Guerrilla. Look, he's waiting. Now he's lifting up his rifle.

REPORTER: Pull out!

PHOTOGRAPHER: The pilot let the bombs go. See? They're traveling down right next to us.

REPORTER: Those?

PHOTOGRAPHER: Uh-huh.

REPORTER: Those are bombs?

PHOTOGRAPHER: Yep.

REPORTER: If they slipped a half a foot they'd blow us up. They're getting closer!

PHOTOGRAPHER: Little man down there is firing!

REPORTER (*To the bomb outside his window*): Down there! Get him! We're your friends!

PHOTOGRAPHER: Yah! Little fucker hit the pilot! Good shot! Woo! (HE *starts snapping pictures*)

REPORTER: We're going to crash!

PHOTOGRAPHER: You bet your ass! We're going down!

REPORTER: Bail out!

PHOTOGRAPHER: You go. I'm staying. You don't think I'm gonna miss this!

REPORTER: Miss what?

PHOTOGRAPHER: When's the last time you saw shots of a plane crash taken *from the plane?*

REPORTER: I'm going! (HE *"bails out"*)

PHOTOGRAPHER: Great shot of your ass, Jim! Wooo!

The PHOTOGRAPHER *whoops and snaps pictures as the scream of the descent increases. The stage goes black as the crash is heard—a colossal explosion. House lights up for:*

Slide: INTERMISSION

ACT TWO

Slide: VILLAGE

Tape: the voice of the EVENT *renders the Ambonese national anthem, which is jerry-built and grandiose. As the lights come up, an* AMBONESE PSYCHOLOGICAL WARFARE OFFICER *is taking his place in front of a group of unseen villagers.* HE *carries a small table arrayed with assorted apparatus for the demonstration* HE *is about to perform. A small cassette player on the table is the source of the anthem.*

The REPORTER *is seated on the ground between us and the* OFFICER, *slightly off to one side.* HE *is dressed like a villager, in black-pajama pants, a conical hat, and sandals. By his feet is a small bundle.* HE *is sitting on his haunches Asian-style, quite relaxed and placid, waiting for the* OFFICER *to start. The* OFFICER *clicks off the cassette.*

OFFICER: Citizens of So Bin Village, you have done a hard day's work. The Government wishes to submit to you a presentation. (HE *arranges his apparatus, which includes a bowl of rice, a basin, chopsticks, a towel, and a quart jug of thick, fetid, poisonous-looking green liquid. While* HE *is thus employed, the* REPORTER *turns to the audience)*

REPORTER: I drifted in my parachute what seemed like miles and miles and I landed over there. I love this village. I've been here—I don't know how long. I think this is my third week. If I had to write a dateline, I'd be out of luck. I don't, though.

OFFICER (*Holding up the jug of green gunk*): This is defoliant. Our friends the Americans use it to improve the jungle so our enemy cannot use it for a hiding place. The enemy has told you that this harmless liquid poisons you and makes your babies come out of your stomachs with no arms and legs. This is not so. You will see for yourself when I have poured some defoliant in this bowl. (HE *does. Then "acting" stiffly*) My but it was hot today. My face is very dirty. I have need to wash my hands and face. (HE *does so, dipping and turning his hands in the green liquid, then splashing it on his face.* HE *looks as happy as the people in TV soap commercials*) Ah! That is refreshing! (HE *wipes himself dry*)

REPORTER (*To the audience*): A company of Government soldiers has been using this village as an outpost. They were here when I arrived. Today at dusk some transport choppers will be coming in to pick them up. I mean to pick *us* up. I'll catch a lift to the airbase, then a plane home. Home *America*. (*Bemusedly*) I don't know why I said that. Home where else?

OFFICER : Mm, my hard day's work has given me an appetite. I think that I will eat some rice. No fish sauce? Very well then, I will pour on some of this. (HE *pours defoliant over the bowl of rice and eats it with the chopsticks*)

REPORTER (*To the audience, referring to his squatting posture*): The villagers all sit this way. I started it because my wound reopened when I hit the ground. But after you get used to it, it's really very comfortable.

OFFICER (*Wiping his mouth*): My! That was good! But now my hearty meal has made me very thirsty. Ah! (HE *"discovers" the defoliant again and drinks the rest of it, straight from the jug; sets the empty on the table with a bang*) The guerrillas are liars. The Government speaks the truth. Goodbye. (HE *clicks the anthem back on and, to its accompaniment, walks off with his gear*)

REPORTER: It's very peaceful in this village. I've picked up bits and snatches of the language and I'm learning how to harvest rice. I spent the morning threshing. When you get the rhythm you can thresh all day. You slap the stalks against a board. The grains go sliding down and drop into a basket. That's all. Slap, slap, slap, slap. . . . Nothing to write about there. No hook. No angle. Slap, slap, slap. . . . (*A* GOVERNMENT SOLDIER *comes on.* HE *is tying the legs of a chicken with a cord that hangs from his belt*) There goes the last of the soldiers. I should go with him. Before I do, I want to show you what I've learned. (*To the* SOLDIER) *Tay dap moung.* (*Translating for the audience*) That means, "Stop please." (*To the* SOLDIER, *in a complimentary tone and with a gesture toward the chicken*) *Kin wau ran faun to bak im brong.* (*The* SOLDIER *stares at him in complete incomprehension. To the audience*) I understand the language better than I speak it. (*To the* SOLDIER *again, more slowly*) *Kin wau ran faun to bak im brong.*

SOLDIER: *Fop nah in gao breet? Rew ksawn ep lam?*

REPORTER (*To the* SOLDIER, *waving away his own words*): *Manh.* (*To the audience*) The trouble is that Ambonese has all these tones. You say the right sounds but the wrong tones and you've got a different meaning. Apparently I told him that his nose was like a bite of tree farm.

SOLDIER (*Challengingly*): *Op feo ting ko bi dang?*

REPORTER: Why? Because I *want* to speak your language. I want to *duc fi rop* what you are saying and to *fan bo doung* to you.

SOLDIER: *Ken hip yan geh wim parn ti brong, ip yuh rat.*

REPORTER (*To the audience*): He says his chicken speaks his language better, and
it's dead. That's an Ambonese joke.

SOLDIER (*Indicating the* REPORTER's *clothes*): *Fawn tip si bah?*

REPORTER: Am I a villager? Yes. Sure. Why not? *Meo.* I'm a villager. I'm happy here.

SOLDIER: *Prig paw yan tsi mah strak.*

REPORTER: You're not protecting me. I landed in a village you were occupy-
ing. *Nik kwan tap.* I wish you hadn't been here.

SOLDIER: *Wep ksi—*

REPORTER (*Cutting him off*): I'm not afraid of the guerrillas. *Manh kip.*

SOLDIER: *Manh kip?*

REPORTER: *Manh.* I'm not their enemy. In fact, I'd like to meet them. If you
think I'm scared, you go ahead without me.

SOLDIER: *Sep?*

REPORTER: You go and catch your helicopter. I'm not leaving yet. *Ping dop.*

SOLDIER: *Ping dop?*

REPORTER: There'll be more troops through here. I can get a ride out anytime.
America won't disappear. *Ping dop.* Go catch your helicopter. (*The* SOLDIER
shrugs and starts out) Goodbye.

SOLDIER (*Turns*): *Dik ram vi clao brong.*

REPORTER (*Translating for himself*): "Now you'll enjoy your chicken." Good.

SOLDIER: *Wep ksi ren—*

REPORTER: Yes, the guerrillas—?

SOLDIER: *—vi clao—*

REPORTER: "—will enjoy—"

SOLDIER (*Points emphatically at the* REPORTER): *—seng.* (HE *goes off*)

REPORTER (*To the audience*): There'll be troops coming back to the village. I
won't be here long. And the guerrillas—well, all right, if I surprise them,
then it's dangerous. I won't though. Probably they almost know already
that I've stayed behind. They'll know before they come. And so I'll have
a chance to talk to them. They'll see I'm not their enemy. (HE *looks up at
the sky*) It's getting dark now. (HE *crosses to his bundle and unwraps it*) I've
been sleeping over here. Sometimes it's rained, and then I've made a lean-
to with my parachute. Tonight, it looks like I can use it for a pillow. (HE
"*fluffs up*" *his parachute—which is mottled shades of green—and stretches out*)
I love the sky at night here. It's not a pretty sky, but it's alive. You can
see the storms far off in all directions. The clouds are gray, and when the
sheet lightning flashes behind them they look like flaps of dead skin, twitch-
ing. I know that that sounds ugly, but it's beautiful. (*A* GUERRILLA *comes
in silently behind him*) The guerrillas can pretend they're animals. They talk
to each other in the dark that way. They also can pretend they're trees and
bushes, rocks and branches, vines. Sometimes they pretend they're nothing

at all. That's when you know they're near. The world is never quite that still. You don't have to tell me. This time I know he's there.

Carefully but decisively, the REPORTER *stands up and turns to face the* GUER-RILLA. *Blackout. Tape: jungle sounds—strange clicking, dripping, hissing of snakes, animal cries, etc.*

Slide: SELF-CRITICISM

A small, bare hut. The REPORTER *is sleeping on the floor. His head is covered by a black hood and his hands are tied behind his back. A* GUERRILLA IN-FORMATION OFFICER *comes in carrying a bowl of rice.*

GUERRILLA: Stand up, please.
REPORTER (*Coming awake*): What?
GUERRILLA: Please stand up.
REPORTER: It's hard with hands behind the back.
GUERRILLA: I will untie them.
REPORTER: That's all right. I'll make it. (*With some clumsiness,* HE *gets to his feet*) There I am.
GUERRILLA: I offered to untie your hands.
REPORTER: I'd just as soon you didn't. When you know that you can trust me, then untie my hands. I'd let you take the hood off.
GUERRILLA (*Takes the hood off*): Tell me why you think that we should trust you.
REPORTER: I'm no threat to you. I've never done you any harm.
GUERRILLA: No harm?
REPORTER: I guess I've wasted your munitions. Part of one of your grenades wound up imbedded in my derriere—my backside.
GUERRILLA: I speak French as well as English. You forget—the French were here before you.
REPORTER: Yes.
GUERRILLA: You told us that you came here as a newsman.
REPORTER: Right.
GUERRILLA: You worked within the system of our enemies and subject to their interests.
REPORTER: Partly subject.
GUERRILLA: Yet you say that you have never done us any harm.
REPORTER: All I found out as a reporter was I'd never find out anything.
GUERRILLA: Do we pardon an enemy sniper if his marksmanship is poor?
REPORTER: Yes, if he's quit the army.
GUERRILLA: Ah, yes. You are not a newsman now.
REPORTER: That's right.

GUERRILLA: What are you?
REPORTER: What am I? (*The* GUERRILLA *is silent*) I'm what you see.
GUERRILLA: What do you do?
REPORTER: I live.
GUERRILLA: You live?
REPORTER: That's all.
GUERRILLA: You live in Am-bo Land.
REPORTER: I'm here right now.
GUERRILLA: Why?
REPORTER: Why? You've got me prisoner.
GUERRILLA: If you were not a prisoner, you would not be here?
REPORTER: No.
GUERRILLA: Where would you be?
REPORTER: By this time, I'd be back in East Dubuque.
GUERRILLA: You were not leaving when we captured you.
REPORTER: I was, though. I was leaving soon.
GUERRILLA: Soon?
REPORTER: Yes.
GUERRILLA: When?
REPORTER: I don't know exactly. Sometime.
GUERRILLA: Sometime.
REPORTER: Yes.
GUERRILLA: You have no right to be here even for a minute. Not to draw one
    breath.
REPORTER: You have no right to tell me that. I'm here. It's where I am.
GUERRILLA: We are a spectacle to you. A land in turmoil.
REPORTER: I don't have to lie to you. Yes, that attracts me.
GUERRILLA: Yes. You love to see us kill each other.
REPORTER: No. I don't.
GUERRILLA: You said you didn't have to lie.
REPORTER: I'm not. It does—excite me that the stakes are life and death here.
    It makes everything—intense.
GUERRILLA: The stakes cannot be life and death unless some people die.
REPORTER: That's true. But I don't make them die. They're dying anyway.
GUERRILLA: You just watch.
REPORTER: That's right.
GUERRILLA: Your standpoint is aesthetic.
REPORTER: Yes, all right, yes.
GUERRILLA: You enjoy our situation here.
REPORTER: I'm filled with pain by things I see.
GUERRILLA: And yet you stay.
REPORTER: I'm here.
GUERRILLA: You are addicted.

REPORTER: Say I am, then! I'm addicted! Yes! I've said it! I'm addicted!

GUERRILLA: Your position in my country is morbid and decadent. It is corrupt, reactionary, and bourgeois. You have no right to live here.

REPORTER: This is where I live. You can't pass judgment.

GUERRILLA: I have not passed judgment. You are useless here. A man must give something in return for the food he eats and the living space he occupies. This is not a moral obligation but a practical necessity in a society where no one is to be exploited.

REPORTER: Am-bo Land isn't such a society, is it?

GUERRILLA: Not yet.

REPORTER: Well, I'm here right now. If you don't like that then I guess you'll have to kill me.

GUERRILLA: We would kill you as we pick the insects from the skin of a valuable animal.

REPORTER: Go ahead, then. If you're going to kill me, kill me.

GUERRILLA: We are not going to kill you.

REPORTER: Why not?

GUERRILLA: For a reason.

REPORTER: What's the reason?

GUERRILLA: We have told the leadership of TransPanGlobal Wire Service when and where to leave one hundred thousand dollars for your ransom.

REPORTER: Ransom? TransPanGlobal?

GUERRILLA: Yes.

REPORTER: But that's no good. I told you, I don't work there anymore.

GUERRILLA: Your former employers have not made the separation public. We have made our offer public. You will not be abandoned in the public view. It would not be good business.

REPORTER (*Truly frightened for the first time in the scene*): Wait. You have to think this out. A hundred thousand dollars is too much. It's much too much. You might get ten.

GUERRILLA: We have demanded one hundred.

REPORTER: They won't pay that. Take ten thousand. That's a lot to you.

GUERRILLA: It is. But we have made our offer.

REPORTER: Change it. You're just throwing away money. Tell them ten. They'll never pay a hundred thousand.

GUERRILLA: We never change a bargaining position we have once set down. This is worth much more than ten thousand dollars or a hundred thousand dollars.

REPORTER: Please—

GUERRILLA: Sit down.

REPORTER (*Obeys; then, quietly*): Please don't kill me.

GUERRILLA: Do not beg your life from me. The circumstances grant your life. Your employers will pay. You will live.

REPORTER: You sound so sure.

GUERRILLA: If we were not sure we would not waste this food on you. (HE *pushes the bowl of rice towards the* REPORTER)

REPORTER: How soon will I know?

GUERRILLA: Soon. Ten days.

REPORTER: That's not soon.

GUERRILLA: This war has lasted all my life. Ten days is soon. (*Untying the* REPORTER'*s hands*) You will be fed on what our soldiers eat. You will think that we are starving you, but these are the rations on which we march toward our inevitable victory. Eat your rice. In three minutes I will tie you again.

The GUERRILLA *goes out. The* REPORTER *eats as best* HE *can. Blackout. Slides: the face of the* EVENT, *each frame now showing two of his features, in somewhat finer half-tone.*

Slide: RESCUE

Lights up on MR. KINGSLEY, *seated at his desk.* HE *is talking on the telephone.*

KINGSLEY: Sure they're going to bring him here, but hell, Dave, you don't really want to talk to him. Why put a crimp in your imagination? Make sure you don't contradict our bulletins. Beyond that, go to town. The sky's the limit. (*The* REPORTER *appears at the door*) Dave, I've got to sign off. Get to work on this right now, check? I'll be firing some more ideas your way as they occur to me. Over and out. (*The* REPORTER *wanders into the office.* HE *looks blown out.* HE *is still in his villager clothes*) So here you are. How far they bring you?

REPORTER: Three guerrillas brought me to the border of the City. Then they gambled with some sticks. One brought me here. He's gone.

KINGSLEY: You look all shot to shit. Sit down.

REPORTER (*Unthinkingly sits down on his haunches; then continues*): He had the longest knife I ever saw. Strapped here, across his back. It would have gone right through me. He took off his thongs and hid them in the underbrush and put on shoes. We started through the streets. He wasn't used to shoes. They came untied. He didn't know how to tie them. So he stood still and I tied them for him. All the time he had this knife. The longest knife I ever saw. (*Pause*) I'd have gone back out with him if he'd have let me.

KINGSLEY: How you fixed for cash?

REPORTER: I have some. (HE *takes some rumpled, pale bills of different colors out of his shirt*) Here.

KINGSLEY: I wasn't asking you to give it to me.

REPORTER: I owe it to you.

KINGSLEY: No you don't.

REPORTER: A hundred thousand dollars.

KINGSLEY: Just forget about it.

REPORTER: Am I supposed to work for you now? I can probably do some kind of work. I can't report the news.

KINGSLEY: We're square. We'll get our value for the hundred grand. You're a four-part feature. Maybe six if we can stretch it. We might try some kind of angle with a girl guerrilla. That's a thought. (HE *picks up the phone*) Get me Dave Feltzer again. (*To the* REPORTER) No, all we ask of you is don't give information to the rival press. We want a clean exclusive. We'll be signing your name to the story, by the way. Don't be surprised.

REPORTER: Why should I be surprised?

KINGSLEY: Well, when you read it.

REPORTER: I won't read it.

KINGSLEY: Okay. Want to catch the movie if you can. We're trying to interest Redford. (*Into the phone*) Yeah, hold on, Dave. (*To the* REPORTER) I think that's all then.

REPORTER: That's all? (*Pause.* KINGSLEY *just sits with the phone in his hand*) Okay. Goodbye, Bob. (HE *turns and leaves*)

KINGSLEY (*Into the phone*): Yeah Dave. Got a little brainstorm for the sequence in the punji pit. He's down there, right, he's got this bamboo sticking through his feet, and he looks up and sees an AK-47 clutched in little tapered fingers and the fingernails are painted red . . . .

Blackout. Tape: tinny Asian-Western rock-and-roll as in Act I, Scene 4 [STRIP]; this time a ballad—say, "Ruby Tuesday."

Slide: PROPOSAL

Lights up on LI*'s room at the Coral Bar. A bed, a doorway made of hanging beads, a screen.* LI *is behind the screen, dressing. The* REPORTER *is lying on the bed.* THEY *have just had sex. The* REPORTER *lies quietly a while before* HE *speaks.*

REPORTER: Li?

LI: Yes?

REPORTER: It's good here. It's so good with you.

LI (*Professionally*): It's good with you too.

REPORTER: When I look in your eyes, your eyes look back. I love that. That's so important to me.

LI: I love that too.

REPORTER: I love to be with you.

LI: I love to be with you too.

REPORTER: Do you love me, Li? You don't, I know.

LI: I love you. Love you best of all my men.

REPORTER: Do you know what? When I come here I pretend we short-time just because we both just want to. I pretend you wouldn't take my money only Mai Wah makes you take it.

LI: Mai Wah makes me or I no take money.

REPORTER: Would you short-time me for love?

LI: Yes.

REPORTER: Are you sure you would?

LI: Yes.

REPORTER: Are you absolutely sure?

LI: Yes.

REPORTER: Li, I don't have any money.

LI (*Emerging from behind the screen*): What you say?

REPORTER: I'm broke. No money.

LI: No. You joke with Li.

REPORTER: I had to see you and I didn't want to spoil it by telling you till after.

LI: I have to pay myself now. Mai Wah writes it down, who comes here, how much time. Now you no pay I have to pay myself.

REPORTER: I didn't know that.

LI: Now you know.

REPORTER: I paid a lot of times, Li. Maybe it's fair that you pay once.

LI: Get out of here.

REPORTER: Li—

LI: Next time I see money first, like you G.I. I thought you nice. You trick me. You get out of here.

REPORTER: Li, marry me.

LI: What you say?

REPORTER: I say I want us to get married.

LI: Now you really joke. You bad man.

REPORTER: I'm not joking, Li. I mean it.

LI: Yes? You marry me?

REPORTER: That's right.

LI: You take me to America?

REPORTER: America? No.

LI: Marry me, not take me to America? You leave me here?

REPORTER: I stay with you, Li. I'm not going to America.

LI: You lie. Sometime you go.

REPORTER: I'm never going to go. I'm going to stay here.

LI: No. America is good. Here no good. You marry me and take me to America.

REPORTER: If I wanted to go to America, I wouldn't want to marry you.

LI: Li just good enough for Am-bo Land. You have round-eye wife, go back to her. I know.

REPORTER: You're wrong, Li. I am never going back.

LI: You say then why you want to marry me.

REPORTER: You make me feel at home here and this country *is* my home. I want to sleep with you, wake up with you. I want to look at you and see you looking back.

LI: Where you live now?

REPORTER: Well, really nowhere just this minute. See, I haven't got a job right now—

LI: You go now.

REPORTER: Wait, Li—

LI: You come back, you show me money first. You owe me for three short-times because you stay so long.

REPORTER: Li, listen—

LI: No. You go away. Not be here when I come back.

LI *goes out through the beaded curtain. Blackout. Tape: a distant foghorn.*

Slide: WORK

Dim lights up on the REPORTER. *It is dusk.* HE *is waiting for someone.* OFFICER X *appears.* HE *wears a stateside class-A army overcoat with the bronze oak leaves of a major on the lapels.*

REPORTER: Officer X? Then you *are* an officer. I didn't know if that might be a code name.

X: What's with the gook suit?

REPORTER: It's just my clothes.

X: They've gotta go. Hawaiian shirts and shiny Harlem slacks is best for couriers. You have to blend in. Give me the card that Kingsley gave you. (*The* REPORTER *hands him the red-white-and-blue card from Act I, Scene 6 [*IMPRINTMENT*]*) You know the number?

REPORTER: No.

X (*Hands back the card*): Learn it. (*The* REPORTER *starts to put the card back in his pocket*) Learn it now. (*The* REPORTER *reads the card, trying to memorize the number. The effort of concentration is hard for him.* OFFICER X *takes the card back*) What's the number?

REPORTER (*With difficulty*): 7 . . . 38 . . . 472 . . . 4.

X: Again.

REPORTER: 738 . . . 47 . . . 24.

X (*Pockets the card*): Remember it. Don't write it down. Here. (HE *hands the* REPORTER *a packet wrapped in paper, tied with string*)

REPORTER: What is it?

X: Don't ask what, ask where.

REPORTER: Where?

X: Lin Cho District. Tan Hoi Street. Number 72.

REPORTER: Number 72 Tan Hoi Street.

X: Better put it under your shirt. But get an overcoat with inside pockets.

REPORTER (*Hiding the package as directed*): I can speak some Ambonese.

X: When we need that, we have interpreters. Be back here with the money in two hours. (*The* REPORTER *starts out*) Hold on. Do you have a weapon?

REPORTER: —Yes.

X: Let's see it. (*The* REPORTER *doesn't move.* X *takes out a handgun*) Here.

REPORTER: That's okay.

X: You'll pay me back in trade. Here, take it.

REPORTER: I don't need it.

X: Hell you don't.

REPORTER: I don't.

X: You've got to have it.

REPORTER: I don't want it.

X: I'll just ask you one more time. You gonna take the pistol? (*The* REPORTER *looks at it but doesn't answer*) Give me back the package.

REPORTER: I can get it where it's going.

X: Give it.

REPORTER: Number 72 Tan Hoi—

X: Nobody carries goods for me unless they're able to protect them.

REPORTER: I'll protect them.

X: If you won't use the gun, don't think I won't.

>X *points the pistol at the* REPORTER. *The* REPORTER *gives him the packet.*

REPORTER: I can speak some Ambonese.

X: You told me. What's my number?

REPORTER: 7 . . . 7 . . . 38 . . . 738 . . . (*His face goes blank*)

X: Good. Don't remember it again.

>X *leaves the way* HE *came. Blackout. Tape: babies crying.*

Slide: ORPHANAGE

The crying of the babies continues into the scene. Lights come up on an AM-BONESE NUN tending children who are imagined to be in a long row of cribs between her and the audience. The REPORTER comes in left.

REPORTER: Excuse me, Sister.

NUN: Yes?

REPORTER: The Mother Superior told me to come up here.

NUN: Yes?

REPORTER: I'm going to adopt a child.

NUN (*Scanning his garments; gently*): Adopt a child?

REPORTER: Yes.

NUN: Have you been interviewed?

REPORTER: Not yet. I have to get a bit more settled first. But the Mother Superior said I could come upstairs and if I chose a child she would keep it for me.

NUN: Ah. How old a child would you want?

REPORTER: He should probably not be very young. And tough. He should be tough. I don't have lots of money.

NUN: You said "he."

REPORTER: A girl would be all right. A girl would be nice.

NUN: It must be a girl. The Government has a law that only girls may be adopted. The boys are wards of the State. When they are older, they will go into the army.

REPORTER: Well, a girl is fine.

NUN (*Starting down the line with him, moving left*): This girl is healthy.

REPORTER: Hello. You're very pretty. You have cheek bones like a grownup, like your mommy must have had. Look. If I pull back my skin as tight as I can, I still don't have skin as tight as you. (HE *pulls his skin back toward his temples. One effect is that this gives him slanted eyes*) Why won't you look at me?

NUN: She is looking at you.

REPORTER: She doesn't trust me. (*To the child*) I won't hurt you. I just want to have a child of your country. Will you be my child? (*To the* NUN) She doesn't like me. Do you see that child down the line there? (*Pointing right*) That one's looking at me. Let's go talk to that child.

NUN: That section is boys. This way. (SHE *leads him to the next crib to the left*)

REPORTER: She's asleep but, look, her little fists are clenched. She wouldn't like me. I don't want to wake her up.

NUN: Here is another.

REPORTER (*To the third child*): Do you like me? I'll take care of you. I understand that you need food, and I'll try and be a friend to you. (*To the* NUN) She doesn't even hear my voice.

NUN: Here.

REPORTER: These aren't children! These are ancient people, shrunken down! Look at their eyes! They've looked at everything! They'll never look at me!

NUN: You're upsetting the children.

REPORTER (*Pointing toward the boys' section*): That child sees me. He's been looking at me since I came in the room. I want that child.

NUN: I've told you that you cannot have a boy—. Wait. Which child?

REPORTER: The one who's standing up and looking at me.

NUN: The child in green?

REPORTER: Yes.

NUN: You can have the child in green. The Government will not object to that. The boy is blind.

REPORTER: Blind?

NUN: Yes.

REPORTER: He isn't blind. He's looking at me.

NUN: He can't see you.

REPORTER: Yes he can.

NUN: He can't.

REPORTER: That child's the only one who sees me. How can he be blind?

NUN: He can't see.

REPORTER: He's looking at me! Can't you see? He's looking at me!

NUN: You'd better go now. Come back when you have made an application and have been approved. The boy will be here.

REPORTER: He's blind.

NUN: Yes.

REPORTER: I'm going to go now. (HE *doesn't move*)

NUN: Yes, please go now.

REPORTER: He's blind. (HE *starts out the way* HE *came*)

NUN: God be with you.

Blackout.

Slide: HOME

A street in the City. It is dead of night. The REPORTER *is walking along the street.* HE *is nearly stumbling from exhaustion. When the lights come up, it is as if—from the* REPORTER*'s point of view—they came up on the audience.* HE *looks at the audience quizzically.*

REPORTER: Hello. You look familiar. I believe I used to talk to you. Are you my readers? I'm doing very well. Last night I found a refrigerator carton that would shelter a whole family with their pigs and chickens. Next to it a trash pile I can live off for a week. If I can find my way back. I kind of get lost on these streets sometimes. (*Pause*) Sometimes I can stand like this and drift in all directions through the City, soaking up the sounds. . . . (*Sitting down on the pavement*) There's a firefight out there beyond the border of the City. Tracers from a helicopter gunship, see, they're streaming down like water from a hose. Green tracers coming up to meet them now, they climb up towards the ship and then they drop and their green fire goes out. They fall and hit some tree somewhere. The lumber industry is almost dead in Am-bo Land. A fact I read. The trees are all so full of metal that the lumber mills just break their sawblades. (*The lights take on bodiless whiteness*) Magnesium flares. They're floating down on little parachutes. I floated down like that once. Everything is turning silver and the shadows are growing and growing. The street looks like the surface of the moon. And listen.

The EVENT's *voice, on tape, has come softly on: elusive Asian music from the opening titles of the play. The* REPORTER *shuts his eyes. As the sounds continue,* HE *falls into a position almost too awkward to be sleep; a position that suggests a drunken stupor or a state of shock. The* EVENT *makes more sounds, blending them together almost soothingly: a helicopter passing overhead; distant mortar and automatic weapons fire; more Asian music, very lulling. From far along the street is heard the creaking sound of dolly wheels. The* PHOTOGRAPHER *comes on, now legless, propelling himself on a platform.*

PHOTOGRAPHER: Hey, is that a body, man? God damn, a Yankee dressed up like a gook. Yeah, that's a picture. Hold it. Smile, Charlie.

The PHOTOGRAPHER *takes a flash photo. Simultaneously with the flash, the stage goes black and the picture appears on the screen. It is the head and shoulders of a body in the same position as the* REPORTER's, *and dressed identically. The face is that of the* EVENT. *The picture holds for several seconds, then clicks off.*

Slide: HOW I GOT THAT STORY

END OF PLAY

MEDAL OF
HONOR RAG

Tom Cole

About Tom Cole

Born in 1933 in Paterson, New Jersey, Tom Cole took his undergraduate degree at Harvard, and, after studying Russian in army language school, returned to Harvard for a graduate degree in Slavic Languages and Literatures. The author of award-winning short stories and a novel, *An End to Chivalry*, Cole became a playwright with *Medal of Honor Rag*. His next play, *Fighting Bob*, was commissioned by Milwaukee Repertory Theater and produced Off Broadway in 1981. Cole's translations/adaptations of Gogol's *Dead Souls* and Ostrovsky's *The Forest* were also first staged by Milwaukee Rep. Since 1970 Cole has enjoyed an active association with film directors Irvin Kershner, Martin Rosen and Joyce Chopra, with whom he has worked on a long series of films both dramatic and documentary. Current projects include a screenplay of a Joyce Carol Oates story, *"Where Are You Going?,"* and both film and stage adaptations of Maxine Hong Kingston's *The Woman Warrior*. Cole has been the recipient of the Atlantic "First" Award, the Rosenthal Award of the National Institute of Arts and Letters, the CINE Golden Eagle and a playwriting fellowship from the National Endowment for the Arts.

Production History

Medal of Honor Rag was first presented by the Theatre Company of Boston in April 1975, under the direction of David Wheeler and Jan Egleson. The first New York production, directed by David Chambers, opened at the Theatre de Lys the following March. In April 1982 *Medal of Honor Rag* was telecast on PBS's *American Playhouse*, in a production directed by Lloyd Richards.

Playwright's Note

The characters in this play are fictional, but the events reported are all drawn from experiences and testimony of the period.

The words of Lyndon B. Johnson are excerpted from remarks made at a Congressional Medal of Honor award ceremony at the White House on November 19, 1968. A tape of the address is housed at the Lyndon B. Johnson Library in Austin, Texas.

Characters

DOCTOR, a white man in his early 40s, informal, hardworking, even overworked—the youngish doctor with simultaneous commitments to hospital, private patients, writing, family, research, teaching, public health, public issues, committees, special projects. White shirt and bow tie, soft jacket, somewhat weary. He is of European background,, but came to this country as a child. Possessor of a dry wit, which he is not averse to using for therapeutic purposes.

DALE JACKSON (D.J.), a black man two weeks before his 24th birthday, erect and even stiff in bearing, intelligent, handsome, restrained. An effect of power and great potential being held in for hidden reasons. Like the doctor, given to his own slants of humor as a way of dealing with people and, apparently, of holding them off.

HOSPITAL GUARD, a sergeant in uniform and on duty. White. An MP, on transitional assignment.

Time

April 23, 1971.

Place

Valley Forge Army Hospital, Pennsylvania.

The Play

Medal Of Honor Rag

An office, but not the doctor's own office. No signs of personal adaptation—looks more like an institutional space used by many different people, which is what it is. Rather small. A desk, a folding metal chair for the patient, a more comfortable chair for the doctor. Wastebasket. Ash tray.

With the lights still low, a squalid sound from a kazoo is heard, which flows into a rendition of the "Fixin' to Die Rag," by Country Joe and the Fish. A few verses: to bring back the mood of Vietnam. While the music plays, door opens stage rear and the DOCTOR *enters. Light pours in from the corridor, but the* DOCTOR *can't find the light switch in the room.* HE *feels about in half-light, then steps outside again, to find the switch there. Fluorescent overhead light comes on, and the* DOCTOR *putters about, hurriedly, in the office.* HE *rearranges the patient's chair. Takes several folders and a notepad out of his briefcase.*

The DOCTOR *studies one of the dossiers and then, after a beat, looks at his wristwatch. Takes out a cigarette, filter-holder, and match; puts cigarette into filter and filter in his mouth and lights the match. Holds the match and lets it burn without lighting the cigarette, while* HE *looks into the folder again. Puts match down, picks up pencil to make hurried notes in the dossier. Takes a small cassette recorder out of his briefcase, rummages for a cassette, checks its title, and puts it into recorder. Lights another match and this time lights*

122

the cigarette. Puts briefcase on floor beside the desk. Looks at watch, starts to make another note, takes a drag on cigarette.

Knock on door, and DALE JACKSON *enters, escorted by* HOSPITAL GUARD. D.J. *wears "hospital blue denims" and slippers or soft shoes.*

GUARD *places paper forms, in triplicate, on* DOCTOR'*s desk, points brusquely to place for signature. Holds out a ball-point pen to* DOCTOR. DOCTOR *signs, glancing at* D.J. GUARD *tears off one sheet for* DOCTOR, *retains others, and holds out his hand to reclaim his pen.* DOCTOR *hands back pen, abstractedly, and* GUARD *(in full sergeant's regalia) salutes him snappily. The* DOCTOR *looks at the* GUARD *as if* HE *were crazy. The* GUARD *still stands there, at attention.* D.J. *watches this. Finally, the doctor gets up halfway from his chair—a funny, inappropriate gesture—and waves at the man.*

DOCTOR: You can leave us alone.

GUARD (*Snappy salute*): Yes, sir! I'll report back for Sergeant Jackson on the hour, sir! (*About face, marches off*)

The DOCTOR *and* D.J. *look at each other.*

DOCTOR: Sergeant Jackson? (D.J. *nods*) Well, they seem to be keeping a pretty close eye on you.

D.J.: Where's the other doctor?

DOCTOR (*Settling back in his chair*): Sit down, please.

D.J.: They keep changing doctors.

DOCTOR: Would you rather see the other doctor?

D.J.: No, man . . . it's just that I have to keep telling the same story over and over again.

DOCTOR: Sometimes that's the only way to set things straight.

D.J.: You're not in the army, huh?

DOCTOR (*Twinkle*): How can you tell?

D.J.: Your salute is not of the snappiest.

DOCTOR: I came down from New York today. To see you.

D.J.: I must be a really bad case.

DOCTOR: You're a complicated case.

D.J.: Like they say, a special case. I am a special case. Did you know that?

DOCTOR: They keep a pretty close eye on you now.

D.J.: I went AWOL twice. From this hospital.

DOCTOR: Oh?

D.J.: But they'll never do anything to me.

DOCTOR: I understand.

D.J.: You understand, huh?

DOCTOR: I understand your situation.

D.J.: Yeah, well, mind telling me what it is?

DOCTOR: You don't need me to tell you that.

D.J.: So what *do* I need you for?

DOCTOR: I don't know—maybe *I* need *you*.

D.J.: That's a new one. That's one they haven't tried yet.

DOCTOR: Oh?

D.J.: Every doctor has his own tricks.

DOCTOR: Oh?

D.J.: That's one of yours.

DOCTOR: Oh? What's that?

D.J.: When it's your turn to talk, you get this look on your face—kind of like an old owl who's been constipated for about five hundred years, you know, and you say (*Imitation of* DOCTOR'*s face*) "Oh?"

The DOCTOR *laughs at this, a little, but* HE *is watching* D.J. *very closely.* D.J. *speaks with sudden anger.*

Man, this is a *farce*! (HE *turns away—as if to "go AWOL" or to charge to the door—but* HE *gets immediate control of himself.* HE *is depressed*)

DOCTOR (*Calmly*): What should we do about it?

D.J.: Who's this "we"?

DOCTOR: Who else is there?

D.J.: We just going to keep asking each other questions?

DOCTOR: I don't know—what do you think?

D.J.: What do *you* think, man? *Do* you think?

DOCTOR: I listen.

D.J.: No, man, I mean, what do you think? You got that folder there. My life is in there. I'm getting near the end of the line with this stuff. I mean, sometimes I feel like there's not much time. You know? (HE *has wandered over to the desk, where* HE *proceeds to thumb through the folders on his case.* HE *does this with a studied casualness*)

DOCTOR: I'm aware of that.

D.J.: You some big-time specialist? (*Suddenly suspicious*)

DOCTOR: In a manner of speaking.

D.J.: What are you a specialist in?

DOCTOR: I do a lot of work with Vietnam veterans and their problems.

D.J.: Well I can *see* that, man. But what do you *specialize* in?

DOCTOR: I specialize in grief.

D.J. (*Laughs, embarrassed*): Shit. Come on.

DOCTOR (*As if taking a leap*): Impacted grief. That's the . . . special area I work in.

D.J. (*Disgusted*): I'm going to spend another hour in jive and riddles and double talk. Only it's not even an hour, right? It's, like, impacted.

DOCTOR: You know the word "impacted"?

D.J.: How dumb do you think I am?

DOCTOR: I don't think you're dumb at all. Matter of fact, the reverse. . . . (HE *has opened the dossier to a sheet, from which* HE *reads aloud*) "Subject is bright. His army G.T. rating is equivalent of 128 I.Q. In first interviews does not volunteer information. . . ." (*Smiles to* D.J., *who allows himself a small smile of recognition in return, then continues reading*) "He related he grew up in a Detroit ghetto and never knew his natural father. He sort of laughed when he said he was a 'good boy' and always did what was expected of him. Was an Explorer Scout and an altar boy. . . ."

D.J.: The other doctor talked a lot about depression.

DOCTOR: What did he say about it?

D.J.: He said I had it.

DOCTOR: Oh? And?

D.J.: He thought I oughta get rid of it. You know? (*The* DOCTOR *reacts*) Yeah, well he was the chief doctor here. The chief doctor for all the psychos in Valley Forge Army Hospital! See what I mean?

DOCTOR: Valley Forge.

D.J.: Yeah. . . .

DOCTOR: Why *don't* you get rid of it?

D.J. (*Animated*): Sometimes that's just what I want to do! Sometimes I want to throw it in their faces! (*Recollecting himself*) Now ain't that stupid? Like, whose face?

DOCTOR (HE *is keenly on the alert, but tries not to show it in the wrong way*): What do you want to throw in their faces?

D.J.: What are we talking about?

DOCTOR: What are you talking about?

> D.J. *stares at him, won't or can't say anything. The* DOCTOR *continues gently, precisely.*

I was talking about depression. You said your doctor said you should try to get rid of it. I asked, simply, why *don't* you get rid of it?

> D.J. *stares at him, still.* D.J. *is a man for whom it is painful to lose control.* HE *is held in, impassive.*

You meant the medal, didn't you, when you said, "throw it in their faces"?

D.J.: Well. That's why you're here, right? Because of the medal?

DOCTOR (*Gentle, persistent*): But I didn't bring it up. You did.

D.J.: You asked me why I don't get rid of it.

DOCTOR (*Repeating*): I was talking about depression.

D.J.: No. You meant the medal.

DOCTOR: *You* meant the medal. I never mentioned it. . . . Are you glad you have it?

D.J.: The depression?

DOCTOR: No. The medal.

D.J. (*Laughs*): Oh, man. . . . Oh, my. . . . Suppose I didn't have that medal. . . . You wouldn't be here, right? You wouldn't know me from a hole in the wall. I mean, I would be invisible to you. Like a hundred thousand other dudes that got themselves sent over there to be shot at by a lot of little Chinamen hiding up in the trees. I mean, you're some famous doctor, right? Because, you know, I'm a special case! Well I am, I am one big tidbit. I am what you call a "hot property" in this man's army. Yes, sir! I am an authentic hero, a showpiece. One look at me, enlistments go up two hundred percent. . . . I am a credit to my race. Did you know that? I am an honor to the city of Detroit, to say nothing of the state of Michigan, of which I am the only living Medal of Honor winner! I am a feather in the cap of the army, a flower in the lapel of the military—I mean, I am *quoting* to you, man! That is what they say at banquets, given in *my* honor! Yes, sir! And look at me! *Look at me!!* (*Pointing to himself in the clothing of a sick man, in an office of an army hospital*)

DOCTOR: I'm here because you're here.

D.J.: What?

DOCTOR: You ask, would I be here if you hadn't been given that medal. But if you hadn't been given that medal, you wouldn't be here, either. If my grandmother had wheels she'd be a trolley car. You know, it's a big *if*. . . .

D.J.: Yeah, but I'm saying a different *if*. If a trolley car didn't have wheels it still wouldn't be nobody's grandmother. It would just be a trolley car that couldn't go nowhere. Am I right?

DOCTOR (*After a pause*): You're right. . . . (*Brisk again*) Do you still have stomach pains?

D.J.: Yup.

DOCTOR: Nightmares?

D.J.: Yup.

DOCTOR: Same one?

D.J.: Yup.

DOCTOR (*Reads from folder*): "An anonymous soldier standing in front of him, the barrel of his AK-47 as big as a railroad tunnel, his finger on the trigger slowly pressing it."

D.J.: That's the one.

DOCTOR: Who is that anonymous soldier?

D.J.: You know who that is.

DOCTOR: No, I don't.

D.J.: Ain't you done your homework? (*Pointing to folder*)

DOCTOR: My memory is shaky. . . . Please?

D.J.: That's the dude who should have killed me.

DOCTOR: "Should have"?

D.J.: Would have.

DOCTOR: What happened?

D.J.: He misfired.

DOCTOR: And?

D.J.: And that's it.

DOCTOR: That's what?

D.J.: That's it, man. What do you want—a flag that pops out of his rifle and says "Bang"?

DOCTOR: They say you then beat him to death with the butt of your weapon. . . . In combat, near—Dakto.

D.J.: That's what they say.

DOCTOR: That is what they say.

D.J.: So I have heard.

DOCTOR: What else have you heard?

D.J.: That I showed "conspicuous gallantry."

DOCTOR: You're quoting to me?

D.J.: That is what they say, at banquets given in my honor.

DOCTOR: It's part of the citation. Is it not?

D.J. (*Quoting; far-away look*): Con-spicuous gallantry, above and beyond the call of duty. . . . (*With Texas accent*) "Ouah hearts and ouah hopes are turned to peace . . . as we assemble heah . . . in the East Room . . . this morning . . ."

DOCTOR: Lyndon B. Johnson?

D.J.: You got it.

DOCTOR: What did you feel?

D.J.: Nothing.

DOCTOR: But when he hung the medal around your neck, you were crying.

D.J.: See, you *done* your homework!

DOCTOR: Are you going to poke fun at me for the whole hour?

D.J.: Anything wrong with fun?

DOCTOR: Dale—

D.J.: D.J! People call me D.J. That's in the folder, too.

DOCTOR: D.J.

D.J.: Yes, Doctor?

DOCTOR: Do you want to listen to me for a moment?

D.J.: You said *you* was the one to listen.

DOCTOR: I can't listen if you won't tell me anything!

D.J.: I am *telling* you, man! If I knew what to tell to make me feel better, I woulda done it a long time ago. I ain't the doctor, I can't cure myself. . . . (*Pause*) Except one way, maybe.

DOCTOR (*Gently, after a beat*): What are you thinking of, right now?

D.J.: Nothing.

DOCTOR: No image? Nothing in your head?

D.J.: It doesn't have nothing to do with me.

DOCTOR: But *you* thought of it.

D.J.: It's about other guys, in The Nam. Stories we used to hear.

DOCTOR: Yes?

D.J.: "Standing up in a firefight. . . . " (*The* DOCTOR *waits*) We used to hear this . . . combat story. I wasn't in much combat, did you know that?

DOCTOR: Except for Dakto.

D.J.: Yeah. These guys, in their tenth or eleventh month—you know, we had to be there for 365 days on the button, right? Like, we got fed into one end of the computer and if we stayed lucky the computer would shit us back out again, one year later. These grunts—that's what we called the infantry . . .

DOCTOR: I know.

D.J.: I was in a tank, myself.

DOCTOR: What happened to these grunts you heard about?

D.J.: Ten months in the jungle, their feet are rotting, they seen torture, burnings, people being skinned alive—stories they're never going to tell no doctor, believe me. . . . Like, *you* never seen anything like that, right, so you can't comprehend this. . . . (*The* DOCTOR *starts to say something in rebuttal, but then waits*) You never seen your best friend's head blown right off his body so you can look right down in his neck-hole. You never seen somebody you loved, I'm telling you like I mean it, somebody you *loved* and you get there and it's nothing but a black lump, smells like a charcoal dinner, and that's your friend, right?—a black lump. You never seen anything like that, am I right?

DOCTOR (*Quietly*): If you say so.

D.J.: Well, *look* at you, man! Look at you, sitting there in your . . . suit!

DOCTOR: What's wrong with my suit?

D.J.: Ain't nothing wrong with your suit! . . . It's the man wearing the suit. That's what we are talking about!

DOCTOR: You were telling me a story. (HE *feels some satisfaction here—that D.J.'s feelings are beginning to pour out, even if obliquely—but tries not to show it*)

D.J.: A story?

DOCTOR (*Looking at words* HE *has jotted down*): About grunts . . . "standing up in a firefight."

D.J. (*Puzzled that* HE *was recalling this*): Oh. Yeah. So, they been through all these things, and they stayed alive so far, they kept their weapons clean, kept their heads down under cover, and then in the middle of a big firefight with 50-caliber rounds, tracers, all kinds of shit flying all over the place, they'll just stand up.

DOCTOR: They stand up?

D.J.: Yes, start firing into the trees, screaming at the enemy to come out and fight. . . . Maybe not screaming. Just standing straight up.

DOCTOR: And? (*Writing*)

D.J.: Get their heads blown off.

DOCTOR: Every time?

D.J.: Oh, man—*guaranteed!* You know how long you last standing up that way?

DOCTOR: A few seconds?

D.J.: You're a bright fella.

DOCTOR: So, why did they stand up?

D.J. (*Retreating again*): Yeah, why?

DOCTOR: Why do you think they stand up?

D.J.: I don't know. You're the doctor. You tell me.

DOCTOR: What made you think of it just now?

D.J.: I don't know.

DOCTOR: What do you feel about it?

D.J.: Nothing.

DOCTOR: Nothing. . . . (*Silence, for a moment.* HE *gets up, restless, takes a step or two—looks at* D.J., *who sits, immobilized*) D.J., I am going to tell you a few things. Right away.

D.J. (*Perking up*): You're breaking the rules, Doc.

DOCTOR: So be it—sometimes there is nothing else to do.

D.J.: I mean, how do you know I won't report you to your superior?

DOCTOR (*Smiling*): My superior?

D.J.: Don't shrinks have superiors? There must be a Shrink Headquarters somewhere. Probably in New York.

DOCTOR: Probably.

D.J.: So, I'll report that *you* did all the talking and made me—a psycho—take notes on everything you said. Here, man—(HE *sits down in the* DOCTOR'S *place at desk, takes pad and pen, sets himself to write*) I'm ready. Tell me, how do you feel now that you're going to get busted into the ranks, emptying bedpans and suchlike? . . . Oh?

DOCTOR (HE *leans forward, to make his words take hold*): You see what's happening: we are playing games with each other. Because that's easy for you, and you are good at it. You could fill this hour, the week, the month that way until it really *is* too late! Do you understand that?

D.J.: Do you?

DOCTOR: How dumb do you think I am?

D.J. (*Trace of a smile*): I ain't decided yet. I don't have a folder on you with your scores in it.

DOCTOR: Yes. You're a very witty man, very quick—as long as the things we touch on don't really matter to you. But when they do, you go numb. You claim to feel nothing. Do you recognize what I'm saying?

D.J. (*Dull*): I don't know.

DOCTOR: Even your voice goes flat. Can you hear the sound of your own voice?

D.J. (*Flat*): I don't know.

DOCTOR: Do you see that?

D.J.: What?

DOCTOR: I merely *mentioned* the fact that you go numb—and you did! What do you think about that?

D.J.: Nothing.

DOCTOR: Nothing! You think nothing about the fact that you just go one-hundred-percent numb, like a stone, in response to everything that matters most in your own life? (HE *surreptitiously glances at his watch.* THEY *are well into the hour*)

D.J.: Well, now I *am* going to tell you something, man! (*Breaks out as if* HE *had been cornered*) I don't know why I'm in this hospital! I don't know why I'm in this room!

DOCTOR: Then why don't you leave it? We're not getting anywhere.

D.J. (*Mocking*): You mean I don't have to stay here till my hour's up?

DOCTOR: No. I'm not your Commanding Officer. So, go.

> D.J. *does start to go. But* HE *stops on the way to the door to return to the* DOC-TOR'*s desk. There,* D.J. *picks up the various folders and drops them into the wastebasket.* HE *does the same thing, pointedly, with the* DOCTOR'*s pen.* D.J. *stares at the* DOCTOR *for a moment, then walks to the door, opens it, and steps out into the corridor. The* DOCTOR *watches him, then heaves a sigh, leans on the desk to think about what has happened. But* D.J. *appears again at the door.*

D.J.: If I go out there, I'll be in the corridors. I hate the corridors. You ever walk the corridors of this place?

DOCTOR: Never had that pleasure.

D.J.: There's seven miles of them. Lined with basket cases. And I've walked them all, man. I've walked them all . . .

DOCTOR: So you're going to stay here with me just to keep out of the corridors for a while?

D.J.: That's right.

DOCTOR (*Not forcing the issue*): Fine. Make yourself comfortable.

> D.J. *smiles, goes to his chair, settles in, stretches, takes off his slippers, wiggles his toes, watches his bare feet as if they were amusing animals. Begins to do a musical beat on the chair, ignoring the* DOCTOR. *The* DOCTOR *calmly goes back to the wastebasket, extracts his folders and notebook, shakes the ashes off them.* HE *takes out his pen, taps it against the side of the basket, in counter-rhythm to* D.J.'*s beat, and blows the dust off. Then the* DOCTOR *settles comfortably at his desk, lights a cigarette, whistles a bit of the Mozart G-minor Symphony, begins to look through the folder as if to do some work on his own.*

Do you mind if I read a bit? To pass the time?

D.J. (*Cool*): Help yourself.

DOCTOR (*After a beat; musingly*): Here's an interesting story . . . a case study

I've been working on . . . trying to write it out for myself . . . about a certain man who was an unusual type for the world he came from. (*Reads from or refers to folder, as if in discussion of a neutral matter*) Rather gentle, and decent in manner . . . almost always easygoing and humorous. Noted for that. As a kid in a tough neighborhood, he had been trained by his mother to survive by combining the virtues of a Christian and a sprinter: he turned the other cheek and ran faster than anyone else. . . . (D.J. *is beginning to listen with interest*) This man was sent by his country to fight in a war. A war unlike any war he might have imagined. Brutal, without glory, without meaning, without good wishes for those who were sent to fight and without gratitude for those who returned. He was trained to kill people of another world in their own homes, in order to help them. How this would help them we do not really know. He was assigned to a tank and grew close with the others in the crew, as men always do in a war. He and his friends in that tank were relatively fortunate—for almost a year they lived through insufferable heat, insects, boredom, but were never drawn into heavy combat. Then one night he was given orders assigning him to a different tank. For what reason?

D.J.: There was no reason.

DOCTOR: There was no reason.

D.J.: It was the army.

DOCTOR: It was the army. The next day, his platoon of four M-48 tanks were driving along a road toward a place called Dakto, which meant nothing to him. Suddenly they were ambushed. First, by enemy rockets, which destroyed two of the tanks. Then, enemy soldiers came out of the woods to attack the two tanks still in commission. This man we were speaking of was in one of those tanks. But the tank with his old friends, the tank he would have been in—

D.J.: Should have been in.

DOCTOR: —the tank that he might have been in—that tank was on fire. It was about sixty feet away, and the crew he had spent eleven months and twenty-two days with in Vietnam was trapped inside it. . . . (D.J. *looks away, in pain*) He hoisted himself out and ran to the other tank. Speaking of standing up in a firefight. . . . Why he wasn't hit by the heavy crossfire we'll never know. He pulled out the first man he came to in the turret. The body was blackened, charred, but still alive. That was one of his friends.

D.J.: He kept making a noise to me, over and over again. Just kept making the same noise, but I couldn't find where his mouth was. . . .

DOCTOR: Then the tank's artillery shells exploded, killing everyone left inside. He saw the bodies of his other friends all burned and blasted, and then— for thirty minutes, armed first with a 45-caliber pistol and then with a submachine gun he hunted the Vietnamese on the ground, killing from ten to twenty enemy soldiers (no one knows for sure) . . . by himself. When he ran out of ammunition, he killed one with the stock of his submachine gun.

D.J.: He kept making this same noise to me . . . over and over.

DOCTOR (*After a pause*): When it was all over, it took three men and three shots of morphine to quiet him down. He was raving. He tried to kill the prisoners they had rounded up. They took him away to a hospital in Pleiku in a straitjacket. Twenty-four hours later he was released from that hospital, and within forty-eight hours he was home again in Detroit, with a medical discharge. . . .

D.J.: My mother didn't even know I was coming. . . .

DOCTOR: Go on.

D.J. (*Looking up*): You go on.

DOCTOR: That is the story.

D.J.: That's not the whole story.

DOCTOR: What happened when you got back to this country?

D.J.: What do you mean, what happened?

DOCTOR: One day you're in the jungle. These catastrophic things happen. Death, screaming, fire. Then suddenly you're sitting in a jet airplane, going home.

D.J.: They had *stewardesses* on that plane! D'you know that?

DOCTOR: Oh?

D.J.: *Stewardesses*, for shit's sake, man! They kept smiling at us.

DOCTOR: Did you smile back?

D.J. (*Straightforward*): I wanted to kill them.

DOCTOR: White girls?

D.J.: That's not the point.

DOCTOR: Are you sure?

D.J.: A white guy would have felt the same way I did. I . . . wanted to throw a hand grenade right in the middle of all those teeth.

DOCTOR: Do you think that was a bad feeling?

D.J.: Blowing up a girl's face, because she's smiling at me? Well, I'll tell you, man, it wasn't the way my mother brought me up to be. Not exactly.

DOCTOR: Neither was the war. Was it?

D.J.: Doc. Am I crazy?

DOCTOR: Maybe a little bit. But it's temporary. . . . It can be cured.

D.J.: *You* can cure me? (*Stares at the* DOCTOR)

DOCTOR: I didn't say that.

D.J.: Yeah, but you mean it, don't you?

DOCTOR: What was it like when you touched ground, in this country?

D.J.: You actually think that you can cure me!

DOCTOR: Did they have a Victory Parade for you?

D.J.: *Victory Parade?!*

DOCTOR: Soldiers always used to get parades, when they came home. Made them feel better.

D.J.: Victory Parades! Man. . . . (*Laughs at the insane wonder of the idea*)

DOCTOR: You mean there wasn't a band playing when you landed in the States?

D.J.: Man, let me tell you something—

DOCTOR: You didn't march together, with your unit?

D.J.: Unit? What unit?

DOCTOR: Well, the people you flew back with.

D.J.: I didn't know a soul in that plane, man! I didn't have no *unit*. Any unit I had, man, they're all burned to a crisp. How'm I supposed to march with that unit?—with a whiskbroom, pushing all these little black crumbs forward down the street, and everybody cheering, "There's Willie! See that little black crumb there? That's our Willie! No, no, that there crumb is my son, Georgie! Hi, Georgie. Glad to have you home, boy!"? Huh? . . . What are you talking about?! This wasn't World War Two, man, they sent us back one by one, when our number came up. I told you that!

DOCTOR: People were burned to a crisp in World War Two.

D.J.: Yeah, well there was a difference, because I *heard* about that war! When people came back from that war they *felt* like somebody. They were made to feel *good*, at least for a while.

DOCTOR: That's just what I was thinking.

D.J.: Then why didn't you just say it?

DOCTOR: I'd rather that you said it.

D.J.: Were you in that war?

DOCTOR: I remember it—very well.

D.J.: And you knew guys who had a parade with their unit.

DOCTOR: I did. Banners. Ticker tape.

D.J. (*Laughs at the thought*): Oh, man. How long ago was that?

DOCTOR: Where did you land?

D.J.: Seattle.

DOCTOR: Daytime? Night?

D.J.: Night.

A pause.

DOCTOR: Nothing?

D.J.: Nothing, man. Nothing.

Pause.

DOCTOR: I had one patient who got spat on, at the Seattle airport.

D.J.: Spat on?

DOCTOR: For not winning the war. He said an American Legionnaire, with a red face, apparently used to wait right at the gate . . . so he could spit on soldiers coming back, the moment they arrived.

D.J.: What are you telling me this for?

DOCTOR: Then, inside the terminal there was a group of young people screaming insults. White kids, with long hair. (*No reaction from* D.J. *The* DOCTOR
watches him carefully) Do you want to know why they were screaming insults?

D.J.: No, Doctor, I do not.

DOCTOR: For burning babies.

D.J.: I didn't burn no babies! (HE *begins to pace.* HE *is agitated. The* DOCTOR
watches, waits) The day I arrived, like, everything was disorganized. There
was a smaller plane took us to the nearest landing strip, know what I
mean?—and then you had to hitch a ride, or whatever, to find your own unit.

DOCTOR: Are you talking about Seattle?

D.J.: No, man. In The Nam. Like, my first day over there. My *first day*, mind
you! So, I hitched a ride on this truck. About six or seven guys in it, heading
toward Danang. I was a F.N.G., so I kept my mouth shut.

DOCTOR: F.N.G.?

D.J. (HE *pulls his chair up closer to the* DOCTOR*'s desk, as if to confide in him, and*
HE *sits*): A F.N.G. is a Fucking New Guy. See? They all pick on you over
there, they hate you just because you're new. Like, nobody trusts you for
the simple fact that you never been through the miseries they been having.
At least, not yet. . . . Then you get friendly with your own little group,
see, your own three or four friends—the guys in my tank—and they mean
everything to you, they're like family—they're like everything you got in
this world—I—see, that was the—thing about—that was the. . . .

D.J. *suddenly can't go on.* HE *buries his face in his hands and is attacked by
a terrible grief—ambushed by it.* HE *tries to pull his hands away to speak again,
but it is impossible.* HE *sobs, or weeps, into his hands. The* DOCTOR *hesitates,
then goes around to the chair where* D.J. *sits, and stays there by him for a moment. The* DOCTOR *begins to lay a hand, lightly, on* D.J.*'s shoulder, so that*
D.J. *will not be completely alone with his grief. But* D.J. *breaks away, violently.*
HE *heads away, as if to escape. The* DOCTOR *moves to block another impetuous
exit, but* D.J. *had no clear intention.* HE *is frozen, sobbing. If his face is visi-
ble, it is painful to see. The* DOCTOR *watches him intently, almost like a hunter.*
HE *seems to be gauging his moment, when* D.J. *will be just in control enough
to hear what the* DOCTOR *is saying, but still vulnerable enough for a deep blow
to be struck. Finally* HE *speaks.*

DOCTOR: Is it the tank? (D.J. *cannot really answer*) Can you say it? (D.J. *almost begins
to speak, but the catch in his throat is still there.* HE *will break down again, if*
HE *speaks.* HE *shakes his head*) Do you want me to say it? (D.J. *cannot answer*)
You don't know why you are alive and they are dead. (D.J. *watches*) You
think you should be dead, too. (D.J. *listens, silent. At times* HE *tries to run
away from the words, but the* DOCTOR *stalks him*) Sometimes you feel that you
are really dead, already. You can't feel anything becasue it's too painful.

You dream about the rifle that should have killed you, with the barrel right in your face. You don't know why it didn't kill you, why just that rifle should have misfired. . . . (D.J. *hangs on these words*) And what about those orders that transferred you out of their tank? Why just that night? Why you? Why did the ambush come the next day? . . . There must be something magical about this, like the AK-47 that misfired for no reason. Perhaps you made all these things happen, just to save yourself. Perhaps it is all your fault, that your friends are dead. If you hadn't been transferred from their tank, then somehow they wouldn't have died. So you should die, too.

D.J. (*Bellowing*): I'm dead already!

DOCTOR (*Quieter*): Yes. You *feel*, sometimes, that you are dead already. You would like to die, to shut your eyes quietly on all this, and you don't know who you can tell about it. You keep it locked up like a terrible secret. . . . (D.J. *remains silent. The* DOCTOR's *words have the power to cause great pain in him. After a pause*) This is our work, D.J. This is what we have to do.

D.J.: I can't, man! I can't!

DOCTOR: You can. I know you can.

D.J. (*Stares at the* DOCTOR; *then speaks*): How do you know all this? From a book?

DOCTOR: I've been through it.

D.J.: *You* were in The Nam?

DOCTOR: No. But I had my own case of survivor guilt.

D.J.: That's jive and doubletalk! Don't start that shit with me.

DOCTOR: It's just shorthand to describe a complicated . . . sickness. It's the kind of thing that can make a man feel so bad that he thinks he wants to die.

D.J.: Where'd you get yours?

DOCTOR: You think it will help you to know that?

D.J.: Man, I take off my skin, and you just piss all over me! And . . .

DOCTOR: You want me to take my skin off, too. That's what you want?

D.J.: I want to get better! I don't want to be crazy!

DOCTOR: Yes. That's why I'm here, to—

D.J. (*Cutting him off*): You're not here!

DOCTOR: I'm not?

D.J.: There's something here. And it's wearing a bowtie. But I don't know *what* it is . . .

DOCTOR: Well, in this treatment, that's the way it works. Normally it's better that you *not* know about your doctor's personal—

D.J.: *Normally?!* Man, this ain't normally!

The DOCTOR *considers this, as a serious proposition. Historically, the abnormal war. The desperation of this man. And* HE *goes ahead, against his own reluctance.*

DOCTOR: All right. All right . . . I wasn't born here. I'm from Poland. I had a Jewish grandmother, but I was brought up as a regular kid. All right? . . . Life in Poland tends to get confusing. Either the Russians or Germans are always rolling in, flattening the villages and setting fire to people. You've got the picture? Anyway, World War Two came, the Nazis, the SS troops, and this time the Jewish kids were supposed to be killed—sent to Camps, gassed, starved, worked to death, beaten to death. That was the program . . . I didn't think of myself as Jewish. We didn't burn candles on Friday night, none of that. I wasn't Jewish. But my mother's mother was. So, to the Nazis I was Jewish. So, I should be dead now. I shouldn't be here. You're looking at someone who "should" be dead, like you. . . . See? (D.J. *nods.* HE *listens intensely*) They sent me to one of those Camps. But I was saved, by an accident. . . . You understand what I'm saying? Someone came along—a businessman—and he said he would buy some Jewish children, and the Nazis could use the money for armaments, or whatever. A deal. One gray morning—it was quite warm—they just lined us up, and started counting heads. When they got to the number the gentleman had paid for, they stopped. I got counted. The ones who didn't—my brother and sister and the others—they all died. But not me. For what reason? *There was no reason.* . . . So, that's it. Eventually, I ended up over here, I lied about my age, got into the army at the end of the war. I thought I wanted revenge. But now I know that I wanted to die, back over there. To get shot. But I failed. Came back, and I even marched in a Victory Parade, with my unit! So I was luckier than you, D.J. . . . But still, I didn't know why I hadn't died when everyone else did. I thought it must have been magic, and that it was my fault the others were dead—a kind of trade-off, you see, where my survival accounted for their deaths. My parents, everybody. I became quite sick. Depressed, dead-feeling . . .

D.J.: How did you get better?

DOCTOR: The same way you will.

D.J.: I thought you was going to cure me.

DOCTOR: No. Essentially, you are going to cure yourself.

D.J.: Wow. (*Shakes his head*)

DOCTOR: Others, men like you, have gone through such things, and they have gotten better. That might make you feel a little better, too, for a start.

D.J.: Yeah, misery loves company. Right?

DOCTOR: Nothing magical happened, D.J. None of this was your fault. (*Glances at his watch*)

D.J.: How much time we got left, Doc?

DOCTOR: Don't worry about the time. We have all the time we'll need.

D.J.: You're the one is always stealing a look at your watch!

DOCTOR: It's just a bad habit. Like picking my nose.

D.J.: I ain't seen you picking your nose.

DOCTOR: You will. You will.

D.J.: I guess that gives me a little something to look forward to, in my hospital stay.

DOCTOR (*Laughs*): I guess it does.

D.J.: A treat instead of a treatment. (*The* DOCTOR *is no longer amused.* HE *stares at* D.J., *expectantly.* D.J. *grows uneasy*) You want something from me.

DOCTOR: Mm. The truck.

D.J.: The truck?

DOCTOR: The story of the first—

D.J. (*Interrupting*): What truck?

DOCTOR: There was a truck.

D.J.: A truck . . . ?

DOCTOR: First day in Vietnam. F.N.G. You hitched a ride in a truck.

D.J.: Jesus.

DOCTOR: Don't feel like talking about it?

D.J.: No. I don't.

DOCTOR: That's as good a reason as any for telling me.

D.J. (*Reacts to this notion, but then goes along with it. Sits down again, as* HE *gets into the story*): Well, uh . . . we were riding along, in the truck. Real hot, you know, and nobody much was around . . . and we see there's a bunch of kids, maybe three, four of them crossing the road up ahead. . . . You know?

DOCTOR: How old were they?

D.J.: Well, it's hard to tell. Those people are all so *small*, you know?—I mean, all dried-up and tiny, man. . . . Maybe ten years old, twelve, I don't know. . . .

DOCTOR: And?

D.J.: Well, we see they're being pretty slow getting out of the road, so we got to swerve a little bit to miss them. . . . Not a lot, you know, but a little bit. This seems to make the guys in the back of the truck really mad. Like, somebody goes, "Little fuckers!" You know? . . . Then those kids, as soon as we pass, they start laughing at us, and give us the finger. Know what I mean? (HE *gives the* DOCTOR *the finger, to illustrate. The* DOCTOR *starts to laugh, but then puts his hand to his head, as if knowing what is to come*) Yeah. So I'm thinking to myself, "Now where did they learn to do that? That ain't some old oriental custom. They musta learned it from our guys." . . . Suddenly the guys on the truck start screaming for the driver to back up. So he jams on the brakes, and in this big cloud of dust he's grinding this thing in reverse as if he means to run those kids down, backwards. The kids start running away, of course, but one of 'em, maybe two, I don't know, they stop, you see, and give us the finger again, from the side of the road. And they're laughing. . . . So, uh . . . everybody on the truck opens fire. I mean, I couldn't believe it, they're like half a platoon, they got M-16s, automatic rifles, they're blasting away, it sounds like a pitched battle, they're pouring all this firepower into these kids. The kids are lying on the ground, they're dead about a hundred times over, and these guys are still firing rounds into their bodies, like they've gone crazy. And the kids' bodies are giving these little jumps into the air like rag dolls, and then they flop down again. . . .

DOCTOR (*Very quiet*): What happened then?

D.J.: They just sorta stopped, and me and these guys drove away. (*The* DOCTOR *waits*) I'm thinking to myself, you know, what *is* going on here? I must be out of tune. *My first day in the country,* and we ain't even reached the Combat Zone! I'm thinking, like, this is the enemy? Kids who make our trucks give a little jog in the road and give us the finger? I mean, come on, man! . . . And one guy, he sees I'm sort of staring back down the road, so he gives me like this, you know— (HE *simulates a jab of the elbow*) and he says, "See how we hose them li'l motherfuckers down, man?" Hose 'em down. You like that? . . . And they're all blowing smoke away from their muzzles and checking their weapons down, like they're a bunch of gunslingers, out of the Old West. . . . (HE *is shaking his head.* HE *still has trouble believing* HE *saw this*)

DOCTOR (*Measured*): Why do you think they did all that?

D.J.: I don't know. They went crazy, that's why!

DOCTOR: Went crazy. . . . Were all those soldiers white?

D.J.: I don't remember.

DOCTOR: What do you think?

D.J. (*A little dangerously*): I think some of them were white.

DOCTOR (*Waits.* D.J. *does not add anything*): And what did you do?

D.J.: What do you mean, what did I do?

DOCTOR: Well, did you report them to a superior officer?

D.J. (*Explodes*): *Superior officer?!* What superior officer? Their fucking lieutenant was *right there in the fucking truck,* he was the first one to open fire! I mean what are you talking about, man? Don't you know what is going on over there?

DOCTOR: Why get mad at me? I didn't shoot those children.

D.J. (*Confused, angry*): God *damn* . . . ! (*Glaring at the* DOCTOR) I mean, what are you accusing me of, man?

DOCTOR: I'm not accusing you of anything.

D.J.: Well, I'm asking you! What would you have done? You think you're so much smarter and better than me? You weren't there, man! That's why you can sit here and be the judge! Right? (*No reaction from the* DOCTOR, *except for a tic of nervousness under the extreme tension that has been created*) I mean, look at you sitting there in your suit, with that shit-eating grin on your face!

DOCTOR: You're getting mad at my suit again? You think my suit has caused these problems?

D.J. can't control his rage and frustration any longer. HE blows up, grabs his chair—as the only object available—and swings it above his head as a weapon. The DOCTOR instinctively ducks away and shouts at D.J. to stop.

Wait a minute! Sergeant! Stop that!

D.J. crashes the chair against the desk, or the floor. HE cannot vent his physical aggression directly against the DOCTOR. After D.J. has torn up the room, HE stands, exhausted, confused, emptyhanded.

Are you all right?

D.J. stares at the DOCTOR, panting. D.J. moves away, into the silence of the room. The DOCTOR speaks neutrally.

How did you feel about being a killer?
D.J.: *I didn't kill those kids, man!*
DOCTOR: I didn't say you did! Did I?

The DOCTOR waits. D.J. glares at him, still full of rage and suspicion. But a deep point has been made, and BOTH MEN are aware of it. A pause.

Did you ever tell people at home about any of this? About Dakto, about the truck?
D.J.: No. I didn't.
DOCTOR: Didn't they ask? Didn't anyone ever wonder why you came home early?
D.J.: Yeah, they asked.
DOCTOR: Who asked?
D.J.: My mother. Little kids, sometimes. My girl, Bea. . . .
DOCTOR: Sounds like everybody.
D.J.: No, not everybody. A lot of people didn't give a shit what happened.
DOCTOR: And you pretended you didn't give a shit, either?
D.J.: What do you want me to say, man?
DOCTOR: But what did you say when your mother or your friends asked you?
D.J.: You guess. You're the specialist.
DOCTOR (*After a pause*): All right, I will. You said, "Nothing happened. Nothing happened over there."
D.J.: Right on. Word for word.
DOCTOR: It's in the folder.
D.J.: Yeah, sure.
DOCTOR (*Takes words from report in the folder*): It also says you "lay up in your room a lot, staring at the ceiling. . . . " (HE *waits, to see if* D.J. *has anything to add*)
D.J.: Read. Read, man. I'm tired.

DOCTOR: Did you do that—did that happen to you right away?

D.J.: Right away . . . ? No. Well, at first I felt pretty good. Considering. . . . (*Trails off*) Considering, uh . . .

DOCTOR: Considering that you had just been heavily narcotized, tied up in a straitjacket, and shipped home in a semi-coma. After surviving a hell of death and horror, which by all odds should have left you dead yourself.

D.J.: Yeah. Considering that.

DOCTOR: You felt lucky that you had survived? At first?

D.J.: I just used to like going to bars with my cousin, William . . . my friends. I was glad to see my girl, Beatrice, and my mama. I joked around with them. I tried to be good to them . . . I shot baskets with the kids, down the block. Understand?

DOCTOR: Of course. And then what happened?

D.J.: It didn't last.

DOCTOR: And?

D.J.: I started laying up in my room. Staring at the ceiling.

DOCTOR: But what happened? What changed you?

D.J.: I don't remember.

DOCTOR: But you did go numb?

D.J.: You're talking me around in circles, Doc!

DOCTOR: I'm sorry. . . . This terrible delayed reaction, after a kind of relief—it seems so mysterious, but it's the common pattern for men who went through your kind of combat trauma . . .

D.J. (*With irony*): Well, I'm glad to hear that. But I sometimes began to suspect that my girl, Bea, might just prefer a man what can see and hear and think and feel things. And *do* things! You follow my meaning? A man what can walk and talk, stuff like that?

DOCTOR: Did you stop having sexual relations with her?

D.J.: Well, I have been trying to send you signals, man! You're none too quick on the pickup.

DOCTOR: Did she criticize you?

D.J.: Not about that. : . . She wanted me to get a job, so we could get married.

DOCTOR: Well. The job situation must have been difficult in Detroit.

D.J.: Especially if you lay up in your room all day, staring at the ceiling. Funny thing about the city of Detroit—not too many people come up through your bedroom offering you a job, on most days. Did you know that?

DOCTOR: I've heard that, yes. . . . Did you stop getting out of bed altogether?

D.J.: No, I put my feet to the floor once in a while. Used to go on down to the V.A. and stand in line for my check.

DOCTOR: How did they treat you down there, at the Veterans' Office?

D.J.: Like shit.

DOCTOR: Did you know why you got treated that way?

D.J.: It wasn't just me personally, man.

DOCTOR: I know. But why?

D.J.: You know that a vet down the block from me flipped out last week—jumped up in the middle of his sleep and shot his woman in bed, because he thought she was the Vietcong laying there to ambush him? . . .

The DOCTOR *goes sharply on the alert at this, but waits for* D.J. *to continue.* D.J. *is profoundly uneasy about his own train of thought.*

Man, if I lose my cool again—just, freak out—what's to stop me from going up and down the streets of Detroit killing everything I see?

DOCTOR (*Concerned, quiet*): Do you actually think you could do that?

D.J.: How can you ask me that?

DOCTOR: I'm asking.

D.J. (*Charging at the* DOCTOR): Well what did I *do*—what did I get that medal for, man? For my good manners and gentle ways?

The DOCTOR *and* D.J. *stare at each other for a tense moment. The* DOCTOR *starts to fit up another cigarette and filter, but throws the filter away and lights up the cigarette.* HE *begins to pace restlessly.* D.J. *watches him. Then the* DOCTOR *abruptly turns back to* D.J.

DOCTOR: Tell me when you actually got the medal.

D.J.: You're making me nervous!

DOCTOR (*Keeps pacing*): As my grandmother used to say, "That should be the worst would ever happen to you."

D.J.: That's the grandmother, could have been a trolley car?

DOCTOR: *If* she had wheels.

D.J.: If she had wheels. Right.

During this colloquy—in which an ease, a trust seems to be forming between the men—the DOCTOR *has restrained himself, but* HE *is impatient now to pick up the thread.*

DOCTOR: Tell me when you actually got the medal!

D.J. (*This story is relatively easy for him to launch into;* HE *settles into his old chair in the course of telling it*): I been home eight, nine months. Then I get this call, they say it's some army office. They want to know if I'm clean—if I had any arrests since I been back, you know. I tell them I'm clean and just leave me alone. Then two MPs come to the door, in uniform, scare the shit out of my mama. They just tell her they want to find out a few things about me—whether I've been a good boy—whether I've been taking any drugs. She makes me roll up my sleeves right there (HE *does so for the* DOCTOR) to show—no tracks, see? When they leave, she is sure I've done something terrible, that I shouldn't be afraid to tell her, that she'll forgive me anything. And all I can do is sit there in the kitchen and laugh at her, which makes her mad, and even more sure I done something weird. . . . Well, about fifteen minutes later a colonel calls up from the Department of Defense in Washington, tells me they're going to give me the Congressional Medal of Honor, and could I come down to Washington right away, with my family, as President Lyndon B. Johnson hisself wants to hang it around my neck, with his own hands. He'll pay for the tickets, he says.

DOCTOR: So, another sudden ride on a jet plane.

D.J.: A goddamn *Honor Guard* meets us at the airport. Beatrice is peeing in her pants, my mother's with me, my cousin, William. . . . They got a dress-blue uniform waiting for me, just my size. Shoes, socks, everything. Escort, sirens. Yesterday afternoon for all they knew I was a junkie on the streets, today the President of the United States can't wait to see me. . . .

The DOCTOR has picked up his cassette recorder while D.J. was finishing the story, and now HE clicks it on. The voice of Lyndon B. Johnson plays, from the award ceremony.

VOICE OF L.B.J.: " . . . Secretary Resor . . . General Westmoreland. . . . Distinguished guests and members of the family. . . . Our hearts and our hopes are turned to peace as we assemble here in the East Room this morning. All our efforts are being bent in its pursuit. But in this company (*The* DOCTOR *points the recorder at* D.J.) we hear again, in our minds, the sounds of distant battle. . . .

The DOCTOR turns the volume down, and the voice of L.B.J. drones quietly in the background, as HE waits for D.J.'s reaction.

D.J.: Ain't that a lot of shit?

DOCTOR: You wept.

D.J.: I don't know, I kind of cracked up. The flashbulbs were popping in my eyes, my mother's hugging me, she's saying, "Honey, what are you crying about? You've made it back." It was *weird*!

The DOCTOR has turned the volume up again to let a few more phrases from the presidential ceremony play, giving D.J. more time for reliving the moment.

VOICE OF L.B.J.: "This room echoes once more to those words that describe the heights of bravery in war, above and beyond the call of duty. Five heroic sons of America come to us today from the tortured fields of Vietnam. They come to remind us that so long as that conflict continues our purpose and our hopes rest on the steadfast bravery of young men in battle. These five soldiers, in their separate moments of supreme testing, summoned a degree of courage that stirs wonder and respect and an overpowering pride in all of us. Through their spectacular courage they set themselves apart in a very select company . . . "

The DOCTOR *underlines these last words—"set themselves apart in a very select company"—with a gesture. Then* HE *flicks off the cassette recorder.*

D.J.: Weird, man.

DOCTOR: Why was it weird?

D.J.: I . . . I don't know?

DOCTOR: You *do* know!

D.J.: What are you driving at?

DOCTOR: What did you get that medal for? (*Repeating* D.J.*'s earlier words*) For your "good manners and gentle ways"?

D.J. (*Stares at the* DOCTOR. *The* DOCTOR *stares back*): I got that medal because I went totally out of my fucking skull and killed everything that crossed my sight! (*Pause*) They say I wanted to kill all the prisoners. *Me.*

DOCTOR: *You don't remember?*

D.J.: Nothing. . . . A few flashes, maybe. Those people are all so small. . . .

DOCTOR (HE *taps a finger on the cassette recorder, trying to recapture the specific moment* THEY *have been talking about—in the White House—but* HE *gradually gets caught up in the intense rush of his own thoughts*): So, your mother was hugging you, in the White House, for doing what she had trained you all your life not to do—for being a killer. And everybody was celebrating you for that. . . . And your dead friends from the tank, whom you had tried so hard to bury, came back again, to haunt you. You had to relive that story, that flash of combat when a man's life is changed forever, when he literally goes crazy, psychotic, in a world of no past and no future, compacted into a few seconds, a wild pounding of the heart, blinding light, explosions, terror, and his whole earlier life slides away from him through a . . . membrane as if lost forever, and all he can do is kill—all *that* was named, broadcast, printed on a banner and waved in your own face so you can never forget. . . . And you wonder why you wept, why you were confused, why you are here in this hospital? You wept for your dead friends, you wept for your dead self, for your whole life that slid away in the first fifteen seconds of that ambush on the road to Dakto. You were choking on your grief, a grief you couldn't share with anyone, and you became paralyzed by your guilt, and you still are, and you're going to be, until *you* decide to make your own journey back through that membrane into some acceptable reality. . . . Some real life, of your own. . . .

Both D.J. *and the* DOCTOR *seem momentarily stunned by the latter's outpouring.*

D.J.: I don't know how to do that, Doc.

DOCTOR: I will tell you. . . . (*Glances at watch, as if recollecting himself*) D.J., do you intend to stay in this hospital for a while?

D.J.: Why do you ask?

DOCTOR (*Reads from folder for an answer*): "Maalox and bland diet prescribed. G.I. series conducted. Results negative. Subject given thirty-day convalescent leave 16 October 1970. Absent Without Leave until 12 January 1971, when subject returned to Army hospital on own volition. Subsequent hearing recommended dismissal of AWOL charge and back pay reinstated . . . in cognizance of subject's outstanding record in Vietnam."

D.J.: Well, yeah, they can't do anything to me.

DOCTOR: Because of the medal?

D.J.: Because of the medal. . . .

DOCTOR (*After a beat*): I'm afraid we have only a few more minutes today. (*Scanning his appointments book*) I can come down the day after tomorrow, and I'd like to talk with you again. After that, if you want, I can see you three or four times a week.

D.J. (HE *automatically readies himself for the end of the hour*): Busy man like you? (*Light mockery*)

DOCTOR: Mm-hm. But I'd like to have you transferred up to New York. I can do that, if you'll make the request. . . . (HE *looks questioningly at* D.J.. D.J. *does not answer—nor does* HE *necessarily imply a "No"*) Well?

D.J.: We'll see.

DOCTOR: We'll see what?

D.J.: We'll see, when you come down again.

DOCTOR: Can I be sure you'll be here?

D.J.: You're looking for too many guarantees in life, man.

DOCTOR: No, I'm not. I'm looking for you to make a decision about yourself.

A knock at the door, and the HOSPITAL GUARD *immediately enters.*

You *can* get better, you know. . . .

GUARD: Reporting in for Sergeant Jackson, sir.

The DOCTOR *and* D.J. *look at each other.* D.J. *gets up, automatically, to go.*

DOCTOR (*To* GUARD): Will you wait outside for a moment? In the corridor?

GUARD: Will do, sir. May I ask, sir, how long?

DOCTOR: Not long. Until the interview is concluded.

GUARD: May I ask, sir, is the interview almost concluded?

DOCTOR: The interview is almost concluded. Just giving a summation.

GUARD: Will wait in corridor, sir, until conclusion of summation of interview. (HE *snaps to, gives salute. The* DOCTOR *waves him off, with his own facsimile of a salute. The* GUARD *wheels into an about-face and exits to station himself outside the door*)

D.J.: Attaboy.

DOCTOR: So?

D.J.: So?

DOCTOR: Do we have a deal?

D.J.: Hit me with the "summation."

DOCTOR (*Closes up his folder*): There is nothing to say that you don't already know. The only question is what to do about it. (D.J. *laughs*) It was a badly damaged self that you brought back to this country, and nothing has happened here, you see, to help you—

D.J. (*Cutting him off*): You're leaving a little something out, ain't you? Man, they gave me the Congressional Medal of Honor!

DOCTOR: So they did. And what happened?

D.J.: Well . . . I became a big hero!

DOCTOR: You became a big hero. . . . You appear on TV. The head of General Motors shakes your hand. You get married. You reenlist—reenlist!—travel around the state making recruiting speeches. You get a new car, a house with a big mortgage. Everybody gives you credit . . . for a while.

D.J.: Rags to riches, man.

DOCTOR: And then? (D.J. *makes a gesture of self-deprecation, meaning, more or less, "Here I am"*) Back to rags again.

D.J. (*Challenging*): But I got the medal! Didn't that medal save me from a lot of shit?

DOCTOR (*Beginning to pack up*): Did it ever occur to you that the medal, in some ways, might have made things worse?

D.J.: *Worse?* What are you talking about, man?

DOCTOR: Well, that's where we can begin our next session. . . . If you will simply commit yourself to being here. That's all I'm asking, you know.

D.J. (*Opening up the* DOCTOR's *folder again*): No! I want to talk about it now. I mean, it sounds like you're just getting down to the nitty-gritty, am I right?

DOCTOR: It's all nitty-gritty, D.J. It's one layer of nitty-gritty after another, until you feel like living again. But we can't just extend this hour arbitrarily—

D.J.: Why not? Just tell the cowboy out there to take a walk. You got the rank here. . . .

DOCTOR: That's not the issue. Look, for one thing I'm a little tired, too. I got up at five this morning, and—

D.J.: Yeah. Well that should be the worst would ever happen to you!

DOCTOR: All right. Let's just say for now, that it's the rules of the game, by which we *both* can—

D.J. (*Pouncing on the word "game"*): So we *are* playing games! You hear?

DOCTOR: We're playing a game for your life!

D.J. (*Studies the* DOCTOR): What do you want from me, man?

DOCTOR: I want you to get better.

D.J.: No, you said you were going to tell me what I had to do.

DOCTOR: I said that?

D.J.: Yeah, you did—after a long speech about killing, when you got all excited. Probably, it slipped out, huh?

DOCTOR: Well, that gives us something else to look into, next time.

D.J. (*Sullen*): No, man. You want something from me. I been getting used to that . . . I think you're a star-fucker.

DOCTOR: A what?

D.J.: A star-fucker. Like, in the Rock world, or in the movies, these chicks who hang around close to the stars. They get their kicks, their thrills out of that.

DOCTOR: I'm not a "chick."

D.J.: But you're like one.

DOCTOR: Meaning?

D.J.: You come down here, you sniff me out. Because in your world, I'm probably a famous case. Because of my medal. Am I right?

DOCTOR (*Gets up, and starts to escort* D.J. *to the door*): I think we're back to where we started the hour. None of this will be easy, D.J., but I will be here the day after tomorrow, and as you say, we'll see what happens . . .

D.J. (*Interrupting*): You want to take that medal away from me, don't you?

DOCTOR (*A little stunned*): No. Why do you say that?

D.J.: Now be honest with me, man. Otherwise you're going to turn my head around backwards, for good. . . .

> The DOCTOR *and* D.J. *look at each other for a long beat.*

DOCTOR: No, D.J., I don't want to take that medal, or anything else away from you. But when the time is ripe, when you are ready, you may not need it anymore. That's why *you* spoke, early this hour, of wanting to get rid of it, sometimes, and of "throwing it in their faces." You see, part of you already wants to throw it away, while—

D.J. (*Pulling away*): Throw it away!? (*Angrily*) You're the one who's crazy. You know what I'd be without that medal? I'd be just another invisible Nigger, waiting on line and getting shit on just for being there! I *told* you about that, man! You just don't *listen*!

DOCTOR: That's one of the very things that's driving you crazy.

D.J.: What is?

DOCTOR: That once again, in Detroit, you have been singled out from all the others.

D.J.: What are you talking about?

DOCTOR (*Pursuing* D.J.): You know what I'm talking about! It's the same story as the tank, all over again. Why are all the others suffering, on the streets, and only you have been spared? But you haven't been spared, and you *are* suffering. . . .

D.J.: So what are *you* doing? You going around telling every dude who has the Congressional Medal of Honor to just throw it away? You just dropping out of the sky into every hospital and nuthouse in the country, scrambling up the brains of everybody who—

DOCTOR (*Pouncing*): You think, then, that everybody with the Medal of Honor must be in some kind of hospital?

D.J.: Did I say that?

DOCTOR: You did. You let it slip out. . . . In some deep way, you agree with me.

D.J.: That what?

DOCTOR: That the medal can make a man sick—drive him into a hospital.

D.J.: The whole thing makes a man sick! There's a lot of sick vets who didn't get no Medal of Honor! And they're mainlining and getting beat up in the streets and sucking on the gin bottle, and they didn't get no Bronze Star, no nothing except maybe a Purple Heart and a *"less than honorable discharge"*—bad paper, man, you can't get a job, you can't get benefits, you can't get nothing if you got bad paper. Now you tell me, what does my medal have to do with *that?*

A knock on the door—on the words "bad paper, man"—and the GUARD *immediately enters. Poker-faced,* HE *listens to the end of* D.J.*'s tirade.*

GUARD: Has the summation been concluded, sir?

D.J.: God *damn.*

DOCTOR: Will you please wait just a minute?

GUARD: You'll have to contact chief of section, sir, about that.

D.J.(*Heated*): Didn't you hear the man? Now, fuck off!

DOCTOR: D.J.—

GUARD: Look, Sergeant. To him you're an important case, but to me you're just another nut.

D.J. (*Makes a threatening move at the* GUARD): Just another nut. Okay. . .

The GUARD *prepares to subdue* D.J. *with his club, if necessary. In no time, a serious scuffle is ready to break out.*

DOCTOR (*Throwing himself between them*): Will both of you stop this! That's an order!

GUARD: Sorry about that, sir. (*Returns to parade rest; stares stonily ahead*)

D.J.: I'll bet you are.

The DOCTOR *looks from one to the other of these near-combatants.* D.J. *is still simmering, with his back to him.*

DOCTOR: D.J. Do you watch TV here?

D.J.: Some.

DOCTOR: The news?

D.J.: Not if I can help it.

DOCTOR: You didn't see it? The other night?

D.J.: What?

DOCTOR: The medals . . . (*Watching* D.J. *closely*) Vietnam vets. Heroes? In wheelchairs, some of them; on crutches? At the Capitol steps? Washington? Throwing their medals away? A kind of miracle-scene, like the old—

D.J. (*Breaking in*): And that's what you want me to do! Hop right on down there and toss it up—

DOCTOR: You saw it?

D.J.: *I didn't see nothing!*

DOCTOR: Some of those men . . . I happen to know some of those men. . . .

D.J.: You cured them?

DOCTOR: They're curing themselves. And they're a lot like you. (D.J. *watches, noncommittal*) . . . But they refuse to stay isolated. They meet, in therapy groups, which they started. Up in New York. "Rap sessions" . . . a new kind of unit, you might say. . . . Everybody tells his story. You see? They're people who have been through the same fires you have, who were *there*, whom you can trust. . . .

D.J. (*After a pause*): Doc, those dudes on TV are all white.

DOCTOR: You *have* been watching them.

D.J.: Yup, and I'm going to tell you something. You got your reasons for wanting to see no more war, right?—and no more warriors. I dig that, for your sake. But a lot of folks don't want the black veteran to throw down *his* weapons so soon. Know what I mean? Like, we are supposed to be preparing ourselves for another war, right back here. Vietnam was just our basic training, see? I'm telling this to both of you, y'see, so you won't be too surprised when it comes.

The GUARD *looks to the* DOCTOR *for instructions.*

DOCTOR (*To* D.J.): Why are you saying this right now?

D.J.: I want you to have something to think about, for the next session. Give us a good starting point. . . .

DOCTOR: Still poking fun at me?

D.J. (HE *waits a moment, then smiles and gives the* DOCTOR *a pat on the arm*): Don't you worry, Doc. I'll be seeing you. You just sit down now, and write your notes. In the folder.

D.J. *walks to the door, where the* GUARD *momentarily blocks him, in order to give a last, official salute to the* DOCTOR. *The* DOCTOR *gives a half-despairing wave as* D.J. *watches.* D.J. *turns to the door, stops, and gives the* GUARD *an imperious cue to open the knob and make way for him. The* GUARD *does so, grudgingly. It is a minor, private triumph for* D.J. THE TWO *exit. The* DOCTOR *reflects for a moment, at his desk. Then, showing his weariness,* HE *packs up his belongings, gives the room a last look, and prepares to leave. Light on stage is reduced until* HE *is alone in the light with darkness around him. The feeling must be of a change in time. The* DOCTOR *steps forward out of the confines of the room, to the edge of the apron, and addresses the audience.*

DOCTOR: When I drove down again from New York, two days later, Dale Jackson did not appear for his hour of therapy. He was in fact AWOL, back in Detroit. He intended to do something about his money troubles. His wife was in a hospital for minor surgery, and he had been unable to pay the deposit. There were numerous protectors he might have gone to in the city for help—people who would not have allowed a Medal of Honor winner to sink into scandalous debt. But he went to none of them, this time. His wife was disturbed about the bill. This was on the evening of April 30. He promised her that he would come back to the hospital that night with a check, and also with her hair curlers and bathrobe. As he was leaving, he said, "Ain't you going to give me a kiss goodbye?" And he put his thumb in his mouth like a little boy, which made her laugh. He asked some friends to drive him to a place where he claimed he could get some money, and asked them to park—in a white section of town. He walked down the block, entered a grocery store and told the manager he was holding it up. He took out a pistol, but never fired a shot while the manager emptied his own gun, at point-blank range, into D.J.'s body. Death came, a few hours later, in Detroit General Hospital, of five gunshot wounds. His body went on a last unexpected jet airplane ride to Arlington National Cemetery, where he was given a hero's burial with an eight-man Army Honor Guard. I wrote to his mother about him, about what a remarkable human being even I could see he was, in only sixty minutes with him. She wrote back: "Sometimes I wonder if Dale tired of this life and needed someone else to pull the trigger." In her living room she keeps a large color photograph of him, in uniform, with the Congressional Medal of Honor around his neck.

Lights slow-fade down to darkness, as the DOCTOR *walks off. Blackout; and then lights up as the* DOCTOR, DALE JACKSON *and the* GUARD *converge, stand side-by-side, and bow to the audience.*

END OF PLAY

MOONCHILDREN

Michael Weller

About Michael Weller

Born in New York in 1942, Michael Weller studied music composition at Brandeis before taking his graduate degree in theatre at the University of Manchester in England. He taught, acted, wrote and directed in England, Italy and Germany for a number of years before returning to the States. *Moonchildren* is the first play of what may be thought of as a Weller trilogy about growing up in America; the middle play, *Fishing*, was premiered by the New York Shakespeare Festival in 1975 and revived by New York's Second Stage in 1981. *Loose Ends*, the third play, opened at Arena Stage in Washington, D.C. and then moved to New York's Circle in the Square in 1979. Originally a one-act, *Split* evolved into *At Home (Split, Part 1)* and *Abroad (Split, Part 2)*, and was so presented by Second Stage in 1980. Weller's most recent play, *The Ballad of Soapy Smith*, was originally produced by Seattle Repertory Theatre before playing at New York's Public Theatre in 1984. Weller is the author of the screenplays for two Milos Forman films, *Hair* and *Ragtime*.

Production History

Moonchildren premiered under the title *Cancer* at the Royal Court Theatre in London in September 1970, in a production co-directed by Roger Hendricks Simon and Peter Gill. The American premiere took place at Arena Stage in November 1970, under the direction of Alan Schneider. Schneider's production opened on Broadway in February 1972.

Characters

MIKE
COOTIE
NORMAN
RUTH
DICK
KATHY
BOB
RALPH
WILLIS

LUCKY
SHELLY
BREAM
EFFING
MURRAY
COOTIE'S FATHER
MILKMAN

Time

1965-66.

Place

A student apartment in an American university town.

The Play

Moonchildren

Scene 1

The stage is dark. You can't see anything.

MIKE: I heard something. She definitely made a noise.

RUTH: Shut up.

MIKE: I'm telling you, I know the noise they make. That was it.

RUTH: For crissakes, be quiet. You keep talking and she'll know we're here.

COOTIE: I was just thinking. I read somewhere about how they can see in the dark.

RUTH: I never read that.

COOTIE: No shit, I read they got these hundreds of thousands of millions of tiny, submicroscopic, photosensitive cells in each eyeball, so when it gets dark they can just turn on these cells and see like it was daytime.

MIKE: He's right, Ruth. Hey, Cootie, you're right. I remember reading that in a back issue of the *Vertebrate Review*.

COOTIE: That's it, that's the one. Special eyeball issue.

MIKE: Yeah, yeah. July.

RUTH: You guys must be pretty stupid if you believe that. What do you think they have whiskers for? The whole point of whiskers in the first place is so you can get around in the dark. That's why they stick out so far, so you don't bump into things. Chairs and refrigerators and that.

MIKE: Hey, shhhh. I think she's starting.

154

RUTH: Well, you're the one that got me going about whiskers in the first place, so don't tell me shhhh.

MIKE: O.K., O.K., I'm sorry, O.K.?

RUTH: So shut up if she's starting.

COOTIE (*Pause*): How many kittens can they have at any one session?

MIKE: There's a recorded case of thirty-eight.

RUTH: Shhhh, for chrissakes.

COOTIE: What I want to know is how are we gonna see her when she starts giving birth?

RUTH: Jesus, how stupid can you get? We'll turn on the light.

COOTIE: Yeah, but the whole thing is how do we know when to turn on the light? Like, what if we're too early?

MIKE: Or too late?

COOTIE: Yeah, what if we're too late?

MIKE: Or right in the middle . . .

COOTIE: Holy shit, yeah, what if we flip on the old lights when she's halfway through a severe uterine contraction? She'll go apeshit and clamp up and kill the kitten. And if the kitty gets really lucky and wriggles free, it'll grow up into a pretty fucked-up animal.

MIKE: We're sowing the seeds of a neurotic adult cathood . . .

COOTIE: . . . doo-wah, doo-wah . . .

RUTH: Hey, shut up, you guys, willya? Willya shut up?

COOTIE: We're just pointing out that's a shitty way to start life.

RUTH: I know the noise, all right?

MIKE: I think there's probably a more scientific way to watch a cat give birth.

RUTH: Everybody shut the fuck up.

A long pause.

NORMAN: How much longer are you guys gonna have the lights out?

COOTIE: Jesus Christ, Norman, why do you have to go creeping up like that? We forgot you were even in here.

NORMAN: I'm not creeping up. I'm just sitting here. Maybe you didn't notice when you came in, but I was reading this book. I mean, I thought you were only gonna have the lights out for maybe a few minutes or something, but you've already been in here for about an hour and . . . I really can't read very well with the lights off. I mean . . . you know . . .

COOTIE: Norman, you can't rush a cat when it's giving birth. You try to rush a cat in those circumstances and you come smack up against nature.

MIKE: Norman . . .

NORMAN: What?

MIKE: Don't fight nature, Norman.

NORMAN: I'm not. I'm just trying to read this book.

COOTIE (*Pause*): Is it a good book?

RUTH: For chrissakes, what's the matter with everyone?

NORMAN: I don't know. It's a pretty good book. I don't follow all of it. It's written in a funny kind of way, so you forget a lot of it right after you've read it. A lot of guys in the mathematics department say it's pretty good. I don't know though.

RUTH: Hey, Norman, can't you go to your room if you want to read?

NORMAN: I don't want to.

MIKE: Why not, Norman?

COOTIE: Yeah, why do you want to creep around in here being all spooky and everything when you could just go to your room and read, huh?

NORMAN: I don't know.

COOTIE: We may be in here for hours and hours, Norman. Maybe even all night. The whole operation from initial labor to the biting off of the umbilical cord could very easily take an entire night. (*Pause*) Norman?

NORMAN: All night, huh?

COOTIE: You never know.

RUTH: Brother, you try to get a few guys to shut up for a little while . . .

MIKE (*Loud*): C'mon, c'mon, hey, everybody, let's have a little quiet around here. I don't want to see anyone panic and lose their heads and start running in all different directions knocking down passersby and trampling on innocent women and children.

RUTH: I swear to Christ, Mike, if you don't shut up I'll kill you.

MIKE: O.K.

> *At this point, the hall door opens and the kitchen is lit up a little.* DICK *is standing in the doorway trying to see into the dark, where* NORMAN *is sitting at a round kitchen table with a book by him, and* RUTH, MIKE *and* COOTIE *are crouched around a cardboard carton with a hole in it.* NORMAN *grabs up his book to take advantage of the crack of light.* DICK *just stands there.* RUTH *and* COOTIE *speak on top of each other.*

RUTH: Hey, c'mon, shut the door, Dick.

COOTIE: Shut the fucking door.

MIKE (*After a pause*): We'd really like you to shut the door, Richard.

> DICK *shuts the door and everything goes black. A moment later it all lights up again because* DICK *has just opened the icebox and it's the kind that has an automatic light inside. So now we see* DICK *squatting in front of the icebox while the* OTHERS *watch him, except for* NORMAN, *who's really trying like mad to read. You can see the kitchen pretty clearly now. The icebox is very old, dating from the time when electricity was replacing the iceman. It's just a box on legs with one of those barrel-shaped coolers with vents on top. You maybe can't see it yet, but on the door of the icebox there's a large inscription that reads "GOD IS COOL." Stacked neatly against one wall are 816 empty two-*

quart milk bottles, layer upon layer with planks between each level. It's a deliberate construction. There's a huge copper stack heater in one corner by the sink, and it has a safety valve at the top with a copper tube coming out of it and snaking into the sink. The floor is vinyl, in imitation cork, alternating light and dark, but the conspicuous thing about this floor is that it's only half-finished. Where the cork tiles end there is a border of black tar, by now hard, and then wooden floor in broad plank. Around the kitchen table are six chairs, all from different sets. Various posters on the wall, but none as conspicuous as a map of Europe near where the telephone hangs. The sink is full of dirty dishes. There is a pad hanging by the icebox, and a pencil. Everyone uses the kitchen in a special way. So DICK is squatting in front of the open icebox.

RUTH: That's very cute, Richard.

MIKE: C'mon, shut the fucking icebox. We were in here first.

NORMAN: I was reading when you guys came in.

> DICK *turns to them, looks, then turns back to the icebox.*

COOTIE: Dick, in my humble opinion you're a miserable cunt and a party pooper.

DICK (*Standing*): All right, now listen. This afternoon I went down to the Star Supermarket and got myself four dozen frozen hamburgers. Now that's forty-eight hamburgers, and I only had two of them for dinner tonight.

RUTH: And you never washed up.

MIKE: Hey, Dick, are those Star hamburgers any good?

DICK: Listen, I should have forty-six hamburgers, and when I counted just now there was only forty-three. Three hamburgers in one night. And for your information I've been keeping track of my hamburgers since the beginning of the semester. There's almost fifty hamburgers I can't account for.

COOTIE: Jesus, Dick, you should have said something before this.

MIKE: Yeah, Dick, you had all them hamburger thefts on your mind, you should have let it out. It's no good keeping quiet about something like that.

DICK: Look, I'm not about to make a stink about a couple of hamburgers here and there, but, Jesus Christ, almost sixty of them. I'm putting it down on common stock and we're gonna all pay for it. (HE *turns on the light*)

RUTH: Dick, willya turn out the light, please?

DICK: I'm sorry, but I've lost too many hamburgers. I'm putting down for four dozen. (HE *goes to the pad on the wall and makes an entry*)

RUTH: Now willya turn the light out?

DICK (*Examining list*): Shit, who put peanut butter down on common stock?

MIKE: I did. I got a jar of chunky last Thursday and when I opened it on Saturday somebody'd already been in there. I didn't eat all that chunky myself.

DICK: Well, I never had your peanut butter. I'm not paying for it.

MIKE: Well, I never had any of your goddamn sixty hamburgers either.

COOTIE: I think I may have had some of that chunky peanut butter. Could you describe your jar of chunky in detail?

MIKE: Elegant little glass jar, beige interior . . .

KATHY *enters through the front door, as opposed to the hall door. The hall door leads to everyone's rooms.*

KATHY: Oh, boy, look out for Bob. (SHE *starts across the kitchen to the hall door.* SHE *carries lots of books in a green canvas waterproof book bag slung over her shoulder*)

RUTH: What's wrong with Bob?

KATHY: He's in a really shitty mood. I've seen the guy act weird before. This is, I don't know, pretty bad, I guess.

MIKE: Where is he?

COOTIE: Yeah, where's Bob?

MIKE: Good old Bob.

COOTIE: Where's good old Bob?

KATHY: And fuck you too. I'm serious.

NORMAN (*Looking up from his book*): Boy, I really can't absorb very much with everyone talking.

KATHY: We were just sitting there, you know, in Hum 105, and that prick Johnson started in about the old cosmic equation again.

NORMAN: What's the cosmic equation?

RUTH: So why'd that upset Bob?

KATHY: I don't know. That's the thing . . .

DICK: I bet Bob's responsible for some of my hamburgers. I notice you and him never go shopping for dinner.

KATHY: It's really weird the way he sort of . . . well, like today, you know . . . I'm not kidding, he might be cracking up or something.

BOB *enters through the front door, carrying his books.* HE *looks all right.* EVERYONE *stares at him.*

RUTH: Hi, Bob.

MIKE: Hi, Bob.

COOTIE: Hi, Bob.

NORMAN: Hello, Bob.

BOB (*Pause*): Hi, Mike, hi, Ruth, hi, Cootie; hello, Norman. (*Pause*) Hi, Dick.

DICK: Listen, do you know anything about . . . ?

BOB: No, I haven't touched your fucking hamburgers.

DICK: Well, someone has.

MIKE: How you been, good old Bob?

COOTIE: How's the old liver and the old pancreas and the old pituitary and the . . .

BOB: Is there any mail?

COOTIE: There's this really big package from Beirut. It took four guys to get it up the stairs.

MIKE: We think it's a harp.

RUTH: There's a letter in your room.

BOB *looks at them quizzically, then goes down the hall.* KATHY *follows him.*

RUTH: I think Kathy's right. There's definitely something wrong with Bob.

DICK: Yeah, he's out of his fucking mind, that's what's wrong with him.

RUTH: You can talk.

MIKE: Hey, c'mon, c'mon, let's have a little order around here . . .

RUTH: Stop fucking around. You heard what Kathy said. Something's troubling Bob.

MIKE: So what?

COOTIE: Yeah, fuck Bob.

MIKE: Fuck good old Bob.

NORMAN: Maybe he's worried about the future. (ALL *look at him*) I mean, you know, maybe he's worried about it. I mean, I don't know him all that well. Just, you know, maybe he's worried about what he's gonna do when, you know, after he graduates and everything.

DICK: He ought to be worried.

MIKE: You bet your ass he oughta be. Same goes for all of you guys. You oughta be worried, Dick. Cootie, you oughta be worried. I oughta be worried. I am. I'm fucking petrified. You watch what happens at the graduation ceremony. There's gonna be this line of green military buses two miles long parked on the road outside and they're gonna pick us up and take us to Vietnam and we'll be walking around one day in the depths of the rain forest looking out for wily enemy snipers and carnivorous insects and tropical snakes that can eat a whole moose in one gulp and earthworms sixteen feet long and then one day when we least expect it this wily sniper'll leap out from behind a blade of grass and powie. Right in the head. I'm worried.

DICK: Anyone that can spell can get out of Vietnam.

NORMAN: I'm in graduate school. They can't get me.

DICK: Norman, you couldn't buy your way into the army.

NORMAN: I wouldn't go.

MIKE: Why wouldn't you go, Norman?

NORMAN: Huh?

COOTIE: Yeah, think of the army. What about them? They need good mathematics graduate students out there in the marshes of Quac Thop Chew Hoy Ben Van Pho Quay Gup Trin.

NORMAN: I don't agree with the war.

MIKE: Well, for God sakes, then, let's stop it.

NORMAN: I had my medical and everything. I passed. I could've pretended I was insane or something.

DICK: Pretended?

RUTH: Hey, doesn't anyone here give a shit about Bob?

MIKE: Hey, c'mon, everyone that gives a shit raise your hand. (COOTIE, MIKE, DICK *and* NORMAN *raise their hands*) See, we all give a shit. So what should we do?

RUTH: Well, I don't know. Maybe we ought to try and find out what's troubling him.

DICK: Maybe he doesn't want us to know. Just maybe.

COOTIE: Yeah, what if he's teetering on the brink of a complete schizophrenic withdrawal and the only thing keeping him sane is knowing we don't know what's troubling him.

MIKE: It's our duty as classmates and favorite turds to leave him alone.

RUTH: Maybe something's wrong between him and Kathy.

DICK: Like what?

RUTH: I don't know. That's what I'm asking.

DICK: He doesn't give a shit about her. Not really. She's just a good lay, that's all.

RUTH: How would you know, Dick?

NORMAN: I thought they were in love.

DICK: Jesus, Norman, where the hell is your head at?

NORMAN: Huh?

MIKE: Define the problem, then solve it.

COOTIE: Yeah, what's troubling good old Bob?

MIKE: I think we oughta all go to bed tonight with notebooks under our pillows, and when we get a well-focused and comprehensive idea about the central dilemma of Bob's existence we oughta write it down in clear, concise sentences, with particular attention to grammar and punctuation.

COOTIE: Yeah, then we can meet in here tomorrow and pool our insights.

MIKE: That's a really great plan.

RUTH: I'd really like to know what's troubling him.

DICK: I'd really like to know who the fuck is eating my hamburgers.

NORMAN: Why don't you talk to him?

RUTH: What?

NORMAN: I mean, you know—Bob. If you want to find out what's troubling him, probably the best thing to do is talk to him and say, What's troubling you, or something like that, and then if he wants to tell you he can and if he doesn't feel like talking about it . . . then . . . well, you know . . . .

RUTH: Yeah, maybe I'll do that.

NORMAN (*Pause*): Yeah, that's what I'd do if I wanted to know. I mean, I'm not saying I wouldn't like to know what's troubling him. I'd really like to know if you find out, but I . . .

MIKE *has been kneeling by the cat box and peering into it.*

MIKE: Jesus Christ. Jesus H. fucking Christ.

NORMAN: What's wrong?

MIKE: She wasn't even in there.

COOTIE: What! All that time we were looking at an empty box and she wasn't even in there?

MIKE: She must've slipped out while we had our backs turned.

COOTIE: Sneaky little beastie.

MIKE: Cootie, you don't understand. She might be out there in the road right now.

COOTIE: Right now.

MIKE: With all the traffic.

COOTIE: Oh, Christ, and all those architects driving home drunk from seeing their mistresses . . .

MIKE: And trying to figure out what to tell the little woman. I mean, she's been waiting up all night in a chartreuse quilted sleeping gown with curlers in her hair . . .

COOTIE: Worrying about the kiddies. Three boys, twenty-seven girls. They all got appendicitis . . .

MIKE: Simultaneously. And when she called the kindly family doctor he was away in Cuba . . .

COOTIE: Doing research for his forthcoming book . . .

MIKE: "Chapter Eight: Peritonitis and Social Democracy."

COOTIE: Jesus, I hope we're not too late. (HE *and* MIKE *rush off down the hall*)

DICK: Hey, Norman, are these your bananas?

NORMAN: You can have one. I don't mind.

> DICK *takes one and puts the others back in the icebox.* COOTIE *sticks his head in around the hall door.*

COOTIE: You coming, Ruth?

RUTH: No.

COOTIE: Your heart is full of bitterness and hate, Ruth. (*His head disappears again*)

DICK: You done the essay for Phil 720?

RUTH: No.

DICK: It's due tomorrow.

RUTH: Yeah?

DICK: Yeah.

NORMAN: Is that a good course, Philosophy 720?

RUTH: Nope. Professor Quinn is an albino dwarf queer with halitosis and he smokes too much.

DICK: He does not.

RUTH: Three packs of Pall Mall a day is too much. He's gonna die of cancer.

DICK: He's a genius.

RUTH: You have a thing about queers.

DICK: Fuck off, Ruth.

RUTH: You started it.

> RUTH *goes into hall.* DICK *stands and eats his banana, chewing slowly.* NORMAN *tries to read but* DICK's *presence distracts him.*

DICK: How come you're reading that book?

NORMAN: I don't know. It's supposed to be pretty good.

DICK: What are you gonna do when you finish it?

NORMAN (*Thinks*): I'll start another one.

DICK: Yeah, but what happens when you forget this one. I mean, it'll be as if you hadn't even read it, so what's the point?

NORMAN: Oh, I don't know. I happen to believe you learn things even when you don't know it. Like, if you're reading something right now . . . I mean, I am reading something right now and maybe I'll forget it in a while . . . I mean, I'm forgetting a lot of it already, but I happen to believe I'm being altered in lots of ways I may not be aware of because of . . . well, you know, books and experiences. (*Pause*) Life.

DICK: That's what you believe, huh?

NORMAN: Um, yes, I believe that.

> MIKE *and* COOTIE *enter, wearing heavy winter parkas and boots.* THEY *look like trappers.*

COOTIE: Boy, if we're too late I hate to think of all the dead cats we'll have on our conscience.

MIKE: You gonna help, Dick?

DICK: Fuck off.

MIKE: How about you, Norman, aren't you gonna do your bit for the world of cats?

NORMAN: I'm just in the middle of this chapter. (MIKE *and* COOTIE *shake their heads in disapproval and rush out.* NORMAN *tries to read again as* DICK *eats the banana, watching him*) Hey, it's really hard to read, you know, when someone's watching you and everything.

DICK: Don't you ever get the feeling you're really irrelevant?

NORMAN: I don't think so.

DICK (*In one breath*): I mean, you go into the mathematics department every day and sit there looking out the window and thinking about cars and women and every now and then a couple of numbers come into your head and there's all these Chinese guys running around solving all the problems worth solving while you sit there wondering what the hell you're doing.

NORMAN: No, it's not like that. Well, you know, it's not that simple. I mean . . . (*Pause*) I guess it's a lot like that. Are you doing anything relevant?

DICK: You can't get more relevant than Far Eastern studies. Ask me anything about the Far East and I'll tell you the answer. That's where everything's happening. China, Vietnam, Japan, Korea. You name it.

NORMAN: I guess I ought to know more about those things. I don't know, I keep thinking there's a lot of things I should know about.

DICK: The thing is, Norman, the way I see it, you're already deeply committed to the system. You take away black ghettos, stop the war in Vietnam, distribute the wealth equally throughout the country, and you wouldn't be in graduate school.

NORMAN: How come?

DICK: You see, you don't know anything about what makes it all work, do you? (HE *throws the banana peel into the cat box*)

NORMAN: Hey, you shouldn't throw that in there.

DICK: Why not?

NORMAN: Well, I mean, that's the box for the cat. Maybe she won't want to have kittens on a banana peel.

DICK: Norman, how long have you been living here?

NORMAN: Well, you know, about three months. A little longer maybe. About three months and two weeks altogether.

DICK: Have you ever seen a cat around here?

NORMAN: Well, I don't know. I'm out a lot of the time.

DICK: Norman, there is no fucking cat. We haven't got a cat. Boy, for a graduate student you got a lot to learn. (HE *starts out but turns to look* NORMAN *over a last time*) Jesus.

Then DICK'*s gone down the hall.* NORMAN *kneels by the cat box and examines it as some muffled piano chords fill the silence. It's* BOB *playing a lazy, rich, drifting progression, moody-Bill-Evans-style.* KATHY *walks through the kitchen in a man's robe carrying a towel.* SHE *lights the stack heater. From inside the hall we hear* DICK'*s voice yelling.*

DICK (*Offstage*): STOP PLAYING THAT FUCKING NOISE. I'M TRYING TO READ. HEY, BOB.

KATHY (*Goes to the hall door and yells down*): Mind your own goddamn business, Richard. (*A door slams, and the music, which had stopped momentarily, starts again, but louder.* SHE *turns*) Hey, listen, Norman. If you're gonna be in here for a while could you do me a favor and make sure no one turns off the water heater, 'cause I'm just taking a shower. And if you get a chance, could you put on some coffee, 'cause I'll be coming out in about ten minutes and I'd like a cup when I come out. O.K.?

NORMAN: Do you have any books on Vietnam?

KATHY (*Pause*): Yeah. A few.

NORMAN: Are they good books?

KATHY: Well, you know, some are, some aren't. Why?

NORMAN: I just, you know, wondered, that's all. (KATHY *watches* NORMAN *go to the stove and fumble around with the coffee percolator.* SHE *shrugs and goes out. We hear the bathroom door close and, moments later, the sound of a shower running*) Actually, I've been thinking I'd like to read some books about Vietnam. I mean it's been going on all this time. I don't know, though. I've never read any books about it. Maybe if I could read one book, then I'd know a little more about it and I could decide if I wanted to read another. Would it be O.K. if I borrowed one of your books to start with? I'd give it back as soon as I finished it. (HE *looks around and sees* HE's *alone.* HE *goes out the door. We hear the bathroom door opening and a yell*)

KATHY (*Offstage*): Goddammit, Norman, what are you doing in here?

NORMAN (*Offstage*): I was wondering if you'd lend me . . .

KATHY (*Offstage*): Hey, get the hell out of here, I'm taking a shower.

A door slams.

NORMAN (*Offstage*): I just wanted to know if it was O.K. for me to borrow one of those books about Vietnam.

KATHY (*Offstage*): Well, Jesus Christ, can't you wait till I'm done?

NORMAN (*Offstage*): Oh . . . yeah, I'm sorry. (*Pause*) Is that all right with you?

KATHY (*Offstage*): Hey, don't stand around out there. You can borrow as many goddamn books as you want, only get away from the door, 'cause it just so happens I don't like a lot of people standing around outside the bathroom door while I'm washing.

NORMAN *comes back into the kitchen.* HE *fixes a little more of the coffee, then goes to the hall door and yells down the hallway.*

NORMAN: I'll just make the coffee first, and when you're finished in there I'll come down to your room with you and get the book. Hey, listen, if you decide to have your coffee in here, could you go down to your room first and bring the book in with you? Yes, that's probably better. Hey, is that O.K.? (*Pause*) Hey, is that O.K.?

No answer. NORMAN *is left baffled, as the lights dim and* BOB's *piano chords keep going and going.*

Scene 2

It's a few days later. NORMAN *is reading.* RUTH *is making sandwiches, and* COOTIE *and* MIKE *are rolling up a banner.*

COOTIE: I don't know about the wording.

MIKE: I think it's pretty good wording.

COOTIE: I'm not too happy about it.

MIKE: You're unhappy about the wording.

COOTIE: Well, I'm not, you know, cut up about it or anything, but I'm definitely not as happy as I could be about it.

MIKE: Ruthie, we need an impartial third voice over here.

RUTH: Who wants orange marmalade?

MIKE: I'd like an orange marmalade.

COOTIE: I want two orange marmalade and one chunky peanut butter, please.

RUTH: How 'bout you, Norman?

COOTIE: And I wouldn't mind a chunky peanut butter and orange marmalade mixed.

RUTH: Hey, Norman, do you want sandwiches or not?

COOTIE: You gotta have sandwiches handy if you're coming, Norman. On your average march you'll find you get through a good two peanut butter and jellies before you even get to where you're supposed to demonstrate, and then after circling round and yelling militant slogans at the monument or park or poison gas plant or nuclear missile establishment for a couple hours, you're just about ready for another peanut butter and jelly.

MIKE: Or cream cheese and olives.

COOTIE: Bacon, lettuce, and tomato. I mean, I know you meet a lotta pretty groovy people at these marches, but you can't count on them having extra sandwiches for a new acquaintance.

RUTH: Hey, Norman, willya please tell me if you're coming with us or not?

NORMAN (*Unfriendly*): I'm going with Dick.

COOTIE: You're lucky there. You'll get hamburger on toasted roll if you go with Dick. He takes sterno and cooks right out there in the middle of lines of charging cops and tear gas and mace and everything.

DICK *enters*.

MIKE: Hey, Dick, you better hurry up and get dressed for the march.

COOTIE: Yeah, Dick, you don't want to be late or all the best ass'll be grabbed up.

DICK (*Indicating banner*): What's it say?

COOTIE: "Buy Government Bonds."

RUTH: You want some of our peanut butter and marmalade?

MIKE: What's this about giving away all our peanut butter and marmalade all of a sudden? He wouldn't give us any of his lousy hamburgers. We had to pay for those hamburgers on common stock.

DICK: Where's Kathy and Bob?

MIKE: Yeah, where's good old Bob? (*Yells*) HEY, YOU GUYS, ARE YOU COMING?

KATHY (*Offstage*): Yeah, hold on a minute, willya?

MIKE: They're coming.

COOTIE: Hey, Norman, I been watching you pretty closely for the last few days and I have this definite impression you've been displaying hostility toward me, Mike, and Ruth, in that order.

NORMAN: I'm just reading this book . . .

COOTIE: Don't be negative, Norman. You're trying to pretend I hadn't noticed your emotions. You happen to be up against a disciple of Freud, Jung, Adler, Pavlov, Skinner, and the honorable L. Ron Hubbard, to mention but a few. It just so happens I can detect subatomic trace particles of hostility within a six-mile radius of anywhere I am.

MIKE: It's no use contradicting him, Norman. If he says he can feel hostility, that's it. I mean, even I can feel it and I'm only moderately sensitive to · hostility up to about a hundred eighty yards.

NORMAN: I'm not feeling hostile . . .

COOTIE: You're not only feeling it, you're dying to tell us about it. That's a basic axiom of hostility.

NORMAN: Oh, boy, you guys.

DICK: Leave him alone.

COOTIE: Dick, that's the worst thing you can do. I know you think you're being a good shit and everything, but if the guy is riddled with hostility and he doesn't get it out of his system, it's gonna go haywire and zing all around inside his body till he's twenty-eight years old and then he'll get cancer.

RUTH: You know, we're gonna be really late if those guys don't hurry up . . .

MIKE: That reminds me of a guy I was reading about. He got so pent up with hostility his head fell right down inside his body, no shit, that's what I was reading, right down between his shoulders.

COOTIE: Fell?

MIKE: Yeah, straight down till all you could see was these two little eyeballs peeping out over his collarbone.

COOTIE: Mike.

MIKE: What, Mel?

COOTIE (*Pause*): Fell?

MIKE (*Pause*): Sank?

COOTIE: Subsided.

MIKE: Right.

COOTIE: In fact, as I remember it, his head eventually disappeared completely.

MIKE: Don't rush me, I'm coming to that. Now, Norman, I want you to pay very close attention because this case is a lesson in itself. You see, everybody used to warn this particular guy to loosen up and maybe see an analyst, but the guy refused on the grounds that it would cost too much, and that turned out to be really stupid economy, because with his head inside him like that he couldn't see anything and he had to hire a guy, full time, seven days a week, to lead him around. The guy was so tight with his money he tried to solve the problem by rigging up this ingenious system of mirrors, like a periscope, but the natural movements of his body kept knocking the mirrors out of alignment, so in addition to the guy that led him around, he had to hire another guy, full time, seven days a week, to keep readjusting the mirrors. You can imagine the expense involved.

COOTIE: There was a very fine article about that guy in the *Hostility Journal*, spring number. Did you happen to catch that article, Norman?

MIKE: Did it tell about what happened to him?

COOTIE: Well, it was one of those stories in two parts, and wouldn't you know it, that's just when my subscription ran out.

MIKE: Oh, well, you missed the best part. You see, when his head got down as . . . *subsided* as far as his stomach . . .

COOTIE: . . . thank you . . .

MIKE: . . . he went and hired a topnotch transplant surgeon to replace his belly button with a flexible, clear plastic window so he could see where he was going.

COOTIE: Jumpin' Jehoshaphat!

MIKE: And I'm happy to announce, the operation was a complete success.

COOTIE: Fantastic! No problems with rejection or anything?

MIKE: Nope. The Dow Chemical Company set up a ten-man, two-woman research team and they developed a type of clear plastic window that matched the guy's antibodies perfectly. In a matter of weeks, the guy was able to live a completely normal life again, skin diving, stamp collecting, a lot of political work. He could even go to the movies when he felt like it, but he had to sit up on the back of the seat and it caused a lot of hard feelings with the people sitting directly behind him. But that's the great thing about the average moviegoing audience; they respected his infirmity.

COOTIE: Fuck a duck!

MIKE: Shut up, sonny boy, I ain't finished yet.

COOTIE: There's more?

MIKE: Yeah, you see, the really incredible thing was when the guy woke up one morning and realized his head was still sinking . . .

COOTIE: . . . subsiding . . .

MIKE: . . . and he went to this doctor to check it out. He was just walking along, you know, and when he got to this corner to stop for a red light a dog peed on his leg, and when he bent forward to see what was making his pants wet a guy up on some scaffolding right behind dropped a pipe wrench on his back, and the impact of this wrench, plus the slightly inclined position of the guy's upper body, knocked his head back into place.

COOTIE: Hot diggity!

MIKE: Well, the guy went apeshit, jumping all over the place, singing songs right out there on the streets . . . and that's just when it all had to happen. This poor guy, after all his suffering, was finally looking forward to a happy and produtive life . . .

COOTIE: Oh, shit, yeah, I remember now. The poor son of a bitch.

MIKE: Yeah, you 'member, he was just standing out there in the street stopping traffic in both directions, tears of humble gratitude streaming down his cheeks and some stupid . . . (HE *sees* KATHY *and* BOB *standing in the hallway door ready for the march*) . . . oh, hi, Bob, hi, Kathy.

RUTH: Hey, do you guys want some of our peanut butter and marmalade?

BOB: I've got an announcement.

COOTIE: We used to have a nearsighted canary . . .

RUTH: Listen, I gotta make these sandwiches and we're gonna end up short if I don't get some cooperation around here.

COOTIE: Hey, Norman hasn't even got a banner. Norman, aren't you gonna bring a banner?

BOB: Mel, willya please shut up? I'm trying to tell you guys something.

COOTIE: Well, fuck you, I'm talking to Norman. You want him to get all the way down to the demonstration and they disqualify him 'cause he doesn't have a banner.

RUTH: Everyone is gonna fucking well eat whatever I make.

DICK: You want some help?

RUTH: Look, it's not like I don't know how to make sandwiches . . .

MIKE: Hey, everyone, c'mon, c'mon, let's have a little order around here. Everybody stay where you are and don't panic. O.K., Bob, I think we got everything under control now.

BOB: Thank you.

MIKE: That's O.K., Bob.

BOB: I've just got this . . .

MIKE: Bob?

BOB: What?

MIKE: Anytime.

BOB: What?

MIKE: Anytime you want a little peace and quiet so you can make an announcement without a lot of people talking over you, just ask me and I'll do what I can for you.

BOB: Thank you, Mike.

MIKE: That's O.K., Bob, you're a good shit.

BOB (*Hesitates, trying to find words to frame his vague thoughts. When* HE *speaks, it is halting*): Look . . . I just thought maybe it was about time somebody around here . . .

MIKE: Do you want some water or anything?

RUTH: Oh, for chrissake, shut up, Mike.

COOTIE (*Cooling things*): Yeah, shut yer mouth, sonny boy, yer creatin' a public nuisance.'

RUTH: Go on, Bob.

BOB: No, no, look, all I want to say is . . . Norman, if there is one way to remain irrelevant and ineffective it's to sit with your nose buried in a book while life is raging all around you. (NORMAN *looks up and closes his book*) Thank you. O.K. Announcement . . . (HE *walks around the room, again trying to think of how to put it. As* HE *starts to speak* . . .)

MIKE: Earthquakes in Singapore . . . ?

RUTH (*Incredible rage*): SHUT UP!

BOB: Never mind.

MIKE: Sorry. I'm sorry.

KATHY: What's wrong, Bob?

BOB: Really, nothing, nothing at all. I just had this stupid thought the other day in humanities. Johnson was saying something idiotic, as usual, and I just started to watch him carefully for the first time talking to us, you know, thirty kids who think he's a prick, and I realized that he probably thinks all of us are pricks . . . and I just started to wonder what we're all doing. You know what I mean? What the fuck are we all doing, seriously, tell me, I'd really like to know . . . in twenty-five words or less . . . . No, no, sorry, come on, carnival time. Let's go marching.

KATHY: I found the letter, Bob.

BOB: What letter? (KATHY *takes an official letter out of her bag*) Kathy, where did you get that? Come on, give it here.

KATHY: We're supposed to be like all together in here. If you can't say it yourself, I'll say it for you.

BOB *is momentarily confused, then realizes that* KATHY *thinks* HE *was trying to tell everyone about the letter.* HE *finds the situation absurd, annoying and funny.*

BOB: Kathy, that letter has nothing to do with anything and it's none of your business and would you please give it back?

KATHY *hands the letter to* RUTH. RUTH *reads.*

RUTH: Oh fuck.

RUTH *hands the letter on.* EACH *reads in turn. It ends in* MIKE's *hands.* BOB *waits impatiently as the letter makes its round.* HE's *embarrassed and then begins to find it funny that* EVERYONE, *especially* KATHY, *has construed the letter as his problem.* MIKE *is by now looking quite seriously at him.*

BOB (*Laughing it off*): It's just for the physical. I mean, I'm not dead yet.

As BOB *says this, something amusing passes through his mind and* HE *stops talking.* MIKE *is looking at the letter again. The* OTHERS *watch* BOB.

MIKE: They misspelled your name?

BOB (*Comes out of his brief daydream*): Huh?

MIKE: Jobert.

BOB (*Amused*): Oh, yeah.

MIKE: Jobert Rettie. Dear Jobert Rettie. Hi, Jobert.

BOB: Hi, Jike.

MIKE: Good old Jobert.

COOTIE: How ya feelin', good old Jobert?

BOB: Dead, how 'bout you?

MIKE (*Sees what's happening and comes to the rescue. Pause*): Hi, Jel.

COOTIE: Hi, Jike.

MIKE: Hi, Jorman.

NORMAN: Huh?

MIKE: Hi, Jorman.

NORMAN: Oh, hi.

MIKE: Hi, Jathy, hi Jick.

DICK: Fuck off.

MIKE: Juck off? Why should I juck off, Jick?

> *The doorbell rings.* COOTIE *rushes over and answers it. At the door, a young man* [RALPH] *in a suit and tie and horn-rimmed glasses, with an attaché case, which* HE *has concealed just out of sight behind the doorframe.*

COOTIE: Hi, Jister.

MIKE: Ask him his name, Jel.

COOTIE: What's your name?

RALPH: Ralph.

COOTIE: Hi, Jalph, I'm Jel and that's Jathy, Jorman, Jike, Jick, and Job, and we're just on our way down to City Hall to beat the shit out of some cops. Wanna come?

RALPH (*Pauses momentarily, then launches his pitch*): I'm from the University of Buffalo and I'm in the neighborhood doing market research. You don't mind my asking you a few questions, do you? (*As* HE *says this last,* HE *reaches down, takes up his concealed attaché case, bends his head like making ready for a dive, and advances swiftly but deliberately into the middle of the room. This swift movement, plus the running patter, is designed to force the average housewife to back away and give ground, but since* COOTIE *merely steps aside when* RALPH *bends down for his attaché case, we are treated to the entire technique out of context.* RALPH *ends up in the middle of the room still bent over, motionless.* HE *looks up and around and straightens himself, laughing nervously at* EVERYONE *watching him*) Do all you people live here?

MIKE: No, we're just using the place for a few days. This is a fantastic coincidence because the guy that lives here just went away for a few days to do a series of special guest lectures at the University of Buffalo.

RALPH: Really? No kidding? That's some coincidence, huh? That's really a fantastic coincidence. Well, ahhh, here's what I'd like to do. I'd like to interview one of you people. I'll choose one of you at random and everybody else can listen and if the guy I choose has a particular opinion that differs significantly from what the rest of you believe, we'll just stop and take a consensus, O.K.? Hey, you guys all work, don't you? I mean, you're not students or anything?

COOTIE: We mostly hold various government jobs.

RALPH: I see. Are any of you married?

RUTH: I'm married to him [MIKE] and she's married to him [KATHY *and* BOB].

BOB: Actually, we're getting a divorce.

RALPH: Oh, I'm very sorry.

BOB (*Very sincerely to* RALPH): No, please. It's just, I've been dying for a while, nothing serious, you know, but now I've decided I'm definitely dead, you see, so I'll have to change my name. It's a legal technicality. We'll marry again under my new name. Jobert. (*Pause*) Job.

RALPH: Oh . . . well . . . that's certainly very unusual. Now this is going to get a little difficult, really. I've got to improvise some of these questions because the standard form is pretty rigid, like, you know, it asks things about your children's opinions and that would hardly apply in a case like . . .

MIKE: I have several kids by a former marriage.

RUTH: Hey, how come you never told me about that?

MIKE: If you remember, dear, we did discuss it.

RALPH: Can I just edge in here, I mean, ha-ha, I don't want to interrupt a little marital tiff or anything, but, ha-ha, you know. (*To* NORMAN) And how about you sir, do you have any children?

NORMAN: I don't have any children. I'm not married.

RALPH: Well, sir, I would guess, am I right, I would guess that you are the oldest person staying here. I only mean that in the sense of responsibility. Am I right?

MIKE: The guy that actually lives here is older, but he's not here right now.

RALPH: No, he's lecturing, right? I remember, ha-ha. Now I'd just like to ask you the following question. Have you ever heard of a teaching program called the World Volumes Encyclopedia?

DICK: Hey, are you selling encyclopedias?

RUTH: Hey, yeah, are you trying to sell us a set of encyclopedias?

RALPH: I'd like to make it very clear that I am not authorized to sell any product, I'm merely doing market research.

MIKE: Jesus Christ, he's not even selling the fucking things. You go and write to the central offices and you wait for a whole year to hear from them and when they finally decide to send a guy around he's not even authorized to sell you a set. I'm not hanging around here listening to a guy that isn't even authorized to sell the World Volumes Encyclopedia while millions of women and children are dying out there in Vietnam.

MIKE *grabs the banner and starts huzzahing as* OTHERS *follow him out the door.* DICK *and* NORMAN *stay behind with* RALPH, *who is yelling after them.*

RALPH: Hey, hey, listen, I can sell you a set if you want one. (HE *turns to* DICK *and* NORMAN) Hey, do you guys really want to buy a set of encyclopedias? I can sell you a set. I got a number of deals and there's a special discount for government employees.

DICK (*To* NORMAN): You going?

NORMAN: Yes, I've been reading a lot about it lately.

DICK: You want to come with me?

NORMAN: Well, yeah, if you don't have any other plans.

DICK: O.K., hold on a minute. (HE *goes out the hall door*)

RALPH: Hey, who are all you people?

NORMAN: We just live here.

RALPH: I go to college. I don't really come from Buffalo. I live in town. I'm trying to earn some money in my spare time. Are you guys really government employees?

NORMAN: I'm a graduate student.

RALPH: Yeah, well, I didn't want to say anything, but I didn't really think you guys were government employees. What are you studying?

NORMAN: Mathematics.

RALPH: I wanted to study mathematics. My father said he wouldn't pay so I'm studying law. Boy, do I hate law. I'm living at home. Do you guys all live here together?

NORMAN: Yes.

RALPH: And . . . and the girls, too?

NORMAN: Yes.

RALPH: Oh, boy, what a life, huh? I'm gonna get me a car pretty soon. I'm saving up. The thing is, I'm not really doing too well selling encyclopedias. I can't pull it off. I wish I could figure out why. I've been thinking about it and I think maybe it's because I can't give the sales pitch credibility. That's pretty bad if I'm gonna be a lawyer because a lot of the time you have to defend people you know are guilty. The thing is, these encyclopedias are really shitty. (HE *blushes*) Sorry. I mean, you know, they're not very good.

DICK *reenters.* HE *is carefully groomed, dressed in a pea jacket and well-laundered jeans.* HE *wears a large, orange Dayglo peace button.*

DICK: You ready?

RALPH: You going out?

DICK: Listen, if you're gonna eat anything, lay off the hamburgers, O.K.?

DICK *and* NORMAN *start out.*

NORMAN: I don't see why he has to go saying he's dead. I mean, that's only for him to have a physical. It's pretty easy to fail a physical. I've heard of guys that pretend . . .

DICK *and* NORMAN *are gone.*

RALPH (*Alone, looks at the open door*): Hey!

Blackout.

Scene 3

A few hours later. KATHY *is sitting in the kitchen, upset.* RUTH *comes in the front door.* SHE *has just returned from the march.*

RUTH: Bob here?

KATHY: No.

RUTH: Hey, what's wrong. You want some coffee?

KATHY: Please. (RUTH *takes off her coat and starts making coffee*) How was it?

RUTH: Weren't you there?

KATHY: No.

RUTH: I thought you and Bob were coming. You were on the bus and everything. I got lost when the cops charged. Boy, they really got some of those guys. Fucking pigs.

KATHY: When we got there he said he didn't feel like marching.

RUTH: Why not?

KATHY: Oh, Ruthie, I don't know. I don't know anything anymore. You devote two years to a guy and what does he give you? He never even told me about the letter. Drafted, and he didn't even tell me.

RUTH: He's not drafted. The letter's for the physical. All he has to do is act queer. They're not gonna take a queer musician.

KATHY: That's what I told him on the bus. He wouldn't even listen until I called him Job.

RUTH: What?

KATHY: He said he was dead. "Bob is dead."

RUTH: Bullshit, he's putting you on.

KATHY: That's what I mean. Me. He's even putting me on. Ungrateful bastard. The things I've done for him, Ruthie. Shit, I sound just like my mother. You know what I mean. I'm not complaining, but you know, you get tired of giving all the time and nothing's coming back. You know what I told him? I said he was the first guy I ever had an orgasm with. I mean, it really made him feel good. Now I gotta live with it. How can you explain something like that.

RUTH: Hey, no shitting around, did he really say he was gonna join?

KATHY: Ruthie, I'm telling you, he's serious. You know what he told me? He thinks the whole antiwar movement is a goddamn farce. I mean, Jesus, I really thought we were relating on that one. It's not like I'm asking the guy to go burn himself or anything but, I mean, he knows how I feel about the war and he's just doing it to be shitty. There's something behind it, I know that. He's like reaching out, trying to relate to me on the personal level by rejecting me but, like, I don't know how to break through. He says he's gonna study engineering in the army and then when he gets out he's gonna get some kind of plastic job and marry a plastic wife and live in a plastic house in some plastic suburb and have two point seven children. Oh, shit, Ruth, it's all too much. He went to a cowboy film.

RUTH: Well, you know, that's how it is.

KATHY: But Ruth, it's not like a fantasy scene. I know the guy. He'll go through with it. I mean, he really thinks he's serious. He doesn't see it's all part of a communication thing between him and me.

RUTH: I don't know. Like, maybe he's really serious. Mike's got this thing about physics. His tutor says he's a genius. O.K., maybe he is, like what do I know about physics? The thing is, he's gonna end up working for his old man in the lumber business. It's all laid out from the start. You have to fit in.

KATHY: You don't want him to do that, do you? If the guy is into physics you've gotta really stand behind him and make it all happen for him.

RUTH: I don't know. You have some kids and everything. I mean it's not like you can't have a meaningful life if you get married and have kids.

KATHY: Wow, I don't believe you really mean that.

RUTH: Look, Kathy, I don't want Mike to saw wood for the rest of his life, but what can I do about it? Why shouldn't he get into wood? Like, what if he does physics for the rest of his life and he's a genius and ends up head of department at some asshole university; you find out one day he's being financed by the C.I.A.

KATHY: These guys. They think they don't need you, so you go away and they freak out. Mike is a really brilliant guy. I mean, we all know that. You could really do things for him if you tried. You should've seen Bob when I first met him.

RUTH: I did.

KATHY: He used to compose all this really shitty music and like when he did something good he didn't even know it. You had to keep telling him yes, it's good, it's really great. A whole year it took for him to believe it. He's writing some fantastic stuff now, ever since, you know, I told him he was the first guy.

RUTH: Yeah, and look at him now.

KATHY (*Upset again*): You think you're really relating like crazy and then, I don't know, it's a whole new scene. It's like you don't even know him anymore.

RUTH: Maybe you ought to stop relating so hard.

KATHY: You don't know him, Ruth. I really know the guy and he needs me.

RUTH: Yeah, but maybe you ought to lay off for a while.

MIKE *bursts in through the front door.*

MIKE: Holy shit, where were you?

RUTH: I got lost and came home.

MIKE: Christ, it was horrible. We got stopped by this line of cops. Me and
    Cootie were right up front so I told him we should get everyone to join
    hands and stand still. We're standing there and this one pig starts running
    toward Cootie and you know how he gets when he sees pigs and he always
    gets diarrhea. I don't know, he should have said something, but he got
    the urge so bad he started to run, you know, trying to find a toilet, and
    this dumb pig thought he was trying to resist arrest.

KATHY: Is he all right?

MIKE: They took him to the hospital. He's, I don't know, they said he'll be
    all right. He got it in the back.

COOTIE *walks in.*

COOTIE: Boy, what a shitty march. You had to go and get separated with all
    the eats. I could've really used a marmalade and chunky peanut butter.

RUTH: Hey, did you know, Bob really wants to join the army? He's not even
    gonna try and get out. He didn't even go to the march.

COOTIE: He didn't miss much.

KATHY: He went to a goddamn cowboy film.

COOTIE: Hey, is that the one with Kirk Douglas and Gina Lollobrigida and
    Curt Jurgens and Orson Welles and Tom Courtenay and . . .

KATHY: You guys are really something. You don't give a shit what happens to
    him. I thought we were, like, all together here. Smug bastards. I'll tell you
    something.

COOTIE: What's that, Kathy?

KATHY: You're no better than the people fighting this war. (SHE *storms out of
    the room down the hall)*

MIKE: She's pretty cut up, huh?

RUTH: She thinks he's serious.

MIKE: Isn't he?

COOTIE *starts jumping and singing, punctuating each note with a leap.* HE
snarls the song.

COOTIE: We shall over cu—u—um,
    We shall over cu—u—um,
    We shall overcome some day—ay-ay-ay-ay
    Oh, oh, oh, deep in my heart
    I do believe.
    We shall over . . .

MIKE: Shut up, Mel.

COOTIE: If Bob's really serious, we gotta stop the war quick so he doesn't get sent over there to get killed by an antipersonnel bullet.

DICK *comes in, livid.*

DICK: Fucking Norman is fucking out of his fucking mind. That's the last time I ever take him with me. (HE *takes a bottle of milk from the icebox, kills it, and places it on the stack*)

MIKE: Hey, what's the matter, Dick, didn't you get yourself some left-wing ass?

COOTIE: Don't be ashamed, sonny. If she's waiting out there in the hallway, bring her in and show us the goods.

DICK: Norman had a fucking gun with him. He took a fucking revolver to the march.

MIKE: Is he a good shot?

DICK: I'm not shitting around. We're sitting on the bus and he's telling me he's reading Ho Chi Minh on guerrilla war and he doesn't think marches are effective. So he says he's gonna use the marchers like an indigenous population and start a guerrilla war against the cops. I mean, I thought he was just fucking around. You know Norman. Then he pulls out this fucking revolver right there on the bus, people looking and everything, and he says he's gonna get a few cops and would I help him create a diversion. He's out of his fucking mind.

MIKE: How many'd he get?

DICK: Fuck you.

COOTIE: He got the girl, huh?

DICK: Where's Kathy and Bob?

RUTH: Bob's not here.

DICK: Kathy here?

RUTH: Leave her alone. She's upset.

COOTIE: Yeah, I wouldn't try to lay her just yet, 'cause she's still going with Bob.

DICK *walks out down the hall.*

MIKE: That was a pretty stupid thing to say.

COOTIE: Just came out.

RUTH: Who cares? Everyone knows what dirty Dicky's up to. Except maybe Bob.

MIKE: And maybe Kathy.

RUTH: Kathy knows.

COOTIE: Do you think a guy could become a homosexual just by willpower? Could someone learn to like guys?

A knock on the front door.

RUTH: It's open.

In walks LUCKY, *the downstairs neighbor, led by* MR. WILLIS, *the landlord.*

WILLIS: Lucky tells me there's been a lotta noise up here. Is that right?

MIKE: Sorry, Mr. Willis, we had a little outburst up here. It's my fault. I just got a letter my sister had a baby.

COOTIE: We were celebrating.

WILLIS: That's all right, but keep it down. Lucky here was saying how you woke his wife up. She's a very ill person. I don't want any more complaints.

MIKE: Don't you worry about that, Mr. Willis, I'll take it on myself to keep this place really quiet.

LUCKY: Listen, I told you kids once before, and I'm not telling you again. You gotta get rid of those galvanized aluminum garbage cans in the yard and get plastic ones like everyone else.

RUTH (*Angry*): I don't see why we can't keep the ones . . .

MIKE: Ruth, now calm down, Ruth. I'm sorry, Lucky, but Ruth's pretty upset. Her father's fallen ill and they don't know for sure if it's . . . you know.

LUCKY: You got the galvanized aluminum ones out there. You'll have to get rid of the galvanized aluminum ones and get plastic.

WILLIS: I'll take care of the rest, Lucky. Thank you for bringing this particular grievance to my attention.

LUCKY: I'll give you till Monday, then I want to see plastic out there. (HE *leaves through front door*)

WILLIS: Whew, I hope I seen the last of that loony today. Nothin' but complaints day and night. The guy was born with a hair across his ass. So who's gonna give the landlord a little coffee?

RUTH *makes a move to get it.*

WILLIS: Thanks, sweetheart. Brother, what a day, what a stinker of a day. Where's Bobby?

MIKE: He's dead.

WILLIS: Dead? He's dead? You guys really kill me, you guys. You got a whole sense of humor like nothin' else. Dead, huh? Smart kid, Bobby. Hey, you been to the march?

COOTIE: Yep.

WILLIS: Great march. I watched it on Channel 8 in color. Brother, clothes you guys wear come out really good on color TV. You know, that guy Lucky can be a lotta trouble. He got a mind, like, you know, the size of a pinhead, you know what I mean? Just one sugar, sweetheart.

MIKE: You want the rent?

WILLIS: Rent, schment. I come to see how you guys are getting along and you talk to me about rent. How many landlords care, tell me that? One in a million, I can tellya. Hey, you decided whatya gonna do when you get out of college?

COOTIE: I'm gonna be a homosexual.

WILLIS: A homo. . . . You guys really slay me, you guys. What a sense of humor. You know, I'd give ten'a my other tenants for any one of you guys. You kids are the future of America, I mean that deeply, not too much milk, beautiful. Yeah, you kids live a great life up here. I got tenants complaining all the time about the way you kids carry on, and I'll tell ya something, you wanna know why they complain? 'Cause they'd give the last piece of hair on their heads to live like you kids are living.

RUTH: How's Mrs. Willis?

WILLIS: Huh? Oh, yeah, great, just great. Well, just between you and me and the wall she's gettin' to be a pain in the ass. She wants me to get rid of you, too. Why? I ask her. She don't like the way you live. O.K., I say, if you know so much, how do they live? She don't know and she don't wanna know. I try to tell her, you know, about the wild parties and stuff and taking drugs to have all new sensations in the body and the orgies with six or seven of you all at once. You should see her eyes light up. Same thing with all the tenants. When they hear what it's really like up here they go all funny. They'd pay me a hunnerd dollars to hear more, but they ain't got the nerve to ask. "Get rid of them." That's all I hear. Wamme to tell you something?

MIKE: If you got something to say you didn't ought to hold back.

WILLIS: Tremendous. You kids are tremendous. Listen. When the neighbors try to tellya about when they was young don't believe it. It's a lotta bull, and I should know. When we was young it was so boring you fell asleep when you was twenty and you never woke up again. You hear them stories Lucky tells about the war? Crap. He's sittin' down there holdin' his dick watchin' Doris Day on television. He'd give his left nut to know what's happenin' up here. This is the best cup of coffee I've had all day. I got a theory about it. It's when the head and the stomach don't talk to each other no more. That's when everything goes to hell. I'm gettin' so I don't know what I want half the time. I got these dreams, really crazy dreams. I got this one where I'm in a clearing, you know, it's right in the middle of the jungle and there's this tribe of Africans, I mean, like I don't know if they're Africans but they're livin' in the jungle and they're black so I figure they must be Africans. They got this skin. It's, you know, black, but really black. This maybe sounds kinda screwy, but it's really beautiful this skin. It's a dream, remember. I'm not sayin' black skin is beautiful, if you see what I mean. I'm in charge of the whole works in this jungle and I got it all organized so the men live in one hut and the women live in another hut and there's a big sort of square in between where nobody's

allowed after lights-out. They live like this all their life. There's no mar-
ryin' or anything. I'm a kind of witch doctor and I got this tribe believing . . . well, you know, they're just, like, Africans, and they don't know
you gotta have a man and a woman to make babies, and I got 'em thinkin'
you get babies when the moon shines down a girl's thing and hits the inside of her womb. And I got this whole ceremony where a girl comes to
me when she wants a baby and I tell her she gotta wait until it gets dark
and the moon comes up. Then I tie her to a plank, face up, and tilt the
plank so her thing is facing the moon and then I go to the hut with the
guys inside and get one of them to jerk off on a leaf, you know, one of
them tropical leafs that's really big. Then I roll this leaf up like it's a tube
and I sneak across the square holding this leaf in my hand all rolled up,
until I get to the girl. She's lying there in the moonlight all black and shiny
and her thing is opened right up 'cause she thinks . . . and I got this tube
full of jis in my hand, and I'm coming closer so I can smell everything
and . . . (*Comes out of it*) Jesus, what am I saying? I'm going crazy. It's just
a dream, what I'm telling you.

RUTH: That's the most beautiful thing I ever heard.

WILLIS: Listen, I got carried away. I didn't mean none of that.

MIKE: Mr. Willis, if you'd've had the opportunities we've had you'd've probably ended up one of the great poets of the century, and I mean that includes Rimbaud, Rilke, Williams, Pasternak, and Ginsberg.

COOTIE: And Whitman.

MIKE: Yes, Whitman included.

WILLIS: Oh, Jesus, you kids. I feel like I can tell you anything. Somebody
could've thought I was pretty screwy if I told them some of them things.

RUTH: How many landlords have poetry in their soul?

WILLIS: Yeah, yeah. Hey, I gotta run now. Listen, it's really great having you
guys around. If I could get some of them other tenants to come up here
and listen to you, the world would be a better place to live in, you know
what I mean?

MIKE: It would be a much better place.

COOTIE: A hundred percent better, at least.

RUTH: You're a beautiful person, Mr. Willis. Never be ashamed of it.

WILLIS: No, I ain't. I ain't ashamed of myself. Hey, you know what I was sayin'
before about all them complaints. I lost a lotta tenants on account of you.
I can't afford any more, so keep it quiet or I'll have to get rid of you.
Wonderful coffee, sweetheart. Seeya. (HE *leaves through front door*)

RUTH: I wonder how long before they put him away?

KATHY, *clothes a bit messed up, flounces into the kitchen and gets a glass of
water.* DICK *follows her as far as the kitchen, as if* HE *was trying to stop her,*

but when HE *gets to the doorframe* HE *stops, feeling the tension in the room.*
HE *tries to button his shirt casually, not sure whether* HE *wants the others
to know what just happened between him and* KATHY.

COOTIE: Hi, Dick, how's it hanging?

KATHY *stiffens at the sink.* DICK *turns and goes down the hall out of sight.*

MIKE: I still can't figure out what to get good old Bob for Christmas.

Before KATHY *can reply, the doorbell rings.* NO ONE *moves.*

COOTIE: Whose turn is it?
KATHY: You're a miserable bastard.
COOTIE: What'd I say? We're just playing a chess tournament.
KATHY: Listen, this is my scene, mine. You guys stay out of it. O.K., Ruth!
RUTH: It's her scene, guys, you stay out of it.
COOTIE: Roger.
MIKE: Sam.
COOTIE: Larry.
MIKE: Richard.
COOTIE: What's Richard getting Bob for Christmas?

The doorbell rings again, and MIKE *jumps up to get it.* SHELLY'*s standing there.*

MIKE: Hello there, I don't know you.
SHELLY: Hi. Does Norman live here?
MIKE: Does anyone here know a Norman?
SHELLY: He said he lived here. I met him at the march today. He said to come
    here and wait for him. I been standing out in the hall 'cause, like, I heard
    someone talking and I didn't want to disturb anyone and then this guy
    just came out so I figured, well, it's now-or-never kind of thing. I'm Shelly.
RUTH: Come on in. I'm Ruth.
SHELLY: Oh, good, then Norman does live here because I wasn't sure when
    he gave me the address. Sometimes you meet a guy at a march and he'll
    like give you an address and you end up waiting for a few days and he never
    shows. Did that ever happen to you? It's happened to me a lot of times.
KATHY: Listen everyone, I'm serious, I don't want him to know. I'll tell him
    when the time's right.
RUTH: It's your scene.

KATHY *exits down the hall.* SHELLY, *meanwhile, goes under the table and sits
down on the floor.*

SHELLY: I'm sorry about this. If you want to laugh go ahead, I'm used to it.
    It's just I've got this thing at the moment where I keep sitting under tables
    and I figured I'd better do it right away instead of pretending for a while

I didn't sit under tables. I mean, sitting under the table is "me" at the moment, so why hide it? Have you ever done it?

RUTH: Want some coffee, Shelly?

SHELLY: I'm a vegetarian.

MIKE: Coffee's made from vegetables.

SHELLY: I don't drink coffee, thanks. I'll just wait for Norman.

COOTIE: Where's Norman?

SHELLY: Well, he was arrested for carrying a concealed weapon, but he said it's O.K. because he has a permit. He's really a total-action freak, and he's very committed to the whole peace thing.

COOTIE: Oh.

MIKE: Well now . . .

COOTIE: How about that?

Fade-out.

Scene 4

NORMAN *is trying to read.* SHELLY *is under the table blowing bubbles.* MIKE *and* COOTIE *are playing chess.*

MIKE: I still think you should've said something, Norman. I mean it's got nothing to do with putting you on. If Dick said we didn't have a cat, all right, I mean he's got a right to think that but, I mean, it's really irresponsible of him to go running all over the place saying we don't.

NORMAN: Well, you turned off the lights that time when you came in. I was trying to read.

MIKE: Yeah, but that was the nitty-gritty, no-nonsense, down-to-earth needs of the moment because a cat just won't give birth with the lights on.

NORMAN: Dick says you don't have a cat.

MIKE: Will you listen to what I'm trying to tell you?

COOTIE: You can't move there.

MIKE: Why not?

COOTIE: Mate in thirty-four.

MIKE: Shit, I didn't see that. O.K., your game. (HE *and* COOTIE *start rearranging the pieces*)

COOTIE: Yeah, you see, Dick gets these things and he'll tell you, like, we don't have a cat or something like that. We would've explained if you'd just come out and asked instead of getting all hostile and paranoid and thinking we were putting you on.

SHELLY: Wow, bubbles are really something else. I think they're maybe divine.

MIKE: Bubbles are divine, Shelly.

COOTIE: So's Bogart.

SHELLY: Oh, Bogart, wow.

COOTIE: You're pretty happy, aren't you, Shelly?

SHELLY: Oh . . . yeah. Like, it's the right foods. And being under the table.

MIKE: You gotta watch the paranoid thing, Norman.

NORMAN: You were putting me on about the cat.

MIKE: See, you got this very paranoid thing about the cat.

NORMAN: I have not . . .

COOTIE: And the worst thing is how you get all defensive about it every time we bring it up. We're not denying your validity to doubt, Norman. We're not rejecting you as a human being. It's just you have a very paranoid personality because your father's a cop and that means you grew up in a very paranoid atmosphere.

SHELLY: Wow, your father's a cop?

NORMAN: Well, you know . . .

SHELLY: You never told me that. I think that's really great. My brother always wanted to be a cop.

COOTIE: My uncle's a cop.

MIKE: Yeah, that's right, our uncle's a cop.

NORMAN: That's what I mean, you see . . .

MIKE: What do you mean?

NORMAN: Well, I mean, you've got to go making fun of my father being a cop.

MIKE: Look, Norman, it just so happens our uncle is a cop and why the hell should you be the only one around here with a cop in the family. You see, you got paranoid again, thinking we're putting you on. I mean, we could do the same thing. How do we know your father's a cop? We don't. We trust you.

COOTIE: Yeah, and if you'd've been more outer-directed maybe you'd've seen you have a lot in common with us. A lot more than you ever expected.

MIKE: Then maybe we could've prevented that whole tragic episode with the gun.

NORMAN: Yeah, well, I don't know about you guys.

MIKE: You're not trying to say it wasn't a tragic episode?

COOTIE: It was an abortion of academic freedom, pure and simple.

MIKE: Hear! Hear!

COOTIE: I mean, when they can kick mathematics graduate students out of school just for trying to murder a few cops . . . . And, by the way, Norman, I've heard that your being kicked out of school was the doing of the Dean of Admissions, a man who is known far and wide to be cornholing his widowed sister in the eye-sockets regularly . . .

MIKE: And without love.

COOTIE: And when the moon comes up he ties her to this plank . . .

MIKE: Mel . . .

COOTIE: So put that in yer pipe and smoke it. And don't try to tell us you enjoy having to schlepp down to the Hays Bick every night to wash dishes for a dollar ten an hour.

NORMAN: Oh, I don't know.

SHELLY: Hey, are you guys brothers?

MIKE: Now there, look at that, Norman. Shelly's wondering about the relationship between Mel and me, and instead of being all paranoid about it and going crazy wondering, she comes right out and asks.

SHELLY: Hey, are you?

COOTIE: Yeah, we're brothers.

SHELLY: Wow, I didn't know that either. I keep learning all these things about you guys.

MIKE: See, everything's cool now. Everybody trusts each other. That's what it's all about.

NORMAN: Well, I mean, with washing dishes I get more time to read. I've been thinking a lot and I guess it's like Dick said. I was pretty irrelevant before. Mathematics is pretty irrelevant no matter how you look at it, and bad mathematics is about as irrelevant as you can get.

SHELLY: I left school after the first month. I'm not saying I'm really relevant, yet, but like, some of my friends in school are really into bad scenes. School is evil. You can't find out where it's at when you're studying all the time to fit your head into exams. I'm getting to where I can read recipes all day and really get something out of it.

NORMAN: Yeah. I'm learning all this stuff about Vietnam. It's really something. I mean, I'm getting to the point where maybe I can do something really relevant about it.

MIKE: I wouldn't call the gun business relevant.

NORMAN: I was still in school when I thought of that.

SHELLY: Norman's got this fantastic idea.

NORMAN: Well, I haven't thought it all out yet . . .

SHELLY: No, Norman-baby, don't like close all up. It's the most relevant thing I ever heard of.

COOTIE: Jesus, Norman, how long have you been walking around with this idea all locked up inside you?

NORMAN: I didn't get it all at once. It sort of came in stages, but I think it's about right.

COOTIE: Man, you're gonna go crazy if you keep everything inside like that.

SHELLY: Tell them the idea, Norman.

NORMAN: Well, you see . . . (*Pause*) I'm gonna set myself on fire as a protest against the war. (COOTIE *and* MIKE *look at him and exchange brief glances*) I've thought about it a lot. I mean, I've read I guess about a hundred books about the war and the more you read the more you see it's no one thing you can put your finger on. It's right in the middle of the whole system, like Dick said. I shouldn't've tried to kill those policemen, but I didn't know then they were part of the system like everything else. No one's got the right to take anyone else's life, that's what I've decided. But I've still got the right to take my own life for something I believe in.

SHELLY: I'm gonna burn with Norman. We're gonna burn together. We've thought it all through and, like, if he burns himself alone that's just one person. Everyone'll say he's insane, but if two of us do it . . . wow. Two people. What are they gonna say if two of us do it?

MIKE (*Pause*): Three of us.

COOTIE: Four of us.

MIKE: You, too, huh?

COOTIE: It's the only way.

NORMAN: Hey, wait a minute. I've read a lot about the whole subject and I really know why I'm gonna do it. I'm not just doing it for fun or anything. You can't just jump into it.

MIKE: Listen, Norman, you don't have to believe this if you don't want to but it's the truth, on my honor. Me and Cootie talked about the exact same thing a year ago. We were all ready to burn ourselves . . .

COOTIE: It was more than a year ago.

MIKE: More than a year?

COOTIE: Almost a year and a half.

MIKE: That's right, a year and a half, boy, time really goes quick . . .

COOTIE: It sure does . . .

MIKE: The thing is, we decided against it because we figured two isn't enough.

COOTIE: You know how the papers can lie. "Brothers Burn!"

MIKE: Yeah, "Hippie Brothers in Suicide Pact." That kind of shit.

COOTIE: But think of it. With four of us!

NORMAN: You really want to do it?

MIKE: It's the only way.

NORMAN: I mean, I wasn't sure yet. I hadn't made up my mind definitely. I was still looking for another way.

SHELLY: No, Norman-baby, it's the only relevant gesture. Like you said.

A long pause while NORMAN *thinks.*

NORMAN: O.K.!

COOTIE: After the Christmas vacation.

MIKE: No, no, after graduation. We'll study like mad and get fantastic grades and graduate with honors so they can't say we were cracking up or anything.

COOTIE: Yeah, we'll get Phi Beta Kappa. I'd like to see them say we're insane when two Phi Beta Kappas go up in flames with the son of a policeman and the daughter of a. . . . Hey, what does your father do?

SHELLY: Well, it's kind of funny. I mean, he's a pretty weird head in his way. He's got, like, six or seven jobs at any one time.

COOTIE: That's O.K. Daughter of a weird head with six or seven jobs at any given time. That covers the whole spectrum.

NORMAN: What does your father do? I mean, I know your uncle's a policeman because I trust you, but you never said what your father did. I was curious. Like if they bring our fathers into it what'll they say about you?

COOTIE: He's a trapper.

SHELLY: Wow, that's really something else. Like, a fur trapper?

MIKE: Furs and hides, you know. Rabbit and mink and muskrat and beaver and elk and reindeer and seal. Some otter. Penguin.

SHELLY: Wow, penguin.

COOTIE: Well, you know, he works the Great Northwest Territory up to the mouth of the St. Lawrence Seaway and over to the Aleutians.

SHELLY: Boy, this'll really blow everyone's mind.

MIKE: Yeah, this'll make everyone think twice, all right.

COOTIE: You know, we can't tell anyone about this. If word gets out they'll send squads of police around here and we'll get arrested and put under psychiatric observation and we'll get subjected to a battery of tests that make you look nuts no matter how you answer.

NORMAN: I won't say anything.

SHELLY: Oh, wow, like you don't even have to worry about me.

NORMAN: I didn't even know there were any trappers left.

A knock on the door.

MIKE: Come in.

VOICE: C'mon, c'mon, open up in there.

MIKE *opens the door and finds two cops standing there.* BREAM *is elderly and* EFFING *is young.*

BREAM: You live here?

MIKE: Yes, sir.

BREAM: Look, you know what I mean, you and who else.

MIKE: Well, there's me and my brother Cootie . . . um, Mel, and there's Norman, Dick, Bob, Kathy, and Ruth.

BREAM: Kathy and Ruth, huh? Those are girls' names.

MIKE: Kathy and Ruth are both girls, sir.

BREAM: Don't block the doorway. (MIKE *stands aside as* BREAM *and* EFFING *enter.* EFFING *wanders around the room, inspecting.* BREAM *indicates* SHELLY) Which one's she? You Kathy or Ruth?

SHELLY: I'm Shelly.

BREAM: Shelly, huh? You didn't say nothin' about no Shelly.

MIKE: She doesn't live here, sir.

BREAM: Visiting?

SHELLY: I'm with Norman.

BREAM: You're Norman, huh?

NORMAN: She's my girlfriend.

BREAM: Good, we got that straight.

EFFING: Hey, Bream, this here's a map of Europe.

BREAM: Yeah. Now listen. There's been a complaint from the people across there. I know you kids are students and you probably think you own the goddamn country, but I got some news for you. There's laws around here and you gotta obey them just like everyone else.

MIKE: We appreciate that, sir.

EFFING: Hey, Bream, look at all them milk bottles.

BREAM: Yeah. Now listen. I don't want to hear any more complaints about you guys. I'm a reasonable man, which is something you can get verified by askin' anyone on the force, but when I gotta put up with a lotta stupid complaints I can cause trouble and I mean real trouble, with a capital T.

EFFING: Hey, look at all them dishes in the sink, Bream.

BREAM: Yeah.

NORMAN: What was the complaint?

BREAM: What do you mean, what was the complaint? The complaint was guys and girls parading around in here bare-ass. Now look, I'm not the kind of dumb cop that goes around throwing his weight everywhere to prove he's some kind of big shot. I don't need to, you follow me. I know what I know and I know what I don't know, and one of the things I know I don't know is what the hell the kids are up to nowadays, but O.K. That's my problem. If you wanna run around naked that's O.K. by me, and I hope you kids take note of the fact that I'm winking one eye when it comes to the law about cohabitation.

MIKE: We appreciate that fact, sir. It was the first thing we noticed.

COOTIE: I sure appreciate it. I think I can speak for Norman and Shelly, and if any of the other guys were here they'd appreciate it a lot.

MIKE: I mean it's not as if we underestimate the life of a cop. For chrissakes, I mean, our uncle's a cop. His father's a cop. A lot of us around here are pretty close to the world of cops.

BREAM: You got cops in the family?

EFFING: Hey, Bream, look at this heater.

BREAM: Yeah.

MIKE: It's not like we don't know what you guys have to put up with. It can be a pretty crappy job.

BREAM: I don't know . . .

MIKE: I'm not saying it doesn't have its rewards. My uncle's life is full of rewards. His father's life is very meaningful.

BREAM: Yeah, that's what I mean.

COOTIE *gets up and starts to leave the room.*

EFFING: Hey, Bream, the kid's leaving the room.

COOTIE: I got a call from nature.

BREAM: That's legit. You go ahead, kid.

COOTIE *goes out the front door.*

EFFING: Hey, Bream, the kid says he's going to the euphemism and what if he's got some stuff on him or something. He can flush it down and come back clean.

BREAM: He's O.K.

EFFING: Jesus, Bream. Sir.

BREAM: The guy's new on the job. He don't know the score yet.

MIKE: You know how some people exaggerate. I mean, look what they say in the papers about you guys. Maybe, like after a shower we'll come in here to get an anchovy snack or chocolate milk or something, and we forget to put something on . . .

EFFING: Look at that, Bream, the girl keeps sitting under there . . .

BREAM: Goddammit, Effing, who's in charge around here?

EFFING: But she's sitting under there . . .

BREAM: Did we come here to investigate a complaint about a girl sitting under the table?

EFFING: No, sir, but . . .

BREAM: The girl happens to be well within her rights as a taxpaying citizen of the community to sit under any table she wants, and until we get complaints about her sitting under there, we leave her alone. Understand?

EFFING: Yeah, yeah, yeah . . .

SHELLY: Thanks.

BREAM: That's O.K., lady. The kid's a rookie. They give us pros a bad name. Now let me tell you something about the people complaining about you. They look in here and see you guys bare-assed and they're complaining because they're so sick of looking at each other they gotta go spying on you. We know about them people. They're strict Roman Catholics. Twelve kids in four rooms. The old man can't keep it in his pants for ten minutes running. So they got troubles, right, and everyone that's got troubles wants to give troubles to someone else. So they make a complaint, and that's well within their rights as law-abiding citizens of this community. I got enough troubles without their goddamn complaints. I got enough to do watching the Vietnam freaks and the niggers and the loonies going up on buildings with high-power rifles picking off everyone down below. Let me give you some good advice. Get curtains. They got some fiberglass curtains at Woolworth's, you can't tell them from real cotton. Twelve dollars and fifty cents a pair and they come in eight colors, plain and patterned. You get some curtain rods for a dollar sixty-nine apiece and for a total of twenty-eight dollars and thirty-eight cents you save yourself from a lot of crazy neighbors. If you can't afford twenty-eight dollars and thirty-eight cents, get some gingham, thirty-nine cents a yard at Penney's. Measure your windows and allow a foot extra at each end. All you gotta do is take up a three-inch hem at each end, fold it over once, and hand-stitch. A couple of curtain rings and you're in business. Can you remember that, or d'you want me to write it down?

SHELLY: Hey, yeah, would you do that?

BREAM *takes out a notebook and starts to write.* EFFING *is nervous.*

EFFING: The kid's been gone a long time.

BREAM: I got eyes, Effing.

EFFING: Yeah, yeah, yeah, O.K.

BREAM (*Writing*): So, what are you kids gonna do with yourselves? (*Pause*) Am I being nosy or something?

MIKE: No, I mean, there's a lot of opportunities all over the place. We're not jumping into anything without we've looked the whole thing over.

BREAM: Smart kids. Boy, that's really something. Cop sending his kid to college. They must pay him pretty good, huh?

NORMAN: I guess so.

BREAM: Yeah, what's he a sergeant . . . lieutenant or something?

NORMAN: He's Chief of Police for Erie County.

BREAM (*Whistles*): Whew! Pretty good. That shut me up O.K. Chief of Police. Oh, boy, that's really something.

NORMAN: It's just his job, you know.

BREAM: Look, ah, here's your instructions. I want them up by Wednesday. Any complaints after that and all of you guys'll be in court, father or no father, you understand me? This ain't Erie County.

MIKE: Yes, sir.

NORMAN: O.K.

COOTIE (*Returns and stands in the door. There's a pause*): That's better.

Scene 5

RUTH *is scraping some cat food into a bowl. A cat comes in and eats.* RUTH *keeps glancing at her watch.*

RUTH: Kitty-kitty-kitty-kitty-kitty. Chomp, chomp. Good girl. Make a lot of milk for the kitties.

KATHY *comes in from the hall and throws herself down on a chair.*

KATHY: Oh, Jesus, Ruth, how am I ever gonna tell him?

RUTH: Who?

KATHY: Bob, for chrissakes. Who else?

RUTH: Well, how should I know?

KATHY: I never slept with Dick. I know you got the idea I did, but it's not true. He never got all the way . . . .

RUTH: . . . O.K. . . .

KATHY: . . . Yet. (*Pause*) I'm not saying I wouldn't like to.

RUTH: So go ahead.

KATHY: Well, don't try to pretend it doesn't mean anything to you. You know as well as I do it'll kill Bob if he ever finds out I'm even thinking of sleeping with Dick.

RUTH: That's how it goes.

KATHY: Ruthie, look, we've know each other since freshman year. I can tell when you're thinking something. This is really a big decision I've gotta make. What am I gonna do about Bob? I mean, it feels like maybe we're you know, finished, but I like the guy. I really like him a lot and I respect his music. But I know he could never relate to me as a friend. It's gotta be tied up with sex. I mean, Richard really seems to dig me, but I don't know. He's pretty together. He's not the kind of guy you could really do something big for. Not like Bob.

RUTH: Oh, for shit's sake, Kathy, Dick is a fucking parasite.

KATHY: That's not fair, Ruth.

RUTH: Fair! Do you know what that guy's doing to get into graduate school? You ever heard of Professor Roper in the Eastern Studies department?

KATHY: He's Dick's adviser.

RUTH: Yeah, and he also happens to be queer as a three-dollar bill, and Dick is fucking his wife to keep her quiet so good old Roper can suck cock with all those graduate students from Thailand or Malaya, or whatever the hell they are.

KATHY: Who said?

RUTH: Who said? For chrissakes, Kathy, the whole goddam school knows about it. "Dirty Dicky."

KATHY: That's why?

RUTH: Yeah, what else? I mean, the guy washes eight times a day.

KATHY: Oh, man, how long have you guys known about this? I mean, why didn't anyone ever tell me? You can't just let him screw up his future like that. Hasn't anyone tried to do anything about it?

RUTH: Like tell him Mrs. Roper's got clap?

KATHY: Ruthie, the guy must be really suffering.

RUTH: Oh, shit, Kathy, let's not have the big savior thing.

KATHY: That's not very funny.

RUTH: Look, we're all gonna graduate pretty soon, and we're all gonna go away, and probably we'll never see each other again except maybe like at

Christmas or something. So why don't you worry about yourself and never mind about Dick and Bob. They'll be O.K.

KATHY: Boy, you sure have changed, Ruth. I don't know. You sure have changed.

> BOB *comes through front door carrying books.*

BOB: I don't believe it. It's incredible. You know what happened today in counterpoint class? Remember I was telling you about Eric Shatz?

RUTH: . . . Three armpits . . . ?

BOB: The very one.

KATHY (*Nicely*): Bob . . .

> BOB, *who has gone to the icebox to steal some of* DICK*'s hamburgers, stops short in whatever gesture* HE *is holding, only for a moment though, just long enough to cut* KATHY. *When* HE *resumes his story,* HE *is talking only to* RUTH, *who is wrapping a Christmas present.*

BOB: Today Shatz turned in this perfect, spotless, clean counterpoint exercise. I mean, for someone as filthy as Shatz, that's a miracle. They say his high-school yearbook voted him "The Most Likely to Attract Infectious Disease." (HE *has the hamburgers out by now.* KATHY, *being all nice, takes the hamburgers from him indicating that* SHE'*ll cook.* HE *goes away from her and sits with* RUTH) He picks his nose and squeezes his pimples right there in class, and his counterpoint exercises have to be seen to be believed. He writes them in pencil, and if he makes a mistake or something, he spits on his eraser and rubs the paper about a hundred times . . . per note, so by the time he hands it to Professor Bolin, it's just this gray sludge with lots of little black things swimming around on it. Anyway, about a week ago, when Shatz handed over his work, Professor Bolin put on a pair of gloves before he'd take it, so Shatz must've got the message and this week when Bolin called for homework, Shatz set this beautiful, clean exercise down on the piano. We couldn't believe it. Boilin just sat there staring at it, and we all sat staring at Bolin, and after about ten minutes, no shit, it took that long, Bolin turned to us and said, "Free will is an illusion." Isn't that too much?

KATHY: Bob, can I talk to you . . . ?

BOB (*Ignores her*): The thing is, Bolin's got a Ph.D. He's also written two books and a couple of hundred symphonies and string quartets and they say he taught himself twenty-two languages in four hours or something . . .

KATHY: Please, Bob, I want to talk to you . . .

BOB: And another thing, Bolin's wife got drunk at a faculty party for the music department last year and she yelled, "Fuck Schönberg, I wanna dance," and then she went and laid the only black professor in the school, which all goes to show that when Bolin tells you free will is an illusion . . . you better believe it.

KATHY (*Pointed*): Bob, I would like to talk to you . . .

BOB: Hey, Ruth, did I ever tell you the one about the guy that died and came back to life as Job?

KATHY: Oh, don't start that shit again.

BOB: Again? It started over a month ago. I mean, even Bolin caught on after two lessons. Of course, he still makes me walk around the music building every time I put down parallel fifths, but that's how it goes, life is trying at the best of times, every cloud has a silver lining, a stitch in time saves nine . . .

RUTH (*Looks at her watch*): I've gotta go.

BOB: Did I say something?

RUTH: No. Kathy wants to talk to you about sleeping with Dick.

KATHY: Ruth . . . bitch!

> RUTH *goes out the front door, grabbing her coat on the way.*

BOB (*Pause*): Meanwhile, back at the ranch. . . . You'll never believe this, but when I came in just now, I didn't expect that. Bedbugs, maybe. Thermonuclear war . . .

KATHY: She had no right.

BOB: I'm trying to think of something appropriate to say, like "Name the first one after me." That's Job. J-O-B. Job.

KATHY: Please, Bob, can I say something . . . ?

BOB: Do you have trouble pronouncing the name Job?

KATHY: Jesus Christ, you're impossible.

BOB: Ah, yes, but I exist, nonetheless.

KATHY: You've just cut me right out. You're not even trying to relate to me anymore. (*Pause*) Well, you're not.

BOB: No, Kathy. The fact is, I like you a lot. I, um, sort of love you, if you know what I mean.

KATHY: I don't really want to sleep with Dick.

BOB: Then don't.

KATHY: It's just, he tried to get me that night after the demonstration.

BOB: I know. He told me.

KATHY: That shit.

BOB: I thought it was pretty good of him.

KATHY: He never got into me, you know.

BOB: That's nice.

KATHY: Oh, Bob. I'm sorry.

BOB: If Bob were around I'm sure he'd forgive you.

KATHY: What'll we do?

BOB: What do you mean? Like study or something?

KATHY: Bob, how does it stand? Is it . . . it's over, isn't it?

BOB: Between us, you mean?

KATHY: Yes.

BOB: If that's what you want.

KATHY: Of course I don't want it. I love you a lot.

BOB: O.K., so let's study for Phil 720.

KATHY: Oh, for chrissakes, show some emotion. I don't know where I'm at with you half the time.

BOB: Look, what's the big hang-up? If you want to stay with me, O.K. If you want to move into Dick's room, go ahead. If you don't know for sure, stay one night with me and one night with him till you start feeling a definite preference for one of us . . .

KATHY: Jesus Christ, Bob, what's the matter with you?

BOB: I'm Job. Bob's dead.

KATHY (*Is in a furious slow burn.* SHE *stands and goes toward the hall door*): All right . . . all right . . .

Before KATHY *can exit a knock on the door stops her. A game. Who's going to open the door?* BOB *picks up a book and starts reading. Another knock.* KATHY *sighs.* SHE's *above these silly games.* SHE *opens the door on a middle-aged man in well-cut coat. A businessman from head to foot. This is* MURRAY, BOB's *uncle.*

MURRAY: Hi. Does Bob Rettie live here?

BOB (*Looks up from his book*): Murray!!

MURRAY: Can I come in?

BOB: What the hell are you doing here?

MURRAY: Guy flies a couple thousand miles to see his nephew, maybe he can come in, huh?

BOB: Yeah, yeah. Come in, come in . . . sit down . . . .

MURRAY: Hey, I bet you're surprised to see me, huh? Maybe a little happy.

BOB: Yeah, I mean I haven't seen you for a couple thousand years or something.

MURRAY (*To* KATHY): It's longer than that since he wrote.

BOB: Oh, ah, that's Kathy. My uncle.

MURRAY: How do you do.

KATHY: Hi.

MURRAY: You drink a lot of milk, huh?

BOB: Yeah.

THEY *laugh*.

MURRAY: Where'd you get that goddamn icebox?

BOB: Oh, you know . . .

MURRAY: Is this the way you been living? Bobby boy, why didn't you tell me. Write a letter, say Murray I need a little cash, I'd've sent you some money for a decent refrigerator.

BOB: Murray, we're living O.K.

MURRAY: So. I'm sorry for breathing. Did I interrupt something?

BOB: No. Nothing at all.

MURRAY: Are you two . . . ah . . .

BOB: Yeah—Murray, look, sit down, take your coat off. . . .

MURRAY: Hey, Bobby, Bobby-boy. You got long hair. . . .

BOB: Yeah, it keeps growing.

MURRAY: Still proud, huh? (*To* KATHY) Just like his mother . . . . (HE *looks at the two of them and shrugs*) Well what can I say . . . ?

KATHY: Look, I think I'll . . .

BOB: How long you in town for?

MURRAY: Oh, you know. Business.

KATHY: Excuse me, I'm gonna . . .

BOB: How's the kids?

MURRAY: Oh, fine, fine, keep asking about you.

BOB: Auntie Stella?

MURRAY: Oh. You know. We got a new house . . .

BOB: Great. Where you going, Kathy?

KATHY (*Has been edging toward the door. Quietly*): I'll be in Dick's room if you want me. (SHE *exits*)

MURRAY: Is she O.K.?

BOB (*Flat*): Yeah. It's her time of the month, you know.

MURRAY: Say no more. You don't have to tell me about that. Nice girl. Very nice. (*Laughs*) So . . .

BOB: Come through New York?

MURRAY: Yeah, you know, passed through.

BOB: You passed through New York, huh?

MURRAY (*Uneasy*): Yeah, sure, you know . . .

BOB: D'you see Mom?

MURRAY: Yeah, yeah, sure. She'd maybe like a letter every now and then. Your own mother.

BOB: It's not like that, Murray. When I see her, I see her.

MURRAY (*Shiver*): Jesus Christ. (HE *drinks*)

BOB: You O.K.?

MURRAY: Sit down, Bobby-boy.

BOB: I'm O.K. like this.

MURRAY: I got something to tell you, you should maybe be sitting down when I tell you.

BOB *sits.* MURRAY *pulls his chair close and takes* BOB*'s head in his hands.* BOB *is stiff.*

MURRAY: Bobby-boy, oh, Bobby. I'd like to see more of you. Me and the family. You maybe come out and visit, huh?

BOB (*Flat*): What's happened, Murray?

MURRAY: How am I supposed to tell you?

Pause.

BOB (*Long pause*): Cancer? (MURRAY *nods*) How long's she got?

MURRAY: A week, two weeks. I don't know. Any time now.

BOB: Those operations . . . kidney trouble. Oh, shit, why didn't someone tell me?

MURRAY: You got your studies, we should worry you to death?

BOB (*Flat*): Fuck you all.

MURRAY: I thought . . . I thought maybe you and me fly to New York tonight.

BOB: Yeah, get in there quick for the payoff. That'll be just great.

MURRAY: She doesn't know yet.

BOB: Yeah. "Hi, Mom, I just came flying in with Murray a couple of weeks before Christmas vacation to see you for no good reason." You think she won't guess?

MURRAY: She doesn't have to. We can always tell her something.

BOB: You planning to keep it from her, too? I bet it's the first thing she thought of. Two years. She had that first operation two years ago. She's been dying for two years and I didn't even fucking know it.

MURRAY: I don't want to hurt anybody.

BOB (*Pause*): I'll pack some stuff. No, you stay here. I want to be alone.

> BOB *goes down the hall.* MURRAY *sits. Very short pause, then* MIKE *and* COOTIE *burst in through the front door, laden with Christmas presents.* THEY *see* MUR- RAY, *cross the kitchen to the hall door, exit, and start arguing loudly just outside in the hallway. After a moment* THEY *reenter,* MIKE *leading. Deferential.*

MIKE: Me and my friend were wondering if you could settle a little argument for us.

MURRAY: What?

MIKE: Were you or weren't you the guy behind the bar in *Key Largo*, starring Humphrey Bogart and Edward G. Robinson?

MURRAY: I'm Bob's uncle.

MIKE (*To* COOTIE): He's Bob's uncle.

COOTIE: Are you a for-real uncle?

MURRAY (*Confused*): Yeah, yeah, I'm his uncle.

COOTIE: Maternal or paternal.

MURRAY: I'm related to Bob through his mother. She was . . . she's my sister.

MIKE: That means you and him have different names.

MURRAY: Yeah, he's a Rettie, I'm a Golden.

MIKE: That's a pretty convincing story, mister.

COOTIE: Most of the pieces fit pretty good.

> MIKE *and* COOTIE *start toward the hall.* SHELLY *comes in the front door.*

SHELLY: Hi, everyone.
MIKE: Hiya, Shelly.
COOTIE: Good old Shelly, hiya.

MIKE *and* COOTIE *are gone down the hall.*

SHELLY: Hey . . . excuse me, do you know if Norman's here?
MURRAY: I don't know who Norman is.
SHELLY: One of the guys here. I mean, like he lives here. You someone's father?
MURRAY: I'm Bob's uncle.
SHELLY: Bob? Oh, yeah, Job. (SHE *sits under the table*) I'm waiting for Norman. Hey, are you, like, a for-real uncle?
MURRAY: You kids keep asking that.
SHELLY: You don't think of him with an uncle.
MURRAY: Look, if you don't want me to stay in here, I'll go and help Bob.
SHELLY: No, you stay here. Like, I enjoy company. Hey, is he here?
MURRAY: I'm afraid I don't know your friend Norman.
SHELLY: I mean Job. Your nephew.
MURRAY: Yes, he's here. I'm waiting for him.
SHELLY: He's, like, in here somewhere? Inside the apartment?
MURRAY: Yes. Look, you want to go down and ask him about Norman, go ahead.
SHELLY: Is he in the toilet?
MURRAY: He's in his room.
SHELLY: Wow, that's like really weird.
MURRAY: He's just packing, that's all.
SHELLY: Yeah, but I mean, if you're his for-real uncle, how come you're like sitting in here when he's down there?
MURRAY: Look, he . . . (*Weeping softly*) . . . I don't know.
SHELLY: Hey, you're really crying like crazy. What's the matter? I thought you were, like, waiting for him to come back here, you know, to the apartment or something. I just wanted to know because I'm waiting for Norman to come back so I thought we could maybe sit here together waiting and that would be something we had in common, then you told me he was in his room packing and everything and I thought that was sorta weird 'cause if you're like his for-real uncle you could just go down there and be with him. Why's he packing?
BOB (*Entering with bag*): O.K. I'm ready.
SHELLY: Hey, Job, you going away?
BOB: I'll be back in a few days.
SHELLY: Like, you mean, you're not just going home early for Christmas vacation?
BOB: No.
SHELLY: Oh. O.K. Hey, Merry Christmas, you guys.

BOB: Merry Christmas.
MURRAY: Merry Christmas.

> DICK *comes in through the front door.* BOB *and* MURRAY *start out.* DICK *is baffled.*

DICK: Hey, you going?
BOB: Yeah. Kathy's in your room. (*Pause*) She doesn't like it from behind.

> BOB *and* MURRAY *are gone.*

DICK: Where's he going?
SHELLY: I don't know, but the guy with him is his for-real uncle and he's a
> weird head.

> KATHY *comes into the kitchen.*

KATHY: Hey, did Bob just go out?
SHELLY: Wow, he didn't even tell you?
DICK: He left with his uncle.
KATHY: Uncle?
SHELLY: Yeah, like it's his for-real uncle, I'm pretty sure.
KATHY: Jesus, why didn't he say something. I mean, I been waiting for him
> down there . . .
SHELLY: Well, the uncle said Job went down to his room to pack, and I mean,
> like if you were in there with him and he started putting a lot of socks and
> underwear and toilet stuff in a suitcase you should've got suspicious and
> asked him something, like where's he going.
KATHY: Look, I went to the bathroom, O.K.?
SHELLY: Ya didn't flush.
KATHY: Mind your own business, Shelly. What does he expect me to do? How
> can I make plans for the Christmas vacation if he just . . . shit, he could've
> said something. (DICK, *in a feeble attempt to avoid* KATHY*'s rage, tries to sneak
> out down the hallway*) And listen, you, you have a lot of nerve telling him
> about that night.
DICK: I didn't say anything.
KATHY: He said you told him.
DICK: Honest, Kathy, I never did.
KATHY (*Vague*): I'm really getting to hate this place. (SHE *starts down the hall.*
> DICK *starts after her*)
DICK: Kathy!

> *Before* DICK *can get down the hall,* RUTH *rushes in through the front door,
> breathless.*

RUTH: Oh, wow, have I ever had the most fantastic experience! (DICK *goes down
> the hall, slamming the door.* SHE *yells*) You're a shit, Dick.

SHELLY: You seen Norman?

RUTH: Oh, hi, Shelly. Hey, let me tell you about what just happened to me. It really blew my mind.

From down the hall, we hear voices singing.

MIKE and COOTIE (*Singing, offstage*):
> We wish you a Merry Christmas
> We wish you a Merry Christmas
> We wish you a Merry Christmas
> We wish you a Merry Christmas
> We wish you a Merry Christmas
> We wish you a Merry Christmas
> We wish you a Merry Christmas
> We wish you a Merry Christmas
> And . . . (THEY *rush in from the hall dressed in Santa Claus costumes and end the song*)
> . . . a Happy New Year.

MIKE: We got a present for you, Ruth.

SHELLY: Hey, where'd you get those?

COOTIE: We're doing collections this year. Yep.

MIKE: You want to see the great old present we got ya?

RUTH: I was just gonna tell Shelly what happened when I went to see Quinn. You know Quinn, the albino dwarf . . .

MIKE: Oh, yeah, old Quinn.

COOTIE: Good old Quinn.

RUTH: Yeah, right. Well, I had to see him about homework for the Christmas vacation and, I mean, like, he was the last person I wanted to see. I always thought he was a vicious little bastard. I mean, he can be pretty shitty.

MIKE: They say he shot a man in Abilene.

COOTIE: In the back.

RUTH: Listen, willya? I went into his office and he's standing by the window, you know, three feet high and everything. I thought he was probably gonna ask why I wasn't doing any homework, and I had this whole speech worked out about how I thought he was a pretentious little snot and how I frankly didn't give a shit about philosophy and even less of a shit about him, if that's possible and . . . oh, you know, I was really going to kill him. Anyway, he told me to come over to the window, so I came over and we both stood there looking out. Snow everywhere, like, white wherever you looked and a lot of snow coming down like in those paperweights you shake up, and there's all these kids down below coming out of the building, all little lumps moving across the white in slow motion, and we're looking at them, just the two of us for, I don't know, about a minute or two, and then he just turns to me, like without any warning, and says this incredibly beautiful thing . . .

MIKE: Hey, don't you want to see the nifty present we got ya?

RUTH: Let me tell you what the guy said, willya?

MIKE: Right, you tell us what Quinn said, then we'll show you the present.

RUTH: Yeah.

MIKE: Will you look at the present first, then tell us what Quinn said?

RUTH: For Christ sake, stop fucking around and listen.

MIKE: All right, what did Quinn say?

COOTIE: I'd like to hear what Quinn said.

As RUTH *is about to speak,* KATHY *runs through from the hall and out the front door with a valise in hand.* DICK *shouts from offstage down the hall.*

DICK (*Offstage*): Kathy. (HE *enters and, on his way across the room and out the front door, buttons his overcoat*) Kathy!

RUTH*'s face shows worry as* SHE *watches this. Seconds after* DICK *exits,* SHE *takes her coat and follows, leaving* MIKE, COOTIE *and* SHELLY *alone. There is a pause.*

COOTIE: What was that all about?

MIKE: Things around here are getting a little out of control, Cootie.

COOTIE: You feel that way, huh?

MIKE: I do.

COOTIE: Well, what are we gonna do about it, movies or roller-skating?

MIKE: Cootie, sometimes you're really a dumb asshole.

COOTIE: But then again sometimes I'm not. (*Gets up and walks down the hall slowly*)

SHELLY: Hey!

MIKE *exits after* COOTIE, *leaving* SHELLY *alone. Slow fade.*

Scene 6

Most of the posters are down. A bare feeling. Around graduation. There's some letters on the table. RUTH, *alone, is reading her letter.* DICK *comes in from outside, dressed for warm weather, perhaps carrying a box.* HE *opens the icebox.*

DICK: Shit, nothing left.

RUTH: We cleaned it.

DICK: Anyone gone yet?

RUTH: No. Why don't you look at your grades?

DICK (*Opens letter*): Jesus.

RUTH: Bad?

DICK: Fucking awful.

RUTH: Do you graduate?

DICK: Yeah, just.

RUTH: They sent Kathy's grades here.

DICK: That was tactful.

RUTH: Maybe she'll be around to pick them up. I got into graduate school.

DICK: Great.

RUTH: Philosophy.

DICK: Philosophy?

RUTH: Yeah! (*Pause*) I mean, you know, why not? (DICK *starts toward the hall*) Hey, Dick, I don't get it. You know that day she left, just before Christmas . . . did you get into her?

DICK: How low can you stoop, Ruth?

RUTH: No, I mean, you know, just, she must've done something to fuck you up this bad.

DICK: Kathy did not fuck me up.

RUTH: Yeah, well, ever since she left you've been looking like really terrible. You never even studied for finals. I mean, you were the academic head around here. Hey, you did get her, didn't you, and I bet she told you you were the first guy that ever turned her on: (DICK *starts out again*) Did she? Oh, come off it, Dick, I just . . . I thought we were friends.

DICK: You know what that goddamn fucking little cunt told me? Just before she left? She told me I was screwing Roper's wife. Me, screwing Roper's wife.

RUTH: Well, you know Kathy.

DICK: She said everybody in the whole fucking school knew about it. It got back to Roper.

RUTH: Wow, I bet he was pretty pissed off, huh?

DICK: He was pretty good about it, considering. He pulled me in after a tutorial and gave me the old "Richard, my boy" speech. He thought I started the rumor. Me. Shit. "Richard, my boy, it's said you're doing unenviable things to my wife. My boy, that particular assignment has already been well seen to. It's not like you to claim credit for someone else's work." You ever tried to do a paper for someone who thinks you've been saying you're screwing his wife? Shit. Poor old fairy. Boy, what a fucking mess.

BOB *comes in the front door.*

RUTH: Hey, Bob, you got your grades.

BOB: Oh, yeah. (HE *looks*)

RUTH: How'd you do?

BOB: O.K. This for Kathy?

RUTH: Yeah. (BOB *starts to open* KATHY*'s letter*) Hey, that's private property.

BOB: What the fuck's gotten into you all of a sudden. (*Reads*) A, A, A, A . . . B minus. B minus in Poetry 210. Man, she really went to pieces without us. I hope she hasn't had a nervous breakdown or anything. Whew, B minus.

A knock on the door. DICK *opens it. It's* LUCKY.

LUCKY: Listen. I just seen Mr. Willis. He wants you out by tomorrow night.

BOB: How ya been, Lucky?

LUCKY: What? Oh, yeah. Well, if you want a hand, you know where to find me.

RUTH: Thanks a lot, buddy.

LUCKY: Don't get fresh, girlie, don't give me lip. You can talk how you want when you're with your own kind, but you show some respect when you're with Lucky. Smart alecks. Think you know everything. You don't . . . you don't know . . . you don't know what it's like living downstairs. That's something I know about. I know about living downstairs. I live downstairs. You seen me . . . you seen me out there, sitting out there. Well, you seen me . . .

BOB: Yeah, yeah, lots of times.

LUCKY: All right. That's what I mean. I sit out there. I'm out there. I got my Budweiser. I got my pretzels. Oh, yeah . . . I'm not just sitting out there, you know. I'm watching. I'm keeping my eyes open. (HE*'s slowly going into a trance*) I see them cars go by, all them cars. Fords. I see Fords out there. Chevies. Lincolns. Oldsmobiles. Plymouths. I see the odd Cadillac, oh, yeah, don't worry about that. It's all up here. You think I'm just sitting there with my Budweiser and pretzels. Think you know it all, oh, yeah.

DICK: Don't worry, we took care of it.

LUCKY: Huh?

DICK: We did like you said. Got rid of those plastic garbage cans and got some galvanized aluminum.

LUCKY: All right, that's what I mean. Now, if you want any help, I'll tell you what you do. You come downstairs. O.K.? (*As* HE *goes, we see him look around and call "Kitty-kitty"*)

RUTH: Guess I'll pack. (*Gets up to leave.* DICK *starts taking down one of his posters*)

BOB: Where's everyone?

RUTH: Mike and Mel went out with Norman. They're meeting Shelly at the flicks. *Casablanca.* You should see the marks they got. They're both magna cum.

DICK: Magna cum. Sneaky bastards.

RUTH: Yep. (SHE *goes out down hall*)

DICK: You staying for graduation?

BOB: No, you?

DICK (*Shakes head no*): Hey, you really going into the army?

BOB: Yeah,.as a hostage. I don't know. What are you doing?

DICK: Shit, I don't know.

BOB: Anything lined up for the summer?

DICK: Yeah, delivering milk. It's your friendly college graduate, Mrs. Miller. "Such a shame, the boy went to college." Maybe I'll get sterilized, save any kids having to go through all this. She really was a bitch, you know.

BOB: I guess so.

DICK: Guess so, shit, I hope she gets cancer of the tits and suffers like crazy while she's dying. Honest to Christ, she's the first person I ever met I could really kill.

BOB: Yeah.

DICK: Oh, great humility scene.

BOB: No, it's just, you know, that's how it goes.

DICK: You know something, Bob? You know what's wrong with you?

BOB: I been waiting all this time for someone to tell me. What's wrong with me, Dick?

DICK: You let her get your balls, Bob.

BOB: That was pretty careless, wasn't it?

DICK: No shit, Bob. I remember when you got stung by that bee in the humanities quadrangle. I always wondered about that. I mean, you're supposed to yell when something like that happens. You don't stand there wondering if you should say something. You really are dead, you know.

BOB: Yeah, well, that's what I was trying to tell everyone right before Christmas. I thought I might just try it out, you know, being dead. Didn't feel any different.

DICK: I don't get it.

BOB: No, it's a pretty weird thing.

DICK: I gotta pack.

BOB: Yeah.

DICK *leaves the room.* MIKE *and* COOTIE *burst in through the front door, panting heavily.*

MIKE: Oh, shit, man, we've really had it. Christ, how could the guy do it? I thought he was kidding.

RUTH (*Comes in with a small suitcase*): Hey, you guys better hurry up and pack. We gotta be out of here tomorrow.

COOTIE: Ruth, sit down, huh? Something pretty bad just happened. Seriously, no shitting around.

RUTH: Where's Norman?

COOTIE: Norman's . . . he just . . . oh, shit.

MIKE: He set himself on fire.

BOB: He what?

MIKE: All that stuff he was reading. He just . . . I don't know. He got this idea. Oh, fuck, how could the stupid bastard ever . . . shit.

RUTH: I thought you guys were going to see *Casablanca*.

MIKE: No, we had to tell you that. He had this plan. Honest to shit, we didn't know he was serious. Him and Shelly. We thought he's just . . . we went to the common and he took all his clothes off and poured gasoline all over himself.

COOTIE: We were just shitting around, Ruth. Honest. If we thought he was serious we'd've stopped him, you know.

MIKE: It was that fucking Shelly.

RUTH: You fucking stupid . . .

MIKE: I'm telling you, it wasn't our fault. He wouldn't have lit the match. I know he poured the gasoline, but he'd never've lit the match.

BOB: He's . . .

MIKE: Oh, shit, it was awful. He just sat there turning black. I didn't want to look, but I couldn't turn away. His skin just, Christ, it just fell away from his face and his blood . . . (*Puts head in hand*)

RUTH: Stupid fucking guys. You should've known. Where's Shelly?

COOTIE: She went crazy, Ruth. She just cracked up. We had to practically knock her out. She's O.K. now.

SHELLY *comes in the front door. Her eyes are closed and her fists clenched.* RUTH *runs to her, doesn't know what to do.*

RUTH: Shelly, oh, Shelly, Jesus . . .

SHELLY (*Teeth clenched*): Fucking guys.

NORMAN *comes in.* HE*'s soaking wet and carries a gasoline can.* MIKE *and* COOTIE *rise.*

MIKE: See, everything's cool now. Everybody trusts each other. That's what it's all about. (HE *smiles oddly at the others*)

COOTIE (*Registering it all*): Holy shit!

MIKE *and* COOTIE *leave the room.*

SHELLY (*Yells*): Creeps. (*To* RUTH) You got any first-aid stuff?

RUTH: Yeah. (SHE *gets a box from the pantry. It's a huge white box with a red cross on it, obviously stolen*)

BOB: Hey, what happened?

NORMAN (*Sits*): I'm all right.

SHELLY: Don't talk, Norman. Would you make him some coffee?

RUTH: Yeah. Those guys said you burned yourself.

NORMAN: No, I'm O.K.

RUTH *makes coffee while* SHELLY *ties a bandage around* NORMAN*'s wrist.*

SHELLY: Sorry if this hurts. Hey, Ruth, those guys are really bastards. They gotta learn you don't joke around sometimes.

BOB: Hey, were you really gonna burn yourself?

NORMAN: Well, you know . . .

SHELLY: We were all supposed to do it. All four of us. We waited all this time for them to graduate with good grades and everything. Six months almost. I mean, like, the war could've ended. Fucking creeps. They went and put water in the gasoline can.

NORMAN: I think I might be getting a cold.

SHELLY: We're making coffee, Norman. Keep cool.

BOB: Hey, were you really serious?

NORMAN: Well, I thought, you know, with the war and everything.

SHELLY: Water, shit.

NORMAN: Well, there was some gas in that can.

SHELLY: Fucking creeps.

NORMAN: I definitely smelled some gas when I poured it over me.

SHELLY: Hold still, Norman.

NORMAN: I mean, I knew there was something wrong when I kept holding the match to my wrist and nothing happened.

SHELLY: What do you mean, nothing happened? What's wrong with you, Norman? You call that burn on your wrist nothing? It's the worst burn I ever saw. We're lucky we didn't get arrested.

NORMAN: I've seen movies of the Buddhist monks setting themselves on fire. They usually go up pretty quick in the movies. I bet it hurts a lot. My wrist really hurts.

RUTH (*Brings* NORMAN *some coffee*): Listen, we have to be out of here by tomorrow.

NORMAN: All right.

RUTH: Well, what are you gonna do?

NORMAN: I haven't thought about it too much. I thought I was going to be dead by now. I hadn't planned beyond that.

RUTH: You got a place to stay?

SHELLY: He'll stay with me.

NORMAN: Yeah, O.K.

RUTH: We'll have to have a big cleanup in case Willis comes around.

NORMAN: I was thinking maybe I'll try to get back into graduate school. I'm getting sick of washing dishes.

> BOB *has been taking down his map of Europe from the wall.*

BOB: I think I'll go to Europe.

NORMAN: I'm not really angry at Mel and Mike. In a way I'm kind of glad I'm not dead.

SHELLY: I think those two guys are really evil.

> RUTH *goes down the hall.*

BOB: You ever been to France?

SHELLY: I went last summer.

BOB: What's it like?

SHELLY: Shitty. They're really uptight in France. I got busted in Calais. Two weeks in prison with the runs. That's no joke.

BOB: Maybe England.

NORMAN: I was in England once.

BOB: What's it like?

NORMAN: I went on a bicycle trip with the Youth Hostel Organization. My father sent me.

BOB: How was it?

NORMAN: It was O.K.

SHELLY: England's a lousy place.

NORMAN: I don't know. I met some nice people. I saw Buckingham Palace. The food's not very good, but it didn't rain much. I guess it was a pretty valuable experience. I remember thinking at the time my horizons were a lot wider after that trip. I don't remember why I thought that. Maybe I'll go back there one day.

BOB: Oh, well, there's always Italy or Greece.

SHELLY: If you go over there, check out Algeria. Algeria's really something else.

MR. WILLIS *opens the door.*

WILLIS: O.K. if I step in? Hey, what have you done to your hand?

NORMAN: It's just a burn.

WILLIS: Too bad, huh? Look, how's about if I see everyone for a minute? Everybody here?

BOB (*Yelling*): DICK, RUTH, MIKE, COOTIE, C'MERE A MINUTE. MR. WILLIS WANTS US.

WILLIS: Hey, hey, hey, you don't have to do that. You don't have to yell on account of me. (ALL *come in*) Hi, how's everybody? Gettin' ready for the big day? You gonna wear them long robes and everything, hey? All that fancy ceremony. Pretty good, huh? Listen, I just wanna give the place a quick once-over because I'll tell you why. I got this tenant moving in pretty soon, so I gotta be sure everything's O.K. Get rid of them milk bottles, that's the first thing, and I'll pick up the rent for this month, O.K.? How 'bout this floor, huh? You gonna finish it? Hey, I asked a question, who's supposed to be doing this floor?

BOB: I am, Mr. Willis.

WILLIS: So how come you leave it half-finished?

BOB: Sorry, I never got the time.

WILLIS: Well, you get it. I give you good money for them tiles, put me back a hunnered bucks. How many landlords you find'll do that?

BOB: Yeah, O.K.

WILLIS: By tomorrow night, understand? Now, let's have a little look round the place. (HE *goes down the hall followed by* BOB, RUTH, COOTIE *and* MIKE)

NORMAN: Mike. (MIKE *turns*) Listen, I just want to tell you, I'm not angry about what happened.

MIKE: What do you mean?

SHELLY: You're a real creep pulling a trick like that.

MIKE: That's what I get for saving his life?

SHELLY: It's none of your business. It's the existential right of every living person to take his own life.

MIKE: No one's stopping you now.

NORMAN: What I wanted to say is, if you and Mel are coming back next year to go to graduate school, maybe we can share a place. I mean, you know, I could come down here early and look around.

MIKE: You going home for the summer?

SHELLY: He's staying with me.

NORMAN: Yeah, well I might go home for a few weeks. Visit my folks. The best way is you write to my father, care of the Police Department, Erie County, and if I'm not at home he'll know where to forward it.

MIKE: Right. Me and Cootie'll be up in the great Northwest Territory helping Dad with the furs. If you don't hear from us, just go ahead and find a place for all of us, 'cause sometimes the mail gets delayed.

NORMAN: Don't worry, I'll get a place.

MIKE: Commissioner of Police, Erie County.

NORMAN: That's right.

MIKE *smiles at him, not without warmth. In come* COOTIE, RUTH, BOB, DICK *and* MR. WILLIS.

WILLIS: Not bad. I'll tellya what I'll do. I'll keep the fifty-dollar deposit for holes in the plaster and the broken window.

COOTIE: Hey, we didn't break that window. That was broken when we moved in.

WILLIS: That's not my problem, Cootie. I keep the fifty and if any of you guys got an objection, you want to take it up with me, let's have it. Look, I got a living to make like everybody else in town. Maybe you think I'm being a rotten guy, but you wait. You go out there in the world and you're gonna see things, you'll think old Willis was Snow White and the Seven Dwarfs all rolled into one. You're gonna see dishonesty, you're gonna see mean people, you see swindlers, killers, queers, you see guys trying to double-park on Saturday morning, you take my word. The thing I love about you kids is you're honest, you're direct. There's no shitting around with you. Yeah, I know it sounds corny, but I'm gonna miss having you guys around. You gotta save this poor fuckin' country, and excuse my language. There was a time, I can remember, when you paid your taxes and you knew your money was goin' into the right things. Good, wholesome things. Look at it nowadays. Two blocks away there's a house full of guys known all over the neighborhood to practice open homosexuality. Open homosexuality two blocks away, and there's kids playing right outside that house every day. I don't know. I'd go jump in the lake if it wasn't for you kids. I never knew anyone like you, and I been around, let me tellya. You know where you are, you know where you're going, and you know how to get there. That's never happened before in the history of this whole fucking country. God bless you kids, and good luck. I'll take a check for the rent.

> COOTIE *starts "For He's a Jolly Good Fellow"; the* OTHERS *join in.*

GROUP (*Singing*):
> For he's a jolly good fellow,
> For he's a jolly good fellow,
> For he's a jolly good fellow,
> That nobody can deny.
> That nobody can deny.
> That nobody can deny.
> (*Etc., all the way through.* WILLIS *beams, entirely unaware of the spoof*)

Scene 7

The next afternoon. The kitchen is bare of furniture. The icebox is gone, only a few milk bottles left. Only one chair left. BOB *is laying the vinyl tiles.* COOTIE *comes into the room with his* FATHER. HE *grabs the last valise by the front door.*

COOTIE: Hey, Bob, I'm going.
BOB: Yeah, we'll see you.
COOTIE: Yeah.
MIKE (*Comes into the kitchen from the hall door*): You going?
COOTIE: Yeah. Oh, this is my father. That's Mike, that's Bob.
BOB: Hi.
MIKE: Hi.
FATHER: A pleasure.
MIKE: What?
FATHER: It's a pleasure meeting you.
MIKE: Oh, yeah, right.
COOTIE: Well, see you guys. Hey, what you doing next year?
BOB: Oh, I got a job in a department store.
COOTIE: Playing piano?
BOB: Harp.
COOTIE: Great. Well, see ya.
BOB: See ya.
MIKE: Yeah, see ya, Cootie.
FATHER: Nice meeting you boys.

COOTIE *leaves with his* FATHER.

MIKE: They don't look like each other. Good old Cootie. Where's Norman?
BOB: He left about an hour ago.
MIKE: Never said good-bye or anything.
BOB: You should've seen it, putting all his stuff in the back of a police car.
MIKE: What?
BOB: Yeah, his old man's Commissioner of Police, or something.
MIKE: I'll be fucked.

RUTH *comes in from the hall with two suitcases and sets them down by some other suitcases near the door.*

RUTH: I guess that's it. Where's Cootie?
MIKE: He just left with his dad.
RUTH: Some friend. No good-bye or anything.
MIKE: We'll see him next year.
RUTH: No we won't.

MIKE *and* RUTH *go down the hall for their last luggage.* DICK *and the* MILKMAN *enter through the front door with empty cartons.* THEY *load the remaining bottles.*

DICK: Hey, I wouldn't mind a little help here. I gotta catch a train.
MILKMAN: I don't understand you guys. You're supposed to be college graduates. Eight hundred and fifty-seven two-quart milk bottles. That's not the kind of thing a grown-up person does. You're supposed to be grown-ups. I don't get it.

The phone is ringing.

DICK: That's the last one.
MILKMAN: O.K. I just hope you guys don't think you can go through life hoarding milk bottles like this. I got enough to do without this. I got a regular route. (*To* DICK) Look, if you want to pick up a lot of bottles, put your fingers right down inside, you get more that way.
DICK: O.K. Hey, you guys, you're a lot of help.

MILKMAN *and* DICK *go out with their cartons.*

BOB (*Answering phone*): Hello, oh, yes, how are you? No, this is Bob. Bob Rettie. No, music. Yes, of course I remember you. No, he's not in right now.

MIKE *and* RUTH *have reentered, motioning* BOB *that* THEY *have to go.* HE *motions back that it's O.K.* HE *waves good-bye as* THEY *pick up their suitcases and begin to leave.*

RUTH: Hey, good luck.

BOB: Yeah, yeah, you too. See ya, Mike.

MIKE: See ya.

RUTH and MIKE exit through front door.

BOB (*Back to phone*): Sorry, Mrs. Roper, I was just saying good-bye to some people I . . . some friends of mine. I don't know if he'll be back or not. Can I leave a message? (*Pause*) Look, Mrs. Roper, I'm very sorry about that but there's nothing I can do if he's gone. I can tell him to call you if he comes back, Mrs. Roper, look, calm down. Listen, I'm hanging up now, all right? I gotta hang up now. Good-bye, Mrs. Roper.

BOB hangs up and returns to the floor tiles. DICK comes in alone through front door.

DICK: Boy, that guy was sure pissed off about the bottles. You should've seen the look on his face.

BOB: Hey, you know that guy you studied with, Professor Roper?

DICK (*Pause*): Yes.

BOB: His wife just called.

DICK: What'd she want?

BOB: She just . . . I don't know. Nothing, I guess. Pretty weird.

DICK: Yeah, pretty weird. (HE *puts on his coat and takes up his bags*)

BOB: Hey, Dick.

DICK: What?

THEY look at each other.

BOB: I don't know. See ya.

DICK: Yeah. (*As* HE *is leaving,* HE *sees* KATHY, *who is standing in the doorway*)

KATHY: Hi. Can I come in? (DICK *moves aside.* HE *and* BOB *stare at her. This makes her a little nervous*) Everyone gone?

DICK and BOB(*Together*): Yeah . . . (THEY *exchange a nervous glance*)

BOB: Except for me and Dick. We're still here. We're right in front of you, as a matter of fact. . . .

DICK: That's a nice coat she's wearing. That's a very nice coat, Kathy.

KATHY (*Knows something is going on but doesn't know what*): Thanks.

BOB: Hey, Dick. (DICK *leaves*) See ya. (*To himself*)

KATHY: Finishing the floor?

BOB: Evidently.

KATHY: Kind of late, isn't it? (*Pause*) Did they send my grades here?

BOB: Right there. You did really shitty.

KATHY (*Gets the letter*): Bob, listen . . . I'm sorry about . . . sounds pretty silly.

BOB: No, I accept your apology for whatever you think you did.

KATHY: I saw Ruth the other day. She said you've been . . . well, pretty bad this semester.

BOB: Did she say that?

KATHY: I wish I'd known . . . couldn't you have . . . you should have told me to stay.

BOB: Well, it slipped my mind. Sorry.

KATHY: You shouldn't be so ashamed of your feelings.

BOB: O.K.

KATHY: I'm serious. You've gotta learn to let go. Like your music. It's all squenched and tidy.

BOB: O.K. I'll work on that.

KATHY: Oh, Bob.

BOB: What?

KATHY: I really wish you'd've told me. I'd've come back. I never really related to Richard.

BOB: I'll tell him when I see him.

KATHY: Yeah, you're right. Why the hell should you be nice? Oh, well, good luck . . . and, you know, when you see your mother say hello for me.

BOB: O.K.

KATHY: How is she?

BOB: She's O.K. Sort of dead.

KATHY: I like her, Bob. You're lucky. She's, you know, she's a real person.

BOB: No, she's you know, a real corpse.

KATHY: All right, have it your way.

BOB: No, it's not what I wanted particularly. No, taken all in all, from various different angles, I'd've preferred it if she lived. I'm pretty sure of that.

KATHY (*Pause*): She's not really . . . ?

BOB: School's over.

KATHY: Bob, do you know what you're saying?

BOB: Kathy, please get the fuck out of here.

KATHY: But, I mean, Ruth never told me. . . . Didn't you tell anyone?

BOB: Yeah, I just told you.

KATHY: But, I mean . . . when . . . when did . . .

BOB: Christmas. No, no, it was the day after.

KATHY (*Sits*): Jesus, Bob, why didn't you tell anyone? I mean, how could you live for six months without telling someone?

BOB (*No emotion*): Oh, I don't know. A little cunning. A little fortitude. A little perseverance. (*Pause*) I couldn't believe it. Not the last time anyway. They put her in this room. I don't know what you call it. They bring everybody there just before they kick the bucket. They just sort of lie there looking at each other, wondering what the hell they got in common to talk about. I couldn't believe that anyone could look like she looked and still be alive. (*Pause*) She knew. I'm sure of that. (*Pause*) Once, I remember, she tried to tell me something. I mean this noise came out of somewhere around her mouth, like somebody running a stick over a fence or something, and I thought maybe she's trying to tell me something. So I leaned over to hear better and I caught a whiff of that breath. Like fried puke. And I was sick all over her. (*Pause. Brighter*) But you want to know something funny, and I mean this really is funny, so you can laugh if you like. There was this lady dying next to my mother and she kept talking about her daughter Susan. Well, Susan came to visit the day I puked on Mom. And you know what? It was only Susan Weinfeld, which doesn't mean anything to you, but she happens to have been the girl I spent a good many of my best months as a sophomore in high school trying to lay. In fact, her virginity almost cost me a B plus in history and here we were, six years later, staring at each other across two dying mothers. I want to tell you something, Kathy. She looked fantastic. And I could tell she was thinking the same thing about me. I mean that kind of scene doesn't happen every day. It was like . . . (*thinks*) . . . it was like how we were the first time. Maybe, just possibly, a little better. So we went out and had a coffee in Mister Donut and started groping each other like crazy under the counter, and I mean we just couldn't keep our hands off each other, so I suggested we get a cab down to my mother's place since, you know, there happened to be no one there at the moment. But the funniest thing was when we get down to Mom's place and you know all those stairs you have to go up and there's Susan all over me practically screaming for it and I start fumbling around with the keys in the lock and none of them would fit. I must've tried every key about fifty fucking times and none of them would fit. Boy, what a drag. (*Pause*) Oh, we got in all right. Finally. I had to go downstairs, through the Salvatores' apartment, out the window, up the fire escape, and through Mom's place, but when I opened the front door, guess what? There's poor old Susan asleep on the landing. She really looked cute. I hated to wake her up. Anyway, by the time we'd made coffee and talked and smoked about a million cigarettes each we didn't feel like it anymore. Not really. We did it anyway but, you know, just to be polite, just to make some sense out of the evening. It was, taken all in all, a pretty ordinary fuck. The next morning we made plans to meet again that night. We even joked about it, you know, about what a super-fucking good time we'd have, and if you ask me, we could've probably really gotten into something incredible if we'd tried again, but when I went to the hospital I found out good old Mom had croaked sometime during the night, and somehow, I still don't know why to this day . . . I never got in touch with Susan again. And vice versa. It's a funny thing, you know. At the funeral there were all these people. Friends of Mom's—I didn't know any of them. They were all crying like crazy and I . . . well . . . (*Pause*) I never even got to the burial. The car I was in broke down on the Merritt Parkway. Just as well. I didn't feel like seeing all those people. I'd sure love to have fucked Susan again, though.

KATHY: Bob . . . I . . .

BOB (*Abstract*): Anyway . . . I just didn't feel like telling anyone. I mean, I wasn't all that upset. I was a little upset, mostly because I thought I ought to be more upset, but as for your actual grief, well. Anything interesting happen to you this semester . . . Kathy? (KATHY *has risen*) Going? (KATHY *is going out the door*) Give my regards to that guy you're rescuing at the moment; what's-his-name? (KATHY *is gone.* HE *shrugs. The cat wanders in from the hallway*) Hey, cat, what are you doing hanging around here? All the humans gone west. (*Puts the cat outside and shuts the door.* HE *nudges the tiles with his toe and looks around at the empty room*) Hey, guys, guess what happened to me? I want to tell you about this really incredible thing that happened to me . . . (HE *is faltering now, choking slightly, but* HE *doesn't know* HE*'s about to crack. His body is doing something strange, unfamiliar*) Hey, what's happening . . . (HE*'s crying now*) Oh, fuck, come on, come on. Shit, no, no . . .

Fade.

END OF PLAY

STILL LIFE

Emily Mann

About Emily Mann

Born in Boston in 1952, Emily Mann received a B.A. from Harvard and an MFA from the University of Minnesota. Her first play, *Annulla Allen: Autobiography of a Survivor*, premiered at The Guthrie Theater's Guthrie 2 under her direction in 1977 and was later produced at Chicago's Goodman Theatre and on *Earplay*. Mann's most recent play, *Execution of Justice*, which depicts the trial of Dan White for the killing of George Moscone and Harvey Milk, was commissioned by the Eureka Theatre Company of San Francisco and first produced by Actors Theatre of Louisville, as co-winner of its 1984 Great American Play Contest. Mann's directorial credits include the BAM Theater Company's productions of *He and She* and *Oedipus the King*, the Guthrie's *The Glass Menagerie* and ATL's *A Weekend near Madison*, which subsequently ran Off Broadway. She has been the recipient of a CAPS grant, a Guggenheim fellowship and an NEA artistic associateship, and is a 1985 McKnight Fellow. In 1983 Mann received the Rosamond Gilder Award from the New Drama Forum for "outstanding creative achievement in the theatre."

Production History

Still Life premiered at the Goodman Studio Theatre in October 1980, and was then produced at American Place Theatre in New York in early 1981. The American Place production, under Mann's direction, won Obies for playwriting, direction and all three performances, as well as for best production. The play has subsequently been performed around the world—in Johannesburg, at the Avignon and Edinburgh festivals, in London and Paris, and in major regional theatres and universities throughout the United States.

Playwright's Note

Still Life is about three people I met in Minnesota during the summer of 1978. It is about violence in America. The Vietnam War is the backdrop to the violence at home. The play is dedicated to the casualties of the war—all of them.

The play is a "documentary" because it is a distillation of interviews I conducted during that summer. I chose the documentary style to insure that the reality of the people and events described could not be denied. Perhaps one could argue about the accuracy of the people's interpretations of events, but one cannot deny that these are actual people describing actual events as they saw and understood them.

The play is also a personal document. A specialist in the brain and its perceptions said to me after seeing *Still Life* that the play is constructed as a traumatic memory. Each character struggles with his traumatic memory of events and the play as a whole is my traumatic memory of their accounts. The characters speak directly to the audience so that the audience can hear what I heard, experience what I experienced.

I have been obsessed with violence in our country since I came of age in the 1960s. I have no answer to the questions I raise in the play but I think the questions are worth asking. The play is a plea for examination and self-examination, an attempt at understanding our own violence and a hope that through understanding we can, as Nadine says, "come out on the other side."

Production Notes

The actors speak directly to the audience. The rhythms are of real people's speech, but may also at times have the sense of improvisation one finds with the best jazz musicians: the monologues should sometimes sound like extended riffs.

The play is written in three acts but this does not denote act breaks. Rather, the acts represent movements and the play should be performed without intermission. The ideal running time is one hour and 30 minutes.

Lyrics for "No More Genocide" by Holly Near

Verse 1
Why do we call them the enemy
This struggling nation that we're bombing 'cross the sea
we put in prison/now independent
Why do we want these people to die
Why do we say North and South
Oh why, Oh why, Oh why?

Chorus
Well, that's just a lie
One of the many and we've had plenty
I don't want more of the same
Genocide in my name
Genocide, no, no, no, no

No more genocide, no, no, no, no
No more genocide in my name

Verse 2:
Why are our history books so full of lies
When no word is spoken of why the Indian dies
Or that the Chicano loves the California land
Do our books all say it was discovered by white man.

Chorus

Verse 3:
Why are the weapons of the war so young
Why are there only older men around when it's done
Why are so many of our soldiers black or brown
Do we say it's because they're good at cutting yellow people down.

Chorus

Characters

MARK, an ex-marine, Vietnam veteran, husband, artist, lover, father.
CHERYL, his wife, mother of his children.
NADINE, his friend, artist, mother of three, divorcee, a woman with many jobs
     and many lives, 10-15 years older than Mark and Cheryl.

Time

The present.

Place

The setting is a long table with ashtrays, water glasses, Mark's pictures and slides upon it. Behind it is a large screen for slide projection. The look is of a conference room or perhaps a trial room.

The director may also choose to place each character in a separate area, i.e. Cheryl in her living room (couch), Mark in his studio (framing table), Nadine at home or at a cafe table.

The Play

Still Life

ACT ONE

I

MARK *snaps on slide of* CHERYL: *young, fragile, thin, hair flowing, quintessentially innocent.*

MARK: This is a picture of my wife before.
(*Lights up on* CHERYL. *Six months pregnant, heavy, rigid*)
This is her now.
She's been through a lot.
(*Snaps on photographic portrait of himself. Face gentle. Halo of light around head*)
This is a portrait Nadine made of me.
(*Lights up on* NADINE)
This is Nadine.
(*Lights out on* NADINE. *Snaps on slide of marine boot and leg just below the knee*)
This is a picture of my foot.
I wanted a picture of it because if I ever lost it,
I wanted to remember what it looked like.
(HE *laughs. Fade out*)

II

CHERYL: If I thought about this too much I'd go crazy.
So I don't think about it much.
I'm not too good with the past.
Now, Mark, he remembers.
That's his problem.
I don't know whether it's 1972 or 1981.
Sometimes I think about divorce.
God, I don't know.
Divorce means a lot of nasty things
like it's over.
It says a lot like
Oh yeah. I been there. I'm a divorcee. . . . Geez.
You could go on forever about that thing.
I gave up on it. No.
You know, I wasn't willing to give up on it,
and I should have,
for my own damn good.

You look:
It's all over now,
it's everywhere.
There are so many men like him now.

You don't have to look far to see how
sucked in you can get.

You got a fifty-fifty chance.

III

NADINE: When I first met Mark, it was the big stuff.
Loss of ego, we shared everything.

The first two hours I spent with him and what I thought
then is what I think now, and I know just about everything
there is to know, possibly.

He told me about it *all* the first week I met him.
We were discussing alcoholism.
I'm very close to that myself.
He said that one of his major projects
was to face all the relationships he'd been in
where he'd violated someone.

His wife is one.

He's so honest he doesn't hide anything.

He told me he beat her very badly.
He doesn't know if he can recover that relationship.

I've met his wife.
I don't know her.
I sometimes even forget . . .

He's the greatest man I've ever known.
I'm still watching him.

We're racing. It's very wild.
No one's gaming.
There are no expectations.
You have a foundation for a lifelong relationship.
He can't disappoint me.

Men have been wonderful to me,
but I've never been treated like this.
All these—yes, all these men—
businessmen, politicians, artists, patriarchs—none of
them, no one has ever demonstrated this to me.

He's beyond consideration.
I have him under a microscope.
I can't be fooled.
I know what natural means.
I know when somebody's studying.
I've been around a long time.
I'm forty-three years old.
I'm not used to being treated like this.

I don't know. I'm being honored, cherished, cared about.

Maybe this is how everybody's treated and I've missed out.
(*Laughs*)

IV

MARK: My biggest question to myself all my life was

How I would act under combat?
That would be who I was as a man.

I read my Hemingway.
You know . . .

The point is,
you don't *need* to go through it.

I would break both my son's legs
before I let him go through it.

CHERYL: I'm telling you—
if I thought about this, I'd go crazy.
So I don't think about it.

MARK: (*To* CHERYL)
I know I did things to you, Cheryl.
But you took it.
I'm sorry.
How many times can I say I'm sorry to you?
(*To audience*)
I've, uh, I've, uh, hurt my wife.

NADINE: He is incredibly gentle. It's madness to be treated this way. I
don't need it. It's great without it.

CHERYL: He blames it all on the war . . . but I want to tell
you . . . don't let him.

MARK: My wife has come close to death a number of times, but
uh . . .

NADINE: Maybe he's in awe of me.

CHERYL: See, I read into things,
and I don't know if you're supposed to, but I do.
Maybe I'm too against his artist world,
but Mark just gets into trouble
when he's into that art world.

NADINE: (*Laughing*)
Maybe he's this way to his mother.

CHERYL: One day I went into the basement to take my clothes out of the
washer,
Jesus I have to clean out that basement,
and I came across this jar . . .

NADINE: Especially from a guy who's done all these dastardly deeds.

CHERYL: He had a naked picture of me in there,
cut out to the form,
tied to a stake with a string.
And there was all this broken glass,
and I know Mark.
Broken glass is a symbol of fire.
(*Thinking*)
What else did he have at the bottom?

NADINE: I accept everything he's done.

CHERYL: Yeah, there was a razor blade in there

and some old negatives of the blood stuff, I think.
I mean, that was so violent.
That jar to me, scared me.
That jar to me said:
Mark wants to kill me.
Literally kill me for what I've done.
He's burning me at the stake like Joan of Arc.
It just blew my mind.

NADINE: Those jars he makes are brilliant, humorous.
He's preserving the war.
I'm intrigued that people think he's violent.
I know all his stories.
He calls himself a time-bomb.
But so are you, aren't you?

MARK: I don't know what it would be for women.
What war is for men.
I've thought about it. A lot.
I saw women brutalized in the war.
I look at what I've done to my wife.

CHERYL: He keeps telling me: He's a murderer.
I gotta believe he can be a husband.

MARK: The truth of it is, it's different
from what we've heard about war before.

NADINE: He's just more angry than any of us.
He's been fighting for years.
Fighting the priests, fighting all of them.

MARK: I don't want this to come off as a combat story.

CHERYL: Well, a lot of things happened that I couldn't handle.

MARK: It's a tragedy is what it is. It happened to a lot of people.

CHERYL: But not too, you know, not anything
dangerous or anything like that—
just crazy things.

NADINE: I guess all my friends are angry.

CHERYL: But, uh, I don't know.
It's really hard for me to bring back those years.

NADINE: Mark's just been demonstrating it, by picking up weapons,
leading a group of men.

CHERYL: Really hard for me to bring back those years.

MARK: My brother . . .
He has a whole bunch of doubts now,
thinking, "Well I wonder what I'd do
if I were in a fight."
And you don't NEED to go through that shit.

It's BULLSHIT.
It just chews people up.

NADINE: Leading a whole group into group sex, vandalism, theft.
That's not uncommon in our culture.

MARK: You go into a VFW hall, that's all men talk about.
Their trips on the war.

NADINE: I don't know anyone who cares so much about his parents.
He's trying to save them.
Like he sent home this bone of a man he killed, from Nam.
It was this neat attempt to demand for them to listen,
about the war.

MARK: I can't talk to these guys.
There's just no communication.
But we just . . . know.
We look and we know.

NADINE: See, he's testing everyone all the time.
In very subtle ways.
He can't believe I'm not shocked.
I think that intrigues him.

CHERYL: Oh. I don't know.
I want it suppressed as fast as possible.

NADINE: He laughed at me once.
He'd just told a whole raft of stories.
He said: "Anyone who understands all this naughtiness
must have been pretty naughty themselves."
Which is a pretty simplistic way of saying we can all do it.

MARK: I thought:
If I gave *you* the information,
I couldn't wash my hands of the guilt,
because I did things over there.
We all did.

CHERYL: I would do anything to help suppress it.

MARK: (*Quietly to audience*)
We all did.

V

NADINE: You know what war is for women?
A friend of mine sent me this line:
I'd rather go into battle three times than give birth once.
She said Medea said that.
I stuck it on my refrigerator.
I showed it to Mark. He laughed for days.

MARK: When Cheryl, uh, my wife and I first met,
I'd just come back from Nam.
I was so frightened of her.
She had this long hair and she was really thin.
I just thought she was really, uh,
really American.

NADINE: Do you know I never talked with my husband
about being pregnant?
For nine months there was something going on down there
and we never mentioned it. Ever.

MARK: You know, it was like I couldn't talk to her.
I didn't know how to respond.

NADINE: We completely ignored it.
We were obsessed with names.
We kept talking constantly about what we would name it.
I gained fifty pounds. It was sheer ignorance.
I was a good Catholic girl
and no one talked about such things.
I never knew what that part of my body was doing.

CHERYL: It was my naivety.
I was so naive to the whole thing, that his craziness
had anything to do with where he'd been.
I mean, I was naive to the whole world
let alone somebody
who had just come back from there.

NADINE: When the labor started, we merrily got in the car
and went to the hospital.
They put me immediately into an operating room.
I didn't even know what dilation meant.
And I couldn't.
I could not dilate.

CHERYL: See, I'd hear a lot from his family.
I worked for his father as a dental assistant.
And it was all they talked about—Mark—so I had to meet the
guy.

NADINE: I was in agony, they knocked me out.

CHERYL: And I saw, I mean, I'd open a drawer and I'd see
these pictures—

NADINE: My lungs filled up with fluid.

CHERYL: . . . dead men. Men hanging. Things like that.
Pictures Mark had sent back.

MARK: Yeah. I kept sending everything back.

NADINE: They had to give me a tracheotomy.

My trachea was too small.
They went running out of the operating room to get
the right equipment.
Everyone thought I was going to die.

CHERYL: Once he sent back a bone of a man he killed. To his mother.

MARK: To my brother, not my mother.

CHERYL: Boy, did that lady freak.

NADINE: My husband saw them burst out of the room in a panic.
He thought I was gone.

CHERYL: Now it doesn't take much for that lady to freak.
Very hyper. I think I'd've gone nuts.
I think I'd wanna take it
and hit him over the head with it.
You just don't do those things.
WHAT THE HECK IS HAPPENING TO YOU? I'd say.
They never asked that though.
I don't think they wanted to know
and I think they were afraid to ask.

MARK: I know. I really wanted them to ask.

CHERYL: I think they felt the sooner forgotten, the better off you'd be.

NADINE: I remember leaving my body.

MARK: I'll never forget that.

CHERYL: They didn't want to bring up a bad subject.

MARK: I came home from a war, walked in the door,
they don't say anything.
I asked for a cup of coffee,
and my mother starts bitching at me about drinking coffee.

NADINE: I looked down at myself on that operating table and felt so free.

CHERYL: Your mother couldn't deal with it.

NADINE: They gave me a C-section.
I don't remember anything else.

CHERYL: My memory's not as good as his.
It's like I put bad things in one half
and in time I erase them.

NADINE: I woke up in the hospital room with tubes in my throat,
stitches in my belly. I could barely breathe.
My husband was there. He said: Have you seen the baby?
WHAT BABY, I said.

Can you believe it?

CHERYL: That's why I say there's a lot of things, weird things,
that happened to us, and I just generally put them
under the title of weird things . . .

and try to forget it.
And to be specific, I'm real vague on a lot of things.

NADINE: I never knew they were in there
and so I guess I didn't want them to come out.

CHERYL: I mean, my whole life has turned around since then.
I mean, gosh, I got a kid and another one on the way.
And I'm thinking of climbing the social ladder.
I've got to start thinking about schools for them,
and I *mean* this, it's a completely
different life,
and I've had to . . .
I've WANTED to change anyway.

It's really hard to bring these things back out.

NADINE: For my second child, the same thing happened.
By the third time around
they had to drag me out of the car.
I thought they were taking me to my death for sure.

MARK: Cheryl is amazing.
Cheryl has always been like chief surgeon.
When the shrapnel came out of my head,
she would be the one to take it out.

CHERYL: It's no big deal.

NADINE: So when people ask me about the birth of my children,
I laugh.

MARK: Just like with Danny.
She delivered Danny herself.

NADINE: My children were EXTRACTED from me.

CHERYL: It's no big deal. Just like pulling teeth.
Once the head comes out, there's nothing to it.

VI

MARK: I want to tell you what a marine is.

NADINE:	CHERYL:
I have so much to do.	See, I got kids now.
Just to keep going.	
	I can't be looking into
Just to keep my kids going.	myself.
I don't sleep at all.	I've got to be looking
	out.

When my kids complain
about supper.

I just say:
I know it's crappy food.
Well, go upstairs
and throw it up.

I was in a cafe today.

For the next five years
at least.

When I'm ready to look
in, look out.

God, don't get into the
kid routine. It'll do
it to you every time.

Because you're getting
their best interests
mixed up with *your* best
interests. And they
don't go together.

I heard the funniest comment:

They go together because
it *should* be your best
interest, and *then their*
best interest. So what
are you gonna do to them
in the meantime?

She must be married.
She spends so much money.

You're talking head-trips.

VII

MARK: There was this whole trip that we were really special.
         And our training was really hard,
         like this whole Spartan attitude.
CHERYL: The war is the base of all our problems.
         He gets crazy talking about it
         and you can't get him to stop
         no matter what he's doing to the people around him.
MARK: And there was this whole thing too
         I told Nadine about that really knocked me out.
         There was this whole ethic:
         You do not leave your man behind on the field.
         I love that.
CHERYL: Well, he's usually talking more than they can handle.
NADINE: You know, we had two months of foreplay.
MARK: I came to a point in there:

Okay, you're here, there's no escape, you're going to get taken,
it's all right to commit suicide.
And it was as rational as that.

We came across a hit at night, we got ambushed,
it was a black guy walking point, and you know,
bang, bang, bang.
You walk into it. It was a surprise.

Well, they got this black guy.
And they took his body and we found him about a week
    later . . .

CHERYL: People start getting really uncomfortable,
and you can see it in his eyes,
the excitement.
NADINE: The first time I met Mark,
I'd gone to his shop to buy supplies.
I didn't think anything about him at first.
(I've never been attracted to younger men.)
But he seemed to know what he was doing.
CHERYL: It's almost like there's fire in his eyes.
MARK: And they had him tied to a palm tree,
and his balls were in his mouth.
They'd opened up his stomach and it had been pulled out.
And I knew . . .
NADINE: I saw some of his work.
MARK: Nobody was going to do that to me.
NADINE: Some of the blood photography I think.
MARK: Better for me to rationalize suicide
because I didn't want . . .
that.
I don't know.
CHERYL: It bothers me because it's better left forgotten.
It's just stirring up clear water.
NADINE: We talked and I left. But I felt strange.
MARK: R.J. was my best friend over there.
He and I got into a whole weird trip.
We found ourselves competing against one another,
setting up ambushes,
getting people on *kills* and things,
being the best at it we could.
NADINE: All of a sudden, he came out of the shop and said:
"You want a cup of tea?"

I was in a hurry,
(I'm always in a hurry)
but I said, "Sure," and we went to a tea shop.
(*Laughs*)

MARK: R.J. is dead.
He got killed in a bank robbery in Chicago.
(He was one of the few friends of mine who survived the war.)

NADINE: Two hours later, we got up from the table.
I'm telling you, neither of us could stand up.
We were gasping for breath.

MARK: See, I got all these people involved
in a Far East smuggling scam when we got back,
and then it all fell apart
and we were waiting to get arrested.

The smack got stashed in this car that was being held
in a custody lot.
Everyone was afraid to go get it.
So I decided to get it.
I did this whole trip Thanksgiving weekend.
I crawled in there,
stole the tires off the car
that were loaded with the smack.
I had R.J. help me.
We were doing the war all over again.
That was the last time I saw him alive.

NADINE: We had said it *all* in two hours.
What I thought then is what I think now
and I think I know everything there is to know.

We must have looked pretty funny staggering out of there.

MARK: I heard from one guy on a regular basis, maybe once a year.
He was green to Vietnam.
We were getting into
some real heavy contact that Christmas.
It was late at night, the VC went to us
while we were sleeping.
They just threw grenades in on us.
The explosion came, I threw this kid in a bush.
All I did was grab him down,
and he got a medical out of there.
But he feels I saved his life.

NADINE: When we got out onto the street we said good-bye

but we both knew that our whole lives had changed.

CHERYL: I know he has other women. I don't know who they are.
At this point I don't really care.
I have a child to think about
and just getting by every day.

NADINE: We used to meet and talk.
We'd meet in the plaza and talk.
We'd go for rides in the car and talk.

CHERYL: See, lots of times people break up.
And then the man goes on to the next one.
And you hear the guy say:
"Oh, my wife was crazy." Or something like that.
"She couldn't take it."

NADINE: Sometimes we'd be driving,
we'd have to stop the car and get our breaths.
We were dizzy, we were gasping for breath,
just from being together.

CHERYL: But the important question to ask is: WHY is she crazy?

MARK: So he wants to see me.
I haven't been able to see him.

CHERYL: My brother is a prime example.
He nearly killed his wife a number of times.
She was a real high-strung person.
She snapped.
The family keeps saying, oh, poor Marge, she was so crazy.

MARK: He was only in the bush maybe five, six weeks,
but it did something to him.
He spent two years, he wrote me a letter,
in a mental institution.
I don't know.

I knew he knew what I knew.

CHERYL: My brother's now got one little girl
that SAW her little brother
get shot in the head by his mother . . .

MARK: I know who's been there.
And they know.

CHERYL: And then saw her mother come after her.

MARK: But in a sense we want to be as far away
from each other as possible.
It's become a *personal* thing. The guilt.
There IS the guilt.
It's getting off on having all that power every day.

Because it was so nice.
I mean, it was power . . .
NADINE: You know they're doing surveys now, medical research on this.
MARK: I had the power of life and death.
NADINE: They think something actually changes
in the blood or the lungs when you feel this way.
CHERYL: I'm sorry. They were married too long
for it just to have been Marge.
MARK: I'm sitting here now deep down thinking about it . . .
NADINE: You watch. Soon there'll be a science of love,
and there should be.
CHERYL: When someone goes so-called crazy in a marriage,
I always think:
IT TAKES TWO.
MARK: It's like the best dope you've ever had,
the best sex you've ever had.
NADINE: It was like dying,
and it was the most beautiful feeling of my life.
CHERYL: My brother's on to a new woman now.
MARK: You never find anything better.
And that's not something
you're supposed to feel good about.
CHERYL: If Mark and I split up, I pity the next one.
MARK: I haven't told you what a marine is yet.
CHERYL: Women should warn each other.

Pause.

NADINE: Everything Mark did was justified.
We've all done it.
Murdered someone we loved, or ourselves.
MARK: I mean, we were trained to do one thing.
That's the one thing about the marines.
We were trained to kill.
NADINE: This is hard to say.
I have been in the jungle so long,
that even with intimates, I protect myself.
But I know that Mark felt good killing.
When he told me that I didn't bat an eye.
I understand.
CHERYL: Look,
I think Mark and R.J. were close
only because they both got off on the war.
And I think they were the only two over there that did.

Doesn't it kill you when they get into this men-talk?
All men don't talk like that,
when they get together to reminisce.
They don't talk about getting laid and dope.
Imagine getting together with your best girlfriend
and talking about what it was like the night before in the sack.
That grosses me out.

NADINE: I judge everyone so harshly
that it is pretty ironic
that I'm not moved by anything he tells me.
I'm not changed. I'm not shocked.
I'm not offended. And he must see that.

MARK: I had the power of life and death.
I wrote home to my brother.
I wrote him, I told him.
I wrote:
I dug it. I enjoyed it.
I really enjoyed it.

NADINE: I understand because I'm *convinced*
that I am even angrier than Mark.
I went off in a different direction, that's all.

CHERYL: Now I don't think Mark and R.J. were rare.
I think the DEGREE is rare.
I mean men would not be going on fighting like this
for centuries if there wasn't something besides
having to do it for their country.
It has to be something like Mark says.
I mean he said it was like orgasm.
He said it was the best sex he ever had.
You know where he can take that remark.
But what better explanation can you want?
And believe me, that is Mark's definition of glory.
Orgasm is GLORY to Mark.

MARK: I talked with R.J. about it.
He got into a hit once at about 8:30 at night.
And there was this "person" . . .
laying down, wounded,
holding onto a grenade.
(It was a high contact.)
We watched R.J. walk over and he just shot . . .
the person . . .
in the face.

He knew it.

As incredibly civilized as we are in this room, these things go
    on.
NADINE: Until you know a lot of Catholics
    you can't understand what hate means.
    I mean I'm a . . . I was a Catholic.
    And Catholics have every right to hate like they do.
    It requires a whole lifetime
    to undo what that training does to them.
MARK: It's getting hard to talk.
    Obviously, I need to tell it,
    but I don't want to be seen as . . .
    a monster.
NADINE: Just start talking to Catholics
    who allow themselves to talk.
    It's unspeakable what's been done to Catholic youths.
    Every aspect of their life from their table manners
    to their sexuality. It's just terrible.
MARK: I'm just moving through society now.

Pause.

VIII

NADINE: I mean my definition of sophistication
    is the inability to be surprised by anything.
MARK: I look at my face in a mirror,
    I look at my hand, and I cannot believe . . .
    I did these things.
CHERYL: Mark's hit me before.
MARK: See, I see the war now through my wife.
    She's a casualty too.
    She doesn't get benefits for combat duties.
    The war busted me up, I busted up my wife . . .
CHERYL: He's hit me more than once.
MARK: I mean I've hit my wife.
NADINE: Have you ever been drunk for a long period of time?
MARK: But I was always drunk.
NADINE: Well, I have.
MARK: We were always drunk.
    It would boil out,
    the anger,
    when we were drunk.
NADINE: I used to drink a lot

and did vicious things when I was drunk.
And until you're there,
you don't *know.*

MARK: When I was sober, I found out what I'd done to her.
It was . . . I just couldn't stop.

CHERYL: I was really into speed—oh, how many years ago?
I'm not good with the past.
I mean Mark knows dates and years.
God I don't know.

MARK: It's like . . .
I feel terrible about it.
The last time it happened
it was about a year ago now.
I made up my mind to quit drinking
because drinking's what's brought it on.

CHERYL: We got into some kind of argument about speed.
And he pushed me down the stairs.
He hit me a couple of times.

NADINE: Yeah it's there and it takes years.
My husband I were
grooving on our fights.
I mean really creative.
And five years ago we got down to the count.
Where we were batting each other around.
Okay, I hit my husband. A lot.
See, I'm capable of it.

MARK: I dropped out of AA.
I put the cork in the bottle myself.

NADINE: Okay—I really was drunk, really mad.
And I beat him up and do you know what he said to me?
He turned to me after he took it and he said:
I didn't know you cared that much.
It was the most incredible thing.
And he stood there and held his face
and took it
and turned around in a state of glory and said:
I didn't think you cared.
I'll never hit another person again.

CHERYL: I went to the hospital
'cause my ribs . . .
I think, I don't know.
I don't remember it real clearly.
It had something to do with speed.

The fact that I wasn't, I was,
I wasn't rational.
No, I must have really tore into him.
I mean I can be nasty.
So anyway that was hard because I couldn't go to work
for a couple of weeks.

NADINE: And I see Mark.
The fact that he beat his wife.
I understand it.
I don't like it.
But I understand it.

MARK: I've been sober so long now, it's terrifying.
See, I really got into photography while I was drunk.
Got involved in the art program at the U.
I mean I could be fine
and then the wrong thing would come up
and it would shut me off.

NADINE: Don't distance yourself from Mark.

MARK: I'd space out and start talking about the war.
See, most of these people
didn't have to deal with it.
They all dealt with the other side.

NADINE: I was "anti-war," I marched, I was "non-violent."
(*Laughs*)

MARK: I brought some photos.
This is a picture of some people who at one point in time
were in my unit. That is,
they were there at the time the photo was taken.
Some of them are dead, some of them made it home,
(*Pause*)
some of them are dead now.

NADINE: But I'm capable of it.

MARK: After I was there, I could never move with people
who were against the war in a real way.
It took a part of our life.
I knew what it was and they didn't.

NADINE: We all are.

MARK: They could get as pissed off as they wanted to
I didn't fight with them.
I didn't bitch with them.
I just shut up. Excuse me.
(*Looks at audience. Sees or thinks* HE *sees they're on the other side. Moment of murderous anger.* HE *shuts up and exits*)

IX

CHERYL: I'm scared knowing that I have to keep my mouth shut.
I don't know this for a fact, but I mean
I fantasize a lot.
I have to.
I've got nothing else to do.
See, I've got no real line of communication at all, on this issue.
If I ever told him I was scared for my life, he'd freak out.
If I ever said anything like that, how would he react?
Would he get angry?
What do you think? Do I want to take that chance?

I got too much to lose.
Before, you know, when we were just single together,
I had nothing to lose. I have a little boy here.
And if I ever caught Mark hurting me
or that little boy again, I'd kill him.
And I don't wanna be up for manslaughter.

Danny means more to me than Mark does.
Only because of what Mark does to me.
He doesn't realize it maybe, but he squelches me.

God, I'm scared.
I don't wanna be alone for the rest of my life
with two kids. And I can't rob my children of what
little father they could have.

NADINE: I've always understood
how people could hurt each other
with weapons.

If you've been hurt to the quick,
and a weapon's around, WHAP.

I signed my divorce papers because
last time he came over, I knew if
there'd been a gun around, I'd've
killed him.

MARK *reenters*.

X

MARK: I'm sorry.
I don't think you understand.

Sure, I was pissed off at myself that I let myself go.
Deep down inside I knew I could have stopped it.

I could just have said:
I won't do it.
Go back in the rear, just not go out,
let them put me in jail. I could have said:
"I got a toothache," gotten out of it.
They couldn't have forced me.
But it was this duty thing.
It was like:
YOU'RE UNDER ORDERS.
You have your orders, you have your job,
you've got to DO it.

Well, it was like crazy.
At night, you could do anything . . .
It was free-fire zones. It was dark, then
all of a sudden, everything would just burn loose.
It was beautiful. . . . You were given all this power to work out-
    side the law.
We all dug it.

But I don't make any excuses for it.
I may even be trying to do that now.
I could have got out.
Everybody could've.
If EVERYBODY had said *no*,
it couldn't have happened.
There were times we'd say:
let's pack up and go, let's quit.
But jokingly.
We knew we were there.
But I think I knew then
we could have got out of it.

NADINE: Oh,
    I'm worried about men.

MARK: See, there was a point, definitely, when I was
    genuinely interested in trying to win the war.
    It was my own area.
    I wanted to do the best I could.
    I mean I could have played it really low-key.
    I could have avoided things, I could have made sure
    we didn't move where we could have contacts.

NADINE: I worry about them a lot.
MARK: And I watched the younger guys.
        Maybe for six weeks there was nothing.
        He'd drift in space wondering what he'd do under fire.
        It only takes once.
        That's all it takes . . .
        and then you dig it.
NADINE: Men are stripped.
MARK: It's shooting fireworks off, the Fourth of July.
NADINE: We took away all their toys . . . their armor.

        When I was younger, I'd see a man in uniform
        and I'd think:
        what a hunk.
        Something would thrill in me.
        Now we look at a man in uniform—
        a Green Beret, a marine—
        and we're embarrassed somehow.
        We don't know who they are anymore.
        What's a man? Where's the model?

        All they had left was being Provider.
        And now with the economics, they're losing it all.
        My father is a farmer.
        This year, my mother learned to plow.
        I talked to my father on the phone the other night and I said:
        Hey, Dad, I hear Mom's learning how to plow.
        Well, sure, he said.
        She's been a farmer's wife for forty, fifty years.
        Yes. But she's just learning to plow now.
        And there was a silence
        and then he said:
        That's a feminist issue I'd rather not discuss
        at the moment.

        So. We don't want them to be the Provider,
        because we want to do that ourselves.
        We don't want them to be heroes,
        and we don't want them to be knights in shining armor, John
            Wayne—
        so what's left for them to be, huh?

        Oh, I'm worried about men.
        They're not coming through.
        (My husband)
        How could I have ever gotten married?

They were programmed to fuck,
now they have to make love.
And they can't do it.
It all comes down to fucking versus loving.

We don't like them in the old way anymore.
And I don't think they like us, much.
Now that's a war, huh?

End of Act One

ACT TWO

I

MARK: This is the photo I showed you.
Of some guys in my unit.

We were south-southwest of Danang—
we were in that whole triangle, not too far
from where My Lai was.
Near the mountains, near the coast.

Everybody knew about My Lai.
But it wasn't different from what was going on.
I mean, the grunts did it all the time.

This fellow up there, that's Michele.
He ended up in the nuthouse,
that's the fellow I pulled out of the bush.
This is the machine gunner.
The kid was so good
he handled the gun like spraying paint.
This kid was from down South.
Smart kid.
He got hit in the head, with grenade shrapnel.
He's alive, but he got rapped in the head.
That was the end of the war for him.

NADINE: I don't know what it is with Mark.
I have a lot of charming friends
that are very quiet, like him—
but they don't have his power.
CHERYL: You know what Mark's power is:
He's got an imagination that just doesn't quit.
NADINE: It got to be coincidental when we'd been somewhere together

and someone said: You know your friend Mark,
I liked the way he was so quiet.

MARK: There were no two ways about it . . .

CHERYL: He's got an imagination that, that embarrasses me . . .

MARK: People who were into it really got a chance to know.

CHERYL: Because I am conservative.

MARK: You knew that you were killing something.
You actually knew it, you saw it, you had the body.
You didn't take wounded. That was it.
You just killed them.
And they did the same to you.

NADINE: (*Laughing*)
I told him his face is a dangerous weapon.
He ought to be real responsible with it.

CHERYL: All his jars . . .

NADINE: I think we'd only known each other for a week and I said:
You should really have a license for that face.

MARK: (That's my friend, that's R.J.)
My friend R.J. used to carry a machete.
I don't know why he never did it.
But he always wanted to cut somebody's head off.

NADINE: You know why they went crazy out there?
It's that totally negative religion.
It makes you fit to kill.
Those commandments . . .

MARK: He wanted to put it on a stick and put it in a village.

NADINE: Every one of them
"Thou shalt not."

MARK: It was an abuse of the dead.
We got very sacred about taking the dead.

NADINE: Take an infant and start him out on the whole world with
THOU SHALT NOT . . .
and you're perpetually in a state of guilt
or a state of revolt.

MARK: There's a whole Buddhist ceremony.
R.J., everybody—got pissed off.
He wanted to let them know.

CHERYL: But he's got an imagination . . .

MARK: I never saw our guys rape women. I heard about it.

CHERYL: And it's usually sexually orientated somehow.

MARK: But you never took prisoners, so you'd have to get
involved with them while they were dying
or you'd wait until they were dead.

CHERYL: Everything Mark does is sexually orientated.

MARK: The Vietnamese got into that.
There was this one instance I told you about
where R.J. shot the person in the face . . .
it was a woman.

CHERYL: I don't know why we got together.

MARK: The Vietnamese carried that body back.
It took them all night long to work that body over.

CHERYL: When I think back on it, he was weird, off the war.

MARK: It was their spoils.
They could do what they wanted.

NADINE: So you send these guys out there
all their lives they've been listening
to nuns and priests
and they start learning to kill.

MARK: (*Snaps on picture of him with medal. Full dress*)
This is a picture of my first Purple Heart.

NADINE: Sure Mark felt great. I understand that.
His senses were finally alive.

CHERYL: His Purple Hearts never got to me.
I was never impressed with the fighting man,
I don't think.

MARK: A lot of people bullshitted that war
for a lot of Purple Hearts.
I heard about a guy who was in the rear
who went to a whorehouse.
He got cut up or something like that.
And he didn't want to pay the woman
or something like that.
He ended up with a Purple Heart.

CHERYL: Well, drugs helped, a lot.
We didn't have much in common.

MARK: I don't know. We were out in the bush.
To me, a Purple Heart meant it was something you got
when you were wounded and you bled.
You were hurt during a contact.
I didn't feel anything getting it.
But I wanted a picture of it.

CHERYL: I mean, I've got to get that basement cleaned out.

MARK: Actually, I was pissed off about getting that medal.

CHERYL: My little boy's getting curious.

MARK: There were South Vietnamese who were sent out with us,
fought with us.

CHERYL: He goes down and sees some of that crap down there Mark's
saved . . .

MARK: They didn't really give a shit.
CHERYL: Never throws anything away.
MARK: If things got too hot you could always
          count on them running.
          Jackasses.
CHERYL: Mark's a packrat . . .
MARK: (*Holds up a belt*)
          I'm a packrat. I never throw anything away.
          This belt is an artifact.
          I took it off of somebody I killed.
          It's an NVA belt.
          I sent it home. I think it was kind of a trophy.

          This is the man's blood.
          That's a bullet hole.
          This particular fellow had a belt of grenades
          that were strapped to his belt.
          See where the rust marks are?

CHERYL: Everything he's done,
          everything is sexually orientated in some way.
          Whether it's nakedness or violence—it's all
          sexually orientated.
          And I don't know where this comes from.
          (MARK *searches for more slides*)
          He can take those slides
          and you know where he can put 'em.
          Right up his butt.
          I mean he's just,
          he'll go down there
          and dig up old slides.
          I won't do that for him anymore.
          I will not,
          no way.
MARK: Here's a picture of me . . .
          (*Snaps on picture of him and some children*)
CHERYL: He asked if he can take pictures of Danny and I . . .
MARK: And some kids. God I LOVED those kids.
CHERYL: I think that's why I'm so against the artist world.
          I just can't handle his work a lot of it.
          It's because he's done that to me.
MARK: Everybody hated them.
          You couldn't trust 'em.

          The VC would send the kids in with a flag.

I never saw this, I heard about it,
the kid would come in asking for C-rations,
try to be your friend, and they'd be maybe wired
with explosives or something
and the kid'd blow up.
There was a whole lot of weirdness . . .

CHERYL: Mark's got this series of blood photographs.
He made me pose for them.
There's a kitchen knife sticking into me,
but all you can see is reddish-purplish blood.
It's about five feet high.
He had it hanging in the shop! In the street!
Boy, did I make him take it out of there.

MARK: I really dug kids. I don't know why.
(*More pictures of kids*)
I did a really bad number . . .
It went contrary, I think,
to everything I knew.
I'm not ready to talk about that yet.

CHERYL: You just don't show people those things.

MARK: These are some pictures of more or less dead bodies and things.
(*Snaps on pictures of mass graves, people half blown apart, gruesome
pictures of this particular war*)
I don't know if you want to see them.
(*Five slides. Last picture comes on of a man, eyes towards us, the bones
of his arm exposed, the flesh torn, eaten away. It is too horrible to
look at.* MARK *looks at the audience, or hears them*)
Oh, Jesus.
Yeah . . .
We have to be patient with each other.
(HE *snaps the pictures off*)

CHERYL: You know. I don't think . . .

MARK: You know, I get panicky
if there's any element of control taken away from me.
(I don't like to be alone in the dark.
I'm scared of it. I'm not armed.)

I don't like fireworks.
If I can control them fine.
I don't like them when I can't control them.

I've had bad dreams
when my wife's had to bring me back out.

Nothing like jumping her, though.
I've heard about vets killing their wives in their sleep.
But this is personal—for me,
the gun was always the instrument, or a grenade.
I never grabbed somebody and slowly killed them.
I've never choked them to death or anything.
I've never beaten anybody up, well . . .

I never killed
with my bare hands.

Pause.

II

CHERYL: You know, I don't think that
men ever really protected women
other than war time.
NADINE: Listen, nobody can do it for you.
Now maybe if I weren't cunning and conniving and
manipulative and courageous,
maybe I wouldn't be able to say that.
MARK: It's still an instinctive reaction to hit the ground.
NADINE: I'll do anything as the times change to protect my stake in life.
CHERYL: And war's the only time man really goes out and protects
woman.
MARK: You know—when I got back, I said I'd never work again.
That's what I said constantly, that'd I'd never work again, for
anyone.
NADINE: I have skills now.
I remember when I didn't have them.
I was still pretty mad, but I wasn't ready.
MARK: I was MAD.
I figured I was *owed* a living.
NADINE: I'm stepping out now, right?
CHERYL: I know my mother protected my father all through his life.
Held things from him, only because she knew it would hurt him.
MARK: And then I got in a position where I couldn't work because
after I got busted and went to prison, no one would hire me.

I did the whole drug thing from a real
thought-out point of view.
I was really highly decorated, awards,
I was wounded twice.
I really looked good.

CHERYL: That's where I get this blurting out when I'm drunk.

Because I'm like my mother—
That's the only time my mother would really let my
father know what's going on in this house.
(When he's not around seven days a week is when she's had a
    couple.)
Otherwise she was protecting him all the time.
Excuse me. I'm going to get another drink.
(SHE *exits*)

MARK: I knew I could get away with a lot.
I knew I could probably walk down the streets
and kill somebody and I'd probably get off.
Simply because of the war.
I was convinced of it.

NADINE: I could have ended my relationship
with my husband years ago.
I sometimes wonder why I didn't.
And I don't want to think it was because of the support.

MARK: I thought about killing people when I got back.

NADINE: I've been pulling my own weight
for about eight years now.
Prior to that, I was doing a tremendous amount of work
that in our society is not measurable.

CHERYL: (*Angry. Reenters*)
My house is not my home.
It's not mine.

NADINE: I kept a house.
I raised my children.

CHERYL: Now, if it were mine I'd be busy at work.

NADINE: I was a model mother.

CHERYL: I'd be painting the walls,
I would be wallpapering the bedroom.
I would be making improvements.
I would be . . . linoleum the floor.
I can't do it.
Because it's not mine.

MARK: I thought of killing people when I got back.
I went to a party with a lady, Cheryl, you know,
later we got married—
She was into seeing people who were into LSD.
And I had tried a little acid this night,
but I wasn't too fucked-up.
And we went to this party.

NADINE: I tried to explain to Mark
that Cheryl may not always want from him what she wants right

now:
looking for him to provide, looking for status.

CHERYL: And Mark will never be ready to have the responsibility
of his own home. Never. Never.

MARK: And there was this big guy.
I was with a friend of mine who tried to rip him off,
or something like that.
He said, the big guy said:
Get the fuck out of here
or I'll take this fucking baseball bat
and split your head wide open.

CHERYL: And I'm being stupid to ever want it from Mark.

MARK: I started to size up what my options were . . .

NADINE: (*Shaking her head*)
Looking for him to provide, looking for status.

MARK: In a split second, I knew I could have him.
He had a baseball bat,
but there was one of these long glass coke bottles.
I knew. . . . Okay, I grabbed that.
I moved toward him, to stick it in his face.
I mean, I killed him.
I mean in my mind.
I cut his throat and everything.

CHERYL: Because your own home means upkeep.
Means, if there's a drip in the ceiling
you gotta come home and take care of it.

NADINE: But between us, I can't understand why a woman her age,
an intelligent woman,
who's lived through the sixties and the seventies,
who's living now in a society where woman have finally been
given permission
to drive and progress and do what they're entitled to do
. . . I mean, how can she think that way?

MARK: My wife saw this and grabbed me.
I couldn't talk to anybody the rest of the night.
I sat and retained the tension and said:
"I want to kill him."
They had to drive me home.
It was only the third time I'd been out with my wife.

CHERYL: That fucking dog in the backyard
—excuse my French—
That dog is so bad. I mean,
there are cow-pies like this out there.
(*Demonstrates size*)

And when I was three months pregnant and alone here—
when Mark and I—
when I finally got Mark to get out of here—
I came back to live
because I just could not go on living at my girlfriend's,
eating their food and not having any money and
—and I came back here
and I had to clean up that yard.

MARK: It wasn't till the next day that I really got shook by it.
My wife said,
"Hey, cool your jets."
She'd say, "Hey, don't do things like that.
You're not over there anymore.
Settle down, it's all right."

CHERYL: I threw up in that backyard picking up dog piles.
That dog hasn't been bathed since I took her over to
this doggie place and paid twenty dollars
to have her bathed.
And that was six months ago. That dog has flies.

You open the back door
and you always get one fly from the fricking dog.
She's like garbage. She . . . she . . .

MARK: I think my wife's scared of me.
I really do.
She'd had this really straight upbringing.
Catholic.
Never had much . . . you know.
Her father was an alcoholic and her mother was too.
I came along and offered her
a certain amount of excitement.

CHERYL: My backyard last year was so gorgeous.
I had flowers.
I had tomatoes.
I had a whole area garden.
That creeping vine stuff all over.
I had everything.
This year I could not do it with that dog back there.

MARK: Just after I got back, I took her up to these races.
I had all this camera equipment.
I started running out on the field.
I started photographing these cars zipping by at
ninety miles an hour.

NADINE: What's important to me is my work.

MARK: It's important to Mark too.

MARK: She'd just gotten out of high school.
          She was just, you know, *at that point.*
          She was amazed at how I moved through space.

NADINE: We talk for hours about our work.

MARK: 'Cuz I didn't take anybody with me.

NADINE: We understand each other's work.

MARK: I moved down everybody's throats verbally.
          First of all it was a physical thing.
          I was loud.
          Then I'd do these trips to outthink people.

NADINE: His jars are amazingly original. Artifacts of the war.
          Very honest.

MARK: I'd do these trips.

NADINE: You should see the portrait Mark did of himself.

MARK: I had a lot of power, drugs,
          I was manipulating large sums of money.

NADINE: He has a halo around his head.
          (*Laughs*)

MARK: She became a real fan.

NADINE: And the face of a devil.

CHERYL: That dog grosses me out so bad.
          That dog slimes all over the place.
          My kid, I don't even let him out in the backyard.
          He plays in the front.
          That's why his bike's out front.
          I'll take the chance of traffic before I'll let him out
          to be slimed over by that dog.

NADINE: She decided to have that child.

MARK: Later on, it got into this whole thing.
          We lived together and with this other couple.

NADINE: It's madness.
          Everyone was against it.

MARK: It was a whole . . . I don't know whether I
          directed it . . . but it became this *big* . . .
          sexual thing . . . between us . . . between them . . .
          between groups of other people . . .
          It was really a fast kind of thing.
          Because no one really gave a shit.

CHERYL: Oh, shut up!

NADINE: His theory is she's punishing him.

MARK: I don't know why I was really into being a stud.

NADINE: Now no man has ever been able to lead *me* into sexual abuse.

MARK: I wasn't that way before I left, so I don't know.

Maybe it was like I was trying to be like all the other people.
NADINE: See, she participated. She had the right to say no.
CHERYL: That dog jumps the fence, takes off.
I have to pay twenty dollars
to get her out of the dog pound.
She is costin' me so damn much money that I hate her.
She eats better than we do.
She eats better than we do.
NADINE: She must have thought it would be fun.
And wow! That was that whole decade
where a whole population of people that age thought that way.
CHERYL: My Danny is getting to the age where there's gotta be food.
I mean he's three years old.
He goes to the freezer he wants ice cream there.
He goes in the icebox there's gotta be pop.
I mean it's not like he's an infant anymore.
NADINE: Every foul thing I've ever done,
I'm not uncomfortable about it.
And I don't blame anyone in my life.
CHERYL: These things have to be there.
And it's not there.
NADINE: I don't blame anyone.
I'm sorry, maybe you have to be older
to look back and say that.
CHERYL: But there's always a bag of dogfood in the place.
Anyways I run out of dogfood,
Mark sends me right up to the store.
But I run out of milk I can always give him Kool-Aid
for two or three days.
Yeah—that's the way it is though.
We haven't been to the grocery store in six months
for anything over ten dollars worth of groceries at a time.
There is no money.

III

MARK: You'd really become an animal out there.
R.J. and I knew what we were doing.

That's why a lot of other kids really got into trouble.
They didn't know what they were doing.

We knew it, we dug it, we knew
we were very good.

IV

CHERYL: I'd turn off to him.
Because I knew that it was hard for me to accept—
you know what he . . . what happened and all that.
And it was hard for me to live with, and him being
drunk and *spreading* it around to others.
(*To* MARK)
How long has it been since anything like that happened?
MARK: Well, last July I hurt you.
CHERYL: Yeah, but Danny was what a year and half so everything was
pretty . . .
MARK: He was exposed to it.
My wife, uh, Cheryl, left one night.
CHERYL: Don't.
MARK: She left with, uh, she had a person come over and pick her up
and take her away.
I walked in on this.
I was drunk. Danny was in her arms.
I attacked this other man and . . .
I did something to him.
I don't know.
What did I do to him?
Something.
CHERYL: You smashed his car up with a sledge hammer.
MARK: I, uh, Dan saw all that.
CHERYL: He was only six months old though.
MARK: No. Dan I think he knows a lot more than we think.
He saw me drunk and incapable of walking up the steps.
Going to the bathroom
half on the floor and half in the bowl.
He's a sharp kid.
Cheryl and I separated this spring.
And he really knew what was going on.
NADINE: Christ, I hate this country.
I hate all of it.
I've never really said it before.
MARK: I come in and apologize when I think about the incidents
that I've done in the past now that I'm sober,
and I feel terribly guilty.
I've exploited Cheryl as a person, sexually . . .
it wasn't exactly rape, but . . .

CHERYL: I can't deal with *that* at all.
But I find that if I can at least put it out of my mind it's easier.

If I had to think about what he's done to me, I'd
have been gone a long time ago.

NADINE: I have yet to be out of this country, by the way.
And I'm criticizing it as if I think it's better everywhere else.

MARK: See, I wanted to get back into the society and
I wanted to live so much life, but I couldn't.
I was constantly experimenting.

CHERYL: It was awful . . .
He'd pick fights with people on the streets.
Just about anyone. It was like a rage.
He'd just whomp on the guy.
Not physically but he would become very obstinate,
very mean and cruel. In bars, handling people . . .
(*To* MARK)
You have to be *nice* to people to have them accept you.

MARK: I don't know.
I was afraid.
I thought people were. . . uh . . . I mean
I was kind of paranoid.
I thought everybody knew . . .
I thought everybody knew what I did over there,
and that they were against me.
I was scared. I felt guilty and a sense of . . .

CHERYL: I can't talk to you.

NADINE: He's trying to judge himself.
One time we were together after a
long period of incredible, sharing times.
I said: "You're so wonderful."
And he started to cry.

MARK: (*To* NADINE)
I've done terrible things.

NADINE: (*To* MARK)
I know.
(*Long pause*)
Christ, I hate this country.

I can remember everything.
Back to being two years old,
and all these terrible things they taught us.
I can't believe we obeyed them *all*.

MARK: (*Very quiet*)
I had two cousins who went through Vietnam.
One was a truck driver and got through it.
My other cousin was in the army.
His unit, about one hundred men were climbing up a hill.
They were all killed except for him and another guy.
And they were lying there.
The VC were going around putting bullets
into people's heads.
Making sure they were dead.
And he had to lay there wounded faking he was dead.
He and I never talked.
Ever.
Someone else communicated his story to me,
and I know he knows my story.

Pause.

V

CHERYL: I feel so sorry for Margie, my brother's wife.
I told you about.
You wonder why there's so much more lesbianism around now?
Look at the men!
You can see where that's turned a lot of women the other way.

NADINE: He possibly is overpowering.
I don't know. She was proud to be his woman.
So he said frog, and they all jumped.
Well, that's terrific.
It cost him a lot
to have that power where he abused it.

CHERYL: Christ!
Mark pushed me into that, once, too.
We were doing this smack deal,
he brought this woman into our room.
He wanted me to play with her.
He wanted me to get it on with her, too.
It just blew my mind.
I mean it just blew me away.

NADINE: I know, I know, I know . . .
But I see when he talks about his wife,
I feel encouraged that there are men that can be that way.
He has never, ever said an unkind word about her.

God, I mean it's incredibly civilized
the way he talks about her.
In fact, had he ever said anything foul about her,
it would have grated on me.
Maybe he just knows what I require.
But I have yet to hear him say
anything bad about anyone;
even those terrible people he had to deal with
in the jungle.

MARK: I saw my cousin at his dad's funeral last December.

CHERYL: Now it's so complex
every time I look . . .
Oh, God . . . every time I look
at a piece of furniture,
it reminds me of something.

MARK: Wherever we moved,
we knew where the other was.
Something radiates between us.

NADINE: I think he's quite superior.
I really do.
I think he's got it all figured out.

MARK: Our eyes will meet, but we can't touch.

NADINE: I think he's gonna make it.
(*Nervous*)
I wonder how you perceive him.

MARK: There's no difference between this war and World War II.
I'm convinced of that.

Maybe it was different in that it was the race thing.
(*Admitting*)
We referred to them as zips, or dinks, or gooks.
But I don't think I would have had any trouble shooting
    anything.

We weren't freaks out there.
Guys in World War II cracked up, too.

We're their children.

I would like to play you a song.

Music: "No More Genocide" by Holly Near. MARK *turns on tape
    recorder.*

End of Act Two

ACT THREE

I

MARK: (*Snaps on slide of him and R.J.*)
        This is a picture of me and R.J.
        We look like a couple of bad-asses.
        It was hot. Shit, I miss him.
        We were so close.
        We talked about everything.
        We talked about how each of us lost our
        virginity, we talked about girls.

CHERYL: (*Agitated*)
        My girlfriend across the street told me
        how babies were made when I was ten years old.
        I just got sick. I hated it.

MARK: We talked about fights, getting back on the streets, drugs.

CHERYL: From that moment on,
        I had a model:
        I wanted kids . . .

MARK: We talked about getting laid . . .

CHERYL: But I didn't want the husband that went along with it.
        I still feel that way.

MARK: We talked about how we would be inseparable
        when we came home.
        We never would have, even if he hadn't died.
        We knew too much about each other.

CHERYL: And this spooks me because I said this
        when I was ten years old.

MARK: (*New slide*)
        This is the place, the Alamo.
        That's where the rocket came in and
        killed a man . . . uh . . .
        (*Indicates in the picture*)
        We got hit one night.
        Some several people were sleeping, this fellow . . .
        (*Picture of him*)
        A rocket came in and blew his head off.

NADINE: I said to Mark:
        "You're still pissed off because they let you go.
        Even assholes stopped their kids from going.
        Your good Catholic parents sent you to slaughter."

MARK: It was near dawn.

We moved his body out of there.
We put his body on a rice-paddy dike.
I watched him. He was dead and he was
very close to me and I don't know.

NADINE: His parents pushed him into going.
They believed all those terrible cliches.

MARK: I didn't want him to lay in that place where he died.
I didn't want him laying in the mud.
And I think I was talking to him.
I was crying, I don't know.

NADINE: Do you know, to this day his father
will not say the word Vietnam.

MARK: His dog came out and started . . .
The dog was eating him.
I just came out and fired at the dog.
I got him killed.
(*Snaps picture*)
Later, I took that picture.

NADINE: But his father talked to everyone but Mark about the war.
He's got his medals on his wall.

MARK: I don't know.
It became a sacred place. It was "the Alamo."
That's what we named it.
I shot the dog because it was desecrating.
The dog was eating our friend . . .
I would have done anything, if I could have,
if I could have kept flies off of him, even.

NADINE: His father's ashamed of himself.
When you let your son go to war
for all the wrong reasons,
you can't face your son.

MARK: (*Crying*)
I just wanted him . . .
He coulda gone home the next day.
The war was over for him.
I wanted him to get home.

Pause.

II

CHERYL: I want to go home.

To the church, to my family.
The sixties are over.

NADINE: The sixties . . .
You know, a lot of us went through that whole
decade pretending to ourselves we were pacifists.

MARK: I wanted to get home so bad.

CHERYL: Well, I mean I'm gonna have another kid.
I'm gonna have to take him to the Cathedral to be
baptized 'cuz our wedding wasn't blessed.
It wasn't in a church.
We had to get married and we had to do it fast.
In South Dakota.
In the clothes we'd been in for three days.

NADINE: As if we didn't know what violence was.

MARK: You know, the biggest thing I had to adjust to
coming home was I didn't have my gun.

CHERYL: My dad had just died so I didn't really care.
My dad and I were really close.
He was the only one who mattered . . .

MARK: I mean, that gun was mine.

CHERYL: I don't know why I'm remembering all this
all of a sudden . . .

MARK: I knew every part of it.

NADINE: God, we hated those vets.

MARK: The barrel burned out of it.
You know, I had a new barrel put in,
but I mean that gun was mine.
I took that gun everywhere I went.
I just couldn't live without that gun.

NADINE: All that nonsense about long hair, flowers and love.

CHERYL: I mean, my family just dug my father's hole
and put him right in there.

NADINE: And the women were exempt!
They were all supposed to be Mother Earths making pots.

CHERYL: My brother's wife went nuts and shot her two-year-old son and
killed him.
I told you.
I mean—all the things we did to him.
He had to come and get me out of jail
at three in the morning and he's not—
he wasn't a strong man.
So my father just jumped into that bottle
and nobody could get him out of it.

NADINE: I think I knew then what I know now.

MARK: When I got on the plane coming home
I was so happy. I didn't miss my gun then.
It was my birthday.

NADINE: I don't know.

MARK: I turned twenty-one.
I did my birthday coming home.

NADINE: Oh, Jesus.

MARK: I did my birthday across the dateline.
I was incredibly happy.
We hit Okinawa.
R.J. was there.
We saw all these guys who were just going over.

NADINE: I only hope I would have done exactly what Mark did.

MARK: All these guys were asking us how it was.
We were really getting off on the fact
that we were done.
These guys were so green and fat.
We were brown, we were skinny.
We were animals.

NADINE: I think he survived
because he became an animal.
I hope I would have wanted to live that bad.

CHERYL: I used to stay up all night with my dad.
I was doing a lot of speed then
and I used to stay up all night with him and talk.
I'd be sewing or something like that at the kitchen table
and he'd be sittin' there drinking and bitching.

MARK: I don't know why I couldn't talk to my parents when I got
back.

NADINE: We just can't face that in ourselves.

MARK: I told my dad everything when I was over there.

CHERYL: My dad was an intelligent, common-sense-type man.
He had no college education, but judging characters . . .

NADINE: Oh, God.

CHERYL: Oh, God.

MARK: The only way I could cry was to write to my dad.
"God, Dad. I'm really scared. I'm really terrified."

CHERYL: Oh, God. He could pick out people.

MARK: When I sent somebody out and they got killed,
I could tell my dad.

CHERYL: My dad told me: Stay away from Mark.

MARK: I got into L.A. . . . , called:

"Hey, I'm back. I'm back."
My dad said: "Oh, great. We're so relieved.
I'm so happy." My mother cried, she was happy.
I said: "I'm going to buy a hamburger."
CHERYL: He told me: Mark can't communicate, his style of dress is weird,
      the war . . .
MARK: I just got on this stool going round and round.
"Hey, I'm back."
No one wanted anything to do with me.
Fuckin' yellow ribbons.
I thought I was tired.
NADINE: The problem now is knowing what to do with what we know.
CHERYL: My dad said:
I want you to forget him.
Just forget him.
Get out of this now, while you can.
MARK: I waited around until 3 A.M.,
caught a flight, got out here.
6:30 in the morning.
Beautiful, beautiful day.
Got my stuff, threw it over my shoulder,
and started walking.
CHERYL: I saw Mark occasionally, anyway.
Shortly after that, my dad had a stroke.
You know, my dad and I are identical.
MARK: I walked in the door and set everything down.
I was home.
My dad looked at me, my mom looked at me.
I sat down. Said:
Could I have some coffee?
That's when my mother started raggin' on me
about drinking coffee.
The whole thing broke down.
NADINE: Oh, God . . .
CHERYL: My sister had a baby when she was seventeen.
They put her in a home, you know, the whole route.
Shortly after that, I was five years younger than her,
I was just starting to date.
MARK: "Well," my mom said, "you better get some sleep.
I've got a lot to do."
I said: like I don't want to sleep.

I got incredibly drunk.

CHERYL: I remember—I'd come home from a date.

The only time I saw my father was late at night.
He would take a look at me and say:
Well, I hope you learned from your sister
that the only way to stay out of trouble
is to keep your legs crossed.

MARK: My mom and dad had to go out that night.
I thought, well, I'd sit down
and talk with them at dinner.
They were gone.

CHERYL: End of conversation.

MARK: We didn't see each other that day.
We never really did see each other.

CHERYL: I mean, he got his point across . . .
more or less.

MARK: I had no idea what was going on.
This was 1970.
My hair was short.
I got really crazed out on junk and stuff.
Then when I was totally avoiding going home
somewhere in that I wanted to . . .
I really wanted bad to . . .
communicate with a woman.

NADINE: You know, all Mark did was—
He brought the war back home
and none of us could look at it.

MARK: I wanted to fuck my brains out.

CHERYL: God, I was naive.
I was naive as they come.
And to sit here and say that now knowing what I know
and what I've been through
just gives me the creeps.

MARK: No one wanted anything to do with me.

NADINE: We couldn't look at ourselves. We still can't.

CHERYL: Because I am so far from being naive.
I mean, just the idea if I ever divorced Mark . . .
I don't think I could ever find anyone who
could handle my past.
I mean, I have a hard time relating to it myself.

III

NADINE: Oh, God.
I'm worried about us.

I keep this quiet little knowledge with me every day.
I don't tell my husband about it
I don't tell my kids,
or Mark.
Or anyone.
But something has fallen apart.
I'm having trouble being a mother.
How can you believe in sending your children to special classes
when you know it doesn't matter?
Oh,
I worry, I worry,
I worry one of my daughters
will be walking down the street
and get raped or mugged by someone who is angry or hungry.
I worry I have these three beautiful daughters (pieces of life)
who I have devoted my whole life to,
who I've put all my energy into—bringing up—raising—
and then somebody up there goes crazy one day
and pushes the "go" button and
phew! bang, finished, the end.
I worry that my daughters won't want to give birth
because of my bad birthing experience.
And I worry that they *will* want to give birth.

I worry that—
Well, one of my daughters does blame me
for the divorce
because I have protected them from knowing
what kind of man their father really is.

(I worry that I worry too much about all this
and I worry that I really don't worry enough about it all.)
I worry so much it makes me sick.

I work eighteen hours a day just to pay the bills.
This year, I work on the feminist caucus,
I do my portraits, run my magazine, organize civic events.
I hold two jobs and more.
I invited my dear, sweet, ninety-one-year-old uncle
to come die at my house.

I go to recitals, shopping, graduation,
I don't go through the ritual
of getting undressed at night.
I sleep with my shoes on.
My husband's alcoholism has ruined us.

(Forty-five thousand dollars in debt.)

I don't dare get angry anymore.
Can you imagine what would happen,
if I got angry?
My children . . .
(*Can't go on*)

MARK: My wife means so much to me.
I don't want to jeopardize what she's giving to me.
I don't want to jeopardize her.

It's like the Marine Corps.
Cheryl is like a comrade. She's walking wounded now.
You don't leave a comrade on the field.

NADINE: It's all out of control.
MARK: Sometimes I think Nadine loses sight of things.
Sometimes, I think she's way ahead of me.
NADINE: I don't know what I'm doing.
MARK: I can't talk to you about Nadine.
NADINE: Oh, men. I have to take care of them.
And they're all cripples.
It's so depressing.
MARK: It's like I know that I'm carrying a time bomb
and there are times that I just don't know
if I'll go off.
I don't know that in the end
I won't destroy myself.
NADINE: And yet, there's that little voice inside me
that reminds me that even though it's hopeless
I have little children that can't survive without me.
MARK: Maybe because I just can't comprehend war.
War that's political enough in terms of
what you have and what you get out of it.

NADINE: I guess I could possibly be the most
vulnerable person of all of us.
But I've also built up all these other devices
which will overrule that.
MARK: I need to tell you what I did.
My wife knows it.
She's come through times
when I got to the very edge of suicide.
She's helped me through a couple of times
that without her help . . .

I'd be dead.
Now, I've been very honest with Nadine
except when she asked me about suicide.
I couldn't tell her that.

NADINE: I couldn't even think about suicide.

IV
The Spaghetti Story

CHERYL: I hate to cook.
Probably because he likes to cook.
I hate to cook.
I don't know how to cook,
and I hate it.

Mark does this spaghetti dinner once a year.
Has he ever told you about that?
Holy Christ!

MARK: Excuse me.
(*Leaves*)

CHERYL: Every day before Thanksgiving
Mark does a spaghetti dinner, and this
is a traditional thing.
This is the one traditional bone Mark has in his body,
and I'd like to break it.

He has 20-45 people come to this thing.
He makes ravioli, lasagne, spaghetti, meatballs,
three different kinds of spaghetti sauce:
shrimp, plain, meat sauce.
Oh, he makes gnocchi! He makes his own noodles!
And it's good.
He's a damn good cook for Italian food.
But you can imagine what I go through
for three weeks for that party
to feed forty people.
Sit-down dinner.
He insists it's a sit-down dinner.

So here I am running around
with no time to cook with him.
I'm trying to get enough shit in my house
to feed forty people sit-down dinner.
We heated the porch last year

because we did not have enough room to seat forty people.
And I run around serving all these slobs,
and this is the first year he's really charged anyone.
And we lose on it every year.
I mean, we lose, first year we lost $300.
This dinner is a $500 deal.
I'm having a baby this November,
and if he thinks he's having
any kind of spaghetti dinner,
he can get his butt out of here.
I can't take it.

Pizzas! He makes homemade pizzas.
You should see my oven.
Oh my God! There's pizza-shit everywhere.
Baked on.
And when it's over with,
he just gets up and walks out.
He's just done.
The cleanup is no big deal to him.
He won't even help.
He rolls up the carpets for this dinner.
People get smashed!
He's got wine everywhere, red wine.
It has to be red so if it gets on my rugs,
my rugs are ruined and my couch is ruined.
I've just said it so many times I hate it.
He knows I hate it.

My brother brought over some speed
to get me through that night.
My brother, Jack, who is a capitalist—
intelligent—makes me sick.
Never got into drugs. Was too old.
Missed that whole scene.
But he now has speed occasionally
on his bad day, you know, drink, two drinks one night,
speed to get him through the day.
Business man.

He brought me some speed to get me through the night
'cause he knew what a basket case I'd be.

And then Mark goes and invites my family.
And they're the last people I want to see at this.
Sure, they love it.
I mean, they all sit around and they

stuff themselves to death.
I'm not kidding!
It is one big stuffing feast.

The first time, the first spaghetti dinner we had was
right after Danny was born.
Danny's baby book got torn up.
I had to start a whole new one.
Mark's crazy friends.
Drunk.
Broken dishes everywhere.
I'm not kidding.
It's just a disaster.

Spaghetti on the walls.
Spaghetti pots dropped in the kitchen.
Spaghetti all over the sink.

That's why I ask him.
I go: "Why?"
"It's traditional. I have to do this every year."
It was three years ago he started.
Tradition, my ass.

I'm telling you.
I mean, he wonders why I can't sleep with him sometimes.
Because I just work up such a hate for him inside that . . .
(MARK *reenters*)
I'm a perfectionist.
My house has to be this way,
and before I go to sleep,
I'll pick up after him.
I'm constantly picking up after him.
Christ Almighty!
In the morning, if he comes in late,
he's read the newspaper
and there's newspaper all over the room.
He *throws* it when he's done with it.
I've broken toes on his shoes.
I broke *this* toe on his shoe.
He always leaves his shoes right out in walking space.
Every morning I trip on
either his tennis or his good shoes.
Whichever pair he doesn't have on.
He's so inconsiderate of other people.
He's so selfish, he's so self-centered.

And this is what I tell him.
I'm just tired of it.
He's so selfish.
Because this spaghetti dinner just ruins me.
Baby or no baby,
it just completely ruins me.
And he's showing off his,
his wonderful cooking that he does once a year.
And I suppose this is why I hate cooking.

V

MARK: (*Shows us slide of wounded children*)
This is a picture of some kids who were hurt.
I used to take care of them,
change their bandages and shit.
I loved these kids.

Oh, God . . .

VI

CHERYL: What am I gonna do? I mean,
someday Danny's gonna have to see Mark
for what he is.
And that just scares the piss right out of me.
NADINE: How do you tell your children their father is an asshole?
CHERYL: I don't wanna be here when Mark tells Danny
about the war.
I don't trust him.
NADINE: How could I tell my children that their father is
in town and hasn't called?
CHERYL: I don't trust what he's gonna tell the kid.
And the way I wanna bring the kid up,
you can't tell him anything.
NADINE: You can't tell your kids
they can't have something they want
because their father has squandered their money.
CHERYL: You're just better off not saying anything.
NADINE: What'm I going to do,
tell them he's off somewhere getting drunk
and has forgotten all about them?
CHERYL: I'm just, you know,

when that sort of thing comes along,
I live from day to day.

NADINE: The counselors tell me and my lawyers tell me
that I should stop protecting them from him.
But it's hard enough, don't you think?
They hurt enough already.

CHERYL: Later on, you know—
there might not be a war going on.
I might not have to deal with that.
And maybe someday *I* can explain to him.

NADINE: One time I told them he was in town
because I couldn't find a way
to cover up the fact that I knew.
They were depressed for weeks.
I have to protect them.

CHERYL: (*Angry*)
See, why do I have to do all this????
And I do.
I find myself doing everything.
Covering for him . . .

NADINE: I don't protect Mark.
He doesn't need it.
He judges himself all the time,
he's devoted to his son.

CHERYL: Sure Mark plays with him.
But when it comes to discipline,
that kid's a little brat,
I mean he is.
And Mark's never around when it comes to discipline.

NADINE: He works hard at his shop. He is supporting his family.

CHERYL: He's never around.

NADINE: He is working his way back into society.
He's beginning to believe in himself
and do his work.

CHERYL: I'm past the sixties.
I want to go back to the Church.
And Mark just will not understand the importance of this for me.
I mean, when there's no father around,
the Church shows some order, you know.

NADINE: He told me he's discovering
who he always thought he was.
I think of him as an artist
and a lifelong friend.

VII

MARK: (*Holding the picture* HE *has framed of the children*)
I'm terrified . . .
I have a son . . .
There's another child on the way . . .
I'm terrified for what I did now . . .

CHERYL: The war is the base of all our problems.

MARK: It's guilt . . .
it's a dumb thing . . .
it makes no sense logically . . .
but I'm afraid there's this karma I built up
of hurting . . .
there are children involved . . .
like it's all going to balance out
at the expense of my kids.

CHERYL: I get so scared when he says that.
I mean, I never did anything.

MARK: There's no logic to it but it's there.
I try . . .
I'm really intense with my boy.

I think what we're beginning to see here is
that it was a different world I was in.
I'd like to be real academic about this . . .
closed case . . .
but this is an ongoing struggle.

NADINE: Mark!

MARK: I don't know.
I just don't know.
Sometimes I look at a news story.
I look at something someone goes to prison for here,
I think about it.
There's no difference.
It's just a different place.
This country had all these rules and regulations
and then all of a sudden they removed these things.

Then you came back and try to make your life
in that society where you had to deal with them.
You find that if you violate them,
which I found,
you go to jail,
which I did.

I sit back here sometimes and watch the news,
watch my mother,
watch my father.
My parents watch the news and say:
"Oh my God somebody did that!
Somebody went in there . . . and started shooting . . .
and killed all those people.
They ought to execute him."
I look at them.
I want to say,
"Hell, what the fuck,
why didn't you ever listen . . .
You want to hear what I did?"
It's real confusion.
I'm guilty and I'm not guilty.
I still want to tell my folks.
I need to tell them what I did.

VIII

CHERYL: There was a time when a man would confess to me,
"I'm a jerk,"
at a private moment
and I would smile
sweetly
and try to comfort him.

Now I believe him.

IX
The Confession

MARK: I . . . I killed three children, a mother and father in cold blood.
(*Crying*)
CHERYL: Don't.
MARK: I killed three children, a mother and father . . .

Long pause.

NADINE: Mark.

MARK: I killed them with a pistol in front of a lot of people.

I demanded something from the parents and then
systematically destroyed them.
And that's . . .

that's the heaviest part of what I'm carrying around.
You know about it now, a few other people know about it,
my wife knows about it, Nadine knows about it,
and nobody else knows about it.
For the rest of my life . . .

I have a son . . .
He's going to die for what I've done.
This is what I'm carrying around;
that's what this logic is about with my children.

A friend hit a booby-trap.
And these people knew about it.
I knew they knew.
I knew that they were working with the VC infrastructure.
I demanded that they tell me.
They wouldn't say anything.
I just wanted them to confess before I killed them.
And they wouldn't.
So I killed their children
and then I killed them.

I was angry.
I was angry with all the power I had.
I couldn't beat them.
They beat me.
(*Crying*)
I lost friends in my unit . . .
I did wrong.
People in the unit watched me kill them.
Some of them tried to stop me.
I don't know.
I can't. . . . Oh, God . . .

A certain amount of stink
went all the way back to the rear.
I almost got into a certain amount of trouble.

It was all rationalized,
that there was a logic behind it.
But they knew.
And everybody who knew had a part in it.
There was enough evidence,
but it wasn't a very good image to put out
in terms of . . .
the marines overseas, so nothing happened.

I have a child . . .
a child who passed through the age
that the little child was.
My son . . . my son
wouldn't know the difference between a VC and a marine.

The children were so little.

I suppose I could find a rationalization.

All that a person can do is try and find words
to try and excuse me,
but I know it's the same damn thing
as lining Jews up.
It's no different
than what the Nazis did.
It's the same thing.

I know that I'm not alone.
I know that other people did it, too.
More people went through more hell than I did . . .
but they didn't do this.

I don't know . . .
I don't know . . .
if it's a terrible flaw of *mine*,
then I guess deep down I'm just everything that's bad.

I guess there is a rationale that says
anyone who wants to live that bad
and gets in that situation . . .
(*Long pause*)
but I should have done better.
I mean, I really strove to be good.
I had a whole set of values.
I had 'em and I didn't.
I don't know.

I want to come to the point
where I tell myself that I've punished myself enough.
In spite of it all,
I don't want to punish myself anymore.
I knew I would want to censor myself for you.

I didn't want you to say:
What kind of a nut, what kind of a bad person is he?
And yet, it's all right.
I'm not gonna lie.

My wife tries to censor me . . .

from people, from certain things.
I can't watch war shows.
I can't drive.
Certain things I can't deal with.
She has to deal with the situation,
us sitting around, a car backfires,
and I hit the deck.

She knows about the graveyards, and R.J. and the woman.
She lives with all this still hanging out.
I'm shell shocked.

X

NADINE: Well, I'm going to look forward to the rest of my life
because of what I know.
I can't wait to test myself.
See, I guess I've known what it is to feel hopeless
politically.
And I've known what it is to plunge
personally.
But Mark has become a conscience for me.
Through him—I've come to understand the violence
in myself . . . and in him, and in all of us.
And I think if we can stay aware of that,
hold on to that knowledge,
maybe we can protect ourselves
and come out on the other side.

MARK: (*Mumbling*)
I'm just a regular guy.
A lot of guys saw worse.

NADINE: If anything I'm on a continuum now.

MARK: See, I didn't want to see people
going through another era of
being so ignorant of the fact that war kills people.

NADINE: And I don't know if it's cynicism or just experience,
but I'm sure I'm never gonna plunge
in the old way again.
I'm not saying that trying to sound tough.
I know about that. I know all about that.

MARK: I feel protective of our children.
Once you're out there, you know there is no justice.
I don't want the children to die.

NADINE: But I have no old expectations anymore.
And when you have none,

you're really free.
And you don't ever plunge.
What do you plunge for?

MARK: It will happen again.

NADINE: I'm just going to work so hard because of what I know.
I do every day.
Did I tell you about not going to sleep at night
because I can't bear to stop thinking about it all?
I'm just going to be so busy for whatever's left.
(But I'm not mad at anyone.)
I don't blame anyone.
I've forgiven everyone.
God, I feel my house is in order at last.

MARK: I DEDICATE . . . this evening to my friends . . .
I'd like a roll call for my friends who died.

NADINE: There's one other thing.
When we all sit around together
with our friends
and we tell women
that no man can do it for you,
we all know it's true,
but I guess for some of us
it never works that way.
At this point in my life,
this curtain has dropped.

MARK: Anderson, Robert.

NADINE: And we see . . .

MARK: Dafoe, Mark.

NADINE: We need them—to be here, questioning themselves
and judging themselves—and us—like Mark.

MARK: Dawson, Mark.

NADINE: I love Mark.

MARK: Fogel, Barry.

NADINE: Well, . . . so . . .
The material has been turning over and over.

MARK: Grant, Tommy.

NADINE: Where is it at now?

MARK: Gunther, Bobby.

NADINE: You see.

MARK: Heinz, Jerry.

NADINE: What do you see, just a cast of characters?

MARK: Jastrow, Alan.
Lawrence, Gordon.
Mullen, Clifford.

Roll call continues through CHERYL's *speech, ending with a conscious decision on* MARK's *part to name* R.J. *among the casualties of Vietnam.*

XI

CHERYL: The men have it all.
MARK: Nelson, Raymond.
CHERYL: They've had it for the longest time.
MARK: Nedelski, Michael.
CHERYL: There's another thing I believe.
There's a lot more people
that are messed up because of the way we were brought up.
MARK: Nevin, Daniel.
CHERYL: Not brought up, but the things we've been through
since we were brought up.
MARK: O'Brien, Stephen.
CHERYL: So I think our generation,
MARK: Rodriguez, Daniel.
CHERYL: the hippie generation, shortly before and after,
are gonna be the ones that suffer.
MARK: Rogers, John.
CHERYL: Because ninety percent of the men never straightened out.
MARK: Ryan, John.
CHERYL: But what I also believe
is that for every woman that has her beliefs,
there's a man that matches.
MARK: Sawyer, Steven.
CHERYL: Whether you find him or not,
is, is like finding a needle in a haystack.
With our population,
I mean, that's the odds you have.
MARK: Simon, Jimmy.
CHERYL: And there's the Women's Libs.
And there's a man for them too.
MARK: Skanolon, John.
CHERYL: See, what we're doing is crossing.
We're meeting the men
that should be with the other ones.
And I truly believe that,
that there is an equal balance.
Even though our group is so fucked-up.
And we are.
MARK: Spaulding, Henry.
CHERYL: You'll look, you'll go in college campuses now

and it's completely back the way it was . . .
and it should stay there.

MARK: Stanton, Ray.

CHERYL: I don't wanna see that shit come back.
I didn't even get that involved in it.
I got involved in it in my own little niche.
But I didn't, you know, get into it
in the school matter.
I went two years and I had it up to here.
And sure I would like to have gone on to school,
but I was competing with Mark.
And I'm not,
I do not like competing with someone.

MARK: Vechhio, Michael.

CHERYL: I'm a happy-go-lucky person.
I used to be anyway, before I met Mark,
where you couldn't depress me on the worst day.
And I had a good day every day of my life.

MARK: Walker,
Pause.

CHERYL: And that is the way life was gonna be for me.

MARK: R.J.
Pause.

XII

MARK *points to his photograph of two grapefruits, an orange, a broken egg,
with a grenade in the center on a dark background. Also some fresh bread,
a fly on the fruit. From far away it looks like an ordinary still life.*

MARK: My unit got blown up.
It was a high contact.
We got hit very, very hard.
The Marine Corps sends you
this extra food, fresh fruit, bread,
a reward
when you've had a heavy loss.

What can I say?
I am still alive—my friends aren't.
It's a still life.
I didn't know what I was doing.

The WOMEN's *eyes meet for the first time as lights go down.*

END OF PLAY

STRANGE SNOW

Stephen Metcalfe

About Stephen Metcalfe

Born in New Haven in 1953, Stephen Metcalfe attended college in Pennsylvania and moved to New York City in 1976. His one-act plays *Jacknife* and *Baseball Play* were staged at New York's Quaigh Theatre in 1980; his full-length play *Vikings* was produced by Manhattan Theatre Club that same year. *Vikings* was later seen at the Edinburgh Festival and heard on *Earplay*. *Half a Lifetime* was also produced, as a one-act, at MTC; the expanded full-length version was first staged by Michigan's BoarsHead Theater, which premiered Metcalfe's *White Linen*, a cowboy play with songs, in 1982. In 1984 *Loves and Hours* was produced by Cincinnati Playhouse in the Park, and Metcalfe's most recent play, *The Incredibly Famous Willy Rivers*, opened at New York's WPA Theatre in December. Metcalfe is the recipient of a 1982 CAPS grant and a 1984 playwriting fellowship from the National Endowment for the Arts.

Production History

Commissioned by Manhattan Theatre Club in 1980, *Strange Snow* opened there in January 1982, in a production directed by Thomas Bullard. The play has subsequently been staged at numerous theatres across the country.

Characters

MEGS
MARTHA
DAVE

Time

The present.

Place

Dave and Martha's home.

The Play

Strange Snow

ACT ONE

Scene 1

The lights come up on MEGS *on the porch, stage left.* HE *looks in the window for signs of life. Nothing.* HE *begins banging on the front door.*

MEGS: Rise and shine, you sweet bear! It's time! The fishy-wishies are waitin' for us like whores in heat! We're the drunkest sailors on the block! Hah!? Hah!? (*Nothing.* HE *comes off the porch, looks upstairs*) Wake up, you great fool! We're gonna dance on Charlie the Tuna's grave! (HE *does a quick dance. Waits. Nothing.* HE *comes onto the porch again.* HE *bangs on the door*) Davey!? You up or what, guy? Hello? Rise and shine! Bed is for lovers or invalids, huh? Davey? Yo, Davey! You awake!?

A light comes on in the stairwell. MARTHA *comes roaring down the stairs.* SHE *is carrying a golf club.* SHE *is in a robe and slippers.* SHE *wears glasses.*

MARTHA: Stop it! Stop that noise! Stop it! (SHE *glares at* MEGS *through the panes of glass in the door.* SHE *brandishes the golf club threateningly*) If I have to come out there, you'll be sorry. I know how to use this!

MEGS *stops banging.* HE *grins.*

MEGS: Well, hi there, little lady. Nice mornin', huh? Kinda cold for golf though. Dark too. You always go golfin' in your PJs? You got mud cleats in your slippers? (MARTHA *glares at him, turns, puts down the club, goes to the phone*) Who you callin'? You're gonna wake'm up.

MARTHA: I'm calling the police.

MEGS: Why you callin' the police, woman?

MARTHA: I suggest you run. The police will come and they'll arrest you.

MEGS: Why would they want to do that?

MARTHA: Hello? Yes, I'd like the police. (*For* MEGS*'s benefit*) I'd like to report a disturbance.

MEGS: Hey, come on, I'm no disturbance. I'm a friend of Davey's!

MARTHA: David?

MEGS: Dave Flanagan. This is his place, ain't it?

MARTHA: David is in bed. At this hour most people are! You'd better have a very good reason for making such a racket.

MEGS (*Grinning*): I wake you?

MARTHA: Of course you woke me! You scared me to death!

MEGS: I'm a buddy a Davey's.

MARTHA: I've never seen you here before.

MEGS: I've never been invited. But I'm a friend. Honest.

Pause.

MARTHA: Yes, hello? Could you please send a squad car to . . .

MEGS: No, wait, listen! You must be Davey's sister, Martha!

Pause.

MARTHA: I don't know you.!

MEGS: I feel like I know you! Davey talked about you all the time. Said you're swell.

Pause.

MARTHA: Never mind.

MARTHA *hangs up the phone. Moves to the door, unlocks it, opens it a crack.* MEGS *sticks his head in, grins.*

MEGS: Joseph Megessey. Everybody calls me Megs.

MARTHA *frowns at* MEGS *as if there is a bad taste in her mouth.*

MARTHA: Megs.

MEGS: That's my name, don't wear it out.

MARTHA: It's a ridiculous name.

MEGS: Ain't it? (*Pause*) Your brother and me, see, we're goin' fishin'.

MARTHA: Fishing.

MEGS: Yeah. It's opening day!

MARTHA: Ridiculous. The sun's not even up.

MEGS: Exactly. See, those trout'll be so bleary-eyed, they'll think our nightcrawlers are filet mignon. They'll go for 'em. Pow! And you know what we'll do, Martha? We'll bring'm home here and cook'm up for your dinner. What a you think a that?

> MARTHA *retreats from the door, letting* MEGS *in.*

MARTHA: I think you're a fool. (SHE *turns on lights in the living room*)

MEGS (*Following*): No-o! It's opening day! The luck is rolling off me in waves! Smell? Perfume, huh?

MARTHA: Don't come near me. You smell like dirt.

MEGS: No! Nightcrawlers! (HE *displays a plastic baggy filled with nightcrawlers*) Hey, Martha! You want to come?

MARTHA: What? Where?

MEGS: Fishin'! I bet there's a rainbow that long just waitin' with your name on it. M-A-R-T-H-A!

MARTHA: Ridiculous.

MEGS: No! Listen, what say you go on upstairs and give your brother a poke in the breadbasket. Get him on down here.

MARTHA (*Brushing past him to close the door that* HE *has left wide open*): I will not! I'll have you know I was up till two in the morning correcting papers!

MEGS: Hey, no you weren't! On a Friday night?

MARTHA: Every night!

MEGS: I bet you was out hullaballooin' under the moon. I bet you got home five minutes ago and you threw on that robe to fool me!

MARTHA: You're preposterous.

MEGS: Ya can't fool me, woman! You got moonburns on your cheeks like roses!

MARTHA: I do not!

MEGS: Do!

MARTHA: Be quiet!

> MARTHA *tries to move past* MEGS *and* HE *sweeps her into his arms.*

MEGS: Opening day, Martha! (*And* HE *dances* MARTHA *around the furniture*) Grab your partner, dance your partner, swing your partner!

MARTHA (*Simultaneously*): How dare you! Stop! You can't just . . . I'm not dressed for . . . stop!

MEGS: Skip to the loo, my darlin'! (*And* HE *deposits* MARTHA *in a chair*) Thank you, ma'am! Ginger Rogers and Fred Astaire better look out, huh? Yeah . . . uh, you think Davey's up?

MARTHA: Joseph, I don't think David remembered he made a date to go fishing with you.

MEGS: Opening day?

MARTHA: He wasn't home when I went to bed at two.

MEGS: Naw, he musta remembered. (*Yelling up the stairs*) C'mon guy! I got my waders in the car! God, it's good to meet you, Martha. Davey, he talked about you all the time, said you're swell. Hey, has he ever mentioned me to you?

MARTHA: I'd of remembered it if he had.

MEGS (*Grinning*): Yeah. (MARTHA *yawns*) Would you look at me keeping you up? You oughta be in dreamland restin' up for good ole Saturday night. Don't worry about me. I'm fine. I'll sit right here and wait. Go. Go to bed. (HE *sits*. HE *"waits"*)

Pause.

MARTHA: I'll tell him you're here. He won't like it. (*Pause*) He hates being woken up. (*Pause*. SHE *starts to leave;* SHE *stops*) He throws alarm clocks through windows. (*No response.* SHE *goes upstairs. Pause.* SHE *comes back down and proceeds briskly to the door with the intention of asking* MEGS *to leave*) I'm not going to do it. He'll take it out on me the rest of the day.

There is the sound of a toilet flushing from upstairs.

MEGS: Somebody's up! I hear something flushing down the drain. Let's hope it's not last night's dinner. (*Calling up the stairs*) 'Bout time, dude! Let's get a move on! I'm borin' your poor sister to death!

MARTHA: Why don't I get coffee on? You'll probably both need it.

MEGS: Hey, I'm fine.

MARTHA: Let me put it this way: David is going to need it.

MEGS: Don't go to any trouble.

MARTHA: I assure you, I won't. I'm up. (*With a touch of sarcasm*) I'm an early riser.

And THEY *move into the kitchen.*

MEGS: Know something? Me too. Up with the milkman every day. Listen, you do coffee and then Davey and I'll go. I got food and drink in the car. I planned ahead. We are gonna eat better'n turkeys on the first a November. Osmosis, see. The trout are gonna feel it in the air that we're fat and happy and they're gonna be so jealous they'll be chompin' on air bubbles. Hey! Look at this! (HE *takes what appears to be a large, brightly colored dustball from his pocket.* HE *places it ceremoniously on the table*)

MARTHA: What is it?

MEGS: It's a fly. I tied it myself. Ya like it?

MARTHA: It's colorful.

MEGS: Oh, goddam, it is that, ain't it? I figure it'll either drive a fish mad with passion or scare'm half to death. Lotta hair and all of it cowlicks. Sorta like you, woman.

MARTHA (*Her hands go to her hair*): What? Oh . . . it's a mess, isn't it?

MEGS: Oh, no, Martha. It's fine. It's just fine . . . uh, I wonder what's keepin' that big guy. Think I oughta go bounce on his belly?

MARTHA: I don't think that would be a wise idea. Joseph . . . there are beer cans in the wastebasket. They're David's discards. From last night. Before he went out.

MEGS (HE *nudges the wastebasket. Cans rattle*): From last night? Oh. He forgot, didn't he!

MARTHA: I'm afraid so.

MEGS: Yeah. Well . . . it's OK. My fault. My dumb mistake.

MARTHA: Joseph . . .

MEGS: No! Davey's a busy guy, drivin' those trucks here and there and back again. Who has time for fishin'? Hey, it's been real good to meet you, Martha. I'm sorry I woke you. I'll let myself out. (HE *begins to exit*)

Pause.

MARTHA: Joseph? This is ridiculous but . . . he's had hangovers before . . . DAVID!? DAVID! GET UP THIS MINUTE! YOU'RE GO-ING FISHING!

MEGS: You think he heard?

MARTHA: I'm sure the whole neighborhood did. DAVID!

MEGS: GET YOUR BUTT IN GEAR, GUY! PULL ON YOUR DRAWERS AND PUT SOME DOUBLE KNOTS IN YOUR SNEAKERS! WE GOTTA CATCH A TROUT FOR MARTHA'S DINNER!

MARTHA: YOU'VE GOT TO CATCH A TROUT FOR MY DINNER!

MEGS: You like trout, do ya?

MARTHA: I've never had them.

MEGS: Well, I've never caught'm but there's a first time for everything.

MARTHA: I bet there's a recipe in one of the cookbooks.

MEGS: You fry'm! You dump'm in corn flour and then whip'm into bacon grease and they come out brown and tasty.

MARTHA: If you catch them and *clean* them, I'll cook them.

MEGS: You will? You're on, Martha. There's one sittin' under a log waitin' for us and know what? It has your name right across the rainbow. M-A-R-T-H-A!! (*And* HE *sweeps* MARTHA *into his arms again*) Swing your part-ner. Dance your partner. Glide your partner round and round. Skip to the loo, my darlin'!

MARTHA (*Simultaneously*): Joseph, put me down . . . you can't just . . . oh!

And MARTHA *breaks into helpless giggles.* DAVE *enters down to the bottom of the stairs.* HE *is in boxer shorts and is horribly hung over.* MARTHA *and* MEGS *stop at the sight of him.*

DAVE: What in hell is goin' on?

MEGS (*Grins; pause*): You're up! (*Pause*) Look at you! Wouldn't go off a high dive in those johns, guy!

DAVE: What do you two think you're doing?

MARTHA: You and Joseph are going fishing, David.

DAVE: You're out of your mind.

MEGS: It's opening day, guy.

DAVE: Rain check.

MARTHA: David, you made a date to go fishing. Joseph has the car loaded and ready to go.

DAVE: Joseph?

MEGS: I got beer, sandwiches. It's a great adventure, guy.

DAVE: We plan this?

MEGS: Hey, last week. McDonald's, remember? How you been, I said. Good, you said. We oughta get together, said me. Fine, said you. Fishing, said me, opening day. Opening day, said you. Hah?! Hah?!Guess what today is, guy!!

DAVE: I thought fishing season was in the fall.

MEGS: No, that's huntin'. Don't worry, we'll do that too when the time comes. Opening day, Davey!

DAVE: I can't.

MEGS: Opening day?

DAVE: Sorry.

MEGS: Rainbows this long.

DAVE: Not up to it.

MEGS: Sure you are, Davey. A big ole nightcrawler on a hook? That'll perk your ass up. I got one here so big those rainbows'll have to be careful he don't eat them.

And MEGS *proudly displays one to* DAVE, *who almost gets sick.*

DAVE: Yech.

MARTHA: Go take a shower. You'll feel better.

DAVE: I'm passing.

MARTHA: You're doing no such thing. Shower and get dressed. I'll make breakfast for you both.

DAVE: I don't want to go fishing, Martha.

MARTHA: You're going.

DAVE: I don't want to go fishing.

MARTHA: David, I want a trout. Fried in corn flour. There's one waiting with my name on it.

MEGS: Davey? Hey, Davey? C'mon, guy. It'll be a great time. There's frost in the air and wondrous strange snow on the ground. The trout streams are gurglin' and singing. Know what they're sayin'? Wake up, Davey. It's time. It's time. Openin' day with your ole buddy, Megs. Damn! Makes me want to paint my face and pretend I'm Hiawatha. Whoo-whoo-whoo-whoo! *Fish*-ing! *Fish*-ing! (HE *keeps up his noise till* DAVE *says OK*)

DAVE: Megs, I . . . I don't . . . ahhh! OK!! (*Exiting*) I must have a screw loose.

MEGS: Never doubted it for a minute.

DAVE: I'm sleeping in the car.

MEGS: You'll sleep, I'll drive. Hey! You're beautiful! Don't you ever forget that.

DAVE (*Offstage*): God.

MARTHA: He didn't look very beautiful to me. Not in those baggy drawers of his.

MEGS: Martha, you're too much, you know that? You are. Something. He was not gonna go and you talked him into it.

MARTHA: I didn't talk him into anything.

MEGS (*Putting his hands affectionately on* MARTHA*'s arms*): Ain't you modest. I saw.

MARTHA (*Coldly*): I was making coffee.

And MARTHA *enters the kitchen.* MEGS *follows.*

MEGS: Hey, y'know, Martha, instant's fine with me. I drink so much instant my stomach's freeze-dried.

MARTHA: I find instant coffee foul. You'll have to make do with ground for drip.

MEGS: Drip? We'll go for it! I'll pretend I fell asleep and woke up in Dunkin Donuts. Hey, you got any milk? (*And* HE *sticks his nose in* MARTHA*'s refrigerator*)

MARTHA (*Annoyed*): Yes, of course I've got milk.

MEGS (*Bringing it out*): Thank God for that. Powdered creamer? I hate that shit. It tastes like powdered mouseballs to me. (*Pause*) Oh goddam, listen to me talk. Give me a bar a soap and I'll wash my mouth out as far down as my tonsils. Maybe it'll learn me to talk like a human being in front of a lady.

MARTHA: A lady? Really . . . besides, I'm used to it. I teach high school students, mouths like spittoons.

MEGS: Rap'm smartly upside the head. That'll learn'm.

MARTHA: My major was in biology, not the martial arts.

MEGS: Well, you ever have any problems, you let me know. I'm not good for much but one thing I could do is put the fear a God into a bunch a young punks. They oughta be bringin' you apples and candy and havin' crushes on you and stuff.

MARTHA: That'll be the day. (*Pause*) You must of been a delightful student.

MEGS: Me? Oh no, I was never any good at school. I specialized in Phys Ed, auto shop and smokin' in the lavatories. I'da driven you crazy.

MARTHA: I doubt it. I've developed a high tolerance level.

MEGS: I woulda. I could never keep my mouth shut. Everybody'd be laughin'. Not with me, at me. I didn't care. I liked the attention. (*Pause*) Hey, you, Martha! I bet you was a hell of a student. (*Pause.* MARTHA *looks at him suspiciously*) Well, were ya?

MARTHA: Yes, I was. I was mad for it.

MEGS: No!

MARTHA (*Proudly*): I loved to study. Straight A's in every subject.

MEGS: You're something, Martha. It must be great to be so smart.

MARTHA (*Gloating*): Yes, it is.

MEGS: I was dumber'n paint. But I sure as hell woulda brought you apples and candy, Martha. You can bet your sweet ass on that! (*And without thinking,* HE *swats* MARTHA *on the rump*) Sorry.

MARTHA: What would you like for breakfast?

MEGS: Hey, anything. Everything. My eyes could be bigger'n basketballs, they still wouldn't be bigger than my stomach.

MARTHA: I like pancakes on Saturday mornings.

MEGS: I do too. I love'm. Give me pancakes and the roadrunner on TV and Saturday morning is complete.

MARTHA: I like sausage too.

MEGS: Squealers? Sausage goes good with pancakes.

MARTHA: You'll have that then?

MEGS: Sausage and pancakes?

MARTHA: Would you rather eggs?

MEGS: Hey, how 'bout all three?

MARTHA: Why didn't I think of that.

MEGS: Goddam, Martha! Eggs and pancakes and sausage, it feels like Easter or something. And do you know what we'll have to go with it? Beer! I got a couple a cases in the car.

MARTHA: For breakfast? That's horrible.

MEGS: Breakfast beer. It's the best kind. Martha, ain't you ever had a beer for breakfast?

MARTHA: Joseph, there are those of us who have never had a beer.

MEGS: No! Woman, you are in for a treat. You sip on a breakfast beer and first thing you know, the cobwebs go, your voice rises two octaves, and God almighty, the sun comes up inside you! I'll go get some! (*And* HE *runs out of the kitchen, through the living room and out the front door*)

MARTHA: Joseph, I hardly . . . all right.

MARTHA *begins to take things from the refrigerator.* DAVE, *dressed, comes down the stairs and into the kitchen.* HE *looks around.*

DAVE: He leave?

MARTHA: He went to the car to get beer.

DAVE: Good. I could use one.

MARTHA: David, it happens to be five in the morning.

DAVE: You better believe it.

MARTHA: The idea is nauseating. You can't drink beer.

DAVE: I can. What an asshole.

MARTHA: Sshh. He'll hear you.

DAVE: I was talking about me. I wish you hadn't sided with him, Martha. He was gonna leave.

MARTHA: He looked so hurt when he thought you might of forgotten.

DAVE: I had forgotten. Martha, why is it you're a hardass with everything but stray animals? Bring'm in, give'm a warm bowl of milk, who ends up cleaning the turds off the floor? Me.

MARTHA: Hardly. Besides, your friend doesn't qualify as an animal.

DAVE (*Preoccupied*): He's not my friend. He's just somebody I know. We were in Vietnam together.

MARTHA (*Interested*): Oh. (*Pause*) I like him.

DAVE: You don't know him, sis.

MARTHA: I'm entitled to my first impressions. He's endearing is what he is.

DAVE: Endearing? (HE *laughs*) God, Martha, what do you know about endearing? (HE *sips from the coffee* MARTHA *has brought him*. HE *makes a face*) I wish he'd hurry up with that beer.

MARTHA: I wouldn't think you could stomach it after all you had last night. I assume the empties were just the start.

DAVE: Come on. I work hard all week. I'm entitled to cut loose on the weekend. You ought to try it sometime. It'd do you good.

Pause.

MARTHA: I'd love to. You can take me with you tonight.

DAVE (*Again preoccupied*): Forget it.

MARTHA: Why not? All you ever do is go out with the boys. I'd think you might like a woman around for a change.

DAVE: Women we can use, a sister we don't need. Besides, I date.

MARTHA: I've seen the kind of woman you date. Their idea of contributing to a conversation is to snap their chewing gum. Don't you think you might like a point of view for a change?

DAVE: I want a point of view, I'll listen to the news.

MARTHA: I'll be silent then. Unresponsive, unobtrusive, the kind of women men like.

DAVE: How do you know what men like? (*Laughing*) God, Martha, you're too much, you know that? You've hardly been out with anybody in your whole life but you're the authority on the subject.

MARTHA: David? Piss up a rope.

DAVE (*Surprised*): What'd I say already?

MARTHA: Just . . . drink your juice.

MEGS *rushes through the front door, through the living room and into the kitchen.* HE *is carrying two sixes of beer.* HE *puts them on the counter.*

MEGS: Beer! We got it! I had to chop it out of the ice chest with a screwdriver! Be careful, it's colder than Alaska. One for you, one for me, and the by-God coldest a the bunch for you, Martha. Blow on it first, otherwise your tongue'll stick to the can. (HE *holds out a beer to* MARTHA)

DAVE: Forget it, Megs. Martha doesn't drink beer.

MEGS: Oh. Well, hey, it is early. (*And* HE *flips it in the air, catches it and sets it down*)

DAVE: Any time of the day is too early for her.

MARTHA: David? (*And* SHE *picks up the can of beer*)

DAVE: Yeah?

MARTHA: To opening day. (SHE *opens it. Shaken, it sprays her. Undaunted,* SHE *takes a mammoth gulp*)

MEGS: To opening day, by damn!

MARTHA *takes the can down from her lips. Her eyes are watering and* SHE *is breathless.*

DAVE (*Sarcastic*): How's it taste, sis?

MARTHA (*Raising the can in toast*): To trout! (SHE *takes an even bigger gulp*)

MEGS (*Impressed*): Are we gonna catch us the limit or what? Breakfast beer, Martha!

Pause as MARTHA *struggles to hold it down.*

MARTHA (*Breathless but with a challenging look at* DAVE): I have a confession, Joseph. I think I like beer.

DAVE: Terrific.

MEGS: I should say so! Finish that one off, I'll crack you another one.

MARTHA: I'll take it upstairs. I'll have to get dressed if I'm coming with you.

DAVE: What?

MEGS: You're coming along, Martha?

MARTHA: You invited me.

MEGS: Oh, this is so great. The rainbows'll never know what hit'm.

MARTHA (*Slapping* DAVE *on the shoulder*): Yes, I'm sure they'll be jumping in my lap dying to hear my women's point of view. (SHE *starts to exit*)

DAVE: Forget it, Martha.

MARTHA: Joseph doesn't mind, do you, Joseph?

MEGS: Mind? I should say not. I'm happy you're coming, Martha. If I'da known you wanted to, I'da asked you twice.

MARTHA (*Exiting*): I'll get ready.

MEGS: And don't you worry about breakfast. We'll stop along the way is what we'll do. We'll eat enough pancakes to build a house. On me! A woman doesn't buy when I'm around.

DAVE (*Sarcastic*): Dress warm, sis.

MARTHA (*Offstage*): David?

DAVE: Yeah?

MARTHA (*Offstage*): Up a rope!

MEGS (*Laughing*): She's great, your sister. I like her. (HE *puts on a Boston Red Sox hat that* HE *pulls from his pocket. It is old and well worn*) Hah!? Hah!? Opening day and we're goin' for it.

DAVE: Let's not.

MEGS: Huh?

DAVE: Let's say we have Martha make us some breakfast, we'll shoot the shit awhile, and you hit the road and let me get some sleep 'cause let me tell you, Megs, I don't feel good.

MEGS: You didn't recognize the hat, did ya? I wear it for luck.

DAVE: Bad luck, huh?

MEGS: It's changed its ways. It didn't like it over there in Nam any better than we did. It's not mine, it's Bobby's.

DAVE: Didn't help ole Bobby much, did it?

MEGS: It's helpin' me.

DAVE: Listen, don't get started.

MEGS: Sorry.

Pause.

DAVE: So . . . don't see you around much, Megs.

MEGS: I been puttin' a lot of hours at the garage. Hey, sweet bear, I opened up my own garage.

DAVE: You quit drivin'?

MEGS: It was time. Time to give those whores a rest, huh?

DAVE: Tell me about it.

MEGS: Yeah, but you're still barrelassin' 'cross them amber waves a grain, ain'tcha?

DAVE: Got a cake run. Produce distribution. Suits me fine.

MEGS: You ride'm, I'll repair'm! Did you know they hide under rocks?

DAVE: Who?

MEGS: Trout, guy! The speckled little bastards, they hide under rocks! Now what kind of a life is that, huh?

DAVE: You ever caught a trout?

MEGS (*Sheepish*): No . . . but I been practicin'! I been casting in the backyard! I had that line singing through the air like a bullwhip! Till I got snagged.

Neighbor's sheet. Ripped the hell out it. Boy, was she pissed. Good fishermen file the barbs off their hooks.

DAVE: Come on. Who told you that?

MEGS: TV! The American Sportsman! Watch Don Meredith hunt anacondas with a bowie knife! Trout fishin'! You file off the barbs so they have a chance.

DAVE: Right. We gonna do that?

MEGS: No fuckin' way, Jose!! Don't tell Martha, stud, but I got a feelin' the only way I'm gonna catch a fish is to drain the pond. We'll see! We'll see! Damn! This trout fishin' is a good time!

DAVE: Great. Terrific.

MEGS: Y'know, I only wear Bobby's hat on special occasions.

DAVE: Megs . . .

MEGS: No, really! Like when one of my kids needs a home run.

DAVE: Kids? What kids?

MEGS: Hey, I coached little league this last summer. Peewees. We screamed and hollered and lost every game. They want me for this year too. They like me.

DAVE: You're just a likable guy. God . . . I gotta lie down.

DAVE *enters the living room.* HE *lies on the couch.* MEGS *follows.*

MEGS: A home run in the ninth!?

DAVE: What?

MEGS: You liked the Yankees, Bobby liked the Red Sox. You guys bet. Bobby won on Carl Yastrzemski's home run in the ninth.

DAVE: That's right. Five bucks we bet.

MEGS: He loved those Red Sox, huh? Ole Bobby? Crazy for'm. He wanted us all to go to Fenway Park, remember? Beer and hot dogs, huh? Scream till we're hoarse. We oughta do that sometime, sweet Davey. Baseball season's just around the corner.

DAVE: Forget it.

MEGS: It'd be fun.

DAVE: Forget it.

MEGS: How come?

Pause.

DAVE: Hold out your hands.

MEGS (*Hiding them*): Aw, Davey . . . I ain't put my fists through glass in a long time.

DAVE: I've heard that before.

MEGS: Look at me now, Davey, huh? Look at me. Fat and happy. I bet you never seen me looking so good, guy.

DAVE: You look the same as before. (*Sarcastic*) Guy.

MEGS (*With an edge*): And you. You look real good too. And you just *stagger* into me in the parking lot of ole McDonaldland. Damn. Fate's a funny thing. (*Pause*) So talk to me some, huh?

DAVE: Talk? About what? (*And* HE *rises, goes to the liquor cabinet, gets a bottle of whiskey from underneath.* HE *takes a sip, offers it to* MEGS)

MEGS: Never touch it, stud. Be wasted on me. Be like puttin' ethyl alcohol in a lawnmower. (HE *is at the trophy case.* HE *picks up a photo*) These your folks, huh?

DAVE: Huh? Yeah.

MEGS: Nice-lookin' mom. Sorta like Martha.

DAVE: She moved to Florida about a year ago. She didn't like the cold. She calls once a week and she and Martha gang up on me.

MEGS: Maybe too many memories of your dad around here too, huh?

DAVE: Maybe.

MEGS: Musta been tough, Davey. Musta been real tough. You come hobblin' off the plane on those crutches a yours and they lay that on you.

DAVE: Yeah. I was pissed. It was my dad's gung-ho vet shit that got me to enlist in the first place and I'd been fantasizing for months on how the first thing I was gonna do was deck the son of a bitch. I felt cheated.

MEGS (*Picking up a photograph*): Hey, is this Martha? (DAVE *looks, laughs*) Whoo, she's changed, stud. Blossomed. (*Picking up a plaque*) And would you look at this? All League!

DAVE: Team captain.

MEGS (*Picking up another photo*): Goddam! Look at you! Nice tie, studhoss. When's this?

DAVE: Senior year.

MEGS: Would ya look at them apple cheeks?

DAVE: Future fuckin' lawyers club.

MEGS: You was gonna be a lawyer, Davey?

DAVE: What?

MEGS: You know, was that what you was, like, plannin'? To be a lawyer? After?

DAVE: I was gonna be everything, man. You name it, I was gonna be it.

MEGS: Hey. Know what all this is, Davey? Memories. Stuff to show your kids.

DAVE: Come off it, man. It's a bad joke. Something out of Archie Comics. (*Calls up the stairs*) Hey, Martha! Let's go if we're going to go!

MEGS (*Calls up to* MARTHA): Dress warm, woman! We want you to catch rainbows, not your death of cold! Hey, sweet Davey, you think maybe she likes me?

DAVE: Come off it, man. You two are from different planets. Only reason she's comin' along is to bust my ass.

MEGS: Oh. Yeah. I guess you're right. (*Pause*) Sun's coming up. Real pretty. Remember the sunrises? Over there? They were beauties, huh? Yeah. Remember what ole Bobby'd say? If it wasn't for the C-rations we could pretend we was in Hawaii. Remember him sayin' that? I do. (*Pause*) Know what I hated? The waiting.

DAVE: Yeah. They always had to let us know in advance when we'd be goin' out.

MEGS: Me, I never got used to it. Made me want to piss my pants every time. Only way I could bear it was to get up for it, y'know? Something set in. It was like I was numb and speedin' at the same time.

DAVE: Christ, you listening to yourself?

MEGS: Just talkin'.

DAVE: What you're talking about! We're not there, we're here!

MEGS: Damn right! We're here and now and that's what counts. Talking doesn't hurt, Davey. (*Pause*) Maybe you don't do it often enough.

DAVE: I was never there, Megs.

MEGS: I ain't followin' that.

DAVE: Look, as far as I'm concerned it never happened. It's done with, understand?

MEGS: How come I'm standin' here then?

DAVE: You got me.

MEGS: How come I'm wearin' Bobby's lucky hat?

DAVE: Burn the fuckin' thing.

MEGS: It was Bobby's.

DAVE: Bury it with him. (*And* HE *suddenly knocks the hat from* MEGS's *head. An ugly silence*) Yeah . . . this trout fishing is a great time. (MEGS *picks up the hat. Pause.* MEGS *begins picking up empty beer cans*) Hey listen . . . Megs . . . leave that stuff. Martha'll do it.

MEGS: My pleasure, stud. (*And* MARTHA *comes down the stairs*) By God, woman, look at you! Straight out of an L.L. Bean catalogue!! The fish are gonna take one look at you and walk out of the water with their hands up!

MARTHA: Thank you.

DAVE: Better get your glasses on or you'll trip over them when they do.

MARTHA: I don't need them. I have on contact lenses.

DAVE: Contacts!?

MARTHA: I've had them. I'll take those, Joseph. They get under foot like marbles, don't they?

And a hard look passes between DAVE *and* MARTHA.

DAVE: Have another beer, sis. Where'd you get the clothes?

MARTHA: I took some of my classes on a field trip to a freshwater pond. I couldn't very well collect samples in a skirt.

MEGS: Hell, no. Would I change a muffler in a three-piece suit? You look terrific, Martha, just terrific. God, are we going to catch the limit or what? Listen, I'll start the car. Opening day, ladies and gentlemen, opening day! Look out, trout, we're on our way! (HE *grabs the beer and exits*)

Pause.

MARTHA: You're drinking.

DAVE: You want to try this too?

MARTHA: I'll pass, thank you. You ready?

DAVE: Who you trying to impress, Martha, huh? Contact lenses? You drinking beer? Give me a break.

MARTHA: What is wrong, David, with me having a good time for once?

DAVE (*Gesturing in* MEGS*'s direction*): You're that desperate?

MARTHA: He's nice.

DAVE: Or maybe he's just as desperate as you.

MARTHA (*Softly*): Fuck you, David.

DAVE: Ooh, Miss Peach! Nice mouth for a schoolteacher. You talk that way to your students?

MARTHA: No. (*Pause*) Go back to bed if you want to. I'm going fishing. (SHE *exits*)

DAVE: Go on. The two of you have a great time! Hell with you both! (*Pause. There is the sound of a car starting up, revving.* HE *runs to the door*) Martha!? I'm coming! (HE *grabs his jacket, a fatigue jacket.* HE *picks up the bottle.* HE *exits*) I wouldn't miss this for the world.

Lights to black.

Scene 2

MARTHA *enters through the kitchen door, stage right.* SHE *has a blanket around her. Her pants and shoes are wet. Her hair is damp.* SHE *is shivering with cold.*

MARTHA: Ohhh . . . (SHE *runs through the kitchen, into the living room and up the stairs*)

Pause.

MEGS: Martha! Hey, Martha!? (HE *enters through the kitchen door.* DAVE *is out cold over his shoulder.* DAVE *groans*) It's A-OK, sweet bear. I gotcha. My wits are weak but my back is strong. (HE *almost slips*) Whoops! Good Christ, guy, there's water on the floor. I almost took us both out. (DAVE *groans*) You gonna be sick again? You alive back there, hah? Hey, nobody ever said trout fishing was gonna be easy. Martha!!? (HE *enters the living room*) Whew, you are heavy, stud. We'll have to make room for you in the trophy case. Have you stuffed and we'll hang a little sign on you. This is what we brought back alive. Barely. Martha, where'd you go, woman!? Don't worry, stud, we'll follow the puddles, we'll find her. Let's get you settled, stud. (HE *puts* DAVE *on the couch*) It's OK, sweet bear, it's A-OK. Some of us, we didn't drink, we'd cut our wrists, huh? You don't have to explain. I know.

You know I know. Looking good, studhoss, looking real good. You and me, we paddled twenty miles a shit creek, huh? Yeah. With our bare hands, we did. Me, I don't forget that. I'm like an elephant, short on smarts, long on memory. You sleep, stud. Ole Megs is on watch. You sleep.

MEGS *takes off his jacket, drapes it over the sleeping* DAVE, *and sits.* MARTHA *enters in warm, dry clothes.*

MARTHA: I was so cold. Is he all right?

MEGS: He's in dreamland is all. His head's gonna feel like a bowling alley when he wakes up but he's fine.

MARTHA: He finished off the whole bottle, the poor fool.

MEGS: Guzzled it is what he did. Wasn't the first time, won't be the last. (HE ' *begins to laugh*)

MARTHA: What?

MEGS: You. You was a bedraggled cat, woman. You looked like you been on the spin cycle of a washing machine for fourteen hours.

MARTHA: If you hadn't had that blanket in the car I'd of frozen to death.

MEGS: You were terrific, Martha.

MARTHA: Every trout for a hundred miles is probably hiding under a rock in a state of shock.

MEGS: Martha, your fish was gettin' away!

MARTHA: Yes, I know! But I never thought you'd push me right in after it!

MEGS: I got excited! I mean, I knew you wanted the brainless thing so badly. God . . . he was beautiful, huh, Martha? A real rainbow. Hey, if I'da known you was gonna throw down the pole and try haulin' him in hand over hand, I'da got you a drop line.

MARTHA: I was startled! I felt as though I'd stepped on a frog. I could feel him through the string.

MEGS: He felt you.

MARTHA: He was heavy.

MEGS: Woman, he was cousin to the Loch Ness monster! Enormous! You got him onto that bank and I thought, look out, Martha! That baby's gonna take your leg off!

MARTHA: No!

MEGS: Yes!!

MARTHA: Really?

MEGS: Hey, would I lie? It's a good thing he threw the hook. He was gettin' pissed!

MARTHA: No. He was desperate. My heart went out to him.

MEGS: You're something, Martha. You are. Didn't I tell you there'd be one waitin' with your name on it? M-A-R-T-H-A! It was a good time?

Pause.

MARTHA: It was a wonderful time, Joseph.

MEGS (*Softly*): Yeah? That's just great.

MARTHA: *You* are having some soup.

MEGS: *Soup* would be great.

MARTHA: Come on. To the kitchen. Sit. Split pea with ham. Homemade.

MEGS: You're kiddin'. By God, if food doesn't come out of a can, I usually have a hard time recognizing it.

MARTHA: I'll have you know I'm a very good cook.

MEGS: Well, goddam, we're a team 'cause I like to eat.

MARTHA: Do your girlfriends cook for you?

MEGS: Tell you the truth, Martha, most a the girls I know don't know a waffle iron from a frisbee. I been keepin' a kinda low profile in the girlfriend department. Got kinda tired of mud wrestlers and hog callers. What about you, Martha? You must have to fight'm off with tomahawks.

MARTHA: I'm sorry to inform you I've given up the fight.

MEGS: Come on, woman, you're built like a brick shithouse!

MARTHA: What?

MEGS: Oh, goddam. Me and my mouth again. Sorry, Martha, but you are. I noticed it straight off.

MARTHA: That's the most ridiculous thing I've ever heard.

MEGS: No.

MARTHA: I'm shapeless.

MEGS: Solid. You're sturdy. You're a battleship!

MARTHA: Agreed. With the face of an icebreaker.

MEGS: No-oh.

MARTHA: Yes.

MEGS: No— . . .

MARTHA: Stop contradicting me! I know what I am. Plain and unattractive.

MEGS: Martha, I saw the picture in there. You used to be.

MARTHA: You're very nice to try and convince me otherwise but I look in the mirror every morning. I live with what I see. The soup will be ready in a moment.

MEGS: Y'know, Martha, some people, they get awful ugly the minute they open their mouths. And other people, like you, Martha, they grow on you. The more you get to know'm, the better lookin' they get.

MARTHA: Very few share your opinion.

MEGS: Oh. You give'm a chance to?

MARTHA: Look, I'm not one of those pieces of fluff you see in men's magazines. Does that make me less a woman? It does not. (*Pause*) And I'm a fool because for some stupid reason I think it does. And so I buy contact lenses and clothes I can't really afford. You think I'd of learned by now. You think I'd of learned at the start. (*Pause*) The soup is almost hot. (*Pause*) David had to even get me a date for my high school formal. I was on the decorations committee, the tickets committee. I put together the whole thing. Nobody asked me to go. David rounded up his friends and told them one of them had to invite me or he'd beat them all up. I think perhaps they drew straws. I didn't know. Suddenly I was invited, that's all that mattered. I was so happy. Well, it was something that couldn't be kept quiet, David's blackmail. I heard rumors. I confronted David. He wouldn't admit what he'd done but I knew.

Pause.

MEGS: You go?

Pause.

MARTHA: I got very sick the night of the prom. A twenty-four hour thing. David meant well.

MEGS: I crashed mine. Yeah, I did. Just walked in wearin' a motorcycle jacket, steel-toed jack boots, and shades, stood there like a madman, grinnin' at all those tuxedos, hopin' somebody'd try to throw me out. I think perhaps I also was very sick on the night of the prom.

MARTHA: Wouldn't we have made a lovely couple.

MEGS: You'da gone with me?

MARTHA: What?

MEGS: If, y'know, I'da like, asked you, you'da gone with me?

MARTHA: Well . . . yes.

MEGS: Nah.

MARTHA: Yes.

MEGS: Nah.

MARTHA (*Angrily*): Why do you always contradict me? Yes, I would have gone with you.

MEGS: Well, goddam, woman! We'da had a great time!! I can see it! (HE *jumps up, moves to the kitchen door*) I come to pick you up. I knock on the door. (HE *exits out the door.* HE *knocks three times*)

MARTHA: What are you doing? What are you doing?

MEGS (*Opening the door, stepping in*): This ain't detention, Martha. It's the prom. Answer the door.

MARTHA: You're in.

MEGS *realizes that* HE *is.* HE *grins.* HE *shuts the door.* HE *does a slow spin as if showing off something.*

MEGS: Hah!? Hah!?

MARTHA: What?

MEGS: Your mom. She thinks I look very dashing in my tuxedo.

MARTHA: Oh, you do.

MEGS (*Whipping off his hat*): The corsage is as big as a goddam dogwood tree. (HE *tosses his hat into the refrigerator*) Your father comes over to shake hands. He smells my breath to see if I've been drinking. (HE *exhales*) I have!

MARTHA: He approves. And offers you an aperitif for the road.

MEGS: Too late! You make your entrance down the stairway! You look . . . terrific!

MARTHA: My gown is silk and gossamer.

MEGS: Yeah. And you look terrific. Your hair is just so. Hey! Know what it is?

MARTHA (*Breaking the spell*): Preposterous.

MEGS: No! It's beautiful.

MARTHA: My shoes?

MEGS: Listen, you could click your heels three times and they'd take you to Kansas.

MARTHA: Ridiculous.

MEGS: No! (HE *retrieves his hat from the refrigerator*) There is a moment of embarrassment as I try to pin on your corsage. I am timid.

MARTHA: Of the occasion?

MEGS: Of your gunboats!

MARTHA (*Giggling, slapping at* MEGS): Stop! (SHE *takes the hat and puts it on her head, the bill facing backwards*) I smile reassuringly. (SHE *does*)

MEGS: And the air is heavy with the portent of things to come! (*Offering his arm*) Shall we go?

MARTHA: The chariot awaits?

MEGS (HE *mimes opening a car door for* MARTHA): '57 Chevy, roars like a PT boat but smooth as glass. In accord with the occasion I have thrown all the empty beer cans in the back seat.

MARTHA: How thoughtful. We arrive?

MEGS: We knock'm dead. You're beautiful.

MARTHA (*Softly*): You're handsome.

MEGS: We dance! (HE *does a ferocious dance: a combination of the jerk and the swim.* HE *sings the instrumental lead to* "En-A-Gada-Da-Vida" *by the Iron Butterfly as* HE *dances.* HE *stops, grinning*) They play a slow one. (HE *begins to sing* "Michelle" *by the Beatles.* HE *opens his arms to* MARTHA. SHE *comes to him.* THEY *sway*) What a terrific dancer you are.

MARTHA (*Shyly*): And you.

MEGS: If I step on your feet you give me a shot to the kidneys, OK?

MEGS *pulls* MARTHA *very close, his hands going down around her waist.* SHE *stiffens.*

MARTHA: This is stupid.

MEGS: Just dancing. (*And* HE *holds* MARTHA *tighter still*)

MARTHA (*With a growing terror at* MEGS's *embrace*): Please. Stop it. Get your hands off me!

MARTHA *struggles free from* MEGS, *rips the hat from her head, tosses it away from her, staggers to the stove. Pause.*

MEGS: That's the thing about shy people, Martha. They think everybody's looking. Nobody is. 'Cept me. (*Unable to hide his anger, his frustration, his hurt*) And I like what I see!

MARTHA: For God's sake, sit down. The soup is ready.

MEGS: That bad a dancer, huh? Yeah . . . (HE *moves to exit out the kitchen door and suddenly, almost without thinking,* HE *punches out one of the panes of glass in the door*) Oh God, I'm sorry . . .

MARTHA (*Simultaneously with* MEGS's *last line*): Joseph! Your hand . . .

MEGS: I'll pay for it, I promise, oh, I'm so sorry, I'll pay for it.

And MEGS *is hiding his hands from* MARTHA. SHE *is trying to see if they're cut.*

MARTHA: I don't care about the glass! Is your hand cut!?

MEGS: No, they're fine! (*And* MARTHA *sees the scars on his hands. Embarrassed,* HE *tries to hide them.* SHE *won't let him*) My hands . . . they ain't so pretty . . . .

MARTHA: You've done it before . . . .

MEGS: Yeah . . . .

MARTHA: Why . . .

MEGS: I dunno why, Martha. I'm real sorry. Listen, you tell Davey so long for me. (HE *starts to leave, going into the living room, heading for the front door*)

MARTHA: Joseph? (MEGS *stops*) I'd have wanted you to take me to the prom.

Pause.

MEGS: Yeah?

MARTHA (*Softly*): Yes.

MEGS: Really?

MARTHA (*Softly*): Yes. (*Pause*) Will you sit and have soup with me?

Pause.

MEGS: Only 'cause you asked 'stead of ordered. (HE *enters the kitchen,* HE *sits.* MARTHA *puts a bowl filled with soup in front of him*) Look at this. China. (*Looking at the plate the bowl is on*) They match too. I almost got a set a tableware once. Every time you bought groceries at the store, they gave you a plate. I just didn't shop often enough.

MARTHA: Go on. Start.

MEGS: No, I'm waitin' for you. It'll stay hot. I hate eating alone. You eat alone much, Martha?

MARTHA *is getting crackers.*

MARTHA: Sometimes I eat with David. David, however, eats alone. (*Pause*) I usually correct papers while I eat.

MEGS: Sounds to me like you give out way too much homework, Martha. (*Pause*) Sure smells good.

MARTHA (*Sitting*): Thank you.

MEGS: Good as Campbell's, I bet. I haven't even tasted it yet and I like it.

MARTHA: Now you can.

MARTHA *puts her napkin in her lap.* MEGS *is on the verge of digging in but notices this.* HE *puts down his spoon and carefully unfolds his napkin, placing it in his lap.* HE *tastes his soup.* HE *tastes it again. Perplexed, yet again.* HE *grins.*

MEGS: Good.

MARTHA *smiles, pleased.* THEY *eat. Pause.*

MARTHA: David said you two were in Vietnam together.

MEGS: Basic right through we were.

MARTHA: He never talks about it.

MEGS: No? Me, I talk about it all the time. To myself when there's no one around to listen. You ever had an ugly melody in your head? You can't get rid of it no matter how hard you try to hum something else.

MARTHA: David gets furious if you even mention it. (*Pause*) Did you know David's friend, Bobby?

MEGS: He told you about ole Bobby? Ole Bobby, Martha, he was . . . . You take a guy who does something well, he practices, right? Well, ole Bobby, he could just look at it once and do it better right off. Yup. And was he smart? He knew things. But see, he knew'm from here (*Tapping his chest*) as well as from here (*Tapping his head*). Ole Bobby was our heart. A regular waterwalker. We loved him. Oh, but we was some trio, Bobby, your brother and me. They thought I was lucky. Davey did anyway. Used to. He was always goin' on about how I was a lucky dollar, a rabbit's foot . . . yeah, I ain't foolin'. Really! Lucky Megs! (*Pause*) That all kinda ended when we lost ole Bobby. It was when, y'know, Davey got hurt and me, I uh . . . I got in the way like I got a habit a doin'. Oh, I'll tell you, Martha. Your brother is one sweet bear but ole Bobby was worth him and me rolled together. (*Pause*) You wouldn't a liked me much when I got home. Crazy. I got in fights a lot, dumb ones, five against one where I got the piss kicked out a me. It was not a nice time. And what it got down to was . . . well . . . one night I was lyin' around, contemplatin' the rafters, wonderin' if they could take my weight, and like . . . don't laugh or nothin', please . . . I prayed. I felt better. What was done, was done, y'know? For some reason we'd lost ole Bobby. And it was up to me to make that reason a good one.

'Cause ole Bobby, he deserved that. I think I've liked myself a little bit more ever since then. (*Pause.* MARTHA *starts to take the bowls*) Hey, no way, Jose! Cook doesn't clean. My turn. (HE *takes the bowls to the sink*)

MARTHA: I think I'm going to cry.

MEGS: Huh?

MARTHA: You make me want to laugh and cry at the same time. I rarely do either one.

MEGS: Oh. Guess I oughta get goin', huh? Sure wish we'd caught some trout. (HE *starts to exit*)

MARTHA: You're coming for dinner anyway!

MEGS (*In disbelief*): I am?

MARTHA: Yes! I'm going to buy steaks and I'm going to make a nice salad and I'm going to put potatoes in the oven and . . . and . . . we'll have wine! I'll get a nice bottle of wine! And pie! I baked a pie this week and we'll put ice cream on it and . . . unless of course you have other plans.

MEGS: Are you kiddin' me?

MARTHA: Yes?

MEGS: Are you kiddin' me?

MARTHA: You'll come?

MEGS: Fuckin' A, I'll come! With fuckin' bells on! You'll pardon the expression. And listen, I'm buyin' the wine!

MARTHA: I don't know wine.

MEGS: Me neither, so what? We'll shoot in the best. Know why? 'Cause you and me, Martha, we deserve it! Goddam, I better get cracking! It's gonna take me a year in the shower to get cleaned up and even then I'd hedge my bets!

MARTHA: Eight o'clock?

MEGS: Eight o'clock is good.

MARTHA: I can be ready earlier.

MEGS: Seven-thirty is earlier.

MARTHA: How about seven?

MEGS: Goddam, woman! Why don't I just stay and watch you change!? Just kiddin', just kiddin'. Opening Day. It feels like Christmas. (HE *puts his lucky hat on* MARTHA) I'll be back.

MARTHA: Bye, Joseph.

MEGS: Joseph. You're too much, Martha. Something. M-A-R-T-H-A!

MEGS *exits out the front door, slamming it behind him.* MARTHA *rushes to the door and peers out watching him go.*

MARTHA: Oh my . . .

DAVE *has stirred at the sound of the slamming door.* HE *sits up on the couch, groggy. A moment.* MARTHA *turns.* SHE *and* DAVE *look at each other.* MARTHA *is suddenly aware* SHE *is wearing the hat.* SHE *quickly takes it off. Lights to black.*

End of Act One

ACT TWO

Scene 1

MARTHA *enters down the stairs into the living room.* SHE *is wearing a beautiful dress in a light pastel color, her hair is carefully brushed back.* SHE *wears a bit of makeup.* DAVE *enters right behind her.* HE *is unchanged, unshaven, and is smoking a cigarette.*

DAVE: What a ya mean you invited him over for dinner?

MARTHA: I thought I spoke English. Invite, a verb, to request the participation of. Dinner. That's a meal if memory serves me.

DAVE: I don't want to eat dinner with him.

MARTHA: Your participation has not been requested. If you'd like to, you may. Go out if you don't.

DAVE: I don't even want the guy in my house.

MARTHA: It's my house too. What shall we do? Call Mother in Florida and ask for a tie-breaking vote?

DAVE: What is this, Martha? Be kind to stranger week? You don't even know Megs.

MARTHA: That's why I invited him over. To get to know him.

DAVE: What you're going to find out, you don't need.

MARTHA: David, I am trying to tidy up. It is difficult with you pretending you're Mount St. Helen's, spewing ashes everywhere.

DAVE: Sis, want to know what he was in Vietnam? Jacknife. That's what he called himself. It's a truckdriving term, sis. It's when you take a big, beautiful eighteen-wheeler and you crash it, turn it to shit. Jacknife. 'Cause he crashed trucks. He was crazy. And Vietnam made him crazier. He's spent more time in the can on assault charges than you can believe.

MARTHA: He's been very nice.

DAVE: Nothing's happened to get him started. Push the right button and he's off. Berserk, Martha.

MARTHA: I'm sorry you don't like him, I do.

DAVE: You want to go out with someone? OK, I'll set you up. Plenty a guys owe me favors; it'll be no problem.

MARTHA: No, thank you.

DAVE: Martha . . .

MARTHA (*Exiting to the kitchen*): I have to put potatoes in the oven.

DAVE (*Following*): He's nothing but a mechanic, Martha. He owns a garage for Christsake.

MARTHA: And you drive a truck, David. I try not to hold it against you.

Pause.

DAVE: Steak. We were gonna have trout for dinner. What a laugh. I froze my ass off.

MARTHA: I should have thought you were too drunk to feel anything.

DAVE: Martha, listen, I have his number someplace. Call him and tell him something came up, the P.T.A.

MARTHA: Are you joining us?

DAVE: The fucking board of education wants to see you!

MARTHA: Do you want a potato!?

DAVE: Yes! (*Pause*) If Dad was alive, he wouldn't let a guy like this on the front porch.

MARTHA: Go out, David. Call up your friends, go to a bar and get drunk and hoarse screaming at the television.

DAVE: No way.

MARTHA: Then not another word if you're staying! Be what you usually are, a presence in the house that eats whatever's put in front of it and grunts when spoken to. I'd be better off living with a Saint Bernard!

DAVE: What is with you today?

MARTHA: What do you care, David? Really, why this sudden concern about who I see?

DAVE: Hey, you're my sister.

MARTHA: I thought I was your housekeeper, your cook. I don't know how long it's been since I heard you say, Martha, how are you? I've been in-vited to a party, come along. Let's get together and do something. How's the old love life, kid?

DAVE: What love life? You never go out.

MARTHA: Exactly.

DAVE: OK, I'm sorry. I'll take more interest from now on, I really will. Hey, we'll go to a movie. How's that sound? But Martha, forget Megs. The guy is not up to your standards.

MARTHA: Has anyone ever been? My so-called standards, David, are merely something I've hidden behind so I could salvage a little pride. (*Pause*) Do you remember that cruise I went on last Easter break?

DAVE: Yeah. You got a nice tan.

MARTHA: It was a swinging singles cruise, a man for every maid. It was a ship filled with depressed, lonely people and I went hoping I might meet . . . what . . . a kindred soul, someone I liked, who liked me, anyone. And I might have. If I could have left my standards at dockside. But I was frightened and so when I went on board my standards walked right up the gangplank behind me. I got a nice tan.

DAVE: Martha, what, you're pissed off you didn't get laid?

MARTHA: Wouldn't you have been?

DAVE: Yeah, but you?

MARTHA: Oh, I'm sorry. Shy, plain women don't desire. When they're in bed at night they keep their hands off themselves and don't fantasize. (*Pause*) David, how many times have you made love?

DAVE: Hey, come on, huh?

MARTHA: Really. Fifteen times? Fifty times? One hundred?

DAVE: Gimme a break.

MARTHA: Good God, David, look at me! I'm almost the perfect image of the virgin schoolmarm. Tending other people's children is supposed to make me feel chaste and noble and fulfilled. Bullshit. I feel helpless and very stupid. I'm not a nun. I wrote boys' names in my notebooks when I was young. I prayed that they'd pull my hair so I'd pay attention to them.

DAVE: Kids don't know shit.

MARTHA: Oh, David, they know. I watch them. Girls are always glancing about. Is anyone looking? Is a boy looking? They are. You call them to the blackboard and they struggle up, bent at the waist, pulling their sweaters down.

DAVE: God, Martha, you checkin' out their boners?

MARTHA: You're horrible. I'm just telling you that they know! When you see a boy walking a girl to class, his arm around her, his mouth close to her ear, you know they know. Why should it be too late for me? (*Pause*. DAVE *suddenly giggles*. SHE *looks at him*. HE *laughs*. SHE *is annoyed*) What?

DAVE: Uh . . . before. About being a virgin schoolmarm? You said almost. I mean, I never thought that you . . . uh, it never occurred to me that . . . (HE *laughs*) Who'd you get it on with? Anybody I know?

MARTHA: You just . . . that's none of your business.

DAVE: Yeah, it is. Come on. Please?

MARTHA: Go away.

DAVE: Martha, I'm curious. Martha? Mar-tha? (HE *is laughing openly now*)

MARTHA: Leave me alone.

DAVE: Loosen the strings, sis. Come on, gossip a little.

Pause.

MARTHA: William Green.

DAVE: Ichabod Crane? I don't believe it. (HE *laughs harder than ever*)

MARTHA: That's why it's so hard for people like me. People like you make fun of someone's rear end or waistline. You turn love into a beauty pageant. Stop laughing!

DAVE (*Trying to stop but not succeeding*): No! No! It's not 'cause a the way you look.

MARTHA: Oh!

DAVE: It's just that . . . I mean, you're not what you'd call experienced. Are you? (HE *laughs*) No! And him . . . he was a shy guy and well . . . (HE *laughs*) Laurel and Hardy! This is another fine mess you've got me into! (HE *laughs*)

MARTHA: Oh, David, I could have died. Neither of us knew what we were doing. We were like two cars that had hooked bumpers . . . both of us pushing and pulling at the wrong times. And he kept apologizing the whole time. I'm terribly sorry. I think he'd hoped I'd changed my mind. (THEY *laugh*) I don't know why I'm laughing . . . it was horrible. No passion. Guilt for him. Frustrated tears for me.

DAVE (*Tenderly*): I'm sorry, kiddo.

MARTHA: He asked me to marry him. He'd been in bed with me so he thought he should.

DAVE (*Considering this a moment*): Y'know, he wasn't such a bad guy.

MARTHA (*Bristling*): Meaning I won't get many chances? Meaning I'm not in any position to pick and choose?

DAVE: Here you go again.

MARTHA: I didn't sleep with him so he'd marry me. We'd have made each other miserable. (*Pause*) Are you having dinner with us?

DAVE: Sis, you make dinner for Megs, he'll latch onto you. He'll be calling, coming by, telling me all sorts of crazy stuff. We won't be able to get rid of him. You're making a mistake, Martha.

MARTHA: It's my mistake then.

DAVE: Jesus, Martha, why won't you listen to me?! Do you know anything about men? No! You'd have a hard time handling the most perfect son of a bitch in the world, let alone this guy! (*Pause*) All right. All right. You'll see. You'll be beggin' him to leave.

MARTHA: Go get cleaned up. You'll feel better.

Pause.

DAVE (*Softly*): Is it really so bad here, Martha?

MARTHA: It's not so bad.

DAVE: I love this place. Every good memory I have is here. (*Pause*) I like having you around here, Martha. (*Pause*) Listen, I'm gonna be more appreciative, you'll see.

MARTHA: The things I want, you can't give me, David.

DAVE: You're gonna leave?

MARTHA: Someday. (*Long pause*) Go get cleaned up.

DAVE: Yeah. I got any clean clothes anywhere?

MARTHA: In the dryer.

DAVE (*Preoccupied*): Get'm for me, huh?

DAVE *exits upstairs.* MARTHA *puts the finishing touches on her table.* MEGS *comes to the front door.* HE *has flowers which* HE *hides behind his back.* HE *is carrying a large bag.*

MEGS (*Knocking*): Hello, it's me! Front door!

MARTHA *scurries around, checking everything to make sure it's perfect.* SHE *checks her reflection in one of the windows.* SHE *hurries to the door, pauses, takes a deep breath, lets* MEGS *in.*

MARTHA: Well now.

MEGS: Just a packhorse, that's me. (HE *displays the flowers, surprising* MARTHA)

MARTHA: Oh, my.

MEGS: Like'm? I told the guy I was a white knight going to meet a fair damsel. Give me your best!

MARTHA: They're beautiful.

MEGS: Wait. Here.

MARTHA: No!

MEGS: Yes! Candy.

MARTHA: Ohh . . .

MEGS: Just a mad seducer, that's me. I got wine too. No idea what goes with what so I got one of every color: white, pink and blood red. And . . . this!

MARTHA: Brandy?

MEGS: If beer for breakfast is sunrise, brandy is sundown. (*And doing a quick "bump and grind,"* HE *takes off his overcoat.* HE *is wearing a very wellmade, dark three-piece suit, a white shirt, a tie*)

MARTHA: Look at you.

MEGS: It looked real good in the store window. I hardly ever get to wear it. I figured what the hell, prom night, y'know? (*Pause*) I'm real glad to be here, Martha.

MARTHA *hesitates, then leans up and kisses* MEGS *on the cheek. Lights go to black.*

Scene 2

MEGS *and* MARTHA *are in the kitchen. Dinner has been finished.* MEGS *has taken off his jacket, loosened his tie, rolled up his sleeves.* HE *sits at the table and sips wine.* MARTHA *is putting the finishing touches on cleanup.*

MEGS: Martha, I feel like I fell asleep and woke up in the Waldorf Astoria.

MARTHA: Go on.

MEGS: I do. Steaks I usually eat are so bad, you put'm down knowin' the restaurant's gotta make up for it by givin' you all the beer you can drink. (*Pause*) Come on, Martha, you sit down.

MARTHA: Joseph . . .

MEGS: Hush, hush, hush. Sit. Have another glass of this Parisian nectar. I'm finishing up here. I'm not taking no for an answer. These hands may finger-paint in axle grease by day but come nightfall they whisper messages to me. Clean us, Megs. Drown us in boraxo. Wash the bathtub or something. So I do. My hands like it.

MARTHA: You're a funny man.

MEGS: I am, ain't I? Aren't. Aren't I. Good wine?

MARTHA: Oh yes. I heartily approve. (*Giggling*) Listen to me. Such an expert. The tip of my nose has gone numb. I'll be swinging from the chandeliers next. Oh, I want to wrap the steak in tinfoil for you so you can take it home.

MEGS: Hey, no way, Jose! That's teacher's lunch for two days.

MARTHA: You're taking it.

MEGS: Oh, God, I'm being ordered again. How can I refuse?

MARTHA: You can't.

MEGS: Are you sure?

MARTHA: I try not to eat lunch. You saw my picture in there. The Hindenburg. My idea of an exceptional Saturday night used to be two pounds of fudge and thirty term papers. I've finally eliminated the two pounds of fudge.

MEGS: And from all the right places too.

Pause.

MARTHA: This will be in the refrigerator. Don't you forget it either. More wine?

MEGS: You?

MARTHA: Yes.

MEGS: Me too.

MARTHA: Why don't you take the wine in the living room and get comfortable. I'll be there in a moment.

MEGS *enters the living room.* MARTHA *prepares a tray for the brandy: a cloth, snifters.* MEGS *is at the trophy case looking at* MARTHA's *picture when* DAVE *comes downstairs.*

MEGS: Hey, some dinner. Can your sister cook!

DAVE: Not bad.

MEGS: Come on, stud, your idea a cooking is to throw the meat in a pan, turn the flame on high and go and take a shower.

DAVE: Yeah . . . (HE *moves to the kitchen*)

MEGS: Hey! Listen, if she asks for my references, lie! Hah!? Hah!?

And MEGS *punches* DAVE *affectionately in the belly.* DAVE *enters the kitchen.* HE *gets a beer from the icebox.*

MARTHA: It's going very well, don't you think?

DAVE: Your steak was pretty good. A little rare for my taste.

MARTHA: You seemed to be enjoying yourself.

DAVE: I didn't think either of you knew I was here. This is great, Martha. Terrific, Martha. Look at you, Martha. And you eating it up. I didn't know who to laugh at.

MEGS: Hey, team captain, big number fifty, like Butkus!

DAVE: Enthusiastic, isn't he?

MARTHA: Positive. Optimistic. It's refreshing.

Pause.

DAVE: He's a loser.

Pause. And MARTHA *suddenly slams an open drawer shut with a loud bang.*

MARTHA: You're the loser, David. Ever since you came home. What is it like to aspire to nothing more than getting drunk on Saturday night?

DAVE: I aspire to be left the fuck alone!

MARTHA: By what? Life in general? Why even be a human being, David?

DAVE: Good question.

MARTHA: The idea of anyone finding anything, even for a moment, offends you, you selfish . . .

DAVE (*Overlapping*): I want you to see what he's like!

MARTHA: I know what he's like. He's gentle and he's kind and we're having a wonderful time. He likes me. You didn't have to threaten to beat him up if he didn't.

DAVE: What?

MARTHA: The time you got me the prom date!

DAVE: Oh, God . . .

MARTHA: That was done out of generosity and love, feelings you've forgotten about. You're willing to keep me in this house just so it won't be empty on the rare occasions you decide to come home! Well, I'm moving, David. I'm leaving! Like Mother! All the tears she shed? Did you really think all of them were for Poppa? Most of them were for you! YOU MIGHT AS WELL HAVE BEEN DEAD TOO!

DAVE: How'd you like a slap in the mouth?

MARTHA: I—dare—you! (*And picking up her tray* SHE *exits to the living room*)

DAVE: You're a shrew, Martha! You got the face of a football cleat and could use a series of shots for distemper! Him tellin' you different doesn't make it so! It doesn't make it so!

MEGS: You shouldn't, Davey.

DAVE: I shouldn't what!?

MEGS: Talk to someone who loves you like that, you shouldn't.

DAVE: I want you to tell me something, man . . .

MARTHA: You don't have to tell him anything, Joseph . . .

DAVE: He does! Just what are you doin', huh? You plannin' on being lucky for my sister!? Like you were for me? Like you were for Bobby?

MARTHA: Just leave, David.

DAVE: He knows what I'm talking about.

MEGS: What bugs you, man? That you thought I was lucky? Or that you was so piss-assed scared, you grabbed hold a that luck like it was rosary beads?

DAVE: I'd give anything to know why it's your face I'm staring at and not Bobby's.

MEGS: Get fucked.

DAVE: He loved it, Martha! He ate it up! Get some! Get some a them gooks! Bap-bap-bap-bap-bap-bap! Blow'm away! Nothin' confusin' about that, huh, Jacknife?

MEGS: It was heartbreaking the things I did. I'll live my whole life being sorry for'm.

DAVE: But you loved it! You never had it so good. It was logical to you. And you just had to carry Bobby and me right along with you.

MEGS: Not Bobby, man. Bobby understood.

DAVE: Bobby is dead! Man! When you gonna remember that!?

MEGS: You fuckin' jocks . . . (*And suddenly* HE *blows.* HE *is at the trophy case and with a sweep of his hand* HE *sends trophies careening into the wall*) You and your fucking jock dreams! I was a truckdriving numbnuts and they drafted me! But you!

DAVE: Yeah!?

MEGS: He enlisted. Mr. High School Hero enlisted! Went marchin' off thinkin' those piranha-eyed, cheesefaced motherfuckers was gonna tackle you 'stead a blow you away!!

DAVE: Jacknife set me straight!

MEGS: I stayed alive the only way I could! I rooted in what was happening around me like a pig in shit! And you ain't gonna blame me or make me feel guilty no more!

DAVE: Thirty feet off the ground in a chopper, Martha, and he's screaming like a rabid dog to get loose!

MEGS: Yeah! And you so close to lucky Megs, I thought you was tryin' to cornhole me, man! No way, Megs. I can't, Megs! Not in a million, Megs! NEVER HAPPEN!

DAVE (*Overlapping*): We shoulda stayed put, motherfucker. We should have stayed! But we went! 'Cause a you!

MEGS: I had to throw him out of the helicopter, Martha! Commanding officer was threatening to shoot him!

DAVE: Bullshit!

MEGS: You chickenshit. I heard you, Davey.

DAVE: You heard what?

MEGS: I heard. You was scared and tight and you landed wrong and your ankles broke. Bobby and I came back for you. I got hit 'cause a that. And I lay there in the mud with the blood pumpin' from my chest, blurp-blurp, and I heard you. No, Bobby! Don't go back for him! Fuck Megs! Jacknife is dead! Don't go back for him, Bobby! But Bobby did go back, huh, Davey? (DAVE *exits*) You can't walk away from that! Bobby did go back! Davey!? Bobby did! BOBBY DID!'(*Pause. Then softly, through tears*) Bobby did . . . (*Pause*) Maybe we never shoulda jumped outta that helicopter. Shoot away, sir. All of us, we don't give a fuck! Dead or alive, we're stayin' right here! No way we're goin' down into that shit! Hindsight.

> *Pause.*

MARTHA (*Softly*): Joseph?
MEGS: Mmm?
MARTHA: Let's go out and do something wonderful.

> *Pause.*

MEGS: Whatcha got in mind, you mad miss?

> *Pause.*

MARTHA: I'd like to see your gas station. (*Pause*) And we'll go by my school after. I'll show you where I work. I have keys. I could show you my classroom. Charts on the wall . . . tick-tack-toe on the blackboard. (*Pause*) Shall I get my coat?

> *Pause.*

MEGS: OK. (MARTHA *gets their coats.* SHE *puts her own on, helps him into his*) Sneakin' back into high school, Martha. If I don't feel notorious or something.

> *Pause.*

MARTHA: I'll protect you, Joseph.

> *Lights to black as* MARTHA *and* MEGS *exit out the front door.*

Scene 3

It is several hours later. MEGS *and* MARTHA *enter through the kitchen door. There is a somberness, a preoccupation to* MEGS *that* MARTHA *is trying desperately to fight.* MEGS *is carrying a case of soda in his arms.* HE *holds the door for* MARTHA.

MARTHA: Thank you. And thank you for the gasoline.

MEGS: Better you than the A-rabs, Martha.

MARTHA: I like my case of soda too. Thank you very much for that.

MEGS: You're welcome.

MARTHA: A whole case of white birch beer. What am I going to do with that? (*Pause*) I suppose I could bathe in it.

MEGS: You don't want it, Martha, I'll take it back.

MARTHA: Joseph, no, I'm teasing.

MEGS: Oh.

MARTHA: You tease me unmercifully and then you can't tell when you're being teased.

MEGS: Sorry.

MARTHA: Teasing, it shows you're cared for, doesn't it? (*Pause.* MEGS *doesn't respond.* SHE *continues softly*) I think it does. (*Pause*) Do you know what white birch beer is, Joseph?

MEGS: No.

MARTHA: I'll tell you if you'd like.

MEGS: Please.

MARTHA: Snow-covered trees in a bottle. (*Pause*) Joseph, what's the matter? You're with me and then you're not with me.

MEGS: Sorry.

MARTHA: You were hoping he'd be home, weren't you? He's not your friend, Joseph.

MEGS: I'm his friend.

Pause.

MARTHA: You're a lovely man. I mean that.

MEGS: No, you don't.

MARTHA: I do and you are.

MEGS: I got big bulgy eyes.

MARTHA: Well . . .

MEGS: And I am sorta losin' my hair.

MARTHA: That's a sign of virility, Joseph.

MEGS: Whoa.

MARTHA: You have a wonderful, open smile.

MEGS: I do not.

MARTHA: You do.

MEGS: You're just leadin' me on, woman, so's you can get into my panties.

MARTHA: Now you're teasing me.

MEGS: Hey, it shows you're cared for. (*Pause. It seems* THEY *are almost going to kiss*) Martha, let's go look for him.

MARTHA (*Desperately*): He's not worth your concern. (*Pause*) Please. Let's have our brandy.

MARTHA *moves to pour.* SHE *is stopped by the sound of* DAVE *entering. There is blood on his face and hands. His shirt is open and there is blood on his T-shirt. His eye is discolored and swollen.* HE *moves as if* HE *is in a daze. Long silence.*

DAVE (*Softly*): I . . . uh . . . I fell down.

MEGS: How's the ground look, stud?

> *Pause.*

DAVE: Martha . . .

MARTHA: What? You want someone to tend your wounds? I'm sorry, David not tonight.

> *Pause.* DAVE *wants to say something, cannot.*

MEGS: Want some ice for that eye, Davey?

DAVE (*Softly*): Martha, I'm sorry . . . .

> *Pause.*

MEGS: Come on, guy, sit. Let's see what you look like under all that blood. Don't worry, it's clean. You know me, I have to wipe my nose, I use my sleeve. (HE *wipes at* DAVE's *mouth*) Hold on. (*Pause*) How can she understand, stud? She doesn't know. She wasn't there. (*Pause*) Hey, we hardly beat you home, guy. Yeah, we been out. I showed Martha my garage. It's just a garage and all but I put a case a pop in her arms so it turned out OK. You want a birch beer, Davey? Good pop. (*Silence*) Maybe Martha'd make us some coffee. (MARTHA *doesn't move*) Then we went and saw Martha's classroom. Whoo, stud, beakers and specimens and microscopes. All we needed was a lightning bolt and we coulda created a monster. And we woulda nicknamed him Davey.

DAVE (*Softly*): Jacknife.

MEGS: That's my name, don't wear it out. That's what Bobby called me.

DAVE: 'Cause you drove the trucks.

MEGS: I did. Crashed a lot of the mothers too. (*Pause*) Why don't you tell Martha what your nickname was. I bet she'd like to know. (*Pause*) No? I will then. High School! 'Cause he loved high school. You was All League and you loved high school. Maybe too much, huh? Ole Bobby had a nickname for everything, didn't he? (*Pause*) Huh? Tell Martha how Bobby could make it seem like Boy Scouts sitting around the campfire. Couldn't he do that? (*Pause*) He could, Martha. (*Pause. It is as if* HE *is suddenly making a decision*) When I first got back, Davey, and was drivin', I'd see ole Bobby standin' at the side of the road with his thumb out. Isn't that something? It'd be late at night maybe and I'd be tired and I'd blink my eyes and there he'd be, standing there in his combat fatigues. Lotta people think they understand what that's like, don't they, studhoss. Well, God love'm for bad liars. They can only try. You and me, we know it like it was yesterday morning. Know what else, Davey? Sometimes I'd even pick ole Bobby up. (DAVE *groans softly*) You believe that? I swear, one time Bobby sat next to me from Pittsburgh, P-A, all the way to Hartford, Connecticut. Wasn't a bad conversation either. You ever do that? Pick'm up? Davey? Did ya? Davey, did you ever do that?

MARTHA: David, did you ever do that?

DAVE (*Softly*): Oh, God, Martha . . .

MEGS: You did, didn't you. What'ja think? Scare ya? Nah. Nothin' scary about ole Red Sock. That was Bobby's nickname, Martha. 'Cause he loved the Red Sox. Didn't he, Davey? Huh? Ole Bobby?

DAVE: He was gonna take us to Fenway Park . . . we were gonna cheer . . . oh, Bobby . . . you shoulda stayed put. You shouldn't have gone back. Bobby didn't help you, Megs.

MEGS: Died reaching down for me. Opened up like a rose in front a my eyes. Never knew what hit him.

DAVE: Christ almighty, if he'd stayed, he would of lived!

MEGS: Guy, how many nights have I stared at the ceiling thinkin' that very thought. But he didn't stay put. Wasn't in him to leave me any more'n it was to leave you!

DAVE: If I hadn't been scared, if I hadn't landed wrong . . .

MEGS: Guy, things happen for a reason!

DAVE: What fucking reason!?

MEGS: I ain't sure. I'm only workin' on it.

DAVE: Then how come you're doin' so much better than me!?

MEGS: Davey . . . I been blamin' myself for things I have no control over since first light. The way I look . . . way I talk . . . way I act . . . I was never no high school hero. I didn't have so far to fall.

DAVE (*So tired*): I just want to be left alone. I want Bobby to leave me alone.

MEGS: Embrace him, stud. Take him in your arms. You and me, we got enough shithole memories to last a lifetime. He ain't one of'm. He was our friend. Our heart. A waterwalker. Did we love him? (*Pause*) What were we gonna do, when we got back, no matter what? (*Pause*) Come on. Help me . . . no matter what.

DAVE: I dunno.

MEGS: Yeah, ya do. Come on. We were gonna . . . Davey!

DAVE: I dunno, go to Fenway Park!

MEGS: Best seats in the house, huh? Huh?

DAVE: Hot dogs and beer.

MEGS: And that green grass, fresh mowed.

DAVE: The sun beating down.

MEGS: Take off our shirts, huh? Soak up some rays!

DAVE: And we were gonna cheer. Cheer for Bobby's favorite team.

MEGS: Cheer so loud, they was gonna start cheerin' us back, yeah. And then?

DAVE: And then we were gonna . . . (HE *stops*)

MEGS: What, Davey? (*Pause*) What?

DAVE: Go fishing . . . opening day. (*A silence.* HE *settles back in his chair, exhausted.* MEGS *moves away, lost in his own thoughts now*) Martha?

MARTHA: Yes?

DAVE: I got in a fight tonight.

MARTHA: I know you did.

DAVE: With kids. The bar was filled with kids in high school letter sweaters, barely eighteen, if they were at all, and I dunno . . . I'd look at them, sis, and it was bringing tears to my eyes looking at them and finally I couldn't anymore and I started pushing one of them. He looked scared. But he pushed back and when he did I just sorta waded into all of them. And Christ, Martha . . . they didn't know how to fight . . . they didn't know how to fight at all. I don't know what to do. I think I might have hurt one of them. Maybe they're still there. Maybe I should go back and see if he's all right.

MARTHA: Maybe you should.

DAVE: I will. (HE *moves to the front door.* HE *stops and turns*) I blame people. I blame people so goddam much. (*Pause*) I'm so sorry, Martha.

MARTHA: I know you are.

> DAVE *turns to leave.* HE *sees Bobby's lucky hat hanging by the door. Pause.* HE *puts on the hat.* HE *turns and looks at* MEGS. *Pause.* HE *exits. Silence.* MEGS *moves to the window, watches* DAVE *go off into the night.*

MEGS: It's snowing. Awful late in the year. Real pretty. Last gasp. (*Pause*) It's hard. Martha, sweet Martha, it's so God-fuckin' hard to put the fatigues to sleep . . . (*Pause.* HE *moves to leave*)

MARTHA: You're leaving?

MEGS: Thought I would. Let things get back to normal.

MARTHA: Has normal been succeeding so well?

MEGS: Your brother loves you, Martha. Well . . .

MARTHA: We never had brandy, Joseph.

MEGS: You're right. We didn't.

MARTHA: One glass. We deserve it.

MEGS: Shoot it in. (MARTHA *pours.* THEY *drink*) Sundown. (HE *moves to leave*)

MARTHA (*In despair*): Stay? (*Pause*) We'll go upstairs.

MEGS: What's there?

MARTHA (*Inaudibly*): Bedrooms. (*Clearing her throat*) Bedrooms.

MEGS (*Not unkindly*): Who the fuck we kiddin', Martha?

MARTHA: Mission accomplished, is that it?

MEGS: A woman like you, a madman like me, who we kiddin' but ourselves?
MARTHA: You brought me flowers and candy and wine. We were having a wonderful time.
MEGS: One a the best I ever had, Martha, but . . .
MARTHA: It doesn't·have to end. If I've been fooling myself, I can fool myself a little longer.
MEGS: I can't, Martha. (HE *exits. Silence. Very slowly, as if* SHE*'s afraid* SHE *might break,* MARTHA *sits. Silence.* HE *returns in a rush, closing the door quickly behind him*) Y'know, I bet we woulda left that prom dance early!
MARTHA: Do you think?
MEGS: Yeah! We woulda gone off for dinner at a fancy restaurant! Partridge maybe!
MARTHA: Partridge?
MEGS: Can't have cheeseburgers, woman! And then maybe we woulda driven someplace. Someplace quiet. And parked. And then . . . who knows?! (*Pause. And the false bravado falls away. Softly*) Who knows . . . (*Pause*) I'm real nervous, Martha.
MARTHA: It's prom night. We've been kissing and hugging in the back of your '57 Chevy for hours. And we've had brandy. (*Pause*) Let's go upstairs. (SHE *takes his hand*) It's time.

As MEGS *and* MARTHA *go up. the stairs, the lights go to black.*

END OF PLAY